FRANKLIN D. ROOSEVELT AND THE ART OF LEADERSHIP

FRANKLIN D. ROOSEVELT AND THE ART OF LEADERSHIP

BATTLING THE GREAT DEPRESSION AND THE AXIS POWERS

WILLIAM NESTER

FRONTLINE
BOOKS

First published in Great Britain in 2024
by Frontline Books
An imprint of
Pen & Sword Books Ltd
Yorkshire - Philadelphia
Copyright © William Nester
ISBN 978 1 03611 090 1

A CIP catalogue record for this book is available from the
British Library

Typeset by Lapiz Digital
Printed and bound in the UK by CPI Group (UK) Ltd,
Croydon, CR0 4YY.

Printed on paper from a sustainable source by
CPI Group (UK) Ltd, Croydon, CR0 4YY

Pen & Sword Books Limited incorporates the imprints of
Archaeology, Atlas, Aviation, Battleground, Digital, Discovery, Family
History, Fiction, History, Local, Local History, Maritime, Military,
Military Classics, Politics, Select, Transport, True Crime, Air World,
Claymore Press, Frontline Publishing, Leo Cooper, Remember
When, Seaforth Publishing, The Praetorian Press, Wharncliffe Books,
Wharncliffe Local History, Wharncliffe Transport, Wharncliffe True
Crime and White Owl.

For a complete list of Pen & Sword titles please contact
PEN & SWORD BOOKS LTD
47 Church Street, Barnsley, South Yorkshire, S70 2AS, England
E-mail: enquiries@pen-and-sword.co.uk
Website: www.pen-and-sword.co.uk
or
PEN & SWORD BOOKS
1950 Lawrence Rd, Havertown, PA 19083, USA
E-mail: uspen-and-sword@casematepublishers.com

TABLE OF CONTENTS

CHARTS

Introduction

FRANKLIN ROOSEVELT AND THE ART OF LEADERSHIP

"Government includes the art of formulating a policy and using the political technique to attain as much of that policy as will receive general support; persuading, leading, sacrificing, teaching always, because the greatest duty of a statesman is to educate." (Franklin Roosevelt)

"Never let your opponent pick the battleground on which to fight. If he picks one, stay out of it and let him fight all by himself." (Franklin Roosevelt)

"It's a terrible thing to look over your shoulder when you are trying to lead – and find no one there." (Franklin Roosevelt)

"Therefore, the only sure bulwark of continuing liberty is a government strong enough to protect the interests of the people, and a people strong enough and well enough informed to maintain its sovereign control over its government." (Franklin Roosevelt)

After their independence and civil wars, Americans never faced a greater threat than the sixteen years of global depression then global war from 1929 to 1945. Franklin Delano Roosevelt was the president for the last dozen of those years during which he led the nation first to alleviate the Great Depression then led an international alliance that vanquished the fascist powers during the Second World War. Along the way, he established the modern presidency with centralized powers to make and implement domestic and foreign policies. He was naturally a master politician who eventually, through daunting trials and errors, became an accomplished statesman.

For all that historians regularly rank Roosevelt among the top three presidents,[1] most historians and countless others criticize Roosevelt for an array of things that he did or failed to do. Conservatives lambast him for creating a welfare state and trying to pack federal courts with liberal judges while liberals condemn him for interning 120,000 Japanese-Americans during the war and doing little to advance civil rights for African Americans. Critics blister war commander Roosevelt for caving into strategies demanded by powerful leaders that squandered countless lives and treasure in literal and figurative dead ends, Prime Minister Churchill's for the Italian peninsula and General MacArthur's for the Philippines. At times, his policies violated his principles. Like President Wilson during the First World War, Roosevelt championed self-determination but not for every nation. He badgered Churchill to break up Britain's empire while bowing to Stalin's brutal communist conquest of eastern Europe. And those are just the opening barrages against Roosevelt. Although he won four presidential elections with overwhelming majorities, nearly as many people reviled as most adored him.

Countless leaders crowd humanity. Their art is the same whether they head households in leafy suburbs or nation-states in a perilous world. They strive to get others willingly to do what they want them to do for a common purpose. Leaders vary greatly in how well or poorly they lead. Roosevelt excelled as a leader. What explains Roosevelt's art of leadership?

Roosevelt was a paradox. He was born into a rich New York family with a three-centuries-old pedigree, yet he genuinely cared about alleviating harsh conditions for poor people. Although he had a patrician accent, he knew how to explain complex issues with simple analogies that virtually anyone could understood. His best asset was not his intellect, which was less than brilliant. Instead, his strengths came from his personality, which was optimistic, confident, and extroverted mingled with his character, which was dutiful, disciplined, honest, just, and pragmatic.

His character and personality empowered him to overcome a tragedy he suffered at the age of 38 that would have devastated most people. Polio paralyzed him from the waist down. After years of therapy and exercises, he learned to stand erect with heavy leg braces and on a cane in one hand, gripping a friend's shoulder with the other, and shifting his hips, he could lunge awkwardly forward. That let him resume his political career. He had been a callow youth and young man. Polio forced him to mature, broaden, and deepen his mind. His wife Eleanor explained the change: "Anyone who has gone through great suffering is bound to have a greater sympathy and understanding of the problems of mankind."[2] In his younger years, Roosevelt loved swimming. After getting polio, he developed his upper body muscles with pullups on rings chained to the ceiling. Tragically, he undercut his health by daily smoking two packs of Camel cigarettes through an ivory holder that did not screen the toxic chemicals he inhaled.

Roosevelt was a stoic who stayed upbeat no matter how dismal the challenges and setbacks he faced, most vitally during the Second World War's darkest moments. Although he never experienced war, he did remain cool and level-headed in a crisis. In February 1933, a nearby assassin fired five pistol shots at Roosevelt and hit four bystanders, including Chicago Mayor Anton Cermak. After police subdued the gunman, Roosevelt calmly reassured Cermak and the others that they would survive. Cermak died of his wound.

As an extrovert, Roosevelt loved being surrounded by adoring people and entertaining them with amusing anecdotes and observations. He favorite time of day was happy hour when he mixed martinis for his guests. His friendliness was at once genuine and shallow. His amiability masked a cold remoteness. His wife Eleanor resented his aloofness but recognized it as a political strength because "it kept him from making mistakes" and helped make him "the kind of person the times required."[3]

Yet the desire always to be liked and in the spotlight could crimp his leadership. At crucial times, a leader must call on his followers to change their beliefs and behaviors for their greater good. Many internationalists then and since have criticized Roosevelt for letting public opinion polls rather than a cleareyed vision of American security interests largely influence his foreign policies from 1933 to 1941. He mostly followed rather than led the prevailing isolationist sentiments. Roosevelt argued that he had to do so to avoid alienating key members of Congress who backed his New Deal policies.

Roosevelt was an expressionistic not a systematic thinker. War Secretary Henry Stimson recalled that: "His mind does not follow easily a consecutive chain of thought but he is full of stories and incidents and hops about in his discussions from suggestion to suggestion and it is very much like chasing a vagrant beam of sunshine around a vacant room."[4] White House advisor Rexford Tugwell explained how he and his colleagues struggled to get him to focus his at times capricious, wandering mind on key issues: "We never could really talk to Roosevelt...If we did not catch his interest, he would shift to another subject; if we did, it became a dialogue...It might be only when

I thought it over afterward that I knew he had not been convinced. It was an exchange but there was not often any conclusion."[5]

Nonetheless, Roosevelt conceived many policy ideas and eagerly shared them with his advisors. Tugwell explained how he did so: "Something occurred to him. After a cautious interval, he began to broach ideas to this or that associate or to someone called in for the purpose. His understanding broadened and deepened satisfactorily, and policy actually began to shape itself. He put someone or a group to work on detail or on verification, and presently there it was, ready for action."[6] Although Roosevelt was not an original thinker, at times he imagined and realized some original ideas that vitally ameliorated America like the Civilian Conservation Corps and G.I. Education Bill of Rights, while his attempts to realize the "Four Policemen" and the United Nations decisively shaped postwar global politics.

Roosevelt's complex of related beliefs, values, and principles was an enormous source of strength. If he was an idealist, he grounded it on his love for America and its founding principles so eloquently expressed by the Declaration of Independence. He wanted to realize those ideals for as many people as possible. He had the liberal view of human nature that almost every individual is self-interested but rational and so open to compromise and developing mutual interests. That usually worked with most American and other western leaders.

He was a problem-solver who explained his approach: "Take a method and try it. If it fails, admit it and try another. But above all try something."[7] He exemplified that during his famed first one hundred days as president in 1933, when he submitted or embraced fifteen laws that established an array of new policies and organizations to fight the worsening vicious cycle of bankruptcies, poverty, joblessness, homelessness, malnutrition, and despair that began with the stock market collapse four years earlier. Then, over the next dozen years, he added, refined, or deleted policies and bureaucracies to adapt to shifting problems and possibilities.

Roosevelt was a Hamiltonian who believed in a muscular problem-solving state as tough as the challenges it faced. He expressed this concise view of how politics should work: "Government includes the art of formulating a policy and using the political technique to attain as much of that policy as will receive general support; persuading, leading, sacrificing, teaching always, because the greatest duty of a statesman is to educate."[8] He invoked Abraham Lincoln's philosophy that, "The legitimate object of a Government is to do for a community of people whatever they need to have done but cannot do at all or cannot do so well for themselves in their separate and individual capacities." To that, he added, "I am not for a return to that definition of liberty under which for many years a people were being gradually regimented into the service of a privileged few. I prefer and I am sure you prefer that broader definition of liberty under which we are moving forward to greater freedom, to greater security for the average man than he has ever before known in the history of America."[9] He was a utilitarian who sought the greatest good for the greatest number of people: "The social objective...is to do what any honest government of any country would do: to try to increase the security and happiness of a larger number of people in all occupations of life and in all parts of the country...to give them assurance that they are not going to starve in old age."[10]

He identified the essential difference between authoritarian and democratic systems: "The issue of Government has always been whether individual men and women will have to serve some Government or economics, or whether a system of Government and economics exists to service individual men and women." A democratic state's most vital duty was defending and enhancing its own democratic principles and institutions: "What is the state? It is the duly constituted representative of an organized society of human beings – created by them for their mutual protection and well-being. The state or government is but the machinery through which such mutual aid and protection is achieved...Our government is not the master but the creature of the people. The duty of the state towards the citizens is the duty of the servant to the master."[11] He adamantly rejected the Jeffersonian or modern conservative ideology of free markets and bare-bones government as a dangerous, self-destructive anachronism: "The opposing or conservative school of thought...does not recognize the need for government itself to step in and take action to meet these new problems. It believes that individual initiative and private philanthropy will solve them."[12]

History repeatedly revealed the paradox of free markets at the national and international level in the industrial era: the freer a market, the sooner it self-destructed. That inevitably happened in one of two ways. The largest corporations wield their power first to bankrupt and buy out smaller companies and then each other until monopolies or oligopolies dominated that industry. The result was high fixed prices and often shoddy goods and services. The other way was when speculators in stocks or land bid up prices to levels far beyond a company or property's real values. At some point, the frenzy of greed that caused prices to skyrocket turned to terror as speculators realized they had to sell before the house of card market collapsed. That became a self-fulfilling prophecy because when collectively they did so they collapsed that market.

To prevent or mitigate market self-destruction, government must be as powerful as the financial and industrial corporations that increasingly dominated not just the economy but also society and politics. Government's duty was not just to overcome existing problems but to anticipate future problems and nip them in the bud before they became overwhelming. In his second inaugural address, Roosevelt explained what his New Deal policies sought to do: "We refuse to leave the problems of our common welfare to be solved by the winds of chance and the hurricanes of disaster. Nearly all of us recognize that as intricacies of human relationships increase, so power to govern them must also increase...[W]e have undertaken to erect on the old foundations a more enduring structure for the establishment of a morally better world."[13]

He distinguished welfare from workfare, and was determined to avoid the moral hazard of people depending on the former: "The Federal Government must and shall quit this business of relief...the giving of cash" that "induces a spiritual disintegration fundamentally destructive to the national fibre. To dole out relief this way is to administer a narcotic, a subtle destroyer of the human spirit."[14]

He understood that politics and psychology are thoroughly tangled, and a leader could not reform one without reforming the other. In a 1926 speech titled, *Whither Bound*, he explained that humanity's problems are "caused as much by those who fear change as much as by those who seek revolution...In government, in science, in the arts, inaction and apathy are the most potent foes." Progressives faced two daunting opponents, "the lack of cohesion on the part of liberal thinkers themselves" and "the solidarity of the opposition to a new outlook."[15]

He had a sophisticated understanding of conditions for and appeal of authoritarianism: "History proves that dictatorships do not grow out of strong and successful governments, but out of weak and helpless governments. If by democratic methods people get a government strong enough to protect them from fear and starvation, their democracy will succeed; but if they do not, they grow impatient. Therefore, the only sure bulwark of continuing liberty is a government strong enough to protect the interests of the people, and a people strong enough and well enough informed to maintain its sovereign control over its government."[16]

The year before Pearl Harbor, Roosevelt remarked that "if war does come we will make it a New Deal war."[17] Although he did not elaborate, that likely meant he would fight the axis powers with the same pragmatism, open-mind, and search for what strategies, organizations, and leaders worked best with which he fought the Great Depression. He undoubtedly also meant that the means of winning the war should also enhance the security and prosperity for America and its citizens after the guns fell silent.

For Roosevelt, the best way to overcome a problem was with a well-funded government organization of experts devoted to doing so. That technocratic approach was central to his struggles to overcome both the Great Depression and the fascist powers during the Second World War. The trouble was that the bureaucracies often had overlapping duties and powers. The result was wasted manpower, money, and other resources, and incessant political squabbles. When conflicts got too debilitating, Roosevelt usually tried trumping them by creating yet another bureaucracy rather than reorganizing and streamlining the existing ones. More often than not, that exacerbated rather than alleviated the confusion.

Among Roosevelt's paradoxes was his faith in rational government and practice of idiosyncratic governance. He asserted himself as the decider-in-chief who would determine all key issues. To that end, he tried to keep policymaking as informal as possible with himself the center. He deliberately played off his advisors against each other to make them more dependent on him to sort out their differences. One advisor observed that Roosevelt "liked conflict, and he was a believer in resolving problems through conflict."[18] He may have liked conflict, but only if it was amical. He hated confrontations, especially firing people, no matter how inept or even disloyal they might be. Eleanor explained that: "His real weakness was – it came out of the strength really, or of a quality – he had great sympathy for people and great understanding, and he couldn't bear to be disagreeable to someone he liked."[19]

During the Second World War, Roosevelt candidly explained his approach: "You know I am a juggler, and I never let my right hand know what my right hand does...I may have one policy for Europe, one diametrically opposed opposite for North and South America. I may be entirely inconsistent, and furthermore I am perfectly willing to mislead and tell untruths if it will help me win the war."[20]

Nicolo Machiavelli would have nodded his approval. What matters above all is preserving and enhancing the state's security and power.

All means must lead to that end. That demands a purely practical approach to politics that wields abstract principles only to mask one's true goals and ways to get there. Roosevelt's willingness to try different possible solutions until he found one that worked was among his most vital leadership skills. Yet, Machiavelli would have raised some caveats.

Deception, of course, only works as long as others believe it. Blatant, easily exposed lies destroy one's credibility and so undermine one's power, the "little boy who cried wolf" syndrome. Another critical problem is the right hand concealing what it's doing from the left hand. A grand strategy that concerts the efforts of the two is the only way to keep the objects in the air and not clattering to the ground in opposed directions. One must constantly align short-term strategy with long-term interests. Too much focus on whirling hands and objects can lead someone toward a cliff rather than the promised land.

Overall, Roosevelt was a first-rate political strategist. Among his key axioms was this: "Never let your opponent pick the battleground on which to fight. If he picks one, stay out of it and let him fight all by himself."[21] He was adept at assessing the strengths and weaknesses, interests and ambitions of others, and appropriately manipulating them.

If Roosevelt was the political system's ringmaster, he relied on three outstanding advisors. Louis Howe, a *New York Herald* journalist, was his campaign manager and closest advisor from his 1912 New York State senator race until his death in 1936. Howe brilliantly nurtured public relations by creating popular images and slogans that attracted most voters. What mattered was subjective, not objective truth. Perhaps his key concept was: "If you say a thing...often enough, it stands a good chance to become a fact."[22] Harry Hopkins was Roosevelt's New Deal trouble-shooter who headed several agencies and became his key advisor after Howe's death. During the White House years, Eleanor was an enormous political asset for Roosevelt as an advisor and stand-in with key individuals, groups, and public appearances. Yet she was controversial. People tended either to love or hate her. Polls indicated that she was more popular than despised. Her outspoken calls for alleviating labor, racial, and other problems angered conservatives.

A critical skill for any leader in a democracy is inspiring as many people as possible to understand and back his policies. In that, a president must be an "educator-in-chief" who provides the public with key information and ideas to comprehend the threats and opportunities facing the nation, and what must be done to defeat the former and seize the latter.

No president has ever spoken to the American people with such clarity and compassion. Roosevelt had the ability to explain complex, entrenched, interrelated problems or outright crises with simple analogies easily understood by most people. Bolstering that was his mellifluous, confident, reassuring voice. He was famed for his "fireside chat" radio broadcasts that he began as governor and continued as president.[23] In the White House, he and his advisors designed each of his thirty-one fireside chats to address listeners' fears and hopes about an erupting crisis or looming challenge with knowledge, comfort, and inspiration to action. Hopkins explained that as Roosevelt crafted his speech, he "wastes little time in forming phrases; he tries to say what is on his mind in the shortest and simplest words...he always thinks of individuals, never a crowd."[24]

Harry Butcher, CBS's Washington bureau chief, actually called Roosevelt's first broadcast as president a "fireside chat."[25] Roosevelt embraced that term as personifying how he imagined addressing each American family as the members gathered beside the hearth. That boosted his confidence and skill to speak simply and intimately with them. Labor Secretary Frances Perkins was among a score of people attending one of his talks and marveled at "how clearly his mind was focused on the people listening at the other end. As he talked his head would nod and his hands would move in simple, natural, comfortable gestures. His face would smile and light up as though he were actually sitting on the front porch or in the parlor with them. People felt this, and it bound them to him in affection."[26]

Roosevelt's gift was vital for keeping American morale high through both the Great Depression and then the Second World War, especially during the uncertainty, humiliation, and rage following Japan's devastating attack on Pearl Harbor and capture of the Philippines. In one fireside chat, he asked Americans to get a world map so that they could follow his explanation in the next one when: "I'm going to speak about strange places that many of them may never have heard of – places that are now the battleground for civilization...I want to tell them in simple terms...so they will understand what is going on and how each battle fits into the picture...If they understand the problem and what we are driving at, I am sure that they can take any kind of bad news right on the chin."[27] Sixty-one million Americans tuned into his broadcast on February 23, 1942, and nearly all later switched off their radios with greater faith and knowledge about their nation's cause.

Roosevelt constructed his speeches with a team of advisors and writers. Among them was Samuel Rosenman who explained the process: "The speeches as finally delivered were his – and his alone – no matter who the collaborators were. He had gone over every point, every word, time and again. He had studied, reviewed, and read aloud each draft, and had changed it again and again...Because of the many hours he spent in his preparation, by the time he delivered a speech he knew it almost by heart."[28]

A leader must also inspire his inner circle of advisors. Perkins explained Roosevelt's power to do that: "I, and everyone else, came away from an interview with the President feeling better. It was not that he had solved my problem or given me a clear direction which I could follow blindly, that he had made me more cheerful, stronger, more determined to do what, while I talked with him, I had clearly seen was my job and not his. It wasn't so much what he said as the spirit he conveyed."[29]

Roosevelt was also adept at manipulating the press with a mix of twice weekly conferences, charm, and rules.[30] He refused to answer hypothetical questions and often diluted serious questions with anecdotes and jocular quips. Among the taboos were never writing about or photographing Roosevelt's handicap nor reporting on any private Roosevelt family matters. The generous time and information that Roosevelt shared with the reporters encouraged most of them to write balanced, objective stories and not reveal off the record information even if their newspaper's editorial page harshly critiqued his policies.

Before Roosevelt, only his cousin Theodore Roosevelt and Abraham Lincoln were as adept with reporters and their editors. Like them and unlike most presidents, Roosevelt enjoyed rather than dreaded the encounters. He held 377 press conferences in his first term and 374 in his second, in contrast to his predecessor, Herbert Hoover, who held only 60 during his one term presidency. However, during the war, he steadily reduced his press conferences with 89 in 1941, 74 in 1942, 58 in 1943, 55 in 1944, and 25 in 1945. He did so because he was busier, spent less time in Washington, and grew more fatigued.[31]

Roosevelt loved the repartee that usually entertained the reporters. He empathized because he had been a journalist and editor for the *Harvard Crimson*, and so understood and appreciated the profession. He saw reporters as allies to help promote his New Deal reform policies designed to alleviate the Great Depression and to help win the Second World War by informing and rallying the American people. Steve Early, the press secretary, was also charming and controlling. He forbade any recorders or cameras. He often planted questions with reporters. He carefully briefed Roosevelt before each conference on what questions were likely and how best to reply.

Nonetheless, conflicts did erupt between journalists and the White House. The most important journalist was Arthur Krock of the *New York Times*. The relationship was at times contentious when Roosevelt thought Krock had distorted elements of a story. In a speech before the National Republic Club on January 26, 1934, Krock blasted the Roosevelt administration for displaying "more ruthlessness, intelligence, and subtlety in trying to suppress legitimate unfavorable comment than any other I have known."[32]

As for family relations, Roosevelt was a dutiful son, an unfaithful husband, and a distant father to their five children. He loved his mother Sara more than anyone else. He was sexually attracted solely to the opposite sex. He loved being with adoring, doting women, especially pretty ones. Relations between Roosevelt and Eleanor were stilted from the start. Sara dominated them both; she insisted at their Hyde Park home that she sit at the dinner table's opposite end from Roosevelt and receive guests in the living room in a chair beside that of her son. In both rooms, Eleanor had to sit elsewhere.

Roosevelt cheated on Eleanor with her secretary Lucy Mercer. In 1918, Eleanor was devastated when she discovered her husband's love letters to her. Thereafter, relations between Franklin and Eleanor were distant and awkward. Yet the ultimate result of a domineering mother-in-law and a cheating husband was Eleanor's liberation. She blossomed both by developing a career as a social reformer, essayist, and speaker, and through a series of loving relationships, likely sexual, with both women and men. She lived with two lesbian couples at different times, and she split their time together between Greenwich Village apartments and her cottage called Val-Kill on the Hyde Park Roosevelt estate.

Roosevelt, meanwhile, developed a loving, likely non-sexual relationship with his secretary, Marguerite "Missy" Lehand, who became his "second wife." Missy was constantly either beside him or on call. No first couple has had a more bizarre living arrangement at the White House. Missy lived upstairs from Roosevelt while Eleanor and her latest love, Lorena Hickok, enjoyed adjacent bedrooms.

Roosevelt had a steadier but aloof relationship with religion. He was an Episcopalian who officially was Hyde Park church's warden. Although he believed in the Christian God and faith, he apparently spent little time questioning them let alone exploring alternatives. His attitude was a mix of conformity and open-mindedness: "I think it is unwise to say you do not believe in anything when you can't prove that it is either true or untrue. There is so much in the world which is always new in the way of discoveries that it is wiser to say that there may be spiritual things which we are simply unable now to fathom."[33]

Franklin Roosevelt and the Art of Leadership explores the dynamic among Roosevelt's character, personality, and presidential power with which he asserted policies that overcame first the Great Depression and then the fascist powers during the Second World War. Along the way, the book raises and answers key questions. What were Roosevelt's leadership skills and how did he develop them over time? Which New Deal policies succeeded, which failed, and what explains those results? Which war strategies succeeded, which failed, and what explains those results? What policies rooted in Roosevelt's instincts proved to be superior to alternatives grounded in thick official reports advocated by his advisors? Finally, how does Roosevelt rank as an American and global leader?

Chapter 1

THE MAKING OF A LEADER

"[W]e intend to stand by the men who are voting for principle. We shall see to it that they are protected in the discharge of their public duty. They shall not suffer because they are faithful to the people." (Franklin Roosevelt)

"In time of war, would we be content like the turtle to withdraw into our own shell and see an enemy supersede us in every outlying part, usurp our commerce, and destroy our influence as a nation throughout the world?" (Franklin Roosevelt)

Franklin Delano Roosevelt was the offspring of a marriage between two rich families with roots in early America.[1] The Delanos sailed with the Mayflower to found Plymouth in 1620. The Roosevelts settled in the Dutch colony of New Amsterdam in the 1650s. Over the centuries, each family steadily acquired more wealth from an array of enterprises. Franklin's father, James Roosevelt, married his mother, Sara Delano, after his first wife died. James was fifty-two years old when he wooed Sara, then twenty-six. Age was not their only clear difference. At five foot ten inches, Sara towered two inches above her husband.

Their only child was born on January 30, 1882. Sara's delivery of him damaged her womb so severely that doctors advised her not to have more children. That determined her to give Franklin as much love and support as possible.[2] Unlike most patrician women, she nursed and nurtured him rather than handed him to a wetnurse to succor and raise. She could not bear sending him off to school so tutors taught him from an early age. Each year, the Roosevelts sojourned for months in different parts of Europe where Franklin learned French and German. They also spent a month or so each summer at their "cottage," actually a huge mansion, on Campobello Island at Maine's east end. From his youth, he enjoyed two pastimes over his lifetime. One was

1

postage stamp collecting and he eventually lovingly mounted over 15,000 stamps. The other was sailing which he learned at Campobello. At age fourteen, Roosevelt entered Groton Academy, a private boys school at Groton, Massachusetts. He started two years behind the other boys because Sara could not be without him. The curriculum was a rigorous immersion in the humanities, ethics, and sports, while the regimen was spartan.

Roosevelt's personality and character were complex. He was at once a stoic and a mama's boy. He was an extrovert who loved being surrounded by admiring others, yet his geniality masked a fear of being too open or intimate. When others disagreed with each other, he was adept at getting each to believe that he backed his or her view. His mother's adoring support gave him an unshakeable confidence in his ability to overcome all challenges.

After graduating from Groton in 1900, Roosevelt entered Harvard. His greatest joy was editing *The Crimson*, the student newspaper. He joined the fraternity Alpha Delta Phi and the Hasty Pudding theatrical club. He was mortified that the most exclusive club, Porcellian, rejected his attempt to join. He also failed his try-out for the football team. During his freshman year, he received the tragic news that a heart attack killed his father. Sara moved into an apartment near Harvard.

Roosevelt was an average student, earning the so-called "gentleman's C" in many classes in that era when strict standards prevailed. One lesson he did learn came later, through hard experience that many academic theories were either useless or damaging when applied to the real world. Looking back from the White House, he reflected that, "I took an economics course in college for four years and everything I was taught was wrong."[3]

He entered Columbia Law School in September 1904, passed New York's bar exam, then dropped out without getting a degree. He pursued law from duty rather than passion. Being a lawyer gave him status, skills, and connections vital for a later political career. He joined the Wall Street legal firm of Carter, Ledyard, and Milburn in September 1907. Meanwhile, he fell in love.

Most young women considered Roosevelt a great catch given he was rich, personable, six foot, two inches tall, lean, and handsome. Yet he did not begin dating until he was in college and he did not marry his first three girlfriends, all from old wealth families. Sara talked him out of marrying the first, Frances Dana, because she was Catholic. The second and third, Dorothy Quincy and Alice Sohier, eventually turned him down because he insisted on having six children. Alice indignantly insisted that "I did not wish to be a cow."[4]

Franklin was twenty-three when he met Anna Eleanor Roosevelt, his fifth cousin, then nineteen, and began courting her. Eleanor was the daughter of Theodore Roosevelt's brother, Eliot.[5] Tragically, Eliot was an alcoholic and womanizer. Although he showered Eleanor with affection, he abandoned her and her mother when Eleanor was six. Her mother Anna was a beautiful, self-centered aloof woman who barely concealed her dismay with her ugly duckling daughter; she died when Eleanor was eight years old. Her aunt and Theodore Roosevelt's sister, Bamie, took in Eleanor and her younger brother Ellie. When Eleanor was ten, a seizure killed her father and diphtheria killed Ellie. Among Eleanor's cousins was Alice Roosevelt Longworth, Theodore's daughter by his first wife who died giving birth to her. Alice recalled that "I saw a lot of Eleanor as a child. We both suffered from being deprived of a parent. But whereas she responded to her insecurity by being do-goody and virtuous, I did by being boisterous and showing off."[6] At age fifteen, Eleanor was sent to a English boarding school called Allenwood. There she became fluent in French, her favorite subject, and enjoying playing field hockey. She became close to Allenwood's headmistress, Marie Souvestre, with whom she traveled during holidays. After graduating, she returned to New York where she joined the Junior League and served as a social worker in the Lower East Side's slums.

What did Roosevelt see in Eleanor? She was not conventionally beautiful. She stood a lanky near six feet tall, and had a recessed chin, buck teeth, and a squeaky voice. She did have pretty blue eyes, thick long blond hair, and a radiant smile that she rarely reveled. She was shy, awkward, melancholic, and insecure. He was attracted to her intelligence and interest in ethical and social issues. She made him think. Yet, mostly, like his law studies and career, Roosevelt appears to have sought Eleanor for propriety and pedigree rather than passion. What did she see in him? He was handsome, wealthy, educated, blue-blooded, kind, and, unlike most men, seemed to genuinely like her. He awakened feelings of romance if not passion in her. Historian Doris Kearns Goodwin brilliantly analyzed the Roosevelt relationship. They were opposites in character and personality. That initially was a powerful attraction as each saw something in the other lacking in oneself. Eleanor contrasted Roosevelt's "confidence, charm, and sociability" with her own "insecurity and shyness" but later saw her husband as "shallow and duplicitous." Roosevelt admired Eleanor's "sincerity, honesty, and high principles" but later saw them as "stiffness and inflexibility."[7]

Upon learning of their engagement, Theodore Roosevelt sent Franklin these lovely congratulatory words: "We are greatly rejoiced over the good news. I am as fond of Eleanor as if she were my daughter, and I like you, and trust you, and believe in you. No other success in life – not the presidency, or anything else – begins to compare with the joy and happiness that come in and from the love of the true man and the true woman...You and Eleanor are true and brave, and I believe you love each other unselfishly; and golden years open before you."[8] Alas, their marriage never came close to that ideal. Franklin and Eleanor married at a relative's New York City townhouse on March 17, 1905. Theodore stood for Eliot to give away Eleanor at their wedding.

They had six children, of whom an infant died but Anna, James, Elliott, Franklin, and John, born from 1906 to 1916, lived long lives. In those prudish days, Eleanor like countless other women distrusted her sexual feelings and did not enjoy sex with her husband. She confessed to her daughter that "sex is a burden to be borne" and that after her sixth birth "that was the end of any marital relationships."[9]

Eleanor was just as dissatisfied with being a mother. She turned over nursing and caring for her babies to nannies and tutors. She later admitted her unfitness for motherhood: "I had never any interest in dolls or little children and I knew absolutely nothing about handling or feeding a baby...It did not come naturally to understand little children or enjoy them."[10] Astonishingly, she actually had a cage built of chicken wire, placed her baby Anna in it, and hung it out the back window, presumably to distance the child's wailing. She only retrieved Anna when a neighbor threatened to report her to the Society for the Prevention of Cruelty to Children.[11]

Franklin was a superficial father. He set aside brief times each day to be with them. He was usually cheerful and positive but emotionally distant and disinterested in them. Eleanor recalled that "Franklin loved his small children. They were a great joy to him; he loved to play with them and I think he took great pleasure in their health and good looks and in their companionship."[12]

Their neglected childhoods probably contributed to the troubled relationships each later had as each went through two or more marriages and apparently many infidelities. By one tally, "Anna was married three times, James four, Elliott five, and John twice. Among them they had twenty-seven children."[13] Unlike their mother, none was ever accused of sexual relations with someone from his or her own gender.

Tammany Hall was the Democratic Party political organization headquartered at Union Square in New York City.[14] Tammany controlled nearly all Democratic Party politicians in New York City and many others across the state. The power came from mobilizing businesses, ethnic groups, and individuals, and dispensing contracts and jobs for kickbacks and votes. Thomas Murphy was currently Tammany's boss; he took over in 1902 and stayed firmly in charge until he died in 1924.[15] Murphy actually backed reforms as long they did not threaten Tammany's power.

Roosevelt deplored Tammany Hall's corruption and sought to avoid and oppose it.[16] Eventually he made peace with it when his political career could not advance without it. When Murphy died, Roosevelt declared that Tammany had "lost probably the strongest and wisest leader it has had in generations…He was a genius who kept harmony, and at the same time recognized that the world moves on. It is well to remember that he helped to accomplish much in the way of progressive and social welfare legislature in our state."[17]

Roosevelt ran for New York's senate in 1910. His district embraced from north to south Columbia, Dutchess, and Putnam counties that stretched between the Hudson River and Massachusetts or Connecticut; the region was around ninety miles north-south and thirty miles east-west. Hyde Park was in Dutchess County overlooking the Hudson River.

Most days from early October to November 6, election day, Roosevelt campaigned through the district in a rented bright-red Maxwell touring car without a windshield or roof. That strategy was risky in a district where most constituents were farm families. Farmers despised automobiles because the sputtering engines spooked their horses. Yet that newfangled machine gave Roosevelt a speed and range greater than a horse and buggy unless it ran out of gas, broke down, or mired in some mudhole on the wretched unpaved roads. In speech after speech to crowds in each town, Roosevelt explained that "I am pledged to no man, to no special interest, to no boss. I want to stay on the job representing you twelve months of the year." He lambasted corruption and incompetence in Albany and New York City, and promised to do what he could to attack it.[18]

One disadvantage Roosevelt carried was his patrician appearance, voice, and attitudes. He somehow had to convince farmers and laborers of his sincerity, empathy, and devotion to serving their interests. He defeated his Republican rival, John Schlosser, by 15,708 votes or 51.88 percent to 14,568 votes or 48.12 percent. Roosevelt rode a Democratic Party wave into power along with John Dix who became governor and majorities in the assembly and senate. Tammany men Alfred Smith and Robert Wagner were respectively the assembly's speaker and senate leader.

New York State's legislature had a 150-seat assembly and 50-seat senate. New York legislative sessions annually lasted ten weeks and paid $1,500, although the governor could call a special session for other periods. Roosevelt bought a three-story brownstone house near the statehouse rather than commute daily by train between Hyde Park and Albany.

The legislature's first priority was electing a United States senator. That took a combined session of both houses with the winner receiving a majority. The current senator was Republican Chauncey Depew but with Democrats occupying 114 of the 200 seats, their party's candidate would easily win. The real dispute was within the party. Tammany's candidate was William Sheehan with a distinguished career as Erie County's political boss, lieutenant governor, and assembly speaker. He was also the law partner of Judge Alton Parker, who as the Democratic Party's presidential nominee in 1904 had run against Theodore Roosevelt. As such, Sheehan was among the most powerful Democrats not just in New York but in the country.

Roosevelt and a group of fellow reform Democrats opposed Sheehan and backed Edward Shepard, a Brooklyn lawyer employed by the Pennsylvania Railroad and dedicated to reform. He assured those who joined him that he would do whatever he could to protect them from Tammany Hall retaliation: "Some of us have means, and we intend to stand by the men who are voting for principle. We shall see to it that they are protected in the discharge of their public duty. They shall not suffer because they are faithful to the people."[19]

The vote within the Democratic caucus resulted in 62 for Sheehan, 22 for Shepard, and seven for Cady Herrick, while ten were not present to vote. The result was that during the subsequent vote for senator, neither Sheehan with 91 nor Depew with 86 had a majority. Roosevelt emerged as the spokesman for those who sought a compromise. Murphy finally agreed to have Sheehan withdraw his candidacy and replaced him with James O'Gorman, a former Tammany underboss and now a state supreme court justice. The final vote was 112 votes for O'Gorman and 80 for Depew. Murphy eventually avenged that humiliating compromise. He mobilized Tammany against the dissidents and was able to replace all but three of them, with Roosevelt among the survivors.

Roosevelt emerged with a national reputation for political courage, compromise, and reform. Murphy and his underlings tried to smear Roosevelt as anti-Catholic and anti-Irish, and some of that stuck in many voter minds. The Sheehan fight's most important legacy was tipping the political balance in favor of direct election for senators.

The Seventeenth Amendment that requires popularly elected senators was ratified on May 13, 1913.

Frances Perkins, who Roosevelt later as president named labor secretary, was then a lobbyist for labor interests in Albany. She described what Roosevelt was like at that time: "I have a vivid picture of him operating on the floor of the Senate; tall and slender, very active and alert, moving around the floor, going in and out of committee rooms, rarely talking with the members, who more or less avoided him, not particularly charming (that came later), artificially serious face, rarely smiling, with an unfortunate habit – so natural that he was unaware of it – of throwing his head up. This, combined with his pince-nez and great height, gave him the appearance of looking down his nose at most people. I think he started that way….because he really didn't like people very much and because he had a youthful lack of humility, a streak of self-righteousness, and a deafness to the hopes, fears, and aspirations which are the common lot."[20]

A horrific tragedy occurred when Roosevelt was a state senator. The Triangle Shirtwaist factory was on the top three floors of the ten-story Asch Bangle Building in Greenwich Village, New York City. Management locked doors to prevent workers from taking unauthorized breaks. A carelessly tossed cigarette caused a raging fire that killed 146 people, 123 women and 23 men, from burning, inhaling smoke, or jumping to escape the flames. Perkins urged Roosevelt and other lawmakers to pass a bill that limited workweeks to 54 hours and imposed safety regulations to reduce the chances of similar tragedies. Roosevelt's callous response stunned Perkins. "No, no," he exclaimed. "More important things….Can't do that now."[21] The legislature passed the bill and Governor Dix signed it into law on April 19, 1912, but Roosevelt was absent for the vote.

Roosevelt was also indifferent to granting women equal political rights with men, including voting and running for office. "I am not opposed to female suffrage," he explained, "but I think it is a very great question whether the people of the state as a whole want it or not." Eleanor was disinterested: "I had never given the question serious thought for I took it for granted that men were superior creatures and knew more about politics than women did. I realized that if my husband were a suffragist I probably must be too [but] I cannot claim to have been a feminist in those early years."[22] Eleanor was a decade or so away from her political and sexual awakening.

Conservation was one area where Roosevelt was genuinely progressive. His cousin Theodore's writings, speeches, and reforms as governor and president inspired him. Franklin Roosevelt chaired the senate's Forest, Fish, and Game Committee that drafted the "Protection of Lands, Forests, and Public Parks Bill." The timber industry mobilized to bribe the bill to death in committee. A majority voted against the bill they had drafted so it never reached the senate floor.

The year 1912 was a presidential election year. Roosevelt was among 1,088 delegates who attended the Democratic Party convention in Baltimore from June 25 to July 2. On the third ballot the delegates unanimously nominated Woodrow Wilson. Roosevelt enthusiastically backed Wilson even though his cousin Theodore Roosevelt had broken with the Republicans, who nominated William Taft, and ran for president as the newly created Progressive Party candidate.

Franklin Roosevelt campaigned for re-election. Fortunately, his manager was Louis Howe, a politically savvy journalist who covered Albany for the *New York Herald*.[23] On November 5, Roosevelt won with 15,590 votes, 48.45 percent of the total, to Republican Jacob Southard's 13,958 votes or 43.38 percent and Progressive George Vossier's 2,628 votes or 8.17 percent. Nationally, the Republicans would have won the White House if the party had not split. Instead, Wilson triumphed with 6,296,284 votes or 41.8 percent with 435 Electoral College votes from 40 states to Roosevelt's 4,122,721 votes or 27.2 percent with 88 Electoral College votes from six states, Taft's 3,468,242 votes or 23.2 percent with eight Electoral College votes from two states, and Socialist Party candidate Eugene Debs with 901,556 votes or 6.0 percent.[24]

Among Wilson's cabinet appointments was Josephus Daniels as Navy Department secretary. Daniels owned and edited the Raleigh, North Carolina *News and Observer*; he knew virtually nothing about the navy, but had endorsed Wilson in a swing state. Roosevelt journeyed to Washington to meet Daniels and William McAdoo, the newly appointed treasury secretary. Roosevelt eagerly accepted Daniels' offer to be assistant naval secretary: "It would please me better than anything in the world. All my life I have loved ships and have been a student of the Navy, and the assistant secretaryship is the one place, above all others, that I would like to hold."[25] He did not mention that his cousin had occupied the same post under President William McKinley's administration. He did not have to do so. Daniels was well aware of that illustrious successor, which was a major reason he made the offer.

The duties of the secretary and assistant secretary were not clearly defined in law. The Navy Department included the bureaus of Navigation, Ordnance, Equipment, Steam Engineering, Construction and Repair, Supplies and Accounts, and Medicine and Surgery. Power was diffused among the bureau chiefs, rendering the secretary and assistant secretary merely supervisors. Daniels and Roosevelt soon established a good working relationship as the secretary accepted his assistant's desire to "get my fingers into just about everything and there's no law against it."[26]

Daniels was not just ignorant of naval affairs, he was a pacifist who dreamed of disarmament. In that he was not alone among Wilson's cabinet appointees. Secretary of State William Jennings Bryan was also a pacifist along with Robert Lansing, his replacement in 1916 and Newton Baker, who replaced Lindsay Garrison as secretary of war in 1916. Never before nor since have pacifists occupied such key posts as the secretaries of states, war, and navy.

Daniels, ably assisted by Roosevelt, pushed through reforms, some controversial. He abolished the four-man board of admirals that shielded him from the rest of the department; limited bureau chiefs to four year terms; required all officers to spend time at sea; had officers wear a more comfortable, looser fitting uniform; opened the Naval Academy to qualified enlisted men as students and qualified civilian professors; encouraged ship captains to organize classes for officers and sailors so that they enjoyed continuous learning; forbade officers from drinking wine and other alcoholic beverages; ended the distribution of condoms to sailors for shore leave; and, most importantly, opened shipbuilding and supply contracts to competitive bids and based promotion on merit rather than seniority. Each of those measures violated the interests of some groups and individuals within the navy or dependent on the navy for business.

On every reform issue, Daniels and Roosevelt worked closely together. Yet, they differed sharply over the navy's mission. As a pacifist, Daniels wanted to confine the navy to defending the nation's ports and shores. To that, Roosevelt retorted, "In time of war, would we be content like the turtle to withdraw into our own shell and see an enemy supersede us in every outlying part, usurp our commerce, and destroy our influence as a nation throughout the world? Yet this will happen...if an enemy...obtains control of the seas. Our national defense must extend all over the western hemisphere, must go out a thousand miles into the sea, must embrace...wherever our commerce may be."[27]

Roosevelt and his family lived in a four story townhouse owned by Bamie Roosevelt, his cousin, Eleanor's aunt, and Theodore Roosevelt's younger sister. Roosevelt joined an array of powerful political and social groups like the Metropolitan Club, Army-Navy Club, University Club, and Chevy Chase Country Club in Washington that bolstered the power dynamic of his long-standing membership in New York's

Harvard Club, Knickerbocker Club, Racquet and Tennis Club, Yacht Club, and City Club. He happily requisitioned voyages aboard warships to inspect distant bases and flotillas. He had his campaign manager Louis Howe serve as his secretary.

Roosevelt's stint as assistant secretary had a short term political cost – resignation of his New York senate seat. In 1914, he suffered a humiliating defeat as one of three contenders for the Democratic Party nomination to run for senator from New York to Congress. In the primary, James Gerrad won 210,865 or 62.68 percent to Roosevelt's 76,888 or 29.64 percent and James McDonough's 17,862 or 8.29 percent.[28] Roosevelt's disappointment was fleeting as he loved being the navy's assistant secretary and life in Washington where he steadily expanded his network of powerful political, corporate, and labor leaders.

That year on August 4, the First World War erupted in Europe initially between allies Britain, France, Belgium and Russia, and central powers Germany and Austro-Hungary. On the western front, the war quickly stalemated as each side dug trench complexes in lines that stretched over 400 miles between Switzerland and the North Sea. Although trench warfare also dominated the eastern front, the vast distances thinned the lines and made breakthroughs less daunting. Machine guns, barbed wire, and rapid firing cannon rendered attacks nearly always suicidal and burrowing deep into the earth the only way to reduce the chance of being killed or maimed.

Wilson officially declared American neutrality on August 4, 1914, and struggled to uphold that over the next two and a half years. The worst challenge was Germany's strategy of unrestricted submarine warfare. That became a crisis when a submarine sank the passenger ship *Lusitania* on May 7, 1915, with 128 Americans among the 1,266 dead. Wilson issued three increasingly strong protests to Berlin on May 13, June 9, and July 21, with the last threatening to break diplomatic relations. He backed his protests by getting Congress to raise both the army and navy budgets. Berlin replied by arguing that the sinking was justified because the *Lusitania* carried military supplies. Worried that America might join the allies, Germany's government announced on September 18 that henceforth its submarines would only sink allied ships within a designated zone.

Wilson asked Congress for a war declaration on April 2, 1917. He did so after Germany resumed unrestricted submarine warfare on January 1, 1917, with three American ships sunk in March. Atop that, British intelligence intercepted and shared with the White House a message from Foreign Minister Arthur Zimmerman to Germany's ambassador in Mexico, to encourage Mexico to war against the United

States in return for which Germany would help Mexico regain territory transferred to the United States by the 1848 Guadeloupe Hidalgo treaty. Congress overwhelmingly voted in favor, the Senate by 82 to 6 and the House of Representatives by 373 to 50, and Wilson signed the war declaration on April 6.

Roosevelt relished his duties amidst war. He presided over the navy budget's expansion from $239,633,000 in 1917 to $2,202,311,000 in 1919; and personnel from 194,617 in 1917 to 448,606 in 1918 then cutback to 272,144 in 1919. During the war, the navy lost two cruisers, two destroyers, and one submarine, while ensuring that no troop or supply transports crossing the Atlantic were sunk by enemy submarines.[29]

Roosevelt visited his counterparts in London and Paris in July and August 1918. His most influential meeting was with Reginald Hall, who directed Britain's Naval Intelligence. Hall inspired Roosevelt to expand the Office of Naval Intelligence (ONI) with agents and listening posts around the world, and its cryptanalysis section in Washington.[30] He also spent several days visiting the war front and was appalled by the death, destruction, squalor, and stench of rotting bodies.

Not all of Roosevelt's affairs during his Washington years were public. He had a love affair with Lucy Mercer, Eleanor's secretary. Lucy was a beautiful, passionate, sweet, and adoring woman, Eleanor's antithesis. Alice Longworth Roosevelt typically had a pointed perspective on the affair: "Franklin deserved a good time. He was married to Eleanor."[31] Their affair lasted from 1916 to 1918.

Eleanor discovered a bundle of love letters from Lucy when she was unpacking Roosevelt's suitcase after he returned from his trip to Britain and France. She confronted her husband and said she was willing to divorce. It was Sara that rejected any notion of divorce that would destroy Roosevelt's political career and social life. She threatened to disinherit him if he did so. Roosevelt lied to Lucy, claiming that Eleanor opposed divorce and informed her that he could never see her again. Lucy married Winthrop Rutherford, a rich man, twenty-eight years her elder in 1920. Lucy and Roosevelt resumed their relationship in 1941, and she was with him when he died. The exposed affair ended all intimate relations between Roosevelt and Eleanor. Thereafter they not only slept separately but soon had separate residences.

Nonetheless, in December 1918, Roosevelt and Eleanor journeyed with Wilson's entourage to Paris for the peace negotiations following the armistice on November 11. Roosevelt thrilled at meeting the array of civilian and military leaders, and learning valuable lessons about diplomacy as he observed the proceedings. He enthusiastically supported the Versailles Treaty, signed on June 28, 1919, especially the tenets authored by Wilson to establish the League of Nations dedicated to collective security and world peace. He was deeply disappointed when the treaty failed to win ratification with the votes of more than two-thirds of senators. That was largely due to Wilson's refusal to compromise with Republicans, most vitally Henry Lodge who chaired the Senate Foreign Relations Committee, compounded by the crippling stroke he suffered during his cross-country whistle-stop tour to convince the public to support the treaty. Wilson's character flaws and political failures provided Roosevelt vivid examples of how not to be and act as president.

Nineteen-twenty was a presidential election year. The Republicans held their convention at Chicago from June 8 to 12, and nominated Senator Warren Harding of Ohio on the twelfth ballot and then Massachusetts Governor Calvin Coolidge as vice president. The Democrats convened at San Francisco from June 28 to July 6. Ohio Governor James Cox beat thirteen rivals for the nomination. Astonishingly, the delegates voted by enthusiastic acclamation that Franklin Roosevelt be his running mate; he was only forty-one and his only previous political experience was a two-year stint as a New York state senator. If his name were not Roosevelt, associated with his cousin Theodore, he would never have been considered.

Roosevelt resigned as assistant naval secretary on August 6, 1920, to embark on a whistle-stop tour of the nation and address crowds at each station. He ran as an internationalist who wanted America to assert its national interests by assuming a leadership role in the world commensurate with its economic power. He explained that: "Modern civilization has become so complex and the lives of civilized men so interwoven with the lives of other men in other countries as to make it impossible to be in this world and not of it."[32] Most Americans rejected that message. Although they were proud of their military's role in winning the war, the 116,516 deaths, 320,000 wounded, and $22 billion financial cost made many believe they should have remained neutral. Now most Americans wanted to withdraw from international politics aside from commerce.

Eleanor joined her husband on the train for four weeks. Louis Howe, Roosevelt's campaign manager, nurtured her latent speaking and writing skills and desire to uplift the poor, sick, and suppressed. He began by asking her advice on strategy and issues. She "was flattered and before long I found myself discussing a wide range of topics...

[and] I came to look with interest and confidence on the writing fraternity and gained a liking for it which I have never lost."[33]

Harding and Coolidge crushed Cox and Roosevelt, winning 16,166,126 votes or 60.35 percent and 34 states with 404 Electoral College votes to 9,140,25 votes or 34.12 percent and 11 states with 127 Electoral College votes. Republicans also swept Congress, ending up with 59 to 37 Senate seats and 303 to 131 House of Representatives seats. Republicans would dominate Washington for the next dozen years until the 1932 election, when, amidst the Great Depression, Roosevelt won the presidency and the Democrats captured Congress.[34]

Roosevelt needed a job. In January 1921, he accepted an offer to become vice president of the Fidelity and Deposit Company, run by William Van-Lear Black, who also owned the *Baltimore Sun* and was a deep-pocketed donor to the Democratic Party. Fidelity and Deposit was the nation's fourth largest surety bonding company. With a $25,000 salary, Roosevelt was in charge of its New York office with operations in New York state and New England. He hired Howe as an advisor. Roosevelt mulled running for New York governor in 1922, and had Howe devise a strategy and build a network of rich and powerful supporters. Meanwhile, Eleanor took business, typing, and cooking classes, and joined the League of Women Voters.

In August 1921, the Roosevelts and their children vacationed at their mansion at Campobello, Maine. Roosevelt delighted in swimming, sailing, and relaxing amidst the natural beauty of the islands and bays. Then, after a swim on August 10, he developed a high fever, paralysis first in his legs then arms and hands, and intense pain. One doctor diagnosed Roosevelt as suffering a blood clot in his lower spinal cord that might take months to dissolve. A second doctor recognized Roosevelt's affliction as poliomyelitis.

Roosevelt fought his plight by being as positive, cheerful, and kind with others as possible. Eventually, he regained power over his upper body, bowels, and bladder but remained paralyzed from the waist down, although, paradoxically he could still get sexually aroused. He began daily exercising his upper body with hand weights and pulling himself with rings attached by chain to the ceiling. Around home, he propelled himself in a wheelchair. He wore fourteen pound braces that extended from his ankles to his waist and let him stand with crutches and totter forward by pivoting his upper body. In public he dispensed with crutches and walked by tightly gripping a cane in one hand and someone's shoulder with his other. He had his car modified so that he could drive it with hand accelerators and brakes. His black valet LeRoy

Jones helped him dress, bath, and anything else he needed help with. Eleanor later wrote that "probably the thing that took the most courage in his life was his… polio and I never heard him complain…He just accepted it as one of those things that was given to you as discipline in life…And with every victory…you are stronger than you were before."[35]

After a fifteen month leave, he returned to work with Fidelity and Deposit. He formed a law partnership with Basil O'Connor, who did both political and legal work. He remained active in politics, attending Democratic Party meetings and dinners, and expanding his network of supporters. During the June 1924 Democratic Party convention, Roosevelt was the floor manager and delivered the nomination speech for New York Governor Al Smith. West Virginian politician John Davies defeated Smith and other rivals for the nomination on the 103rd ballot. Sitting President Calvin Coolidge decisively won with 15,723,789 votes or 54.0 percent and 392 Electoral College votes from 35 states to Davies' 8,386,242 votes or 28.8 percent and 136 Electoral College votes from 12 states and Progressive Socialist Party Robert La Follette 4,831,706 votes or 16.6 percent and 13 Electoral Colleges from one state.[36]

After the convention, Roosevelt journeyed to Warm Springs, Georgia where his friend George Peabody, a rich Wall Street investor, had recently bought and renovated the Merriweather Inn, a spa with magnesium-rich waters. Those waters and vigorous massages alleviated some of Roosevelt's physical and psychic pain. Roosevelt bought the inn in 1926 and had a separate cottage built for himself on the extensive grounds. He established the Warm Springs Foundation, later called the National Foundation for Infantile Paralysis, devoted to providing care for the afflicted and researching a cure for polio. For $42 a week, polio victims received a room, three daily meals, and therapy. From 1924 to 1928, Roosevelt spent more than half his time administering the foundation and enjoying the waters, patients, and staff.

The Roosevelt children grew up and left home for universities, careers, and marriages. That freed Eleanor to devote herself full time to her work with the League of Women Voters. She developed her own network of friends and became especially close to Marion Dickerman and Nancy Cook who shared a Greenwich Village apartment. Roosevelt had a cottage built for them on the Hyde Park estate where part of each year the three lived together. The women initially called their home the "Honeymoon Cottage" and later "Val-Kill." Eleanor became a teacher of history, English, and politics at the Todhunter School for Girls in Manhattan.

Meanwhile, Roosevelt mulled with Howe various ways that he could make a political comeback. Then, fortuitously, an opportunity arose.

Chapter 2

THE GOVERNOR

"It has always been my belief that it is far more important to ascertain as fully as possible, and consider with an open mind, the criticism of those who do not agree with you on important public questions than it is to read the plaudits and encomiums of friends." (Franklin Roosevelt)

"I assert that modern society, acting through its government, owes the definite obligation to prevent the starvation or dire want of any of its fellow men and women who try to maintain themselves but cannot...To those unfortunate citizens aid must be extended by government – not as a matter of charity but as a matter of social duty." (Franklin Roosevelt)

Al Smith was New York's popular governor from 1923 to 1928, having previously served as a state assemblyman from 1904 to 1915, sheriff of New York County from 1916 to 1917, and governor from 1918 to 1920, then losing a re-election bid.[1] He was born in New York City and owed his rise to being an enterprising Tammany Hall member. For the 1928 national election, Smith overwhelmingly won the Democratic Party's presidential nomination on the first ballot at the convention at Houston from June 26 to 28.

That left New York's governor's mansion an open contest for whoever wanted it. Roosevelt was considered a leading contender with powerful backers, most vitally Governor Smith himself, National Democratic Party Chairman John Raskob, and the New York *World* that endorsed him.[2] Yet, he had mixed feelings about running. He wanted to be governor but was not sure that he could first defeat party rivals like Owen Young, Robert Wagner, and Herbert Lehman backed by Tammany Hall, then defeat the Republican candidate after years of national prosperity with Republicans in the White House and dominating Congress. He was also uncertain about his health, and was taking the waters at Warm Springs, Georgia. He announced that he would not be a candidate, although he told Smith that "if, in the final analysis, the convention insisted on nominating me, I should feel under definite obligation to accept the nomination."[3]

That is exactly what happened after the Democratic convention opened at Rochester on October 2. New York Mayor Jimmy Walker nominated Roosevelt for governor and the delegates voted overwhelmingly to approve him, and then Herbert Lehman as lieutenant governor. The party platform endorsed public control of hydroelectric power, expanding the state's park and parkway system, a four-year term for governor and senators, and two-year term for assemblymen, an eight-hour work day and forty-eight hour work week for women and children, expansion of workmen's compensation to include occupational diseases, direct primaries for all elected state positions, and campaign spending limitation. The only ambivalent stand was on prohibition with a vague call to let states choose whether and how to regulate alcoholic beverages.

Roosevelt faced Republican candidate Albert Ottinger, with an impressive resume as a New York state senator, Assistant to United States Attorney General in Washington, and New York State Attorney General. Ottinger campaigned for cutting the state's crime, corruption, taxes, and red-tape, abolishing the national income tax, and raising national tariffs for revenues and to promote American industries and wages, although like Democrats, he equivocated on prohibition.

Roosevelt narrowly defeated Ottinger by 2,130,238 votes or 48.96 percent to 2,104,630 or 48.34 percent, with a 25,608 vote gap between them. Meanwhile, Republican candidate Herbert Hoover crushed Smith by 21,427123 votes or 58.2 percent and 444 Electoral College votes from 40 states to 15,015,464 or 40.8 percent and 87 Electoral College votes from 8 states.[4] Republicans won majorities in Congress and Albany's legislature.

Roosevelt took the oath to be New York's governor on January 1, 1929. He inherited his predecessor's personnel and policies, and retained sixteen of eighteen department heads. The most formidable person he faced was Robert Moses, the secretary of state, chair of the State Council for Parks, and the Long Island Parks Commissioner.[5] Moses wielded his powers to build a network of parkways and bridges linking New York City to the surrounding regions of Long Island and the Hudson River Valley. Although that spurred New York's economic development, Moses was criticized for the ruthless ways he asserted eminent domain by legally condemning thousands of homes and businesses along the way. Roosevelt was among those who disliked Moses, "who rubs me the wrong way." Typically, Moses was scathing, castigating Roosevelt as a "poor excuse for a man" and "not quite bright."[6] Roosevelt fired Moses as secretary of state but retained him in his chairmanships.

Roosevelt established an unofficial inner state government of loyalists. He named his friend Al Flynn secretary of state; Flynn led Tammany Hall's Bronx organization. Roosevelt used Flynn to trade patronage for votes, money, and other support. He had Jim Farley chair the New York State Democratic Party. For policymaking, Roosevelt's right-hand man was Raymond Morley, who taught politics at Columbia University's Barnard College. Roosevelt appointed him to the Commission on the Administration of Justice where he drafted Roosevelt's judicial and prison reforms.

Louis Howe remained his closest advisor, seconded by Sam Rosenman. His first and second personal secretaries were Marguerite "Missy" LeHand and Grace Tully. Howe was with him most of the day and evenings while Missy was constantly beside him or nearby, and enjoyed her nickname as his "second wife." Both Howe and Missy had bedrooms in the governor's mansion.

Howe was brilliant at public relations. He got New York's Democratic Party to raise $100,000 for the Democratic Publicity Bureau. He also helped Roosevelt develop the folksy style of his radio broadcast that would later be called his "fireside chats." Roosevelt delivered his first broadcast in April 1929, shortly after taking office. He also met with the press almost daily for off the record question and answer sessions.

Roosevelt generally stayed at the governor's suite at the Capitol from ten in the morning until five in the afternoon on weekdays. After work, he often went for a swim before dinner. As an extrovert, he loved being surrounded by and entertaining others. He insisted on mixing cocktails for his guests each evening. Once a week he had a movie evening when he let all seventeen mansion employees join him, his family, and other guests. He also had poker nights for friends, advisors, and key politicians. Although he was informal with others and called them by their first names, he expected to be called governor and later Mr. President.

Eleanor remained peripheral to Roosevelt's life, private and public. When a reporter asked her feelings about her husband's election as New York's governor, she tartly replied, "I don't care. What difference can it make to me?"[7] Actually, it enormously affected her in ways that she believed harmed her. She initially resented Roosevelt's election to be first governor and later president. She dreaded having to fulfill traditional first lady duties of serving tea and chitchat to endless guests.

She had established her own career that bolstered her confidence and contentment. Now she had to set that aside and resubmerge her identity within her husband's. She eventually reconciled herself to the governor's mansion and White House: "I accepted his nomination and later his election as I accepted most of the things that had happened in life thus far; one did whatever seemed necessary and adjusted one's personal life to the developments in other people's lives."[8]

Having Earl Miller as her bodyguard helped Eleanor make the transition. Miller was a charming, handsome, and tough New York State policeman who became her close friend and perhaps lover. She was then forty-four, a dozen years older than him. She had a room for him at both Val-Kill and her Greenwich Village apartment. Her friends Marion Dickerson and Nancy Cook were dismayed and jealous of her "romantic involvement" and public affection between them. He taught her to shoot a pistol, and become a better tennis player and horseback rider, and, most vitally according to her son James Roosevelt, "to take pride in herself, to be herself, to be unafraid of facing the world."[9]

With a Republican controlled legislature, Roosevelt had to make the most of his political skills at nurturing relationships, finding common ground, and forging compromises to get anything done. He explained his attitude: "It has always been my belief that it is far more important to ascertain as fully as possible, and consider with an open mind, the criticism of those who do not agree with you on important public questions than it is to read the plaudits and encomiums of friends."[10]

Roosevelt's first battle with Republicans was over the budget. Two years earlier, New York's constitution was amended to have a unified state budget whose composition the governor determined for the legislature to approve or reject. Republicans preferred having assembly and senate committees determine the components so they could dole benefits to those individuals and businesses that benefited them. Roosevelt worked with Budget Director Joseph Wilson to draft a $256 million budget, $23 million more than the previous year, and submit it on January 28, and a supplemental budget on March 18, 1929. Republicans sought and received approval for drafting their own budget from Attorney General Hamilton Ward, a Republican. Roosevelt asked the Court of Appeals to overturn that opinion. The Court of Appeals did so, forcing Republicans to accept the new budget system established by the constitutional amendment. After prolonged horse-trading, they approved revised regular and supplemental budgets.

Prison conditions in New York, like most other states, were abysmal with overcrowding, brutality, filth, wretched food, and foul plumbing.

The 1926 Baumes Law obliged judges to sentence for life anyone convicted for the fourth time of the same felony. That gave desperate lifers little to lose. Inmates at the Clinton and Auburn state prison revolted in July 1929. As guards struggled to crush those revolts, Roosevelt endorsed the State Crime Commission's prison reform proposals that included $10 million for rehabilitating old or building new prisons, better food, more guards, and a parole commission with three members appointed by the governor with the senate's approval. The legislature eventually passed and the governor signed laws that implemented those reforms.

Roosevelt's worst worry was how to improve the dismal farm economy. As a gentleman farmer in upstate New York, he knew well how dropping crop and livestock prices devastated farmers. Farm income had peaked during the First World War with Europe's growing demand for food then declining steadily as mechanization, fertilizers, pesticides, improved crops and livestock, and Europe's agrarian recovery caused supplies to exceed demand.

Roosevelt formed a twenty-one member Agricultural Advisory Commission and asked his neighbor and friend Henry Morgenthau to head it. Morgenthau was the scion of a wealthy New York City Jewish family that got rich through finance. Farming rather than finance fascinated Morgenthau. He talked his father into letting him attend the New York College of Agriculture, buy a dairy and fruit farm, and publish *The American Agriculturalist*, the nation's second oldest weekly farm magazine. His farm was renowned for the quality of its fruits and milk from prize Holstein cattle.

Roosevelt asked the Commission to find answers for this question: "What can the state of New York do to aid agriculture, give farmers a square deal, and help make the farm dollar go as far as the dollar of the city man."[11] With Republicans a majority on the Commission, its report concluded that tax cuts, not welfare, could best help farmers. Counties paid 35 percent of the tax burden for school and road building and maintenance. The report called for eliminating that tax along with the state tax on real estate, and filling the revenue gap with a gasoline tax. That report became the basis for a bill that passed both houses and Roosevelt signed into law on April 1, 1929. Those tax cuts provided some relief not just to farmers, but also the rich. Only around 300,000 of New York's population of 12,588,066 people in 1930 paid the state's income tax; the tax was mild and progressive, rising in steps to 2.33 percent on incomes of $100,000 or more.

Governor Roosevelt was amicably managing problems of prison reform and farming when the nation's economy collapsed in what became a decade of Great Depression. The measures he took to alleviate poverty, joblessness, and hunger in the state would later shape his White House policies.

Periodically, America's economy has collapsed leading to high levels of bankruptcies, joblessness, poverty, and despair. The worst nineteenth century depressions or panics as they were traditionally called were in 1819, 1837, 1857, 1873, and 1893. The causes varied but usually unbridled speculation in stocks or land led to skyrocketing prices increasingly remote from the assets' real value. At some point the frenzied greed that pushed up prices morphed into frenzied panic by speculators that the paper titles they held were worthless. Their panicked selloffs caused domino effects of plummeting prices and bankruptcies across the nation.

That much was generally understood. The problem was that no one knew how to prevent a panic or reverse one after it began. For either challenge, the prevailing attitude was that the federal and state governments could and should do nothing. Sooner or later, the economy would revive as people, especially entrepreneurs, did whatever they could to survive, including starting new businesses for which they demanded goods, services, and employees. Eventually the collective choices of tens of millions of Americans would restore the related dynamic forces of growth and confidence.

The stock market crash in October 1929 typically resulted from uninhibited greed followed by terror.[12] A half dozen years of "roaring twenties" preceded the plummet. During that time, Americans enjoyed a consumer revolution as prices fell for mass produced cars, refrigerators, vacuum cleaners, radios, record players, and other goods. Wages rose as jobless ranks fell and employers expanded their businesses.

The soaring economy obscured four weaknesses. One was that many Americans borrowed money to buy goods along with houses, and thus had greater debts. Another was the farm sector that employed one of five Americans and suffered falling prices and profits as supplies of harvested crops and livestock grew; the result was more farm debt and bankruptcies that economically hollowed out rural regions across the country. A third was the unregulated stock market where speculators increasingly bought stocks on margin or borrowed money that they could only repay as long as prices rose. The fourth was the widening gap between the rich and everyone else; in 1929, the top 0.1 percent owned more wealth than the bottom 43 percent. Although from 1920 to 1929, average income rose 9 percent, the top 1 percent's share shot from 12 percent to 19 percent.[13] That made the economy's fate increasingly dependent on the rich whose wealth increasingly reflected the mirage of skyrocketing stock prices.

Three Republican presidents – Warren Harding, Calvin Coolidge, and Herbert Hoover – helped fuel the "roaring twenties" by cutting taxes and dismissing increasingly dire warnings that the speculative bubble eventually would burst with disastrous results.[14] Massive selloffs caused the stock market to plunge in December 1928 and March 1929, only to skyrocket as speculators scrambled to buy suddenly much cheaper stock certificates. But the plummets of October 24 and 29, 1929, were so severe that speculators shunned the market from fear of penury.

President Hoover had the intellect, experience, and expertise to understand the reasons for the collapse and ways to revive the economy.[15] Tragically, his faith in self-correcting free markets blinded him to those complex realities. Hoover was a self-made millionaire who got rich as the chief engineer for mining corporations. He was a philanthropist who led the Commission for Relief in Belgium that saved hundreds of thousands of lives from disease and starvation during the First World War. As commerce secretary under Harding and Coolidge, he spearheaded many of the policies that expanded the economy while leading the American Relief Administration that provided food and medicine for millions of Russians facing starvation after years of the First World War, the communist revolution, and the civil war. He was an idealist who celebrated enterpreneurs and free markets that he believed would overcome all problems by creating more wealth. When he accepted the Republican Party's nomination for president in 1928, he declared: "We in America today are nearer to the final triumph over poverty than ever before....We shall soon...be in sight of the day when poverty will be banished from this nation."[16]

Despite his brilliance, Hoover could not imagine reacting to the stock market collapse beyond trying to reassure Americans that the problem was not serious and that business leaders would soon begin buying and selling again. As tax revenues plunged, he cut government spending to balance the federal budget. As revenues kept falling while the national debt climbed, he signed the 1932 Tax Bill that raised taxes. All those measures worsened the economy. In 1932, he reluctantly signed a bill that established the Reconstruction Finance Company (RFC) with $300 million that gave low-interest federal loans to states, banks, and corporations. That measure helped but was too little too late. The RFC distributed only $30 million by 1932's end.[17]

The Dow Jones Industrial Average fell to 220.1 in November 1929, rose to 257.3 in April 1930, then fell to 196.1 in December 1930, 116.6

in December 1931, and 84.8 in December 1932. The New York Stock Exchange's total value plummeted in a series from $89.6 billion on September 1, 1929 to $15.6 billion on July 1, 1932. Among the most powerful corporations devastated by the crash were United States Steel whose share dollar prices dropped from 262 to bottom at 22, American Telephone and Telegraph from 304 to 72, Montgomery Ward from 138 to 4, and General Motors from 72 to 8.[18]

From 1929 to 1933, the depression halved the nation's economy and average income from $103 billion to $55.6 billion and from $847 to $442, respectively while joblessness skyrocketed from 3.2 percent to 24.9 of the workforce.[19] The value of America's farms plunged from $57.7 billion in 1929 to $36.3 billion in 1933. Bank closures soared with 499 in 1928, 659 in 1929, 1,358 in 1930, 2,294 in 1931, 1,456 in 1932, and 4,004 in 1933; those 9,490 closures were 40 percent of 23,697 banks and wiped out $7 billion of depositors' savings. The number of home mortgage foreclosures where families lost their homes was around 100,000 in 1929, 150,000 in 1930, 200,000 in 1931, and 273,000 in 1932.[20]

Homelessness soared. Many people lived in "hobo" shanty towns they called "Hoovervilles" or "rode the rails" by hopping freight trains in a search for jobs and freedom. Eric Sevareid, who later became a famous television journalist, hoboed during some of those years. He recalled "the great underground world, peopled by tens of thousands of American men, women, and children, white, black, brown, and yellow, who inhabit the 'jungle,' eat from blackened tin cans, find warmth at night in boxcars...steal one day, beg with cap in hand the next, fight with fists and often razors, hold sexual intercourse under a blanket in a dark corner of a crowded car...wander from town to town, anxious for the next place, tired of it in a day, fretting to be gone again, happy only when the wheels are clicking under them, the telephone poles slipping by."[21]

Governor Roosevelt responded to the Great Depression by calling the legislature into special session and explaining to the members his political philosophy's essence: "I assert that modern society, acting through its government, owes the definite obligation to prevent the starvation or dire want of any of its fellow men and women who try to maintain themselves but cannot...To those unfortunate citizens aid must be extended by government – not as a matter of charity but as a matter of social duty."[22]

As usual, his first act was to amass information about the problem. He got the Department of Social Welfare, the Department of Labor, and the Charities Aid Association to form a task force to tour the state to determine the severity of joblessness, homelessness, malnutrition, and poverty. Armed with that task force's dire statistics, he asked the legislature to establish a Temporary Emergency Relief Administration (TERA) and appropriate $20 million for it to disperse to the needy. To pay for that, he called for a 50 percent raise in the state's income tax. Astonishingly, Roosevelt's TERA was the first relief organization by any state.

Meanwhile, he appointed a commission to determine why the banking system failed and how to revive it. As with other commissions, he gave most seats to Republicans since they dominated the senate and assembly. Subsequently, the Banking Commission's report reflected Republican Party ideals rather than hard economic realities. Democrats on the commission called for strict laws against speculation, corruption, and theft; requiring banks to hold a share of their assets in state bonds; and for separating savings and investment banks. The commission's report became the foundation for the 1930 Banking Law that increased the State Banking Department's personnel and right to examine the books of any financial institution.

Roosevelt signed that law even though it lacked the power to deter or punish speculators and fraudsters. He explained that: "Government cannot prevent some individuals from making errors of judgment. But Government can prevent to a very great degree the fooling of sensible people through misstatements and through the withholding of information on the part of private organizations, great and small, which seek to sell investments to the people of the nation."[23]

The unregulated financial market continued to implode. The State Banking Department was forced to close the fifty-seven branches of the Bank of the United States as it teetered at the brink of collapse, precipitated by rampant speculation, fraud, and theft by high-ranking insiders. An investigation by New York Special Prosecutor Max Steuer eventually indicted twenty-eight directors and their underlings for conspiracy and neglect of duty, including Joseph Broderick, the State Banking Department supervisor. A jury found Broderick not guilty.

Roosevelt formed the Commission on Old Age Security to investigate problems suffered by elderly working and retired people. As usual, he had to yield most seats to Republicans and as usual the final report reflected that party's principles rather than genuine problems. In February 1930, the commission reported that only 15 percent of people seventy years and older needed any assistance while everyone else was just fine, and recommended against any public institution interfering with elderly living with their families and friends. Nonetheless, Republican Senator Seabury Mastick, the chair, did sponsor the Public

Welfare Law that declared the "care and relief of aged people...a special matter of State concern," but provided for no new institution or funding for that "concern." Roosevelt signed the bill anyway, hoping eventually to build something substantial on that principle.

Nineteen-thirty was an election year. Charles Tuttle was Roosevelt's Republican challenger, picked during the party's convention at Albany on September 28. Tuttle was the tough U.S. Attorney for the Southern District of New York. By acclamation, the Democratic Party renominated Roosevelt for governor during its convention at Syracuse on September 30.

Campaign manager Louis Howe got the Democratic Publicity Bureau to spend $25,000 on radio advertisements. He also had a short film called "The Roosevelt Record" made and distributed to two hundred movie theaters across the state to be shown before the Hollywood features.[24] Among the attributes that made Howe such an excellent political advisor was that he confronted accusations with openness rather than denial, and showed rather than told. Rumors about Roosevelt's health persisted ever since polio crippled him. During the campaign, Republican politicians and newspaper editors vented the latest barrage of questions and assertions about Roosevelt's health, Howe invited a group of insurance company physicians to examine Roosevelt at his New York City townhouse on East Sixty-Fifth Street. The doctors released their report on October 18, two weeks before the election. Dr. Edgar Beckwith spoke for them by declaring Roosevelt's health "gilt-edged for a man of forty-eight." His only problem was his withered legs from polio. But Beckwith had "never before observed such a complete recovery in organic function and such a remarkable degree of recovery of muscles and limbs in an individual who had passed through an attack of infantile paralysis."[25]

Roosevelt enjoyed overwhelming support from workers. He received this glowing endorsement from William Green, the American Federation of Labor (AFL) director: "Labor has very seldom secured the enactment of so many measures which so favorably affect their economic, social, and industrial welfare during a single session of a legislative body."[26]

Roosevelt won 1,770,342 votes or 56.4 percent to Tuttle's 1,045,341 or 33.4 percent, Law Preservation Party Robert Carroll with 190,666 votes or 6.08 percent, and the rest spread among the Socialist, Communist, and Socialist-Labor Parties. That done, Roosevelt got back to governing.

As a gentleman farmer, Roosevelt understood the value of rich soil for crops, pastureland for livestock, and woods. Many farmers enhanced their income by clearcutting trees on their property and plowing or grazing marginal lands. Hard rains washed away soil to the bedrock. The result was denuded landscapes filled with tree stumps and barren eroded ground. Farmers fled their devastated farms then banks and real estate firms that acquired the property could not sell it. Recently, farmers were annually abandoning over 250,000 acres.

For Roosevelt, that problem's solution was clear. In 1931, he worked with the legislature to pass a proposed amendment for New York's constitution to empower the state's Conservation Department to buy lands at least 500 acres large and reforest them, paid for with a $19 million bond issue that covered a $1 million budget in 1932 that rose $250,000 a year to peak at $2 million in 1937. The people vote on amendments proposed by the legislature, and approved this amendment by 778,192 to 554,550. The reforestation program eventually employed 10,000 jobless men to plant seedling trees in newly acquired state lands.[27]

Despite Roosevelt's efforts, New York's economy worsened along with the rest of America. Across the state over 2 million people were jobless while wages for factory workers lucky enough to keep their jobs fell from a 101.7 index in 1929 to 46.5 in 1932. Roosevelt was able to get the legislature to pass a $30 million bond issue to use for welfare in 1932, but that was less than half what experts calculated was needed.[28]

Roosevelt realized that economic problems immersed all states and the more states that cooperated in policies that alleviated conditions and boosted growth, the likelier they would succeed. In January 1931, he invited the governors of Connecticut, Massachusetts, New Jersey, Ohio, Pennsylvania, and Rhode Island to meet with him in Albany. The conference's theme was "Government Responsibility for Relief and the Prevention of Unemployment." Although the governors had a vigorous exchange of ideas and information, they forged no common policies. They did agree to form an Interstate Commission for the Study of Unemployment Insurance.

That effort inspired two legislators, Republican Senator Seabury Mastick and Democrat Irwin Steingut, the Assembly Speaker, to co-sponsor a bill that established a compulsory unemployment insurance system. The American Federation of Labor (AFL) enthusiastically backed that bill while the National Association of Manufacturers and other business groups adamantly opposed it. Roosevelt was equivocal, not openly supporting or rejecting the bill. He did express this principle: "An enlightened government…should help its citizens insure themselves during good times against the evil days of hard times to come. The worker, the industry, and the State should all assist in making this insurance possible."[29] Without the governor's endorsement, the bill failed.

The Interstate Commission issued its report in February 1932 and recommended that employers contribute 2 percent of each worker's payroll to an insurance fund and the establishment of State Unemployment Administrations with representatives of officials, employers, and workers to cooperate in overcoming common problems. That inspired Mastick and Steingut to draft the latest version of an unemployment insurance bill. Once again business interests denounced the bill and Roosevelt refused to endorse it so it died.

Roosevelt did ask the legislature to pass a bill that capped the workweek for women and children at forty-eight hours along with the principle that human labor was not a commodity. No committee passed that proposal. Then, in August 1931, he got the legislature to pass a bill that provided a forty-hour and five day work week for state highway construction workers. He signed that bill on December 1, 1932.

Roosevelt sought to provide statewide electricity for industries, businesses, and households. The best energy source was the St. Lawrence River where a dam could generate hydroelectricity. As the first decisive step to that end, he got the legislature to establish the St. Lawrence Power Authority. He then established a five-person St. Lawrence Power Development Commission to investigate how to achieve that. On January 13, 1931, the Commission issued its report that provided estimates for construction costs and electricity rates. In March 1931, Republican assemblyman Jasper Cornaire sponsored the St. Lawrence Authority Bill that embraced the Commission's recommendations. The Assembly passed the bill but Senate Republicans blocked the bill in committee. They insisted that the Power Authority should be a privately owned company subsidized by the state rather than a state-owned corporation. Roosevelt eventually got key lawmakers to make enough changes that got both houses to pass the bill, which he signed on April 27, 1931.

That was a critical but far from final step. Roosevelt had to get President Hoover to support the project and get an agreement with Canadian Prime Minister Mackenzie King on issues like St. Lawrence navigation and Canadian contributions. On July 18, American and Canadian diplomats signed a treaty, but Hoover did not intend to submit it to the Senate for ratification before that year's presidential election. He did not want the political spotlight cast favorably on someone who might contest him for the White House in 1932.

Chapter 3

THE FIRST HUNDRED DAYS

"The day of the great promoter or financial Titan, to whom we granted everything is over. Our task now is...the...business of administering resources and plans already in hand, of seeking to re-establish foreign markets for our excess production, of meeting the problem of underconsumption, of adjusting production to consumption, of distributing wealth and products more equitably."

"The country demands bold, persistent experimentation. It is common sense to take a method and try it: If it fails, admit it frankly and try another. But above all try something." (Franklin Roosevelt)

Franklin Roosevelt no sooner won re-election as New York's governor in 1930, when his campaign manager Louis Howe began systematically preparing for his presidential campaign in 1932.[1] Howe organized a "Friends of Roosevelt" club in New York City and then branches in major cities across the country. He got *Liberty* magazine to publish a dozen 400-word essays on public affairs with Roosevelt the author but actually ghost-written by Earle Looker. Those essays were published as a book called *Government, Not Politics*, in 1932. Looker wrote a fawning biography of the governor called *The Man Roosevelt*. Howe got Ernest Lindley, an Albany based *New York World* reporter, to write his own favorable biography titled *Franklin D. Roosevelt* in 1932, and then in 1933, *The American Way: F.D.R. in Action* about his first year as president.

Republican politicians and newspaper editors criticized Roosevelt's character and policies, and disparaged his health, claiming he was unfit to be president. Howe countered that barrage by calling in a panel of physicians to thoroughly examine Roosevelt. On April 29, 1931, the panel reported that Roosevelt's "health and powers of endurance are such as to allow him to meet any demand of private and public life. We find that his organs and functions are sound in all respects... Governor Roosevelt can walk all necessary distances and can maintain a standing position without fatigue." Earle Looker summed up the panel's finding: "I am able to say unhesitatingly that every rumor of Franklin Roosevelt's physical incapacity is false."[2]

And then there were criticisms by former allies. Walter Lippman, the New York *World*'s editor, had endorsed Roosevelt's campaign for the governorship but thereafter had mixed feelings about him. He dismissed Roosevelt as an "amiable man with many philanthropic impulses, but he is not the dangerous enemy of anything...for F.D.R. is no crusader. He is no more a tribune of the people. He is no enemy of entrenched privilege. He is a pleasant man who, without any important qualifications for the office, would very much like to be president."[3] All that was then stingingly true. But Roosevelt was determined to change each negative point while staying thoroughly pleasant.

Roosevelt announced his presidential campaign on January 23, 1932, with the first of a series of speeches blasting President Herbert Hoover's administration. On April 7, he condemned the White House for exacerbating rather than alleviating the Great Depression, for mistaking the symptoms for the causes of economic disease: "It has sought temporary relief from the top down rather than permanent relief from the bottom up. These unhappy times call for the building of plans that put their faith once more in the forgotten man at the bottom of the economic pyramid."[4]

Roosevelt shifted position on two key issues. He had enthusiastically backed the League of Nations a dozen years earlier and was willing to forgive or reduce the debt that Europeans owed America. For that William Randolph Hearst blistered him as an "internationalist" in his various newspapers. To placate Hearst, Roosevelt explained on February 2 that he no longer supported the League because it failed to fulfill the promises and principles of collective security and peace that President Woodrow Wilson and others had envisioned for it, and now insisted that Europeans pay all they owed the United States. That won Heart's approval.

Meanwhile, Hoover compounded his unpopularity by the heavy-handed way he dealt with the "Bonus Army" of nearly 15,000 veterans, many with families, who gathered in Washington and demanded compensation in April 1932. They camped in makeshift shelters beyond the Anacostia River which they crossed daily to protest near the Capitol and White House. On July 28, Hoover ordered General Douglas MacArthur to mass troops armed with bayoneted rifles and tear gas and drive them from the city but let them retreat back to their camp.

MacArthur disobeyed orders by leading his soldiers to follow the veterans across the river and rout them from and burn their camp.

Roosevelt recognized that Hoover had blundered politically. He told his advisor Rexford Tugwell that, "What Hoover should have done was to meet with the leaders of the Bonus Army when they asked for an interview. When two hundred or so marched up to the White House, Hoover should have sent out coffee and sandwiches and asked a delegation in." Later that day, Roosevelt got a call from Huey Long, currently the Senator from and former governor of Louisiana. Roosevelt described Long as "the second most dangerous man in this country. Huey's a whiz on the radio. He screams at people and they love it. He makes them think they belong to some kind of church. He knows there is a promised land and he'll lead 'em to it." When Tugwell asked Roosevelt who was most dangerous, he replied, "The first is Douglas MacArthur. You saw how he strutted down Pennsylvania Avenue… Did you ever see anyone more self-satisfied? There's a potential Mussolini for you." During the Second World War as commander in chief, Roosevelt struggled and often succumbed to the charisma and intellect of that "potential Mussolini."[5]

The Republicans convened at Chicago from June 14 to 16. Hoover received 1,126 votes on the first ballot and the votes of all 1,154 delegates on the second. The delegates unanimously renominated Charles Curtis for vice president.

The Democrats held their convention at Chicago from June 27 to July 2. Roosevelt faced two main rivals along with nine other candidates who got votes. Al Smith, New York's former governor, had Tammany Hall's backing. Senator John Garner of Texas, known as Mustang or Cactus Jack, had the backing of Hearst and his publishing empire. During the first three ballots, Roosevelt got three times more votes than Smith and six times more than Garner but was short of the two-thirds needed for victory. His repudiation of the League of Nations and insistence that Europeans repay their debt earlier that year led Hearst to broker a deal whereby Garner pledged his delegates to Roosevelt for being nominated for the vice presidency. That enabled Roosevelt to win on the fourth ballot with 945 votes to Smith's 190.

Roosevelt upended precedent by flying to Chicago and personally accepting the nomination. In doing so, he declared: "Let it also be symbolic that in doing so I broke traditions. Let it be from now on the task of our Party to break foolish traditions." He asserted these remarkable lines: "I warn those nominal Democrats who squint at the future with their faces turned to the past, and who feel no responsibility to the demands of the new times, that they are out of step with their party. Ours must be a party of liberal thought, of planned action, of enlightened international outlook, and the greatest good to the greatest number of our citizens." His core promise was this: "I pledge you, I pledge myself, to a new deal for the American people."[6]

Roosevelt's latest triumph typically depressed and angered rather than elated Eleanor. She later wrote that "I did not want my husband to be president. I realized that it was impossible to keep a man out of public service if that was what he wanted and was undoubtedly well equipped for. It was pure selfishness on my part."[7]

The jaunty ditty "Happy Days Are Here Again!" became Roosevelt's campaign song and theme. Roosevelt embarked on what became a thirteen thousand mile whistle-stop campaign around the country. All along he pulled no political punches. He clearly explained what was wrong with the economy and how to reform it. Above all, pragmatism, not theory, would guide his policies. He insisted that "the country demands bold, persistent experimentation. It is common sense to take a method and try it: If it fails, admit it frankly and try another. But above all try something."[8]

He picked a haven of big business mavens – San Francisco's Commonwealth Club – to boldly deliver a blistering critique of unbridled corporate power. He argued that: "The history of the last half century is in large measure a history of a group of financial titans...A mere builder of more industrial plants, a creator of more railroad systems, an organizer of more corporations, is as likely to be a danger as a help. The day of the great promoter or financial Titan, to whom we granted everything if only he would build or develop, is over. Our task now is not discovery, or exploitation of natural resources, or necessarily producing more goods. It is the soberer, less dramatic business of administering resources and plants already in hand, of seeking to re-establish foreign markets for our excess production, of meeting the problem of underconsumption, of adjusting production to consumption, of distributing wealth and products more equitably."[9] Emphasizing the distribution of wealth and redirection of production over the unbridled markets and the creation of wealth, enraged conservatives.

Republicans slightly outraised Democrats in fundraising, $2.6 million to $2.4 million. Republicans outspent Democrats on radio advertisements by $551,972 to $343,415.[10] Those advantages could not overcome the prevailing image of Hoover as a failed president and dour, angry, resentful man, especially when contrasted with Roosevelt's ebullient, confident image in newsreels.

Roosevelt crushed Hoover, winning 22,821,277 votes or 57.4 percent and 472 Electoral College votes from 42 states to 15,761,254 or 39.6 percent and 59 from six states. Democrats captured Congress with overwhelming majorities. In the House of Representatives, the Democrats gained 91 seats to control 313 while the Republicans fell 101 seats to control 117. The Farmer-Labor Party picked up four seats to total five. In the Senate, the Democrats picked up 11 seats to total 59 while the Republicans lost 11 and dropped to 37. The sole Farmer-Labor Party senator retained his seat.

Typically, Eleanor felt loss rather than elation for her husband's victory. She later admitted that: "I felt happy for my husband because I knew that in many ways it would make up for the blow that fate had dealt him when he was stricken with infantile paralysis; and I had implicit confidence in his ability to help the country in crisis...But for myself, I was probably more deeply troubled than ever....As I saw it, this meant the end of any personal life of my own. I knew what traditionally should lie before me...By earning my own money, I had recently enjoyed a certain amount of financial independence and had been able to do things in which I was personally interested."[11]

Like his predecessors, Roosevelt had three months between his election and inauguration to pick advisors and department chiefs. As in New York's governor's mansion, Louis Howe and Missy LeHand would live at the White House. Howe inhabited the Lincoln bedroom and LeHand had a small bedroom on the third floor. The White House physician was Admiral Ross McIntire.

Roosevelt's Albany "brain trust" followed him to the White House. His closest advisors, included Raymond Moley, a Columbia University politics professor; Rexford Tugwell, a Columbia economics professor; Adolf Berle, a Columbia Law School professor; Basil O'Connor, Roosevelt's law partner; Hugh Johnson, a financier; Samuel Rosenman, a longtime confident; and Felix Frankfurter, a Harvard Law School professor. As a second brain trust, he formed a Business Advisory Council that included such corporate leaders as Gerard Swope of General Electric, Averill Harriman of Union Pacific Railroad, Winthrop Aldrich of Chase Manhattan Bank, and Walter Gifford of American Telephone and Telegraph (ATT). Among the more important scholarly books that guided Roosevelt's administration were *Concentration and Control: A Solution of the Trust Problem in America* (1912) by Charles Van Hise; *The Modern Corporation and Private Property* (1932) by Berle and Gardiner Means; and *Industrial Discipline and the Governmental Arts* (1933) by Tugwell. The consensus among these works was that only commensurate government regulatory power could check and channel corporate power to benefit rather than harm society. Tugwell explained how Roosevelt faced the challenge of working with his advisors to overcome the Great Depression: "All the members of the Brains Trust and their associates will testify…to the flexibility of the Roosevelt mind even when the presidency approached. He was a progressive vessel yet to be filled with content."[12]

During his presidency, Roosevelt increasingly depended on Eleanor as his conscience on social issues. He listened carefully to her and sent her on investigative trips around the country and even overseas. That complicated her own busy schedule as an advisor to various groups, her daily newspaper column "My Day," weekly radio address, and frequent speaking engagements across the nation. They rarely met. Eleanor had her getaways, an apartment in New York's Greenwich Village and her Val-Kill cottage on the Roosevelt estate at Hyde Park ninety miles up the Hudson. But more often she traveled around the country meeting with various groups and investigating problems.

For his cabinet, political payback rather than expertise determined many of Roosevelt's choices. Utah Governor George Dern became the war secretary because he helped swing western voters behind Roosevelt, and despite his lack of military experience. Likewise Claude Swanson headed the navy although he never served in any armed service. He was a former Virginia governor and current senator who served on the foreign relations committee. His first choice for treasury secretary was Carter Glass, a former representative and current senator from Virginia who had helped draft the Federal Reserve Act. Glass declined. Roosevelt then turned to William Woodin, a New York financier who had helped underwrite his campaign. His candidate for attorney general, Senator Thomas Walsh of Montana had chaired the 1924 and 1932 Democratic conventions; tragically, that 74 year old suffered a fatal heart attack on the train for the inaugural following his honeymoon with a much younger wife in Havana. Roosevelt replaced him with Homer Cummings, a corporate lawyer and Roosevelt backer. For commerce, he tapped Daniel Roper, a South Carolinian who had served in several administrative posts in Washington and for two years in the House of Representatives. Harold Ickes, a Chicago political activist, became Interior secretary. Henry Wallace, an Iowa farmer and essayist, became agriculture; secretary. For labor secretary, Roosevelt chose Frances Perkins, a tireless and articulate lobbyist on worker issues; Perkins was the first female to head a department. For commerce secretary, he picked Harry Hopkins.

Before his inauguration, Franklin Roosevelt suffered a near death experience. On February 15, 1933, he was scheduled to address a veteran's convention in Miami. He was seated in the back of a convertible car chatting with Chicago Mayor Anton Cernak before a crowd. Suddenly, five shots blasted and each hit someone near Roosevelt, including Cernak, a secret service agent, and three other people; Cernak soon died while the others recovered. The gunman was Giuseppe Zangara, an anarchist and jobless bricklayer, who had bought the .32 caliber revolver that morning at a pawn shop. A woman standing beside Zangara swatted his gun-hand with her purse and so may have saved Roosevelt's life. Police tackled and arrested Zangara who admitted his crime and motive. He wanted to kill Roosevelt for symbolizing all that he detested: "I have always hated the rich and powerful. I do not hate Mr. Roosevelt personally. I hate all presidents, no matter from what country they come." Zangara was swiftly indicted, tried, and executed on March 20. It is astonishing to think how the subsequent fate of America and the world would have differed had a bullet killed Roosevelt, leaving John "Texas Jack" Garner to be inaugurated as president on March 4, 1933.[13]

Roosevelt faced the Great Depression at its worst. In 1933, the economy was half its size four years earlier and one of four workers or 13 million were jobless, including 400,000 women. Homelessness and malnutrition afflicted millions of Americans. The economy was locked into a vicious cycle of worsening bankruptcies, joblessness, and poverty. The depression persisted from underconsumption and overproduction. The key to economic expansion was getting consumers to buy more and producers to make less. That would raise prices, profits, and employment.

In his inaugural address, Roosevelt famously declared that: "The only thing we have to fear, is fear itself." He then targeted "unscrupulous money-changers in the temple" as the Great Depression's worst villains: "The rulers of the exchange of mankind's goods have failed through their own stubbornness and their own incompetence, have admitted their failure, and have abdicated. The money changers have fled from their high seats in the temple of our civililzation. We may now restore that temple to the ancient truths. The measure of the restoration lies in the extent to which we apply social values more noble than mere monetary profit...If I read the temper of our people correctly, we now realize as we have never realized before our interdependence on each other, that we cannot merely take but we must give as well." He promised to call a congressional special session to approve an array of programs to fight the Great Depression. He then darkly added that if Congress failed its duty, "I shall ask the Congress for the one remaining instrument to meet the crisis – broad Executive power to wage a war against the emergency, as great as the power that would be given to me if we were in fact invaded by a foreign foe."[14]

That night Roosevelt was the first president to throw an inauguration ball since William Taft in 1909. For varying reasons the intervening presidents had neglected the joyous custom that George Washington began. The irony, of course, is that Roosevelt, paralyzed, could not have launched the ball by dancing with Eleanor. Indeed, he did not appear, but Eleanor did. Couples paid $150 to attend and the money was donated to charity. Cousin Alice Roosevelt Longworth was among the guests at that "riot of pleasure. I went with great alacrity and enthusiasm and had a lovely, malicious time."[15] That evening Alice had been a widow for nearly two years. Her husband, Nicolas Longworth, was the House of Representatives Speaker but pneumonia killed him in April 1931.

Roosevelt enacted much of his New Deal agenda in his first one-hundred days in the White House.[16] The day after his inauguration, he issued two executive orders – for Congress to convene for a special session beginning on March 9 and for wielding the Trading with the Enemy Act to assert a four-day banking holiday and halt all gold payments. He had Treasury Secretary Woodin draft a bill that empowered the president to determine the criteria for a bank to reopen. For clout over senators and representatives, he pointedly withheld filling thousands of political posts in the federal government until after the Special Session finished the work he assigned it. If necessary, he would trade posts for recalcitrant votes.

The Special Session lasted from March 9 to June 15. During that time, Roosevelt sent to Congress fifteen bills or calls to adopt a bill already in committee and Congress passed all of them. That "One Hundred Days" of lawmaking was among the most critical in American history.[17]

On its first day in special session, Congress overwhelmingly passed the Emergency Banking Act by acclamation in the House of Representatives and by 91 to 7 in the Senate.[18] That bill amended the 1917 Trading with the Enemy Act that empowered the president to impose financial, trade, and other economic restrictions in a national emergency, including suspending gold transactions; let the twelve Federal Reserve Banks issue enough money to member banks so they could fulfill their obligations after they reopened; letting the Reconstruction Finance Corporation (RFC) invest in banks; and let the

Federal Deposit Insurance Corporation guarantee bank accounts up to $2,500. Eventually the RFC saved the banking system by investing $1,171,000,000 in 6,000 banks; among them only 106 failed and the RFC lost merely $13,600,000.[19]

The evening before the banks opened, Roosevelt gave his first presidential "fireside chat" radio broadcast. He explained in simple terms how the Emergency Banking Act saved the banking system and assured Americans "that it is safer to keep your money in a reopened bank than under the mattress...We have provided the machinery to restore our financial system; and it is up to you to support and make it work."[20] The next morning on March 13, countless Americans lined up at banks to deposit rather than withdraw money.

Roosevelt withdrew the dollar from the gold standard on April 18. Congress reinforced that policy by passing on June 5 a law that eliminated the gold clause for public and private contracts. That caused the dollar's value to drop, thus making imports more and exports less expensive. Americans and foreigners alike bought more American goods, which stimulated America's economy as money circulated, production expanded to meet greater demand, unemployment fell, and stock prices rose. Meanwhile, the Treasury Department bought gold that helped raise its price from $20.67 to $34 an ounce by January 1934, when the program ended.

Roosevelt and Congress took two major steps to reduce the speculation that fueled financial bubbles. The Truth in Securities Act that became law on May 27, required businesses with publicly traded stocks to file reports on their companies with the Federal Trade Commission that published them. The Glass-Steagall Act separated commercial and investment banking and established the Federal Deposit Insurance Corporation (FDIC) that guaranteed bank deposits up to $2,500 in 1933 and $5,000. Different versions of Glass-Steagall passed by 262 to 19 in the House and acclamation in the Senate. A reconciled version passed the House by 191 to 6 and Senate acclamation, and Roosevelt signed it on June 16.

Roosevelt potentially undercut his New Deal on March 10, by getting Congress to approve his Economy Act that empowered him to cut the $3.6 billion budget by half a million dollars that included eliminating some bureaucracies, consolidating others, reducing salaries for federal employees, and halving veterans' payments. In doing so, he conceded to fiscal conservatives in Congress and Bernard Baruch, a key Democratic Party financier.

Undoubtedly, the most toasted New Deal measure repealed the Eighteenth Amendment prohibiting alcohol that was ratified on

January 16, 1919, and took effect a year later on January 16, 1920. Prohibition was a disaster for America as it distorted the economy, boosted organized crime and violence, made criminals of anyone who indulged, and undermined the legitimacy of law and government authority. On February 20, 1933, Congress passed the Twenty-first Amendment that repealed the Eighteenth Amendment and sent it to the states for ratification. On March 22, Congress passed the Beer-Wine Revenue Act that let the federal government tax those and other alcoholic beverages as soon as the states passed repeal. The Twenty-first Amendment was ratified on December 5, 1933.

As he had in Albany, Roosevelt did whatever he could to revive the depressed farm economy.[21] Most farmers peaked in prosperity during the First World War with extraordinary global demand, then declined steadily during the 1920s as mechanization, fertilizers, pesticides, and genetically enhanced seeds and livestock led to overproduction. Then prices plummeted with the Great Depression. The farm price index of 100 in 1928 was 41 in 1932 while the prices that farmers paid for goods fell from 101 to 70. That bankrupted countless farms across the country. Banks acquired ever more property that they could not sell, which helped bankrupt them, thus exacerbating the economic collapse.[22] Only one of ten farms had inside toilets and electricity. Sharecropping and tenant farming existed in all states but was especially virulent in the south. Average annual incomes for white and black sharecroppers were $350 and $294, respectively, in 1934.[23]

Roosevelt submitted the Agricultural Adjustment Act (AAA) on March 16, the House passed it by 315 to 98, the Senate by 64 to 20, and the president signed it on May 12. The law empowered the president to establish the Farm Credit Administration (FCA) whose Commodity Credit Corporation (CCC) sought to reduce crop and livestock surpluses by paying farmers not to plant and ranchers not to breed beyond set quotas. The six crops targeted for floor prices were corn, wheat, cotton, rice, peanuts, and tobacco. Taxes paid for the subsidies. Roosevelt asked his friend Henry Morgenthau to organize and head the FCA.

Roosevelt conceived the Civilian Conservation Corps (CCC) as a civilian army that managed the nation's federal lands and natural resources.[24] By acclamation the House and Senate approved the Civilian Conservation Act that created the CCC and Roosevelt signed the bill on March 31. To head the CCC, Roosevelt chose Robert Fechner, vice president of the American Labor Federation (AFL). Over the next nine years under Fechner's able leadership, the CCC employed over 2,750,000 men, including 200,000 blacks, at 2,500 camps for six month stints renewable for two years. They received a monthly salary of $30, with $25 sent to their families, lived in barracks, ate three daily meals, and worked on such conservation projects as flood control, reforestation, and constructing roads, bridges, trails, and fire outlooks, and they also fought wild fires. In all, they built 3,475 fire towers, strung 65,100 miles of telephone lines, planted 1.3 billion seedling trees, and devoted 4.1 million work hours to fighting forest fires. The army ran the camps and the Forest Service supervised the projects. The CCC gave those who served not just jobs, food and lodging, but dignity, a hand up rather than hand out. It also injected often desperately needed money and infrastructure into remote, poverty-stricken regions, boosting their chance of developing.

The Emergency Relief Administration Act passed the Senate by 55 to 17 and House by 326 to 42, and became law on May 12. The Act established the Federal Emergency Relief Administration (FERA) that Roosevelt had Harry Hopkins direct. From May 1933 until it expired in December 1935, FERA distributed $3.1 billion, with half directly dispensed and the other half matched with the states for impoverished people. Those who applied for relief had to pass a "means test" by a social worker to the home to determine that family's residents' income, debts, savings, diet, and health. FERA helped over 20 million people.

The Tennessee Valley Authority (TVA) passed the Senate by 63 to 30 and the House by 306 to 91, and became law on May 18.[25] The TVA eventually brought hydroelectricity, flood control, and paved roads to a mostly impoverished seven-state southern region with a complex of dams and related infrastructure projects. The TVA increased the number of electrified farms from 2 percent in 1933 to 75 percent in 1945.[26]

The Home Owners Loan Corporation Act, signed on June 13, established the Federal Home Loan Bank Administration (HOLC) that issued bonds to banks for default mortgages then let homeowners pay back their loans at lower interest rates over longer years. That program saved countless families from losing their homes to banks when they failed to make mortgage payments. The loan ceiling was $20,000 to ensure the program benefited inexpensive homes. From 1933 to its expiration in December 1936, HOLC issued more than 1 million loans worth $3.1 billion.

Congress's most sweeping and controversial program came on June 16, with passage of the National Industrial Recovery Act. That law provided a minimum wage; let workers unionize and collectively bargain with employers; and created the three-person National Labor Relations Board to help resolve disputes; established the

National Recovery Administration (NRA) empowered with creating and managing industrial cartels with production, price, and wage caps; and established the Public Works Administration (PWA) with $3.3 billion to help industries rationalize and modernize themselves.

Businesses that took federal money agreed to forty-hour work weeks; minimum wages that varied for unskilled workers in the northern, central, and southern states with sixty cents, forty-five cents, and forty cents, respectively; and good faith bargaining with employees. In return for that package, known as a "code," they received a Blue Eagle seal of government approval which they could display, and, most importantly exemption from anti-trust laws. By February 1934, the NRA had approved 557 basic codes and 200 supplementary codes.[27]

Roosevelt tapped Brigadier General Hugh "Iron Pants" Johnson to head the NRA. The NRA had a Labor Board and Consumer Advisory Board. Johnson awarded compliant businesses, unions, and other organization a Blue Eagle award with the saying, "We Do Our Part." Johnson proved to be a failure as a manager and man. He was an alcoholic often absent from work or impaired on the job and failed to fulfill the NRA's mission. Roosevelt fired him in 1934.

Roosevelt had Interior Secretary Ickes head PWA. Ickes was a fiscal conservative who approved only $110 million worth of projects by December 1933. Although Roosevelt chaffed at Ickes' glacial pace, he did not fire him. Instead, on November 9, 1933, he created an alternative bureaucracy, the Civil Works Administration (CWA), with his most trusted advisor, Harry Hopkins in charge. He hoped to spur a dynamic rivalry between the two organizations and chiefs similar to that between the Engineer Corps and Reclamation Bureau. Roosevelt explained that: "Ickes is a good administrator but often too slow. Harry gets things done."[28] Hopkins and Ickes often clashed as heads of rival departments and with different policy priorities and outlooks. At one point, Hopkins rebutted Ickes' assertion that they had to anticipate their policies' long-term results by declaring, "People don't eat in the long run. They eat every day."[29]

Hopkins proved to be a managerial genius. He enrolled 4.2 million people and spent $833 million in the half year ending on March 31, 1934, when CWA was scheduled to expire. During that time, CWA workers "laid 12 million feet of sewer pipe and built or ungraded 500,000 miles of secondary roads, 40,000 schools, 3,700 recreation areas, and nearly a thousand airports. It employed 50,000 teachers to keep rural schools open and to provide adult education in the cities. It hired 3,000 artists and writers."[30] The average CWA wage was $15.04 compared to weekly federal relief payments of $4.25. As astonishingly,

Hopkins kept CWA's administrative costs to just 2 percent and spent 80 percent on salaries.[31]

The PWA expanded steadily. From July 1933 to March 1939, PWA built 34,000 projects totally worth $6 billion and employed 1.2 million that included La Guardia Airport, the Triborough Bridge, and the Lincoln Tunnel in New York City, the Skyline Drive in Virginia, the hundred mile Oversea Highway linking south Florida with Key West, and the aircraft carriers *Enterprise* and *Yorktown*.

That array of "Hundred Day" policies reignited the economy. The industrial index nearly doubled from 56 in March to 101 in July 1933. By June, 90 percent of banks had reopened flush with money from depositors and Washington. Indeed, the economy expanded despite being battered by 1,672 strikes involving 1.1 million workers in 1933. Of those strikes, two of three won workers more pay and better conditions.[32] Yet those policies, laws, and institutions alleviated the depression but could not end it. For that Roosevelt searched for other remedies.

Chapter 4

THE CORRECTIONS

"We have earned the hatred of entrenched greed. They seek the restoration of their selfish power...Give them their way and they will take the course of every autocracy of the past – power for themselves, enslavement for the public." (Franklin Roosevelt)

"But the simplest way for each of you to judge recovery lies in the plain facts of your own individual economic situation. Are you better off than you were last year? Are your debts less burdensome? Is your bank account more secure? Are your working conditions better? Is your faith in your own individual future more firmly grounded?" (Franklin Roosevelt)

After that frenzied first hundred days the White House settled into a relaxed routine around the president. After waking, Franklin Roosevelt lingered in bed for several hours. There he had a simple breakfast of eggs, toast, bacon, and coffee, read a pile of newspapers including the *New York Times, Washington Post, Baltimore Sun, Chicago Tribune*, and *Times Herald* while chatting with his closest aide Louis Howe and "second wife" Missy LeHand, his secretary. Around ten thirty each morning, he appeared in the Oval Office where he stayed until five in the afternoon. He met a series of advisors or distinguished congressional or business leaders usually at fifteen minute intervals. He had cabinet meetings every Thursday afternoon, although he used them to solicit information and ideas rather than make decisions. He chatted with the press for an hour on Wednesday and Friday mornings at ten. He dictated letters. He spent a couple of hours each day on the telephone talking to administrators and politicians. He had a light lunch at his desk.

After work, he usually went for a short swim then was dressed for dinner. At seven he mixed martinis for whoever would join him for dinner at eight. Both his martinis and the dinners were infamous for their dreadful taste. Apparently Roosevelt used cheap gin and vermouth. Henrietta Nesbitt was his cook at the governor's mansion and the White House, and she churned out bland meatloaf, roast beef, and boiled vegetables. The most common after dinner activity was seeing a movie. Once a week he usually had a poker night. Without guests he relaxed by working on his stamp collection. He usually went to bed around midnight and slept soundly until six the next morning.

For most vacations, Roosevelt stayed at his health resort at Warm Springs, Georgia, that became known as the Little White House. He would die there. From 1942 when it opened, Roosevelt passed many weekends at Camp David, a 125-acre complex of rustic buildings in the Catoctin Mountain range sixty-two miles northwest of the White House. The Civilian Conservation Corps originally built Camp David as a summer camp for boys and girls until the federal government designated it the president's retreat. Roosevelt loved relaxing at Camp David which he called Shangri-La. He also spent time at his mansion at Hyde Park, New York

When ill health forced Treasury Secretary William Woodin to resign, Roosevelt replaced him with a curious choice on January 1, 1934. Henry Morgenthau owned an estate and farm near Roosevelt's Hyde Park home.[1] They had long been close friends with shy Morgenthau admiring Roosevelt for his confident extroversion. Morgenthau was Jewish by heritage but not by practice. His father had made a fortune in New York City's real estate market, contributed generously to the Democratic Party, and was chosen by President Wilson to serve as ambassador to the Ottoman Empire. Much to his father's disappointment, Morgenthau had dropped out of Cornell University and spurred law or business to be a gentleman farmer in the Hudson River valley. He edited the journal *American Agriculturalist* but neither that publication nor his farm made a profit. After winning the presidency, Roosevelt appointed Morgenthau to head the Federal Farm Board rather than the Agriculture Department that he had requested. Apparently, Roosevelt named Morgenthau treasury secretary over guilt at not earlier making him agriculture secretary. Without any financial expertise, Morgenthau could merely preside over the department and let the professionals run it. He would be best known for his Morgenthau Plan to strip Germany of its industries and break it up into agrarian states after the Second World War.

Roosevelt was a master at spinning the news with reporters and editors.[2] He usually had two weekly press conferences that began at ten o'clock on Wednesday and Friday mornings for the 125 revolving press club members managed by his press secretary Steven Early. Roosevelt designated what information he shared either as "background" and attributed to "a White House source" or "off the record." He refused to answer hypothetical questions. Sessions usually lasted an hour. Roosevelt enjoyed fielding questions and did so usually with wit and insouciance if not always insight. Arthur Krock of the *New York Times* admitted to Rosevelt that: "You charm me so much that I go back to write comments on the proceedings, I can't keep it in balance."[3] The president undoubtedly grinned knowingly when he heard that while silently confirming, yes, that indeed was the intent.

The accredited Washington press corps numbered 504 during the New Deal years and around 750 during the Second World War. It was mostly a man's profession. For instance, of 363 reporters registered with the White House press pool in 1934, only fifteen were women. Both the National Press Club and White House Correspondents' Dinner banned them. Jostling with the reporters were 85 members of the White House News Photographers Association.[4]

While Early managed the White House press pool, Louis Howe sought to influence the national media. He nurtured journalists for such influential magazines as *Saturday Evening Post*, *Cosmopolitan*, *Liberty*, and *American Magazine* to write favorable articles about the administration and its policies. He wrote his own stories called *Howe's Daily Bugle*, and distributed them to hundreds of newspapers and magazines.

Howe had a team of twenty-five investigators compile statistics on whether the stories and editorials were favorable or not. That effort expanded in August 1934, when the National Recovery Administration established the Division of Press Intelligence with a couple of hundred employees. The National Emergency Council subsumed that outfit in July 1935. In July 1939, the White House dissolved the National Emergency Council and transferred the Division of Press Intelligence to the newly established Office of Government Reports, headed by Lowell Mellet, the former *Washington Daily News* editor.

As for policymaking, with Democrats dominating each congressional chamber, Roosevelt's proposed bills and other measures faced little opposition. Nonetheless, he had to work closely with key members of each house to devise and pass bills. Joseph Robinson was the Senate Majority Leader and Henry Rainey of Illinois was the House of Representatives Speaker. Senator Carter Glass and Representative Henry Steagall each chaired his chamber's banking and finance committee. Sam Rayburn of Texas chaired the House Committee on

Interstate and Foreign Commerce. Roosevelt also worked closely with four pragmatic Republicans, Hiram Johnson of California, George Norris of Nebraska, Gerald Nye of North Dakota, and Bronson Cutting of New Mexico.

Roosevelt worked with Congress in 1934 to bolster the financial system with new laws and policies built on the previous year's measures. First came the Gold Reserve Act, signed on January 30, that shifted the exchange rate for gold from $20.67 to $35.00 an ounce. That higher price stimulated gold mining in the United States and around the world, and the federal government's steadily increasing supply which was stored at Fort Knox, Kentucky. Not to be outdone, western silver mining interests influenced enough members of Congress to pass the Silver Purchase Act, that Roosevelt reluctantly signed on June 19, 1934. That law required the federal government to buy silver until it was one-quarter of the monetary reserve or $1.29 an ounce.

The Securities Exchange Act passed the House by 281 to 84 and the Senate by 62 to 13, and Roosevelt signed it on June 6, 1934. That law established the Securities and Exchange Commission (SEC) to oversee the stock market by promoting fair and punishing fraudulent transactions like insider trading and false marketing; and requiring publicly traded corporations to compile and issue financial reports of all their transactions. Roosevelt named Joseph Kennedy to head the SEC. Kennedy had gotten rich by manipulating the stock market. When asked why he picked Kennedy for that watchdog duty, Roosevelt quipped, "Set a thief to catch a thief."[5] The Federal Reserve Bill, signed into law on August 24, 1935, gave the Federal Reserve Board of Governors direct control over the Open Market Committee that buys and sells federal bonds.

The National Housing Act, signed on June 27, 1934, established the Federal Housing Administration and the Federal Savings and Loan Insurance Corporation to encourage a larger market and lower interest rates for home mortgages. The Home Owners Loan Corporation (HOLC) soon underwrote 20 percent of all mortgages.

The Federal Communications Act, signed on June 19, 1934, established the Federal Communications Commission to regulate the radio and telephone industries, and later the television, internet, and satellite industries.

The Reciprocal Trade Act empowered the president to negotiate trade deals with foreign countries whereby tariffs were reduced by up to 50 percent. That bill tried to undo some of the damage inflicted on the global trade system by the 1930 Smoot-Hawley Act that raised tariffs 50 percent, which provoked other countries to reciprocate, thus collapsing international commerce. The bill passed the Senate by 57 to 33 and the House by 271 to 111.

The plight of farmers remained bleak, and that was partly self-inflicted. Overplowing and overgrazing severely eroded once rich soils and pastures across the nation, especially in the arid West. Senator Edward Taylor of Colorado deplored the "waste, competition, over-use, and abuse of valuable range lands and watersheds eating into the heart of western economy...Erosion, yes, even human erosion, had taken root. The livestock industry...was headed for self-strangulation."[6]

A prolonged drought and series of wind storms caused what was called the "Dust Bowl" in the mid-1930s.[7] Just one storm on May 11, 1934, stripped 300 million tons of topsoil and blew it across the country as far as the east coast. By 1936, over 9 million acres were completely ruined and 50 million acres severely degraded. The Dust Bowl's epicenter was a region around Oklahoma's panhandle that included nearby regions of Kansas, Colorado, New Mexico, and Texas. By 1936, erosion afflicted 97.6 percent of those lands, with 53.4 percent suffering severe loss.[8] The Dust Bowl did not just ruin land, it fouled the lungs of millions of people and livestock. Atop that, western farmers suffered Biblical-scale hailstorms that flattened their crops and billions of grasshoppers that devoured them.

The losses were devastating with 400,000 families and $5 billion worth of wealth ruined. For instance, Kansan farmers harvested only 10.5 million bushels in 1934 compared to an average 137.7 million annual bushels from 1927 to 1931. Farmers went bankrupt and moved elsewhere after banks seized their land. From 1930 to 1940, several Great Plains states lost population, including Oklahoma by 2.5 percent (59,606), North Dakota by 3 percent (38,910), South Dakota by 7 percent (49,586), Kansas by 4 percent (79,971), and Nebraska by 5 percent (62,179); Vermont was the only other state to lose people during that decade, although the 380 net loss was negligible.[9]

Around half a million high plains people emigrated elsewhere, with most following Route 66 or other roads west to California. California's government tried stemming those refugees by deploying the state highway patrol at the sixteen major roads leading from other states where they turned back anyone without proof of a job or enough money. Hundreds of thousands of people managed to meet or evade those checkpoints and enter California whose population soared from 5,674,259 in 1930 to 6,907,387 in 1940. By 1940, there were 8,000 labor camps across the state.

The White House mobilized several New Deal institutions to alleviate conditions on the Great Plains. The Civilian Conservation Corps' Shelterbelt Project planted 220 million trees to cut the wind and contain and make soil; around 80 percent of the planted trees survived. In 1934, the Interior Department established the Soil Conservation Service to work with farmers to reduce their erosion and recover degraded lands by planting trees and leaving more land unplowed. The Soil Conservation Act, signed on April 27, 1935, transferred the Soil Conservative Service to the Agriculture Department. The Soil Conservation and Allotment Act that Roosevelt signed into law on February 29, 1936, authorized the Soil Conservation Service to pay farmers to reduce acreage for crops that depleted soil quality; leave natural borders around crop fields; use contour and strip plowing to reduce erosion; and rotate crops to replenish minerals.

The Jones-Connally Farm Relief Act, signed on April 7, 1934, included $200 million in relief to desperate farmers and ranchers. The money was distributed through the Federal Surplus Relief Corporation. More than half – $111,546,204 – purchased 8.3 million dairy and beef cattle for butchering that yielded 657,346,312 pounds of fresh or canned beef.[10] That helped reduce overgrazing. The Bankhead-Jones Farm Tenancy Act that became law on July 27, 1937, established the Farm Security Administration to provide low interest loans and conservation services to tenants to buy and farm their own land.

Roosevelt established the Rural Electrification Administration (REA) on May 11, 1935. The REA organized nonprofit rural cooperatives to build generators and power lines underwritten with federal loans with 3 percent interest rates. Hydroelectricity was the most important source with power lines eventually emanating from Boulder Dam on the Colorado, Grand Coulee Dam and Bonneville Dam on the Columbia River, Fort Peck Dam on the Missouri River, and 29 dams of the Tennessee Valley Authority (TVA). Thus did the REA raise the number of farms with electricity from 11 percent to 90 percent within half a dozen years. Roosevelt reinforced those measures with an executive order that created the Electric Home and Farm Authority to provide cheap loans for farmers to buy electric equipment and appliances.

The Supreme Court's 1935 ruling that the 1933 Agricultural Adjustment Act was unconstitutional forced the president and Congress to rewrite the law to avoid another successful legal challenge. On February 18, 1938, Roosevelt signed the Agricultural Adjustment Act that re-established the Commodity Credit Corporation (CCC) to provide price support for cotton, corn, and wheat if prices fell below 75 percent of parity.

Edward Taylor, a Colorado congressman, worked with Interior Secretary Harold Ickes to draft and sponsor the Taylor Grazing Act that established a Grazing Division within the Interior Department that would withdraw 173 million acres of federal grasslands into carefully managed reserves split among districts. In each district, officials would survey the land and determine the carrying capacity or maximum number of livestock that could graze there to allow the grasses to recover. Ranchers would pay a small fee – 5 cents a month – for each animal they grazed on federal land. Stockholder interests whittled the reserves to 140 million acres. Roosevelt signed the Taylor Grazing Act on June 28, 1934, withdrew 80 million acres in November 1934 and 62 million more acres in June 1936. The Interior Department split those 142 million acres into nine regions, each with an undersecretary in charge and divided among scores of districts.

Eleven million livestock including cattle, sheep, horses, and goats grazed public lands by 1940. The Taylor Grazing Act stabilized but did not recover most of those lands. Stockholder interests pressured those who drafted the bill to let local ranchers dominate the district advisory councils. The usual result was for districts to let more livestock graze than the range could sustain.

The Resettlement Administration sought to buy 75,000,000 acres of marginal lands owned by 450,000 poor farm families and resettle them in richer soils or other livelihoods. They succeeded in buying only 11,300,000 acres and resettling only 10,000 families.[11] However bleak their conditions, most people preferred staying in their homes on their land within their communities and often near cemeteries where loved ones were buried. Swaths of purchased lands became national grasslands.

The National Forest System had 162,009,145 acres, of which 133,490,204 acres were in the west in October 1934. Yet less than one of three forest acres were federal lands. There were 395,000,000 other forest acres of which state and local governments owned 15,000,000 acres and the other 380,000,000 acres were privately owned, usually by logging corporations. Those businesses varied greatly whether their practiced clearcutting that destroyed the forest or selective cutting and replanting that sustained the forest. Most corporations put short-term profits before long-term profits by chopping down and selling every tree for lumber or pulp. They then sought to sell the devastated landscape. The Forest Service was eager to buy and restore those lands. From 1934 to 1941, the National Forest Service paid $54 million for 12,500,000 acres.[12]

After clearcutting, fire destroyed most forest. Fire is actually a natural part of western forests where lightning strikes periodically spark conflagrations. That can actually be good for the forest if the fire burns undergrowth but spares larger trees. But if too much debris from dead trees accumulates on the ground that can fuel firestorms that devastate the forest. That was why the Forest Service's policy of fire suppression actually made fires worse over the long-term.

Two New Deal laws tried to improve National Forests. The Fulmer Act of August 29, 1935, sought to coordinate forest management by federal and state forests. The Farm Forestry Act of May 18, 1937, expanded tree planting and watershed protection in the National Forests. Tragically, logging corporations clearcut countless swaths of once healthy forests into oblivion with soils so eroded and dry that seedlings withered.

For people living across the bone-dry West, getting enough water for their homes, crops, livestock, and other businesses was critical. Two federal bureaucracies provided nearly all the water for westerners and a lot for people in other regions. The Army Corps of Engineers and the Interior Department's Bureau of Reclamation competed to dam the nation's rivers. The Corps did so primarily to improve navigation and control flooding, while the Bureau had the additional goals of providing hydroelectricity, irrigation, and drinking water. During the New Deal years, the Bureau constructed twenty-six projects worth $335,480,000.[13]

The 1922 Colorado River Compact split that river's waters among seven states, with Colorado, Utah, Wyoming, and New Mexico in the Upper Basin and California, Arizona, and Nevada in the Lower Basin. Hoover Dam on the Colorado River was the Bureau's largest and at $49 million and a hundred lives, its most expensive project. A consortium of six companies began construction in early 1931 and finished on March 1, 1936, two years ahead of schedule; the dam began storing water on February 1, 1935. Hoover Dam is 727 feet high or as tall as a fifty-story building, 660 feet thick at the base, 45 feet thick at the top, and 1,244 feet wide at the top. It created 115-mile long Lake Mead, then the world's largest artificial lake. The Bureau also completed Parker Dam on the Colorado River 155 miles below Boulder Dam in 1938. In 1937, Congress approved the Colorado-Big Thompson Project that bore a thirteen mile tunnel through the Rocky Mountains to deliver water from the Colorado River to irrigate 615,000 acres of farms on the high plains.

Elsewhere, the Bureau constructed Bonneville Dam and Grand Coulee Dam on the Columbia River, completing them in 1938 and

1942, respectively. The Bureau built the Central Valley Project of dams, canals, and irrigation for California's Central Valley from 1937 to 1947; Shasta was the largest dam, 602 feet high and 3,460 feet long and was constructed from 1938 to 1945.

Meanwhile, the Corps built earthen Fort Peck Dam on the Missouri River for $49 million; the dam was a half mile wide at its base, 3.68 miles across, and created a 180-mile long reservoir when it was completed in 1940.

Historian Richard Lowitt sums up the Bureau of Reclamation's New Deal feats: "By 1940, one-fifth of the entire installed hydroelectric capacity in the West was generated by 23 plants operating on Bureau of Reclamation projects...It had also constructed more than 20,000 miles of canals, ditches, and drains; 4,600 miles of telephone lines; 13,000 bridges; and almost 200,000 other irrigation structures....[that] irrigated fully 6 million acres of arid land, supporting approximately one million people whose homes, farms, villages, and town represented a stabilizing investment in an unstable region. Annual crop production was valued at more than $100 million, and the annual market for nationwide business created through these projects was...double this figure."[14]

No people in America suffered worse poverty and discrimination than the original inhabitants. Roosevelt hoped to alleviate their plight by appointing John Collier to head the Interior Department's Bureau of Indian Affairs in 1933. Collier served in that post until 1945. He was an excellent choice with his knowledge of and compassion for Indians. He worked with sponsors to draft two laws in 1934 designed to improve reservation life. The Johnson-O'Mally Act of April 16 required the federal and states governments to improve or create education, health, jobs, and welfare programs for Indians. The Wheeler-Burton or Indian Organization Act of June 18 empowered tribes to write constitutions for modern self-governments, establish corporations to manage their own land and minerals, and increased tribal lands by 7,400,000 acres. Those laws sought to reverse the devastation inflicted on the tribes by the 1887 Dawes Act that privatized communal lands by giving each family a tract to own that they could keep or sell. Over the next five decades, Indians desperate for income sold nearly half their land with the total falling from 140 million acres to 75 million acres. The Dawes Act also created boarding schools where Indian children were sent to Americanize them by stripping them of their culture and language. Poverty, malnutrition, disease, joblessness, and despair plagued most Indians on most reservations. Collier explained that his law aimed "to help the Indians to keep and consolidate what lands they have now and to provide more and better lands upon which they may effectively carry on their lives."[15]

Most tribes welcomed the opportunities. By 1940, 192 tribes had voted to establish modern governments and corporations while 77 rejected the proposal. The Indian reservation population rose from 320,454 in 1933 to 361,816 in 1940, largely because Indians moved back for better health, education, infrastructure, and job opportunities. The Civilian Conservation Corps employed 77,000 Indians. The New Deal began the revitalization of tribal life.[16]

Roosevelt lost a key New Deal bureaucracy when the Supreme Court ruled on May 27, 1935, that the National Recovery Administration (NRA) was unconstitutional for regulating commerce within states, a power confined to the states themselves; the federal government could only regulate "interstate commerce." Anticipating that ruling, he established the Works Progress Administration (WPA) by executive order on May 6, 1935, and put indefatigable Harry Hopkins in charge. From then through its termination in 1943, the WPA employed 8.5 million people for $11 billion worth of infrastructure projects including building or renovating 100,000 bridges, 572,000 miles of roads, 8,000 parks, 13,000 playgrounds, 5,900 schools, and 2,500 hospitals.[17] The WPA also included four programs that subsidized creative people including art, literature, theater, and music. Roosevelt issued an executive order that required the WPA to serve needy white and black people equally. WPA funds and programs eventually provided money to over a million black families and enrolled over three hundred thousand black teenagers in training programs.

Fearing the Supreme Court would systematically declare unconstitutional his other New Deal programs, Roosevelt worked with congressional leaders to draft laws impervious to being overridden called the Second New Deal that included the Emergency Relief Appropriation Act, the Banking Act, the Wagner National Labor Relations Act, the Public Utility Holding Company Act, the Social Security Act, and the Wealth Tax Act. The Emergency Relief Appropriation Bill authorized $4 billion for various programs after being signed into law on April 8. The 1936 Patman Act imposed price-floors for products sold by chain stores to prevent them from bankrupting family businesses with rock-bottom prices then recouping those losses by raising prices. Two laws reformed the coal industry, the 1935 Guffey-Synder Act and 1937 Guffey-Vinson Act. Together they formed a national coal commission that established and tried to enforce a floor price for coal and wage and safety floor for miners.

The Wagner National Labor Relations Act legalized trade unions and collective bargaining; empowered the National Labor Relations Board to oversee union elections; and outlawed such "unfair labor practices" by employers as company unions, retaliation against union members, and refusal to negotiate. The Senate overwhelmingly passed the Wagner Act by 62 to 12, the House by acclamation, and Roosevelt signed it on July 5, 1935,

America's federal tax system imposed the worst burden on those least capable of paying. In 1934, indirect taxes on consumer goods accounted for 55 percent of all federal taxes, while income. Roosevelt asked Congress to pass a bill that raised taxes on very rich people, very rich inheritances, and the intercorporate income of holding company conglomerates. He argued for stiff taxes on the rich and their inheritances because "the transmission from generation to generation of vast fortunes…is not consistent with the ideals and sentiments of the American people."[18]

The Revenue Act, signed on August 30, 1935, imposed graduated income and corporate taxes.[19] For households, rates began at 4 percent for incomes from $2,000 to $11,999, then rose in stages to the top 75 percent for incomes of $1 million to $4.999 million and 79 percent for incomes of $5 million or more; the 79 percent tax actually applied to only one person – John D. Rockefeller. One in a hundred Americans made more than $12,000 and paid 6 percent. The rich also had to pay estate and gift taxes. Corporations paid taxes on profits, capital stocks, and undistributed dividends but could claim tax reductions for charitable donations. The top one percent's share rose slightly from 28.3 percent in 1933 to 30.6 percent in 1939. Those income and inheritance taxes were popular because nineteen of twenty Americans made less than $2,000 and so paid no federal income taxes.

For his tax policies, conservative critics lambasted Roosevelt as a "traitor to his class," pointing out his own inherited wealth that helped finance his path to the White House. To that, Roosevelt retorted, "We have earned the hatred of entrenched greed. They seek the restoration of their selfish power…Give them their way and they will take the course of every autocracy of the past – power for themselves, enslavement for the public."[20] Not all corporate leaders hated the New Deal. Edward Filene got very rich as the founder of Filene's Basement and other retail shopping chains. As for paying higher taxes, Filene replied, "Why shouldn't the American people take half my money from me? I took it from them."[21] Few big business chiefs have ever been as candid or philosophical.

Social Security was the New Deal's most enduring program. That program addressed a enduring, deep rooted problem. Around one in ten Americans was sixty or more years old and most of them lived in poverty. A populist and patriot spurred Roosevelt to create Social Security.

Francis Townsend was a sixty-six year old physician in September 1934, when he sent a letter proposing an old-age pension plan to the *Long Beach Press Telegram*'s editor. His Townsend Plan would establish an Old-Age Revolving Pension Fund that monthly would give $200 to everyone over sixty years old, paid by a national 2 percent sales tax. The only requirement was for recipients to spend all the money that month which would at once enhance their needs and desires while that demand stimulated the economy to produce more goods, jobs, and tax revenues that underwrote the pensions. That inspired people to form Townsend Clubs across the country with over 2 million members in more than 5,000 clubs by December. In January 1935, Townsend organized those clubs into the Old Age Revolving Pension, incorporated, and began publishing the *Townsend National Weekly*. Eventually 25 million Americans signed petitions calling for the federal government to implement the Townsend Plan. Townsend championed his proposal as deeply conservative. He described himself and his followers as folks "who believe in the Bible, believe in God, cheer when the flag passes by, the Bible Belt solid Americans."[22]

Roosevelt convened a cabinet Committee on Economic Security that included Relief Administrator Harry Hopkins, Treasury Secretary Henry Morgenthau, Agriculture Secretary Henry Wallace, Labor Secretary Frances Perkins, and Attorney General Homer Cummings. Their report became the foundation for Roosevelt's Social Security plan to alleviate elderly poverty that he unveiled on January 17, 1935.

Roosevelt argued that: "I see no reason why every child, from the day he is born, shouldn't be part of the social security system. When he begins to grow up, he should know he will have old-age benefits direct from the insurance system to which he will belong all his life. If he is out of work, he gets a benefit. If he is sick or crippled, he gets a benefit... Cradle to grave...everyone ought to be in the social security system."[23]

Of course, not everyone agreed. The National Association of Manufacturing was the most powerful interest group that condemned the proposed social security bill as "socialism." It took half a year before Congress finished debating social security and voted in favor. The House of Representatives approved its version by 371 to 33 on April 19, and the Senate its version by 76 to 6 on June 19. A joint committee reconciled those versions into the Social Security Act that Roosevelt signed into law on August 14, 1935.

The Social Security Administration provided pensions for elderly and handicapped people, unemployment insurance, and $50 million in Aid to Dependent Children, later called Families with Dependent Children. The unemployment plan was financed by a tax of 1 percent on employers with eight or more workers that rose to 2 percent in 1937 and 3 percent in 1942. The Social Security Act eventually diminished poverty for elders living alone from eight in ten to one in five, an extraordinary feat.

Chapter 5

THE OPPONENTS

"But it is more than the recovery of the material basis of our individual lives. It is the recovery of confidence in our democratic processes, our republican institutions...Confidence is growing on every side, renewed faith in the vast possibilities of human beings to improve their material and spiritual status through the instrumentality of the democratic form of government." (Franklin Roosevelt)

"The true conservative is the man who has a real concern for injustices and...seeks to protect the system of private property and free enterprise by arresting such injustices that arise from it."

Franklin Roosevelt and his New Deal and foreign policies provoked an array of enemies who mercilessly castigated them. In a fireside chat in June 1934, he explained that his critics, "A few timid people, who fear progress, will try to give you new and strange names for what we are doing. Sometimes they will call it 'Fascism,' sometimes 'Communism,' sometimes 'regimentation,' sometimes 'Socialism.' But in so doing they are really trying to make very complex and theoretical something that is really very simple and very practical." He warned American people that "Plausible self-seekers and theoretical die-hards will tell you of the loss of individual liberty. Answer this question...out of the facts of your own life. Have you lost any of your rights or liberty or constitutional freedom of action and choice?"[1]

Naturally, the Republican Party provided the largest, best organized opposition to the Roosevelt administration.[2] Former President Herbert Hoover was a bitter critic through speeches and his book *The Challenge to Liberty* (1935). Yet Roosevelt had plenty of critics from within the Democratic Party, both the extreme left and right wings, with the former denouncing his New Deal policies for not going far enough and the latter because they went too far.[3]

53

Democratic Party conservatives deplored the New Deal's big government welfare and business regulations. On August 22, 1934, to oppose what they called "state socialism," former New York governor Al Smith, former party chair Jacob Raskob, and former presidential candidate John Davies were the most prominent leaders who formed the American Liberty League, underwritten by corporate chiefs like General Motors chair Alfred Sloan and Montgomery Ward president Sewell Avery. Jouett Shouse was the Liberty League's first president. The Liberty League espoused free enterprise, private property, free markets, and minimal government.

Like an intellectual judo master, Roosevelt countered those conservative shibboleths with his own "true" version that some call liberalism. He argued that he was a conservative in the sense that he thought to conserve what was best about America while overcoming its deep-rooted problems and creating ever more prosperity and justice for ever more people: "The true conservative is the man who has a real concern for injustices and...seeks to protect the system of private property and free enterprise by correcting such injustices and inequities that arise from it. The most serious threat to our institutions comes from those who refuse to face the need for change. Liberalism becomes the protection for the far-sighted conservative...I am that kind of conservative because I am that kind of liberal." What he sought was a balance between individual liberty and social justice by promoting the best of both: "I believe in individualism up to the point where the individualist starts to operate at the expense of society...I do not believe in abandoning the system of individual enterprise...the freedom and opportunity that have characterized American in the past...but only if we recognize the fact that individualism needs reform, and the collaboration of all of us to provide security for all of us."[4]

Roosevelt and General Douglas MacArthur, the Army Chief of Staff, loathed each other. Roosevelt's attempts to cut the military budget in 1933 provoked an enraged response by MacArthur during a White House meeting. The general told the president that "when we lost the next war, and an American boy, lying in the mud with an enemy bayonet through his belly and an enemy foot on his dying throat spat out the last curse, I wanted the name not to be MacArthur but Roosevelt." That in turn provoked Roosevelt angrily to say, "You must not talk that way to the President!" MacArthur apologized and offered to resign. Roosevelt rejected the offer, but insisted that "you and the budget must get together on this."[5]

Most independent and chain newspapers opposed Roosevelt and their numbers swelled each year of his presidency. Roosevelt had support from 41 percent of dailies and 45 percent of weeklies in 1932, 37 percent of dailies and 40 percent of weeklies in 1936, and 25 percent of dailies and 33 percent of weeklies in 1940.[6] Robert McCormick's *Chicago Tribune* sold the most copies of daily newspapers whose editorial page persistently blistered the Roosevelt administration. Other major opposition newspapers were the *New York Herald-Tribune, Los Angeles Times, New York Sun,* and *Detroit Free Press* along with the Scripps Howard chain. William Randolph Hearst remained a powerful media mogul who owned 13 percent of all daily newspapers, thirteen magazines, eight radio stations, and two movie companies. Hearst initially backed Roosevelt but by 1934 turned against him.

Henry Luce exceeded Hearst in power as a media mogul during the Roosevelt years. He was the conservative Republican publisher of weekly *Time* and monthly *Life* and *Fortune* magazines, founded respectively in 1923, 1883, and 1929. He began the "March of Time" of news stories first as a radio broadcast in 1931 and then as a thirty-mile newsreel in 500 movie theaters in 1935. He increasingly despised and opposed Roosevelt and his New Deal. In 1937, he violated one of the White House press conference rules by having *Life* publish a photo of Roosevelt in a wheelchair, the first time any publication did that. Over time more newspapers and magazines broke that taboo and published their own.

Two charismatic demagogues – a priest and a senator – were the most powerful voices attacking Roosevelt and the New Deal.[7] Each claimed that the president did too little to alleviate the depression and plight of the poor.

Father Charles Coughlin was a Canadian-born Catholic priest who, at age thirty-four in 1926, received the parish of Saint Theresa of the Little Flower in a working class Detroit neighborhood.[8] Coughlin fathered what some call "talk" radio and its critics "rant" or "hate" radio. With a microphone in the pulpit, he began broadcasting his Sunday sermons via radio station WJR from October 17, 1926. His increasingly fiery sermons that castigated an array of evils won him a 1930 contract with Columbia Broadcasting Company (CBS) for a national audience. At his peak, 40 million Americans tuned in to his broadcasts from a network of 26 stations, and his magazine *Social Justice* had a 200,000 circulation. After Roosevelt's election in 1932, Coughlin first embraced then blistered the president and his New Deal policies for not going far enough. On November 11, 1934, he announced the inauguration of his political movement, the National Union for Social Justice with sixteen principles that included the federal takeover of industries and workers' rights. On January 27, 1935, he denounced Roosevelt's proposal for the United States to join the World Court.

Huey Long was Louisiana's flamboyant governor from 1928 to 1932 who was elected to the Senate in 1932.[9] He initially backed Roosevelt and his New Deal, then argued that the federal government had to assume far greater powers to control the economy for "the people." During one speech, he warned his colleagues that: "Men, it will not be long until there will be a mob assembling here to hang Senators from the rafters of the Senate. I have to determine whether I will stay and be hung with you, or go out and lead the mob." His autobiography *Every Man a King* appeared in October 1933.

Long unveiled his "Share Our Wealth Society" scheme that he claimed would make "every man a king" in January 1934. Every family would receive annual incomes of at least $2,500 and $5,000 as a downpayment for a home while no one could make more than $1.5 million annually or have more than $5 million of wealth; taxes on the rich would subsidize everyone else. By 1935, Long's movement had 27,000 chapters and 8 million adherents. He launched his presidential campaign "My First Days in the White House" in 1935.

Roosevelt and his allies feared that Long could upstage him in the 1936 presidential race either by seizing the Democratic Party nomination or as a third candidate. Then something unexpected happened to end that fear. Dr. Carl Weiss hated Long for his radicalism and harm his political machine inflicted on his father-in-law. Weiss shot to death Long as he strode into Louisiana's Capitol in Baton Rouge on September 8, 1935. Long's bodyguards shot Weiss to death. Long's last words were, "God don't let me die! I have so much to do."[10] Gerald Smith took over the Share Our Wealth Society movement and was as fiery a demagogue as Long.

The Roosevelt White House feared the swelling power of those demagogues. The exasperated president griped that, "I am fighting Communism, Huey Longism, Coughlinism, [and] Townsendism." Yet the president was optimistic that: "Some well-timed, common sense campaigning on my part this spring or summer will bring people to their senses."[11] National Recovery Administration chief Hugh Johnson warned that Coughlin and Long, "with nothing of learning, knowledge, nor experience to lead us through a labyrinth that has perplexed the minds of men since the beginning of time...These two men are raging up and down this land preaching not construction but destruction – not reform but revolution. You can laugh at Father Coughlin, you can snort at Huey Long – but this country was never under a greater menace."[12]

Despite the constant attacks by conservatives and socialists, Roosevelt and the Democratic Party remained popular. During a fireside chat on June 28, 1934, Roosevelt asked the American people to evaluate his New Deal policies by looking within themselves: "But the simplest way for each of you to judge recovery lies in the plain facts of your own individual economic situation. Are you better off than you were last year? Are your debts less burdensome? Is your bank account more secure? Are your working conditions better? Is your faith in your own individual future more firmly grounded?"[13]

Midterm elections almost always result in losses for the president and his party as voters react against policies that fail to alleviate problems or worsen them. Roosevelt's New Deal inspired and helped most Americans. Democrats widened their domination of Congress in the 1934 midterm elections. In the House, Democrats ended up with 322 House seats, up nine, while Republicans dropped by 14 to 103 Republicans; the Progressive Party and Farmer Labor Party respectively won seven and three. In the Senate, Democrats emerged with 69 seats, nine more, while Republicans lost 10 net seats, falling to 25; the Farmer-Labor Party senator retained his seat and the Progressive Party won a seat. The last midterm election when a party in power actually gained seats was 1902, when President Theodore Roosevelt's Republican emerged with eleven more.

Roosevelt was up for re-election in 1936.[14] Democrats convened at Philadelphia from June 23 to June 27, and nominated Roosevelt by acclamation. The Republicans had already chosen their candidate. During their convention at Cleveland from June 10 to 12, they nominated for president Kansas Governor Alf Landon, a wealthy centrist over Idaho Senator William Borah, an isolationist by 984 to 19 votes. For his running mate, the delegates picked Frank Knox, a retired army colonel and newspaper editor.

Roosevelt assembled the modern Democratic Party coalition of workers, farmers, blacks, Catholics, Jews, and big city bosses. Unions replaced corporations for more valued endorsements. He campaigned as the people's champion against the greedy rich and powerful elite. During a speech at Madison Square Garden, he condemned "business and financial monopoly, speculation, reckless banking, class antagonism...Never before in all our history have these forces been so united against one candidate as they stand today. They are unanimous in their hate for me – and I welcome their hatred."[15]

Amidst the campaign, Roosevelt mourned the death of Louis Howe on April 18. For over two decades Howe had been his friend, advisor, and alter-ego. Roosevelt replaced him with Harry Hopkins as his closest advisor and unofficial chief of staff.[16] Hopkins had already performed wonders directing the Federal Emergency Relief Administration, the Civil Works Administration, and the Works Progress Administration. He appointed Hopkins commerce secretary in 1938 and during the Second World War sent him on numerous diplomatic missions to Winston Churchill, Joseph Stalin, and other foreign leaders. Like Roosevelt, Hopkins was a supremely confident extrovert. He was also a lady's man and had three marriages. He suffered from bad health. Like Roosevelt, he was addicted to tobacco and chain smoked cigarettes. In 1939, he was diagnosed with stomach cancer and survived an operation and radiation treatment. He outlived Roosevelt, finally succumbing to cancer on January 29, 1946.

Roosevelt trounced Landon by an even greater margin than his first Republican challenger, scoring 27,747,636 or 60.8 percent of the vote and 523 Electoral College votes from 46 states to 16679,543 or 35.6 percent and 8 Electoral College votes from 2 states. In the Senate, the Democrats gained five to total 75 while the Republicans fell five to hang on to 17. In the House, the Democrats raised their total 12 seats from 324 to 336, while the Republicans lost 15 to end up with 88. The Progressive Party and Farmer-Labor Party won respectively eight and five seats.

Perhaps the most interesting state political race in 1934 was for California's governorship. Novelist Upton Sinclair, most famed for his muckraking novel *The Jungle* (1906), had previously run twice before but as a socialist and got few votes.[17] Nonetheless, believing that he had good name recognition and charisma, a group of Democratic Party's leaders asked him to be their candidate. For his campaign, Sinclair created the *End Poverty in California* (EPIC) movement and wrote and distributed his pamphlet, *"I, Governor of California, and How I Ended Poverty: A True Story of the Future"* that called for nationalizing industries and unworked lands for the common good. Among his supporters were fellow novelists Theodore Dreiser and John Dos Passos along with the International Ladies Garment Union. Sinclair won the Democratic Party primary in August. In a three man race, Frank Merriam, the Republican candidate and sitting governor, won 1,138,629 or 48.87 percent to Sinclair's 879,537 or 37.75 percent, and Progressive Party Raymond Haight's 302,519 or 12.99 percent of the vote. Sinclair would have won had Haight stayed out of the race, but the two candidates split the vote among those who favored socialist programs. Sinclair assuaged his painful defeat by writing the tract, *"I, Candidate for Governor: And How I Got Licked."*

The Twentieth Amendment, ratified on January 23, 1933, moved the inaugural date from March 4 to January 20. In 1937, Roosevelt was the first president to take the oath on this new date. In his second inaugural address, he declared, "I see one-third of the nation ill-housed, ill-clad, ill-nourished…The test of our progress is not whether we add more to the abundance of those who have much; it is whether we provide enough to those who have too little."[18] Roosevelt identified many reasons for those harsh realities, but one above all was the most obstructionist and had to be overwhelmed before progress could advance.

Among his foes, Roosevelt prominently included most Supreme Court justices.[19] The Supreme Court tilted right. The four most conservative justices that Roosevelt dubbed the Four Horsemen of the Apocalypse – James McReynolds, Willis Van Devanter, George Sutherland, and Pierce Butler – were septuagenarians. Liberal-leaning judges were Louis Brandeis, Benjamin Cardozo, and Harlan Stone, while Chief Justice Charles Hughes and Owen Roberts were swing votes. During his first term, Roosevelt became the first full term president who never appointed a Supreme Court justice.

The Supreme Court ruled unconstitutional several key New Deal laws by five to four votes: the Railroad Retirement Act on May 6, 1935; the National Industrial Recovery Act in *Schechter Poultry Corporation versus the United States* on May 27, 1935; and the Agricultural Adjustment Act (AAA) in *United States versus Butler* on January 5, 1936. The Supreme Court straitjacketed state power to regulate the economy including imposing minimum wage laws in *Morehead versus New York ex rel. Tipaldo* on June 1, 1936.

Roosevelt feared that eventually the Supreme Court would destroy the entire New Deal. To pre-empt that, he sent Congress a message that stunned most Americans on February 5, 1937. The Judicial Reform Bill empowered Congress to expand the Supreme Court by up to six new members for each sitting justice older than seventy years who refused to resign, and designated fifty new federal judges at lower levels. That plan was a blatant attempt to pack the Supreme Court with justices who backed the New Deal. Yet, that would have been constitutional since the Constitution empowers Congress to determine the number of justices and regulate the judicial system.

That proposal provoked a chorus of condemnation in Congress and editorial pages. A Gallup Poll revealed that 53 percent of Americans opposed Roosevelt's court packing scheme. In Congress, the bill was bottled up in both houses and never received a formal floor vote.

Roosevelt tried to break that deadlock by appealing to the public. In a March fireside chat, he explained that his bill would first, "make the administration of all federal justice, from the bottom to the top, speedier and...less costly; secondly, to bring to the decision of social and economic problems younger men who have had personal experience and contract with modern facts and circumstances under which average men have to live and work. This plan will save our national Constitution from hardening of the judicial arteries."[20]

Although Roosevelt's bill died, that threat sobered most justices. Thereafter they mostly upheld rather than struck down federal and state New Deal measures. The first came with the five to four vote that upheld Washington's minimum wage law in *West Coast Hotel versus Parrish* on March 29, 1937. Justice Owen Roberts had voted against minimum wage laws in *Tipaldo* but voted in favor in this case. A wag dubbed that "the switch in time that saved nine." That same five to four split upheld the Wagner National Labor Relations Act in *NLBR versus Jones and Laughlin* on April 12. Roosevelt locked in a liberal majority after Willis Van Devanter announced his retirement on May 18 and a heart attack killed Justice Joseph Robinson on July 14. He named Hugo Black and Stanley Reed to replace the conservatives.

Roosevelt loathed John Lewis who was president of the United Mine Workers (UMW) and vice president of the American Federation of Labor (AFL).[21] Lewis had long felt that the AFL was too passive in asserting workers' rights through strikes. As UMW chief, he formed the Committee for Industrial Organizations (CIO) with David Dubinsky of the International Ladies Garment Workers Union and Sidney Hillman of the Amalgamated Clothing Workers (ACW) on November 9 and resigned as AFL vice-president on November 23, 1935. In 1936, Lewis established the Steel Workers Organizing Committee (SWOC) to demand an eight-hour day, forty-hour week, and pay rises. He renamed the CIO the Congress of Industrial Organizations when it formally broke with the AFL in September 1938.

General Motors (GM) was the world's largest corporation. The United Auto Workers (UAW), led by Walter Reuther, struck against GM at its Flint, Michigan industrial complex on December 30, 1936. The workers demanded more pay, fewer weekly hours, and a grievance process. GM"S automobile production plummeted from 50,000 in December 1936 to 125 in February's first week. Rivals Ford and Chrysler boosted their own production to profit from GM's strike. Michigan Governor Frank Murphy had state officials join the talks between management and labor representatives. Roosevelt was the key to resolving the strike by calling GM President William Knudsen and talking him into compromising. GM resolved the strike by recognizing the UAW as the sole representative of the workers.

Meanwhile, the United States Steel Corporation's workers went on strike. Violence erupted in Chicago on May 31, when police fired on protesters, killing ten and wounding thirty. Police killed five other strikers that summer. That prompted U.S. Steel Corporation to accept SWOC's demands. Across the country, workers walked to pressure management into granting them better wages, hours, and other conditions. Strikes peaked in 1937, with 2,200 involving 941,802 workers, of whom 711,000 won concessions. Those labor victories caused union membership to soar. From July 1936 to September 1937, the UAW's rolls soared 88,000 to 400,000, and the CIO's from 1,296,500 in July 1936 to 3,718,000 in September 1937.[22]

The economy nosedived in 1937 and went into recession in 1938. Strike disruptions partly caused that. More important were government policies. The Federal Reserve raised its reserve requirements by 50 percent; new social security taxes reduced consumer spending; and Roosevelt cut the budget deficit from $4.3 billion in 1936 to $2.7 billion in 1937, and planned a deficit of only $700 million for 1938 and a balanced budget for 1939. The Dow Jones Industrial Average plunged from 190 to 115 from August to October 1937. The jobless rate soared.

Roosevelt called Congress into a special session from November 15, 1937, and gave them the latest batch of New Deal programs to approve, including to manage industry and agriculture, impose minimum wage and work standards, and establish "Seven Little TVAs" for dams, hydroelectricity, and flood control on other rivers. But when the special session ended on December 21, Congress had not enacted any of those proposals. The New Deal had reached a political saturation point where exhaustion rather than enthusiasm prevailed. A bipartisan group of representatives and senators issued on December 19, a ten point "Conservative Manifesto" that included demands for lower taxes, fewer regulations, a balance budget, and the rights of business leaders over their employees. Most southern Democrats were conservatives who embraced these principles.

The Housing or Wagner-Steagall Act, signed on September 1, 1937, bolstered the 1934 National Housing Act by creating the Federal Housing Agency that subsidized renovation of old housing and construction of new housing, and worked with the Home Owners Loan Corporation to help people acquire that housing. Roosevelt and Congress further developed the housing market by establishing the Federal National Mortgage Association, better known as Fannie Mae, on February 10, 1938, as a secondary mortgage system with secure government packed bonds that encouraged banks to lend more money at lower interest rates for homeowners.

Roosevelt also got Congress to approve the Fair Labor Standard Act that established a twenty-five cent an hour wage and forty-hour work week for most workers that would rise to forty cents and forty hours two years later, and banned child labor for interstate businesses. He signed that bill on June 25, 1938.

Over the next several years, Congress passed and the president signed other reform bills. The 1938 Civil Aeronautics Act established the Civil Aeronautics Board (CAB) to subsidize the development of private airlines with low interest loans, construction of airports, regulating routes, letting airlines carry mail, freeing the industry from anti-trust laws, and providing a national air control system. The 1939 Hatch Act forbad federal employees from engaging in political activity while on the job. Congress expanded benefits distributed by the Aid for Dependent Children program. But Congress dismantled some New Deal programs. The 1939 Relief Act fired all WPA workers who had served more than eighteen months that resulted in 770,000 WPA workers losing their jobs in July and August. The 1939 Executive Reorganization Act established the White House Office and the Executive Office of the President. Three new national parks emerged during the New Deal years, Mount Olympic in Washington on June 29, 1938, King's Canyon in California on March 4, 1940, and Big Bend in Texas on June 4, 1944.

The one issue that Roosevelt avoided confronting was racism.[23] In varying degrees and ways, blacks suffered discrimination across the nation. That racism was worst in southern states where "Jim Crow" or "Black Code" laws imposed strict segregation in public schools, housing, transportation, banking, lodging, dining, and restrooms, and limited the ability of blacks to vote and run for office. A mere 5 percent of blacks were registered to vote in the eleven former rebel states in 1940.[24] In *Grovey versus Townsend* (1935), the Supreme Court reinforced discrimination by ruling that Texas law allowing white primary elections that excluded blacks was not unconstitutional.

Black poverty was most severe in rural southern states where nearly four of five blacks still lived. A federal study revealed that black men in 1930 were 40 percent of the south's 2.1 million farmworkers but only 12.8 percent or 107,000 of the 835,000 black laborers owned the farms where they worked and lived. The number of white sharecroppers and tenants actually outnumbered blacks by 581,000 to 486,000. The average annual income was $312 for all sharecroppers and $417 for all tenants.

Tenants and sharecroppers kept about 50 percent and 25 percent of the value of the respective crops or livestock that they harvested.[25] Landless blacks and whites tried to better their conditions through the Share Croppers Union and Southern Tenant Farmers Union, respectively founded in 1931 and 1934, but landowners and politicians worked together to stymie those efforts. Millions of southern blacks alleviated their poverty by migrating from southern farms to northern or west coast factories during both the First and Second World Wars.

Most egregious, lynchings mostly of blacks accused of crimes, usually rape, by white mobs persisted. From 1889 to 1933, 3,745 people were lynched, of whom 2,954 were black and 791 were white; with 1,406 blacks accused of murder, 878 of rape, and 67 of insults to whites. Many were tortured before they were executed. Of those who committed lynchings, only 49 were indicted and only four convicted of murder. From 1933 to 1937, 83 blacks were lynched, nearly all in the south.[26]

Two New Yorkers, Senator Robert Wagner and Joseph Gavagan, first introduced an anti-lynching bill in January 1934, but opponents bottled it in committee that year and senators filibustered it in 1935. The bill empowered the Justice Department to investigate a lynching if local authorities failed to do so thirty days after it occurred and could impose fines up to $5,000 and up to five years in prison against local officials who protected lynchers.

Most Americans favored an anti-lynching bill by January 1937, with Gallup finding 70 percent across the country and 63 percent of southerners.[27] That month, Wagner and Gavagan introduced the bill in their respective chambers. The House of Representatives passed it by 277 to 120 on April 15, but Texas Senator Tom Connally filibustered it to death. Roosevelt privately supported the bill but refused publicly to endorse it. He explained to Walter White, chair of the National Association for the Advancement of Colored Peoples (NAACP) the harsh political dilemma he faced: "Southerners, by reason of the seniority rule in Congress, are chairmen or occupy strategic positions on most of the Senate and House committees. If I come out for the anti-lynching bill now, they will block every bill I ask Congress to pass to keep America from collapsing. I just can't take that risk."[28] Undaunted, Wagner reintroduced the bill on January 6, 1938, but opponents forced him to withdraw it on February 24. Roosevelt was just as publicly mum during that latest round.

Eleanor tried to be her husband's conscience as she prioritized civil rights for blacks. She befriended Walter White, the NAACP's head, and Mary MacLeod Bethune, who founded and directed Bethune-Cook College in Daytona Beach, Florida. In April 1939, she resigned from the Daughters of the American Revolution when they opposed black contralto Marian Anderson from singing at Constitutional Hall in Washington. Eleanor arranged for Anderson to sing before the Lincoln Memorial on April 9.

Harold Ickes warned Roosevelt that: "She is becoming altogether too active in public affairs and I think she is harmful rather than helpful." Roosevelt replied, "I can always say, 'Well, that's my wife; I can't do anything about her.'"[29] Historian Doris Kearns Goodwin explained that "Franklin tolerated Eleanor because she represented the more generous, idealistic side of his own nature, the humanitarian values...But it was also good politics. While he kept the party intact in the South, Eleanor was building new allies in the North among tens of thousands of migrating blacks."[30]

Roosevelt valued the insights that Eleanor provided him about the harsh economic, political, and social conditions that black people faced. His policies, however, were cosmetic. He made the first black appointment to a federal court when he named William Hastie a district judge for the Virgin Islands. He had an informal group of black advisors led by Mary MacLeod Bethune whose advice he solicited. He courted blacks to abandon the Republican Party for the Democratic Party, arguing that the Grand Old Party (GOP) was no longer the party of Lincoln but of financial and industrial corporations. In the 1934 election, more blacks voted for Democrats than Republicans. In Chicago's south side congressional district, challenger Arthur Mitchell beat incumbent black Republican Oscar de Priest and so became the first black Democratic Party member of Congress.

During the mid-1930s, several fascist groups emerged of which the largest was the neo-Nazi German American Bund with around 100,000 members. Twenty-thousand of them, many dressed in Nazi uniforms with swastika armbands, held a "Mass Demonstration for True Americanism" at Madison Square Garden in New York City on February 20, 1939.

The Communist Party peaked in popularity during the 1930s.[31] It's strength was not in elections. The Communist Party's best showing was during the 1932 election when its presidential candidate William Foster and black running mate James Ford won 103,307 votes or 0.3 percent compared to the average 0.1 percent share for communist presidential candidates.

The communist threat was not at voting booths but on factory floors and in committee rooms. Communists infiltrated and influenced many labor union, civil rights, and humanitarian groups. Such prominent novelists as John Dos Passos and Sherwood Anderson, scholars Sidney Hook and Edmund Wilson, and poet Langston Hughes were among those who signed a manifesto declaring that, "as responsible intellectual workers we have aligned ourselves with the frankly revolutionary Communist Party."[32]

Communism's simple Manichean creed of class struggle and justification for the exploited masses to overthrow their oppressors and confiscate their wealth appeals enormously to downtrodden people. Paul Robeson, the black singer and actor, was a communist who visited the Soviet Union in 1934. He recalled feeling "like a human being for the first time since I grew up. Here I am not a Negro but a human being. Before I came I could hardly believe that such a thing could be."[33]

Of course, what communist believers in America received, including those who visited the Soviet Union, was a sanitized idealist version. They dismissed rumors that Stalin was a genocidal tyrant responsible for murder by gunshot or starvation of twenty million or more people and that most of the survivors existed fearfully as exploited laborers with minimal food, clothing, shelter, and stipend.

Moscow directed the global communist movement with the Communist International (Comintern), headquartered in Moscow. Around the world, Comintern agents either worked through existing communist parties or founded new ones. They brought back members for training in revolution in Moscow. In December 1934, Comintern ordered Communist Party chief Foster to dissolve the communist Trade Union Unity League (TUUL) and instead infiltrated the mainstream American Federal of Labor (AFL).

Worsening fears about subversive radicals within the nation led to a 194 to 41 vote by the House of Representatives to establish the House Special Committee to Investigate Un-American Activities on May 26, 1938. Texas representative Martin Dies chaired the twelve person committee. Under Dies leadership, the Committee focused on investigating the communist infiltration of labor unions and federal programs. The revelations helped end the Federal Theater Project and win passage of the Act to Prevent Pernicious Political Activities or Hatch Act that forbade federal officials from engaging in political activities in 1939.

Isolationism ran deep in 1930s America, especially in Congress, editorial boardrooms, and college campuses.[34] The most powerful pacifist groups were the National Council for the Prevention of War, National Peace Conference, Federal Council of Churches, Women's International League for Peace and Freedom, League of Nations

Association, and Carnegie Endowment for International Peace. College students were especially committed. A 1932 poll of college students found that 72 percent opposed serving in the military and 50 percent even if an enemy attacked the United States.[35] In 1933, 15,000 students on 65 campuses signed a pledge either to uphold complete pacifism or fight for America only if it was invaded. On April 12, 1935, pacificists organized a one-hour "Strike against War" that attracted 175,000 students across the nation; they opposed any people or institutions involved with war including the Reserve Officers' Training Corps (ROTC).

Leading Senate isolationists included Republicans William Borah of Idaho, Hiram Johnson of California, Gerald Nye of North Dakota, Arthur Capper of Kansas, Arthur Vandenburg of Michigan, Bronson Cutting of New Mexico, Robert La Follette, Jr. of Wisconsin, and Robert Taft of Ohio; and Democrats George Norris of Nebraska and Burton Wheeler of Montana; and Progressive. Complicating the politics was that Republicans Borah, Johnson, Nye, La Follette, and Cutting were progressives who voted for most of Roosevelt's New Deal policies.

Roosevelt bowed to the prevailing sentiment in Congress and beyond by reluctantly signing a series of "Neutrality Acts" from 1935 to 1939 that prevented the president from backing a side in a foreign war and for American businesses to sell directly to either side although belligerents could buy American war goods if they paid cash and carried it away in their own ships. After war broke out in Europe in 1939, Roosevelt sought to transform public opinion from prevailing isolationism into prevailing internationalism.[36]

A dilemma plagued Roosevelt's effort. Trying to educate the public about the worsening threats posed by fascist Japan, Germany, and Italy provoked an isolationist backlash. On September 4, 1940, General Robert Wood, the chair of Sears Roebuck, and six other pacifists formed the America First Committee committed to staying at peace and building an impregnable defense to deter any attack on the United States. Within a year, the America First Committee claimed 450 chapters and 850,000 members. The America First Committee included a political array with Herbert Hoover, Henry Ford, and Charles Lindberg on the right and Socialist Party leader Norman Thomas, historian Charles Beard, and novelist Sinclair Lewis on the left.

America's most famous isolationist was Charles Lindberg, who became a national hero when he flew solo across the Atlantic on May 20 and 21, 1927.[37] For that, President Coolidge awarded him the Medal of Honor and promoted him from captain to colonel, and New York gave him a tickertape parade. Lindberg looked and acted like a hero as he was tall, lanky, handsome, self-effacing, and eloquent. He graduated top of his class in the Army Air Service in 1925. He married Anne Morrow, a gifted writer and the daughter of America's ambassador to Mexico, in 1929. They suffered a tragedy in 1932 when a man kidnaped and killed their first-born son. To escape the incessant hounding by reporters eager for a story, they fled to a country home in England in 1935.

The first step in what would be Lindberg's increasingly controversial stances on American foreign policy came in May 1936, when he accepted an invitation by Major Truman Smith, America's military attaché at the embassy in Berlin, to visit Germany to access their air force. Lindberg sojourned three times in Germany, in July and August 1936, October 1937, and October 1938. German Air Marshal Hermann Goering awarded Lindberg the Knight of the German Eagle in October 1938.

Lindberg made his first radio broadcast of dozens calling for America to stay out of Europe's latest war on September 15, 1939, that grew more critical of Roosevelt and other internationalists. On May 29, 1941, he declared: "Mr. Roosevelt claims that Hitler wants to dominate the world. But it is Mr. Roosevelt himself who advocates world domination when he says it is our business to control the wars of Europe and Asia."[38] Roosevelt organized an internationalist counterattack that attacked not just Lindberg's positions but his character, including accusations of being a traitor and Nazi agent.

Eventually two internationalist lobby groups emerged, the Committee to Defend America by Aiding the Allies led by progressive Republican William White, who published the *Emporia Gazette*, in May 1940, and the Fight for Freedom Incorporated led by Francis Miller, a financier, April 1941. On May 20, 1941, Roosevelt signed an executive order that established an Office of Civilian Defense to "facilitate constructive civilian participation in the defense program, and to sustain national morale," and appointed New York Republican Mayor Fiorella La Guardia to head it and Eleanor Roosevelt to assist it.

The New Deal was over by 1940. Roosevelt proposed no new welfare or development programs in the year's January State of the Union address. That ended half a dozen years of the White House and Congress working together to find practical ways to alleviate the Great Depression's poverty, malnutrition, and joblessness; providing roads, schools, electricity, flood control, and running water; and restoring forests, grasslands, dignity, and enterprise. When a program fell short, the New Dealers tried something else. Historian Richard Hofstadter described that dynamic process: "At the heart of the New Deal there was not a philosophy but a temperament."[39]

Chapter 6

THE CREATORS

"Hell, they've got to eat just like other people." (Harry Hopkins)

"This land is your land, this land is my land." (Woodie Guthrie)

"During boon times conservatism is a thing to be ridiculed, but under unsettling conditions it becomes a virtue." (Grant Wood)

The Great Depression and the Second World War affected all creative genres – film, painting, theater, literature, music, and commentary. Politically, red tinged most 1930s novelists, playwrights, painters, journalists, and commentators until Pearl Harbor, after which red, white, and blue prevailed. All along, Roosevelt recognized the creative class's importance as potential supporters for his policies, and with his advisors devised policies and programs to enlist them.

The economic collapse shook the faith of countless people in the alleged virtues of private property and free markets. The prevailing attitude among creative people during the 1930s was to expose all that was economically, politically, and socially wrong with America like oligopolies, inside trading, corruption, incompetence, authoritarianism, exploitation of workers, and racism against blacks and other minorities. Ironically, it was the allegedly repressive federal government that lifted briefly from poverty or joblessness many of those creators along with tens of millions of other Americans.

Never before or since has Washington more systematically and generously patronized creative people.[1] The Works Progress Administration (WPA) sponsored four programs for creative individuals and groups, the Federal Art Project, the Federal Writers Project, the Federal Music Project, and the Federal Theater Project. Initially there was a fifth program, the Historical Records Survey that inventoried the nation's local historical archives, but it became autonomous in 1936. Harry Hopkins justified these programs on relief rather than cultural grounds: "Hell, they've got to eat just like other people."[2]

The Federal Writers Project annually employed from 4,500 to 5,200 writers from 1935 to its termination in 1943; those writers produced 276 books and 700 pamphlets, a rather light output for so many.[3] Among later famous authors that enjoyed Writers Program paychecks were Richard Wright, Ralph Ellison, Saul Bellow, Kenneth Rexroth, Nelson Algren, Nora Neale Huston, Mari Sandoz, and John Cheever.

The American Guide Series employed writers to write guidebooks for states and cities, thus encouraging tourism and economic development for those places. Literary critic Alfred Kazin lauded that series as "an extraordinary contemporary epic. Out of the need to find something to say about every community and the country around it, out of the vast storehouse of facts behind the guides...there emerged an America unexamined in density and regional diversity."[4]

The Writers Program's most vital project was to record the folklore, memories, and music of rural folks and minorities, and eventually compiled over 14,000 documents including interviews with over 2,000 former slaves.[5] The book *These Are Our Lives* (1939) depicted poverty-stricken but resourceful people in the deep south and Appalachia. Alan Lomax and Charles Seegey worked respectively for the Writers and Music Programs. They teamed up to record the folk music of most rural white and black people, including Delta Blues and Appalachian Bluegrass.

The Federal Theater Project headed by Hallie Flanagan employed over 12,000 actors, stagehands, playwrights, and designers for 64,000 performances of plays, musicals, and dance attended by over 30 million viewers by 1939. Later famous theater and film directors and actors that enjoyed Theater Project paychecks included Orson Welles, Arthur Miller, John Huston, and Burt Lancaster. The most controversial staging was the theater version of Sinclair Lewis' *It Can't Happen Here*, about a charismatic demagogue taking power in a coup and transforming America from a democracy into a dictatorship. The play opened at twenty-one theaters in seventeen states on the evening of October 27, 1936. Other provocative works included an all-black version of William Shakespeare's *MacBeth* and *Triple A Ploughed Under and One Third of Our Nation* for extolling New Deal programs.

Holger Cahill headed the Federal Art Project that employed over 5,000 artists that created 108,000 easel paintings, 18,000 sculptures, 11,300 prints, and 2,500 murals for public buildings, post offices, and schools.[6] Post office murals usually depicted local history. Talents among the painters varied greatly. Regardless, a large mural could earn the artist $1,500. Later famous artists that got Art Project paychecks included Thomas Hart Benton, Grant Wood, Jackson Pollock, and Wilhem de Kooning. The greatest Federal Art film documentaries were Pare Lorentz's film *The Plow that Broke the Plains* (1937) and *The River* (1938), both with musical scores composed by Virgil Thompson. The Federal Music Project underwrote 224,698 concerts with 15,000 musicians for 150 million people in audiences. The number of symphony orchestras rose from eleven in 1935 to thirty-four in 1936.

The Farm Security Administration (FSA) had a Historical Section whose photographic division was headed by Roy Stryker. It was Stryker who hired photographers like Dorothea Lange, Walker Evans, Arthur Rothstein, Marion Post Walcott, Russell Lee, and Ben Shahn who captured some of the Great Depression's most haunting images. In addition to paying them salaries of $2,300 to $3,200, he let them sell their photos to popular magazines like *Time, Fortune,* and *Life* or publish them with essays in books.

Whether or not their day jobs came with a federal pay check, writers kept writing. Many extraordinary novels, short stories, and poems appeared during the Roosevelt years.[7]

The most prolific and profound books that depicted America during those dozen years were those of John Steinbeck. California was mostly the setting for his *The Red Pony* (1933), *Tortilla Flats* (1935), *Dubious Battle* (1936), *Of Mice and Men* (1937), *The Grapes of Wrath* (1939), *The Moon Is Done* (1942), and *Cannery Row* (1945).

Arguably, Steinbeck's Pulitzer Prize winning *Grapes of Wrath* was the greatest novel of the Roosevelt years and among the greatest American novels.[8] The novel explores the Joad family of Oklahoma that loses their farm to the Dust Bowl and bank, piles into their jalopy, and heads west on Route 66 to the promised land of California. Tom Joad is the ex-con son, just out of prison. He is tough, bitter, and cruel, but he loves his family. His mother, Ma Joad, provides the moral compass for him and the rest of the family and other characters. Steinbeck brilliantly depicted the dilemmas of class, poverty, property, freedom, privilege, justice, law, morality, rights, love, and America. He reached deep into the characters to reveal how often each put his or her own interest before the needs of others. Chapter Five pits land owners against tenants who they evict for not paying their debts. This passage shows how each emotionally dealt with that harsh but legally justified act: "Some of the owner men were kind because they hated what they had to do, and some of them were angry because they hated to be cruel, and some of them were cold because they long ago found that one could not be an owner unless one were cold. And all of them were caught in something larger than themselves." He then gives the tenant's anguished response: "Sure, cried the tenant farmers, but it's our land. We were born on it, and got killed on it, and we died on it. Even if it's no good, it's still ours. That's what makes it ours – being born on it, working on it, dying on it. That makes ownership, not a paper with numbers on it." Land owners and tenants alike are prisoners of a banking system, "the monster," that gives and takes away money along with one's dignity, livelihood, and peace of mind. These exchanges capture that: "Yes, but the bank is made of men" and "No, you're wrong there...The bank is something more than men...Men made it but they can't control it."[9] There is similar conflict between the tractor driver hired by the owners to tear down the shacks of evicted tenants and those who lose their homes. "Well, what you doing this kind of work for – against your own people?" "Three dollars a day...I got a wife and kids. We got to eat. "That's right," the tenant said. "But for your three dollars a day fifteen or twenty families can't eat at all. Nearly a hundred people have to go out and wander on the roads for your three dollars a day. Is that right?"[10] Like most other impoverished and uprooted depression-era families, the Joads eventually find a new home and livelihoods, but suffered terrible losses along the way. Toward the end, Tom leaves home to become a labor organizer, while his sister, Rose of Sharon, who lost her husband and baby, nurses with breast milk an old man from death's brink.

During the Roosevelt years, an astonishing number of writers came from and wrote about the American south. Of them, William Faulkner and Eudora Welty reigned as the region's literary king and queen. In Oxford, Mississippi, Faulkner wrote *Light in August* (1932), *Absolum! Absolum!* (1936), *The Unvanquished* (1938), *The Hamlet* (1940), and *Go Down, Moses* (1942). In Jackson, Mississippi, Welty wrote scores of short stories, including her collection *A Curtain of Green and Other Stories* (1941), *The Wide Net and Other Stories* (1942), and *Livvie Is Back* (1943) that respectively won a second place O'Henry Award and two first places, and the novella *The Robber Bridegroom* (1942). Thomas Sigismund "T.S." Stribling's trilogy of novels explores generations of a southern family, *The Forge* (1931), *The Store* (1932), which won a Pulitzer Prize, and *The Unfinished Cathedral* (1934). Caroline Miller's Pulitzer Prize winning *Lamb in His Bosum* (1933) was set in poverty-stricken Georgia. Majorie Kinnan Rawlings's Pulitzer Prize winning *The Yearling* (1939) takes place in rural poverty-stricken rural Florida.

Robert Penn Warren's novels included *Night Rider* (1939), *At Heaven's Gate*, and *All the King's Men* (1946) about a southern populist like Huey Long that won a Pulitzer Prize. Carson McCuller's *The Heart Is a Lonely Hunter* (1940) is about down and out people in a Georgia mill town and *Reflection in a Golden Eye* (1941) about sexually ambivalent officers and privates at a southern army base. Thomas Wolfe produced two elegiac novels inspired by growing up in a boarding house full of characters in Asheville, North Carolina, *Look Homeward, Angel* (1929) and *Of Time and the River* (1935).

Several memorable novels were set in New England. George Santayana's *The Last Puritan: A Memoir in the Form of a Novel* (1935) is a coming of age novel that takes place in nineteenth century small town Connecticut. Frances Winwar's *Gallows Hill* (1937) was about the Salem witch trials. John Marquand's *The Late George Apley* (1937) is a contemporary satire.

For the American trans-Mississippi West, Wallace Stegner was the leading writer with his many lyrical novels and histories, most notably *On a Darking Plain* (1940), *Fire and Ice* (1941), and *Big Rock Candy Mountain* (1943). Ethel Hueston's *Star of the West* (1935) recounted the Lewis and Clark expedition with Sacagawea the heroine. Although Willa Cather is perhaps best recalled for her historical novels set in the West like *My Antonia* (1919) and *Death Comes to the Archbishop* (1927), more take place in the East or elsewhere like *Shadow on the Rock* (1931), *Lucy Gayheart* (1935), and *Sapphira and the Slave Girl* (1940). Clyde Davis's *The Anointed* (1937) and *The Great American Novel* (1938) were picaresque tales of footloose, free-spirited American adventurers.

Notable war novels appeared during this era. For the Civil War, there were Robert Chambers' *Whistling Cat* (1932), and *Secret Service Agent 13* (1934), Harold Sinclair's *American Years* (1938), and, most acclaimed and popular, Margaret Mitchell's *Gone With the Wind* (1936). World War I novels included John Dos Passos's *Nineteen-Nineteen* (1932), William Marsh's *Company K* (1932), and Herbert Gorman's *Suzy* (1934). Ernest Hemingway grounded his novel, *For Whom the Bell Tolls* (1940), on his experiences as a correspondent covering Spain's civil war.

As for colonial America, Kenneth Roberts wrote several brilliant novels, including his masterpiece *Northwest Passage* (1937) along with *Arundel* (1929), *Lively Lady* (1931), *Rabble in Arms* (1933), *Captain Cautious* (1934), and *Oliver Wiswell* (1940). He was a Cornell University graduate who served as an army intelligence officer in France during the First World War, and as a journalist for the *Saturday Evening Post* from 1919 to 1928, before devoting himself to fiction. Other first-rate novels depicting America's Revolutionary War included James Adams' *The Epic of America* (1933), Maxwell Anderson's *Valley Forge* (1934), Walter Edmonds's *Drums Along the Mohawk* (1936), Katharine Mayo's *General Washington's Dilemma* (1938), and Bruce Lancaster's *Guns for Burgoyne* (1939). A few writers set their novels overseas. Pearl Buck grew up in China as the child of missionary parents; her Pulitzer Prize winning novel *The Good Earth* (1931) depicts the poverty and war afflicting China. Herbert Gorman's *The Mountain and the Plain* (1936) is a French Revolution epic.

Plenty of novels depicted contemporary America. Dalton Trumbo's novels *Eclipse* (1935), *Washington Jitters* (1936), and *Johnny Got His Gun* (1939) respectively explored a successful salesman's decline, a political satire, and existence of a First World War veteran who lost his arms, legs, hearing, and sight or in his words, "a dead man with a mind that could still think." In her Pulitzer Prizing winning *Years of Grace* (1931), Margaret Myer Barnes depicted the first fifty years of Jane Ward's upwardly mobile life through setbacks, tragedies, and moral dilemmas. William Saroyan's *My Name Is Aram* (1940) is a short story collection about a boy growing up in small town California. Novels that depicted hardscrabble rural life included Erskine Caldwell's tawdry *Tobacco Road* (1932) and Josephine Winslow Johnson's elegiac *Now in November* (1934). Michael Gold's *Heaven's My Destination* (1935) and Tom Kromer's *Waiting for Nothing* (1935) respectively depicted the picaresque lives of a door-to-door salesman and a hobo during the depression. Nathaniel West's novels *The Dream Life of Balso Snell* (1931), *Miss Lonely Hearts* (1933), *A Cool Million* (1934), and *Day of the Locust* (1939) expose often perverse, sadistic relationships.

Several writers wrote "noir" novels like James Cain's *The Postman Always Rings Twice* (1938), Horace McCoy's *They Shoot Horses Don't They?* (1939), and Edward Anderson's *Thieves like Us* (1937). The finest "noir" writer set most of his novels in sunny Los Angeles. Raymond Chandler's hardboiled private detective Philip Marlow solved crimes in *The Big Sleep* (1939), *Farewell My Lovely* (1940), *The High Window* (1942), and *The Lady in the Lake* (1943). Chandler was influenced by the brilliant crime novels of Dashiell Hammett, especially *The Maltese Falcon* (1930), *The Glass Key* (1931), and *The Thin Man* (1934).

The novels of two writers were so explicitly sexual that the United States government banned them. Henry Miller's *Tropic of Cancer* (1935), *Black Spring* (1936), and *Tropic of Capricorn* (1939) are erotic novels inspired by his own experiences as an expatriate in Paris and other exotic foreign cities. Anais Nin, who for a while had a menage a trois with Miller and his wife June, wrote her own erotic novels, *House of Incest* (1936) and *Winter of the Artifice* (1939).

The Great Depression devastated Harlem's Renaissance of writers and artists as many dispersed in search of elusive day jobs but kept creating. Average income in Harlem was already below New York City's average, $1,300 to $1,750 in 1929, then plunged 43 percent from 1929 to 1932, when 54 percent of black families had annual incomes below $500.[11] Among those who kept writing was Richard Wright, author of the novels *Native Son* (1940) and *Black Boy* (1945). Wright lampooned many of his fellow black writers as "prim and decorous ambassadors who went a-begging to white America... dressed in the kneepads of servility, curtseying to show that the Negro was not inferior, that he was human."[12] The most diverse writer was Zora Neale Hurston whose *Mules and Men* (1935) was a collection of her essays, *Their Eyes Were Watching God* (1937) and *Moses, Man of the Mountain* (1939) were novels set in the depression, and *Dust Tracks on a Road* (1942) was her autobiography. Arna Bontemps's *Black Thunder* (1936) concerns a slave uprising. Three playwrights celebrated black heroes, Sheppard Randolph Edmonds with *Nat Turner* (1935), May Miller with *Harriet Tubman* (1935), and Langston Hughes with *Emperor of Haiti* (1936). Langston Hughes's *Ways of White Folks* (1934) included fourteen short stories.

Communists tried mobilizing writers with the American Writers Congress and League of American Writers. John Dos Passos, Sherwood Anderson, Lincoln Steffens, Sidney Hook, and Erskine Caldwell were among fifty-two believers that signed a letter supporting Communist Party Chair William Foster's candidacy for president of the United States in 1932. For each declared adherent, one must ask whether that embrace came mostly from conviction, naivety, or fashion. Many writers flirted with communism and held fleeting affiliations before becoming disillusioned, while some were hardcore disciples.

Among the era's Marxist novels of bleak working class lives were James Farrell's *Studs Lonigan*, Edward Anderson's *Hungry Men* and Tom Kromer's *Waiting for Nothing* appeared in 1935. Gene Marsay's heroes liberate themselves and others by embracing communism in *You Can't Sleep Her* (1934) and *This Is Your Day* (1937). Josephine Herbst explored what Marxists condemn as the hypocrisy and delusions of bourgeoisie life through her trilogy *Pity Is Not Enough* (1933), *The Executioner Waits* (1934), and *Rope of Gold* (1939). Farrel was eventually an apostate who denounced Stalinist communism with his 1936 "Note on Literary Criticism."

Dos Passos also broke with the communists. He was America's most prominent political novelist during the interwar years. His "U.S.A. Trilogy" included *The 42nd Parallel* (1930), *Nineteen Nineteen* (1932), and *The Big Money* (1936) that spotlighted the nation's materialism, shallowness, corruption, and vulgarity. Along the way, he blistered business corporations and communists alike.

Two writers depicted the depravities of dictatorship. Ayn Rand excoriated communism and collectivism in her novels, most notably through the hero Howard Roark of *The Fountainhead* (1943) who epitomizes individualism, enterprise, and courage. Sinclair Lewis's most important novel during this time was *It Can't Happen Here* (1935) about a demagogic populist politician who takes power and transforms America into a fascist dictatorship; sales revived during and after Donald Trump's presidency and attempted coup in 2020.

Two writers that exemplified two starkly opposed images of the 1920s, F. Scott Fitzgerald for the decadent "roaring twenties" and Ernest Hemingway for the expatriate "Lost Generation" declined as writers during the Roosevelt years. Fitzgerald wrote three novels that captured the 1920s' exuberant, excessive materialism, *This Side of Paradise* (1920), *The Beautiful and the Damned* (1922), and, especially *The Great Gatsby* (1925). His own decadent lifestyle including alcoholism and tobacco addiction took its toll. During the 1930s, he was a hack screenwriter in Hollywood where a heart attack killed him at age forty-four in 1940. He did produce one last complete novel, *Tender Is the Night* (1934) and the unfinished *The Last Tycoon* (1941). Alcoholism also afflicted Hemingway whose 1930s novels *Death in the Afternoon* (1932), *Winner Take Nothing* (1933), and *To Have and Have Not* (1937) did not excite the critical acclaim of his earlier *The Sun Also Rises* (1926) and *A Farewell to Arms* (1929). Yet many critics consider his *For Whom the Bell Tolls* (1940) among his best novels.

During the Roosevelt era, playwrights continued to produce notable plays even though many theaters shuttered their doors and audiences thinned for the survivors. Eugene O'Neil continued to turn out brilliant, thought-provoking plays like *Mourning Becomes Electra* (1931), *The Iceman Cometh* (1939), *Long Day's Journey into Night* (1941), after earlier Pulitzer Prize-winners like *Beyond the Horizon* (1920), *Anna Christie* (1920) and *Strange Interlude* (1928). Thornton Wilder's *Our Town* (1938) depicts conflicts among the townspeople of imaginary Grovers Corners, New Hampshire, on three summer days in 1901, 1904, and 1913 narrated by a graveyard ghost. His *The Skin of Our Teeth* (1942) parable was even more ambitious with conflicts among characters set in contemporary New Jersey with allusions to Biblical times. Maxwell

Anderson wrote a series of plays set in different historic times and places including *Night Over Taos* (1932), *Mary of Scotland* (1933), expanding his earlier repertoire of *White Desert* (1923) and *Elizabeth the Queen* (1930). Tennessee Williams wrote seven plays before creating his first masterpiece, his *Glass Menagerie* (1944). Arthur Miller's career was just beginning with two plays, of which the second, *The Man Who Had All the Luck* (1944) closed after four performances.

The Great Depression dimmed Broadway with its work force plunging from 25,000 to 4,000 from 1929 to 1933. Broadway made a comeback in 1933 when sixteen new plays – ten dramas and six musicals – opened. Such already or soon to be famous movie stars like Henry Fonda, Melvyn Douglas, Tallulah Bankhead, Ethel Merman, Jimmy Stewart, and Walter Huston appeared on stage. *As Thousands Cheer*, with Irving Berlin's songs and Moss Hart's dialogue, was a hit Broadway musical from its opening in September 1933. The show's satirical depictions of international financiers proved as popular as the jaunty tunes and repartee. Composer Richard Rogers collaborated with lyricist Lorenz Hart to create *On Your Toes* (1936) and *Pal Joey* (1940), and with lyricist Oscar Hammerstein for Pulitzer Prize winning *Oklahoma!* (1943) and *Carousel* (1945). George Gershwin produced a series of beautiful single songs and musicals during the 1920s and 1930s, with "Variations on I Got Rhythm," "Porgy and Bess," and "Shall We Dance" his most acclaimed during the Roosevelt years.

A portion of the theater world was openly Marxist. Group Theatre was a commune of fellow traveling playwrights, actors, stage hands, and directors. Marxist influenced plays included Clifford Odets's *Waiting for Lefty* (1935) and Elmer Rice's *We the People* (1933) and *Judgment Day* (1934) that depicted various ways that corporate greed blights working class lives. There were far left off-Broadway musicals. Kurt Weill teamed with Paul Green to compose anti-war *Johnny Johnny* (1936), with Maxwell Anderson for anti-fascist *Knickerbocker Holiday* (1938), and with Moss Hart and Ira Gershwin for the psychological drama *Lady in the Dark* (1941). Marc Blitzstein wrote the leftist musicals *The Cradle Will Rock* (1937) and *No For an Answer* (1941).

First-rate non-fiction books also proliferated during the Roosevelt years. Among the better autobiographies were General John "Black Jack" Pershing's bestselling *My Experiences in the World War* (1931), architect Frank Lloyd Wright's *An Autobiography* of 1932, and communist Louis Adamic's *Autobiography of an Immigrant in America* (1932) and *My America* (1938). The best autobiographies of writers were muckraking journalist Lincoln Steffen's in 1931, novelist Edith

Wharton's *A Backward Glance* (1934), Harriet Monroe's *A Poet's Life* (1938), and Langston Hughes' *The Big Sea* (1940). With her *The Grass Roof* (1931) and *East Goes West* (1937), Younghill Kang wrote the first autobiographies of a Korean-American. Marxist Malcolm Cowley wrote of his jarring transition from American expatriate to resident in *Exile's Return* (1934).

As for biographies, Marquis James won a Pulitzer Prize for his *The Life of Andrew Jackson* (1938), as did Arthur Schlesinger who put that life in a broader historic horizon with his *The Age of Jackson* (1945). Carl Sandburg's two volume biography of Abraham Lincoln, *The Prairie Years* (1926) and *The War Years* (1939), mingles poetic fiction with fact. Three biographies illuminated individuals obscure beyond their immediate social circles. John Neihardt, a Nebraska poet, wrote the biography of his friend, a Sioux medicine man, called *Black Elk Speaks* (1932). Pearl Buck's *The Exile* and *The Fighting Angel*, both published in 1936, revealed the lives of her mother and father as missionaries in China. Expatriate and salon chief Gertrude Stein's most accessible and popular book was her *Autobiography of Alice B. Toklas* (1937), the story of her life partner.

For general histories, none surpassed Arnold Toynbee's three-volume *A Study of History* that appeared in 1934. W.E.B. Du Bois's *Black Reconstruction* (1935) was a revisionist Marxist history of the post-Civil War era. Stuart Chase's *Rich Land, Poor Land* (1936) was a pioneering environmental history of America. Paul Buck's *The Road to Reunion, 1865–1900* (1937) won a Pulitzer Prize. Carl Van Doren's *The American Novel, 1789–1939* (1940) was a groundbreaking literary history of America.

Notable books appeared in other liberal arts. The most influential book on economics was Englishman John Maynard Keyes's *General Theory of Employment, Interest, and Money* (1936). Anthropologist Ruth Benedict's *Patterns of Culture* (1934) sold over a million copies. Anthropologist Frank Boas summed up a lifetime of studies and influential books and articles with his *Race, Language, and Culture* (1941). Sociologists Robert and Helen Lynde's *Middletown in Transition* (1937) was the sequel to their *Middletown* (1929), a study of a "typical" mid-sized American city, Evanston, Indiana, given a cover name. Wilbur Cash explored an entire region in his *The Mind of the South* (1941). Lewis Mumford's *Techics and Civilization* (1932) and *The Culture of Cities* (1938) displayed the dilemmas of modern urban life as did Frank Lloyd Wright in his *The Disappearing City* (1932). The federal government produced its own massive study of urban life: *Our Cities: Their Role in the National Economy* (1937).

Several thought-provoking books on ethics and philosophy appeared, most notably Reinhart Niebuhr's *Moral Man and Immoral*

Society (1934), John Dewey's *The Common Faith* (1934), and Shailer Mathews *New Faith for Old* (1936). The best-selling self-help book was Dale Carnegie's *How to Win Friends and Influence People* (1936). Anne Morrow Lindbergh, Charles's wife, wrote elegiac travel and mediation books like *North to the Orient* (1935) and *Listen, the Wind* (1938).

Many writers depicted the nation's class and racial divides. Gunnar Myrdal was a leading Swedish economist and sociologist who first lived in the United States from 1929 to 1930 as a Rockefeller Foundation Fellow. He returned in 1938 on a Carnegie Foundation grant to study America's economic, social, and racial problems. In 1944, he published his fourteen hundred page *An American Dilemma: The Negro Problem and Modern Democracy*, which exposed the gap between American ideals and discrimination against blacks. Wendell Willkie, the failed Republican candidate for the White House in 1940, called for what became the United Nations and independence for colonized peoples in his best-selling book *One World* (1943). Walter White, the NAACP director, wrote *A Rising World* (1945) to advocate racial equality in the United States.

Conservatives asserted their views themselves through several key works during this time. Twelve southern writers, most prominently Robert Penn Warren, wrote essays celebrating their region, agrarianism, and "the lost cause" in *I'll Take My Stand* (1930). In his *Revolt against the City* (1935), artist Grant Wood argued that: "During boon times conservatism is a thing to be ridiculed, but under unsettling conditions it become a virtue."[13] Fredrich Hayek's *The Road to Serfdom* (1944) became an iconic conservative text. Hayek was an Austrian economist who migrated to the United States and taught at the University of Chicago. He presented the classic liberal argument for free markets and against big government, and castigated Roosevelt's New Deal programs as a form of tyranny.

During the 1930s, many novelists turned to journalism to directly record the Great Depression's impact on ordinary Americans. Among the more prominent writings were Theodore Dreiser's *Tragic America* (1931), Edmund Wilson's *American Jitters* (1932), Erskine Caldwell's *Some American People* (1935), Sherwood Anderson's *Puzzled America* (1935) and *Hometown* (1940), Charles Wilson's *Roots of America* (1936), and Nathan Asch's *The Road: In Search of America* (1937). In his *Boy and Girl Tramps of America* (1934), Thomas Minehan interviewed scores of homeless young people living in shanty towns, hitchhiking, or hopping freight trains across the country.

Lorena Hickok was the among the era's leading investigative journalists. During the 1932 election, the Associated Press assigned

Hickok to cover Eleanor. The two soon became close friends. Hickok's editor fired her after learning she let Eleanor proofread the stories she wrote about her. Eleanor got Harry Hopkins to employ her along with fifteen other journalists on assignments to investigate political, social, and economic conditions across America. For her first in July 1933, Hopkins told her: "What I want you to do is to go out around the country and look this thing over. I don't want statistics from you. I don't want the social worker angle. I just want your own reaction as an ordinary citizen."[14] Eleanor and Lorena forged a deep relationship, with Lorena given a bedroom near Eleanor's at the White House and Eleanor's home of Val-Kill in Hyde Park.[15]

The Great Depression did not harm the newspaper and magazine industry as badly as most other industries and it recovered quicker than most. Henry Luce built a magazine empire with *Time* from 1925 and *Life* from 1936. Popular magazines included the *Saturday Evening Post* and *Collier's*, and leading women's magazines included *Cosmopolitan* and *Woman's Home Companion*. The leading liberal intellectual magazine was the *New Republic* edited by Malcolm Crowley was from 1929 to 1940. A leading conservative newspaper was William Allen White's *Emporia Gazette* in Emporia, Kansas; White's editorials reappeared in newspapers across the country. He was a progressive Republican who backed Theodore Roosevelt and Thomas Dewey. A leading progressive writer was Walter Lippman with his weekly essay in the *New York Herald Tribune*.

Writers and photographers collaborated on some notable books. Novelist Erskine Caldwell and photographer Margaret Bourke-White depicted the poverty stricken south in *You Have Seen Their Faces* (1937), and married the following year. Married couple, photographer Dorothea Lange and economist Paul Taylor, traveled the Dust Bowl region to reveal the life of migrants searching for job, food, and shelter in *An American Exodus: A Record of Human Erosion* (1939). Henry Luce, *Fortune's* editor, commissioned poet James Agee and photographer Walker Evans to investigate southern poverty. The result was *Let Us Now Praise Great Men* (1941).

Most photographers depicted their images without written commentary while the magazines *Look* and *Life* provided the best show cases for dramatic photos. Among the best male photographers of rural poverty were Russell Lee and Arthur Rothstein. Lee's "Christmas Dinner" (1936) depicted four small children standing beside a battered table and eating potatoes and cabbage. Rothstein's "Plantation Owner's Daughter Checks Weight of Cotton" (1936) showed a teenage white girl with a bonnet and white dress weighing a cotton bale before a family of black sharecroppers with a wagon and the cotton field beyond. His "Farmer and Sons Walking in the Face of a Dust Storm, Cimarron County, Oklahoma" (1936) to their shack is another iconic photo. Lewis Hine's book *Men at Work* (1932) displayed an astonishing collection of blue-collar laborers with the most dizzying, a downward shot of "Man on Girders, Mooring Mast, Empire State Building" (1931). Gordon Parks was the greatest black photographer of the Roosevelt years, with his best-known photo "American Gothic, Washington D.C." (1942) of a black cleaning lady with a mop in one hand and broom in the other standing before an American flag.

Dorothea Lange, Margaret Bouke-White, Marion Post Wolcott, and Berenice Abbott were the era's leading female photographers. Lange and Bourke-White had similar back stories growing up in middle-class suburban New York families, going to college, and developing an interest in photography into a career. They started as fashion photographers then focused on portraying down-and-out, marginalized people. Among Lange's most famed photos were "Migrant Mother," "Drought Refugees from Oklahoma Camping by Road," and "Former Slave" from 1936, "Abandoned Farm House on Large Mechanized Cotton Farm" and "White Angel Breadline" from 1938, and "Former Nebraska Farmer, Now a Migrant Farm Workers" (1939). Her "Near Los Angeles, California" (1939) shows two hoboes with suitcases walking down an empty road with a huge billboard of a well-dressed man in an easy chair titled, "Next Time Try the Train, Relax, Southern Pacific." Lange's first husband was Maynard Dixon who painted sweeping western scenes. They lived in Taos, New Mexico, and were part of Mabel Dodge's salon of creative people. Bourke-White spent a couple of years photographing industrial sites before switching to striking human characters and dilemmas. Her "Otis Steel Company" (1928) shows nine soaring black chimneys dwarfing two tiny workers at their base. Wolcott grew up in a New Jersey suburb then fled to Paris where she studied photography. She returned to America and focused on the Great Depression's victims. Abbott was also among the expatriates in Europe, mostly Paris, during the 1920s into the 1930s, and specialized in cityscapes with odd juxtapositions of light and shadow. Many of her most powerful photos appeared in her book *Changing New York* (1939).

Several California photographers that called themselves Group f/64, the most precise aperture, specialized in nature. Ansel Adams was the most brilliant with hundreds of shots of soaring mountains and forbidding deserts; among them his "Clearing Winter Storm"

(1935), "Moonrise, Hernandez, New Mexico" (1941), and "The Tetons and Snake River" (1942) along with his book *Sierra Nevada: The John Muir Trail* (1938) are the most iconic. Edward Weston's subjects were as sensual and abstract as Adams's were epic and realistic. His most innovative photos were of the twisted bodies of naked women and bell peppers.

With the Photo League, communists tried to organize and control photographers as they did every profession. Members had an outlet for their photos of workers, sharecroppers, and protesters in *New Masses* magazine. Walker Evans was the best known Photo League member with his book, *American Photographs* (1936), and later collections. He spent much of 1938 and 1941 in New York with a camera hidden in his overcoat, squeezing photos of weary subway riders. Arthur Fellig, known as Weegee, produced gritty scenes of New York's underworld, collected in two books, *Naked City* (1945) and *Weegee's People* (1946).

A number of painters created provocative works during the Roosevelt years. Two excelled at realism. Rockwell Kent's stark seascapes and landscapes are so powerful that viewers can feel the sharp chill and breeze as in "Early November, North Greenland" (1933), "Seal Hunter" (1933), and "Moonlight, Winter" (1940). Among America's iconic paintings is Edward Hopper's "The Night Hawks" (1942) with two men and a woman at a diner counter with a white clad waiter nearby and the ominous dark city beyond the knee to ceiling windows. His paintings depict isolated people, buildings, and landscapes. Couples in the same room are absorbed in their own separate worlds of work, reading, and gazing without talking or even looking at each other as in "New York Room" (1932) and "Summer in the City" (1932).

Three Midwesterners mostly painted landscapes from their region in styles realistic enough to be accepted if not beloved by most Americans. Thomas Hart Benton's most ambitious work was his 250 square foot mural "A Social History of Indiana" (1933) with twenty-two panels depicting farmers, workers, businessmen, housewives, and kids interacting. His figures are fluid, his colors gaudy, and his subjects often tawdry as in "Hollywood" (1939) and "Persephone" (1939). Grant Wood's "American Gothic" (1930) of a stern farm couple standing before their home, the old man with a pitchfork, was at once an icon and parody as was his "Daughters of Revolution" (1932) of three frosty old ladies and "Parson Weems' Fable" (1939) of George Washington, his father, and a felled cherry tree. John Stewart's war paintings included "The Parade to War" (1938) of soldiers marching off cheered by pretty girls and "The Return of Private Davis from the Argonne" of his funeral (1938). His most powerful painting was "Tragic Prelude" (1937) of a wild-eyed John Brown, arms spread, a rifle in his right hand and a Bible in the other, with Kansas settlers behind him.

A few painters depicted contemporary political themes including Bernarda Shahn's "Saco and Vanzetti" (1931), Reginald Marsh's "Breadline – No One Has Starved" (1932) and "This Is Her First Lynching" (1934), William Gropper's "Youngstown Strike" (1936), Joseph Hirsh's "Landscape with Tear Gas" (1937), and Philip Evergood's "American Tragedy" (1937) of police suppressing a demonstration and "Toiling Hands" (1939).

The most enduring artist was Georgia O'Keefe whose career spanned the twentieth century's first eight decades. From 1917, photographer Alfred Stieglitz helped develop her painting career first as her patron, then lover, and eventually husband in New York. During the 1910s, she mostly did colorful abstractions followed during the 1920s mostly by cityscapes. She first visited Taos, New Mexico in 1929, was enchanted, and moved there in 1934. Thereafter she painted western landscapes, closeups of flowers, and juxtapositions of objects like cow skulls and flowers floating above western landscapes.

As for applied arts, Norman Geddes pioneered the "Streamline Design" for automobiles and train locomotives. That style and other modern wonders were displayed at two world fairs held during the Roosevelt years, Chicago's Century of Progress from 1933 to 1934 and New York's World of Tomorrow from 1939 to 1940. Roosevelt opened New York's version on April 30. The highlight was Futurama that conveyed viewers in moving chairs with commentary from a speaker through vignettes of what American life might be like in 1960. The combined attendance was 85 million, or two of three Americans.

Art Deco remained the most striking urban architectural style with such magnificent skyscrapers as New York's 1,048 foot tall, 77 story Chrysler and 1,472 foot tall, 102 story Empire State buildings completed respectively in 1930 and 1931. The Rockefeller complex of art deco buildings included 6,000-seat Radio City Music Hall that opened in 1932 and the 70-story flagship from 1939. More down to earth, the Supreme Court occupied its current magnificent Greek temple style building in 1936. Frank Lloyd Wright, who pioneered the organic style of architecture, created such stunning buildings as the headquarters for J.C. Johnson Company in Racine, Wisconsin and Falling Water, a home straddling a stream in southwest Pennsylvania's woods, both finished in 1936. Wright expressed these provocative thoughts about the greatest creators: "The effect of any genius is seldom seen in his own lifetime. Nor can the full effects of genius ever be traced or seen… What we call life is…a becoming, in spite of all efforts to fix it with names, and all endeavors to make it static to man's will…For genius is an expression of principle."[16]

Spectacular displays of engineering and design appeared as bridges during the Great Depression including New York's George Washington (1931), Triborough (1939), and Whitestone (1939), New Orleans' Huey Long (1936), and San Francisco's Golden Gate (1937) and San Francisco-Oakland (1937), with each surpassing 3,000 feet. Meanwhile, Gutzon Borglum designed and directed a jackhammer team to carve the sixty-foot tall faces of George Washington, Abraham Lincoln, Theodore Roosevelt, and Thomas Jefferson from granite Mount Rushmore in South Dakota's Black Hills from 1927 to 1941. The completed work is a stunning American icon.

Listening to the radio was America's favorite home pastime. Prices for radios steadily dropped while the number of broadcasters steadily increased. By 1930, nearly nine of ten households had a radio. They tuned in to such shows as "Amos 'n' Andy," "The Lone Ranger," and "The Green Hornet." Will Rogers, Fred Allen, and Jack Benny provoked laughter during their weekly comedy hour shows. Music like jazz and country filled most broadcasts. Orson Welles inadvertently provoked panic among some listeners when on Halloween eve, 1938, he broadcasted a news story version of H.G. Welles's novel *War of the Worlds*, about the Martian invasion of Earth, even though he opened by explaining he was presenting a drama.

American music diversified in genres and artists throughout the twentieth century. During the 1920s, the proliferation of inexpensive radios, record players, and records let music-lovers indulge their tastes and provided income for music groups. The Great Depression was disastrous for the music industry as thousands of players, singers, and technicians lost their jobs. The number of records sold peaked at 100 million in 1929 then plummeted to 6 million in 1932, a 94 percent decline. Thereafter the industry slowly revived as New Deal policies created jobs and income. Ever more folks could buy records and afford an occasional evening out listening or dancing to music at some city club or county fair.

For jazz, the 1930s was the heyday of swing Big Bands like those of Edward "Duke" Ellington, William "Count" Basie, Fletcher Henderson, Coleman Hawkins, Tommy and Jimmie Dorsey, Artie Shaw, Glen Miller, and Benny Goodman.[17] Of them, Ellington created some of the most bequiling pieces like "Mood Indigo," "Sophisticated Lady," "In a Sentimental Mood," or "It Don't' Mean a Thing (If It Ain't Got that Swing)," and complex prolonged compositions like "Symphony in Black" and "Reminiscing in Tempo." In 1938, Ellington welcomed Billy Strayhorn into his band and the two collaborated on over two hundred sophisticated compositions. Meanwhile, Louis Armstrong's band mostly played Dixieland. Extraordinary singers like Ella Fitzgerald and Bille Holiday toured with bands. New York's Cotton, Apollo, Roseland, and Famous Door clubs were the most famed for the bands that performed there. In the early 1940s, Charlie Parker and Dizzy Gillespie developed a new style for quartets and quintets called Bebop with a faster pace and more improvisation.

Country music likely exceeded jazz in popularity. Nashville's Grand Ole Opry was country music's epicenter. From 1925, radio station WSM broadcasted the live performances to over a million radio owners across much of the nation. The other leading country stations were WLS at Chicago, Illinois, WCHS at Charleston, West Virginia, and WLW at Cincinnati, Ohio. Among the most popular performers were the Carter Family, Bob Wills and the Texas Playboys, Roy Acuff, Uncle Dave Macon, Moon Mullican, Cliff Brown, and Hollywood singing cowboys like Gene Autry, Roy Rogers, and Gail Davis. Hank Williams and his Drifting Cowboys had a radio show in the late 1930s. Bill Monroe and his Bluegrass Boys popularized bluegrass music in the early 1940s.

Woody Guthrie was America's wandering folk troubadour, hitch-hiking, hopping freight trains, strumming his guitar, and singing haunting songs like "This Land is Your Land," "Tom Joad," "Dusty Old Dust," and any from his 1940 album *Dust Bowl Ballads*. Guthrie might never have won fame without his discovery by John Lomax, an English professor and music lover, who traveled through rural America, eventually with his son Alan, recording songs that he presented in his *American Ballads and Folk Songs* (1934).

Three composers developed classical music during the Roosevelt years. Aaron Copeland was born to an immigrant Jewish family in Brooklyn, yet created music that captured America's mythic essence through compositions like *El Salon Mexico* (1936), ballet *Billy the Kid* (1938), *Fanfare for the Common Man* (1942), ballet *Rodeo* (1942) with Agnes de Mille's choreography, *Lincoln Portrait* (1942), *The Second Hurricane* (1943), and *Appalachian Spring* (1944). Among Virgil Thompson's most powerful works were the scores for the films *The Plow That Broke the Plains* (1936) and *The River* (1937), the Second Symphony (1941), and Eight Portraits for Orchestra (1942–44). Leonard Bernstein composed the music and Jerome Robbins the choreography for *Fancy Free* (1944), and the music and Betty Comden and Adolph Green the lyrics for *On the Town* (1944), about three sailors on leave in New York, with "New York, New York" its best known song.

Movie going dropped during the depression as people had less money for leisure. Weekly attendance was around 100 million in 1930 and 60 million in 1933, while around 5,000 of the nation's 16,000 theaters closed. The five "majors" included Radio-Keith-Orpheum (RKO), Paramount, Metro-Goldwyn-Mayer (MGM), 20th Century Fox, and Warner Brothers. Collectively their assets plummeted from $1 billion to $200 million, and only MGM stayed profitable.[18]

The film industry revived with the New Deal economy as weekly attendance steadily rose to around 80 million by 1940. Indeed, many critics consider the late 1930s and early 1940s Hollywood's golden age.[19] Arguably 1939 was the peak year with such great films as *Gone with the Wind*, *The Wizard of Oz*, *Stagecoach*, *Mr. Smith Goes to Washington*, and *Ninotchka*.

Although it was panned when it appeared, *Citizen Kane* (1940) is the choice of countless critics for best film of all time.[20] Orson Welles wrote, directed, and starred in the film inspired by the life of William Randolph Hearst, the publishing titan with multiple conflicting points of view. He did enjoy good reviews for his more conventional *The Magnificent Andersons* (1942).

Frank Capra was America's most popular director during the 1930s, adept at evoking both laughter and pathos. Perhaps his best light-hearted film was the "screwball" romantic comedy *It Happened One Night* (1933) starring Clark Gable and Claudette Colbert that delighted audiences and won the three of them Academy Awards. Capra provided a lone political hero overcoming corrupt, inept politicians and bureaucrats in *Mr. Deeds Goes to Town* (1936) and *Mr. Smith Goes to Washington* (1939) that respectively starred Gary Cooper and Jimmy Stewart. John Ford directed three great films during the Roosevelt years. He hit his stride as a director with his western *Stagecoach* (1939) starring John Wayne, then *Grapes of Wrath* (1940) starring Henry Fonda and based on Steinbeck's novel, and *How Green Was My Valley* (1941) starring Wayne that won an Academy Award.

The range of movies from 1933 to 1945 was astonishing from tear-jerking dramas like William Wyler's *Mrs. Miniver* (1942) to zany comedies like the Marx Brothers' *Duck Soup* (1934). Femme fatales provided both role-models for aspiring woman and warning tales. For that no one surpassed Greta Garbo, especially in *Grand Hotel* (1932), *Queen Christina* (1933), *Anna Karenina* (1935), and *Ninotchka* (1939).

Among her leading rivals were Ginger Rogers in *Gold Diggers*, Bette Davis in *Ex-Lady*, Barbara Stanwix in *Baby Face*, and Mae West in *I'm No Angel*, all in 1933. Musicals were highly popular. The most prolific and spectacular director and choreographer was Busby Berkeley with thirty-three from 1933 to 1943, including *The Gold Diggers* (1933), *Footlight Parade* (1933), and *42nd Street* (1933). The greatest movie dance couple was Fred Astaire and Ginger Rogers who starred in nine musicals from 1933 to 1939, with most acclaimed *The Gay Divorcee* (1934), *Top Hat* (1935), and *Swing Time* (1936). Criminals and crime-fighters alike excited audiences. Versions of Chicago crime boss Al Capone appeared with pseudonyms played by Edward G. Robinson in *Little Caesar* (1930) and James Cagney in *Public Enemy* (1931). Pretty Boy Floyd was the hero of *I am a Fugitive from a Chain Gang* (1932), starring Paul Muni. Robinson and Cagney played incorruptible cops fighting crime respectively in *Bullets or Ballots* and *G-Man*, both in 1935. *Double Indemnity* (1944) and *Murder, My Sweet* (1945) became film noir classics. In the early thirties, a spate of popular monster movies appeared that included *Freaks* (1932), *Frankenstein* (1932), and *King Kong* (1933). For stark realism, few surpassed King Vidor's film drama *Our Daily Bread* (1934) that depicted the hard lives of a farming community. Walt Disney produced a string of brilliant animated films that all ages could enjoy like *Snow White and the Seven Dwarfs* (1937), *Pinocchio* (1940), *Fantasia* (1940), *Dumbo* (1941), and *Bambi* (1942). There were costume dramas like *A Tale of Two Cities* (1935) and *Conquest* (1938), and thrilling westerns like *Way Out West* (1937), *Destry Rides Again* (1939), and *Union Pacific* (1939).

All along, Will Hays, the Motion Picture Production Code chief, strictly enforced a long list of forbidden scenes and attitudes like nudity, atheism, and profanity. Preceding feature films were newsreel series like the March of Time, News of the Day, and Fox Movietone. Lowell Thomas was Movietone's sonorous, reassuring voice that reported from numerous battle fronts during the Second World War.

Enlisting artists for any cause is usually as easy as herding cats. During the Second World War, President Roosevelt pulled that off when philanthropist Mary Ingraham acted on his request to found an organization dedicated to providing light entertainment for America's military personnel. On February 4, 1941, she incorporated the United Service Organization (USO) as a partnership among the Young Men's Christian Association (YMCA), Young Woman's Christian Association (YWCA), Salvation Army, National Catholic Community Service, National Jewish Welfare Board, and National Traveler's Aid Association. She got New York Governor Thomas Dewey and Senator Prescott Bush of Connecticut to serve as the chairman and deputy.

That first year, they raised $16 million for two programs. One was a network of rooms in train and bus stations for traveling military personnel where they might get a cup of coffee and directions from cheerful volunteers. The other was variety shows of comedians, actors, and musicians that performed at bases. Among the most famed volunteers were Bob Hope, Marlene Dietrich, Betty Grable, George Raft, and Edward G. Robinson. Meanwhile, the Department of the Army enlisted film directors to promote the war, of which Frank Capra's seven "Why We Fight" movies was the most powerful.

For his millions of fans, Glenn Miller's big band provided a sound track for the war years. He and his band hold the record for Top Ten hits with 69, including popular classics like "Moonlight," "Chattanooga Choo Choo," and "In the Mood." In October 1942, he received an army air force captain's commission and took his act to London where it was renamed "Captain Glenn Miller and His American Band of the Supreme Command." The BBC and American military radio broadcasted their live performances. Tragically, Miller and his colleagues died when their plane crashed into the English Channel on December 15, 1944.

Meanwhile, composers and musicians boosted morale with such popular songs including "Don't Sit Under the Apple Tree," "Tonight We Love," "Blues to the Night," "Deep in the Heart of Texas," "I'll Walk Alone," "Strangers in the Night," "It Could Happen to You," "Time Waits for No One," "I'll Get By," "Swinging on a Star," and "It Had to Be You." The Broadway musical *This Is the Army, Mr. Jones* (1943), included Irving Berlin's "I Left My Heart at the Stage Door Canteen," "Oh How I Hate to Get Up in the Morning," "I'm Getting So Hard I Can't Sleep." The show had 112 performances in New York before touring the nation. The most popular song writers were Irving Berlin, Johnny Mercer, and Cole Porter, and the most popular crooners were Frank Sinatra, Burl Ives, and Bing Crosby along with female singers like Peggy Lee, Lena Horne, and the Andrew Sisters.

As for art, illustrator Norman Rockwell painted several iconic images during World War II. He expressed Roosevelt's Four Freedoms through four paintings in 1943, "Of Speech" with a middle-aged workers standing with his mouth open in an assembly of fellow citizens; "Of Worship" with profiles of four people with heads bowed or uplifted; "From Want" of a middle-aged father presenting a platter with a roasted turkey on its to his beaming family; and "From Fear" of parents tucking in their daughter at night. With the slogan "Buy Victory Bonds," he depicts a slender veteran returning to a tenement's backyard where his family and neighbors joyfully greet him. Rockwell painted a version of "Rosie the Riveter" (1943) with a muscular women in overalls, a huge rivet gun across her lap, a ham sandwich in one hand, eyes closed, and a halo behind her head. A year earlier, Howard Miller created the more famous version of Rosie in overalls, red bandana binding her hair, sleeve rolled up, an upheld fist, her firm gaze at the viewer, and the written assertion, "We Can Do It!"

Popular films during the war years included three about war, *Casablanca* (1942), *For Whom the Bell Tolls* (1943), and *The White Cliffs of Dover* (1944) but also *Lassie Come Home* (1943), *Meet Me in St. Louis* (1944), *Jane Eyre* (1944), *National Velvet* (1945), and *A Tree Grows in Brooklyn* (1945).[21] Of those, *Casablanca* was the greatest. Many critics saw *Casablanca* as a metaphor for neutral America as a world war worsens. Humphry Bogart plays a cynical bar owner in Casablanca, Morocco, nominally a French colony. But Germany's conquest of France in 1940 and imposition of the puppet Vichy regime, has transformed France and thus its empire into German colonies. Bogart tries to avoid politics when his ex-girlfriend played by Ingrid Bergman appears to complicate the moral dilemmas.

Hundreds of courageous journalists covered World War II's front lines. Of them, Ernie Pyle provided some of the most vivid and visceral reporting through the eyes of combat soldiers in his columns and two books, *Here Is Your War* (1943) and *Brave Men* (1944); a Japanese sniper killed him on Okinawa. John Hershey was just as brilliant. His *Men on Bataan* (1942) depicted the doomed American defense of that Philippine peninsula and his Pulitzer Prize winning *Hiroshima* (1946) was a stunning account of the atomic bombing of that city. Ernest Hemingway wrote stories for *Colliers* while following the European front, first in London and later in France from May 1944 to March 1945; although he came under fire several times his best recalled feat was liberating the Ritz Hotel's bar after Paris's liberation on August 25. The *Saturday Evening Post* presented a series written by soldiers and sailors called "What I am Fighting For." Ethal Gorman, a *New York Times* journalist, wrote the best-selling *So Your Husband's Gone to War* (1943). *Stars and Stripes* was and remains the military's daily newspaper. In it, Bill Mauldin's cartoon, "Willie and Joe," humorously depicted the absurdities and ironies of army life at the front and behind the lines.

A few authors explored World War II. John Steinbeck's *The Moon Is Down* (1942) took place in a Norwegian village with people split bitterly and dangerously between collaborators and resisters to the pro-Nazi regime and German occupation. Helen MacInnes set her espionage novels *Above Suspicion* (1941) and *Assignment in Brittany* (1942) in Nazi dominated Europe. Glenway Wescott's *Apartment in Athens* (1945) took place in German occupied Greece. Upton Sinclair's *Presidential Agent* (1944) is an espionage tale in Germany during the mid-1930s. John Hershey's *Bell for Adano* (1944) won the 1945 Pulitzer Prize for his novel set on the Italian front.

Shortly after the war, eight acclaimed novels appeared written by participants, Gore Vidal's *Williwaw* (1946), James Michener's Pulitzer Prize winning *Tales of the South Pacific* (1947), John Burns's *The Gallery* (1947), Thomas Heggen's *Mister Roberts* (1946), Norman Mailer's *The Naked and the Dead* (1948), Irwin Shaw's *The Young Lions* (1948), James Jones' *From Here to Eternity* (1951), Herman Wouk's Pulitzer Prize-winning *The Cain Mutiny* (1952), and eventually Joseph Heller's *Catch-22* (1961) and Kurt Vonnegut's *Slaughter-House Five* (1969).

World War II inspired numerous playwrights. Lilian Hellman wrote two plays on the war, *Watch on the Rhine* (1941) about freedom fighters trying to undermine Hitler's regime, and *The Searching Wind* (1944), about financiers who collaborated with Hitler. Others included Robert Sherwood's *There Shall Be No Night* (1940), Elmer Rice's *Flight to the West* (1940), Norman Krasna's *The Man with the Blond Hair* (1941), Maxwell Anderson's *Candle in the Wind* (1941), *The Eve of St. Mark* (1942), *Tomorrow the World* (1943), and *Storm Operation* (1944), Paul Osborn's adaption of John Hershey's novel *A Bell for Adano* (1944), Rose Franken's *Soldier's Wife* (1944), Laurence Stalling's *The Streets Are Guarded* (1944), John Patrick's *The Hasty Heart* (1945), and Arthur Laurent's *Home of the Brave* (1945). Few directly depicted combat but mostly explored the war's indirect effects in an array of situations including occupied towns, hospitals, and home fronts.

Among the more noted poetry collections during the war were Babette Deutsch's *Take Them, Stranger* (1942), Karl Shapiro's *Person, Place, and Thing* (1942), Melvin Tolson's *Rendezvous with America* (1944), and Stanley Kunitz's *Passport to the War* (1944). Among the more vivid war poems were Marianne Moore's "In Distrust of Merits," Winfield Scott's "The U.S. Sailor with a Japanese Skull," Richard Eberhardt's "The Fury of Aerial Bombardment," Robert Lowell's "The Bomber," Melvin Tolson's "The Unknown Soldier," John Nims's "Shot Down at Night," and especially Karl Shapiro's "Full Moon New Guinea," "The Leg," "V-Letter," and "Elegy for a Dead Soldier."

Finally, America was enriched culturally and scientifically during the Roosevelt years by the hundreds of brilliant minds that escaped Europe. There were painters like Wassily Kandinsky, Salvador Dali, Joann Miro, Marcel Duchamp, Lyonel Feininger, Piet Mondrian, Marc Chagall, Max Ernst, and Ferdinand Leger; architects like Ludwig Mies van der Rohe and Walter Gropius; composers like Kurt Weill; writers like Thomas Mann; and film-makers like Ernst Lubitsch, Henry Koster, and Billy Wilder. As for the war, the greatest contribution was by European physicists like Albert Einstein, Edward Teller, Leo Szilard, Enrico Fermi, and Niels Bohr for the atomic bomb project.

Chapter 7

THE STRIDES TO WORLD WAR

"We must be the great arsenal of democracy." (Franklin Roosevelt)

"When you see a rattlesnake poised to strike, you do not wait until he struck you before you crush him." (Franklin Roosevelt)

"Our civilization cannot endure unless we, as individuals, realize our responsibility to and dependence on the rest of the world. For it is literally true that the 'self-supporting' man or woman has become as extinct as the man of the stone age." (Franklin Roosevelt)

"[I]f American democracy ceases to move forward as a living force, seeking day and night by peaceful means to better the lot of our citizens, then Fascism and Communism will grow in strength in our land." (Franklin Roosevelt)

"We have learned that when we deliberately try to legislate neutrality, our neutrality laws may operate unevenly and unfairly – may actually give aid to an aggressor and deny it to the victim. The instinct of self-preservation should warn us that we ought not to let that happen anymore." (Franklin Roosevelt)

"No matter how long it may take us to overcome this premeditated invasion, the American people in their righteous might will win through to absolute victory." (Franklin Roosevelt)

Three foreign policy camps competed during Franklin Roosevelt's dozen years in the White House, isolationists, unilateralists, and internationalists.[1] Depending on the issue and time, Roosevelt could be found in any of those camps although occasionally he tried awkwardly to straddle two or even all three. An array of forces determined his position, including the issue's relative importance, prevailing public opinion, prevailing congressional opinion, prevailing advisor opinion, powerful interest groups with a stake, and his own gut instincts.

He naturally leaned toward internationalism because he understood the benefits of free trade and investments, amicable resolutions of differences, and promotion of common interests with other countries. He struggled against America's dominant isolationism during the 1930s. Most citizens, newspaper editors, and members of Congress opposed any American involvement in foreign crises and wars. He provoked blistering criticisms when he tried to shift opinion with speeches that explained how ignoring foreign threats worsened them. In what was called his Quarantine Speech on October 5, 1937, he suggested the international isolation of imperialist countries much as diseased people are quarantined. Reacting to the subsequent chorus of vitriol, Roosevelt allegedly quipped, "It's a terrible thing to look over your shoulder when you are trying to lead – and find no one there."[2]

Yet, embracing isolationism was among the political prices that Roosevelt paid to win the presidency. He had been a Wilsonian internationalist since 1913, when Wilson appointed him the assistant naval secretary. Roosevelt supported the League of Nations and other internationalist treaties like those of the 1922 Washington conference and 1928 Kellogg-Briand Pact. Then, in a campaign speech on February 2, 1932, he declared that "American participation in the League would not serve the highest purpose of the prevention of war and a settlement of international difficulties in accordance with fundamental American ideals."[3] With that, he repudiated the League of Nations' core reason for being, collective security or for all members to unite against any potential aggressors.

Roosevelt changed his tune after winning the presidency. On December 28, 1933, in his address to the Woodrow Wilson Foundation dinner, he reassured the internationalist audience that his administration would give "cooperation to the League in every matter which is not primarily political and in every matter which obviously represents the views and good of the peoples of the world as distinguished from the views and good of political leaders, of privileged classes, and of imperialistic aims."[4]

Roosevelt's first major foreign policy bolstered American isolationism. London hosted the World Economic Conference of 66 states to devise measures to counter the global depression from June 12 to July 27, 1933. Roosevelt essentially scuttled that forum on June 30, when he told reporters that the United States would not join efforts to stabilize currency values and would not return to the gold standard for the foreseeable future. On July 3, he doubled down on his economic nationalism by having Secretary of State Cordell Hull release this statement: "The sound internal economic system of a nation is a greater factor in its well-being than the price of its currency in changing terms of the currencies of other nations...When the world works out concerted policies in the majority of nations to produce balanced budgets and living within their means, then we can properly discuss a better distribution of the world's gold and silver supply to act as a reserve base of national currencies."[5] In other words, each nation had to get its economic house in order before the United States would discuss currency exchange.

Likewise, the Roosevelt administration refused to cancel the debt that other countries amassed by borrowing from American financiers during and after the First World War. In 1934, Senator Hiram Johnson of California sponsored a bill that prevented American financiers from making new loans to countries unless they repaid their existing loans. Roosevelt signed that into law in April.

Ironically, the Roosevelt administration refused to reduce the debts of other democratic countries but wrote off most of the $600 million debt owed by a communist tyranny. The outstanding issue between the United States and the Soviet Union was the communist regime's policy in 1919 of repudiating Russia's foreign debt and nationalizing foreign investments. In response, Washington refused to recognize the communist regime. On November 17, 1933, Roosevelt invited Foreign Minister Maxim Litvinov to discuss those and other issues at the White House. Roosevelt accepted Litvinov's offer partly to pay what Moscow owed by letting the federal government confiscate some of its assets in the United States, although that value was a fraction of the $150 million that the president sought. Nonetheless, with that "gentleman's agreement," Roosevelt recognized the Soviet Union and agreed on an exchange of ambassadors.

Roosevelt backed the efforts of the ongoing Geneva Conference to reduce arms by all League of Nations members along with the United States and Switzerland. The conference opened on February 1, 1932, and persisted mostly in stalemate until it broke up in December 1934. The biggest obstacles were Japan and Germany that denounced any restrictions and resigned from the League and Geneva conference.

Roosevelt took a major step from isolationism to internationalism when he got Congress to pass the Reciprocal Trade Act, which empowered the president to negotiate with foreign governments mutual tariff cuts up to 50 percent. The House approved by 274 to 111 on March 29, the Senate by 57 to 33 on June 4, and the president signed it on June 12, 1934. The law amended and canceled the 1930 Smoot-Hawley Law that had raised tariffs up to 50 percent and provoked an international trade war of retaliatory protection that worsened the global depression. The law included a most-favored-nation clause that extended tariff reductions to countries that reciprocated. Congress renewed the Reciprocal Trade Act in 1937 and 1940.

Roosevelt expanded Herbert Hoover's "Good Neighbor Policy" to reduce American military commitments in the Western Hemisphere.[6] On April 12, 1933, he announced that for "I would dedicate this Nation to the policy of the good neighbor." He had Secretary of State Hull vote a resolution that "no state has the right to interfere in the internal or external affairs of another" at the Pan-American Conference in Montevideo, Uruguay in December 1933. That refuted President Theodore Roosevelt's 1904 Roosevelt Corollary to the 1823 Monroe Doctrine that asserted Washington's right militarily to intervene in countries where civil war or radicalism threatened American economic and strategic interests. A bilateral treaty in May 1934 released Cuba from the Platt Amendment that let the United States supervise its foreign and financial policies and withdrew the last marines from Haiti. On March 24, 1934, he signed the Philippine Independence or Tydings-McDuffie Act that would grant that colony independence a decade later.

Roosevelt still asserted American power to restore stability or democracy to vital Latin American states, but he did so with diplomatic and economic not military means. For instance, he had Undersecretary of State Sumner Welles negotiate the ousting of Ramon Saint Martin Grau, Cuba's revolutionary dictator, and replacement by Army Chief of Staff Fulgencio Batista after refusing to recognize and cutting economic ties with his regime while promising a $4 million loan to his successor. That prompted Grau's bitter quip that America had asserted "a new type of intervention – intervention by inertia."[7]

Roosevelt called for the Senate to approve a treaty whereby the United States joined the Permanent Court of International Justice, called the World Court, during his State of the Union address on January 16, 1935. That provoked a firestorm of debate between internationalists and isolationists. The Senate voted 52 to 36, short of the two-thirds necessary for ratification on January 29. Bitter at the loss, Roosevelt wrote Majority Leader Joseph Robinson that: "As to the 36 Gentlemen who voted against the principle of a World Court, I am inclined to think that if they ever get to Heaven they will be doing a great deal of apologizing for a very long time – that is if God is against war – and I think he is."[8]

The worst and worsening threat to international peace was aggression by the fascist states of Japan, Italy, and Germany.[9] Benito Mussolini and his coterie of theorists and advisors had invented the ideology of fascism as an authoritarian political system with a dictator that developed the economy by a partnership between the state and businesses, the devotion of people to the nation, and the nation's territorial expansion by conquering other countries. Mussolini and his Fascist Party took power in Italy legally in October 1922, when King Victor Emannuel named him prime minister after he threatened to march with his followers on Rome, presumably to take over the government. Once in power, Mussolini got parliament to grant him dictatorial powers and outlaw all parties except the Fascist Party. Mussolini enacted policies that developed the economy by investing in infrastructure like electricity, water, roads, and railroads that stimulated the creation and distribution of wealth. He steadily expanded Italy's military and called for recreating the Roman Empire.

Adolf Hitler also legally took power and established a dictatorship.[10] Mussolini inspired Hitler's demagogic style and the ideology, organization, and tactics of the National Socialist and Workers (Nazi) Party he had led since 1920. The Great Depression devastated Germany's economy and discredited its democratic political system and the coalition of centrist parties that struggled to govern. Ever more voters sought salvation by supporting either the Nazi or Communist parties. The Nazis won 2.6 percent of the vote in 1928, 18.25 in 1930, and 37.27 percent in July 1932, when it took the largest share of Reichstag (Parliament) seats. Although the Nazi's support slipped to 33.69 percent in the November 1932 election, it remained the largest party. Meanwhile, the Communist Party's share rose from 10.5 percent in 1928 to 16.9 percent in November 1932. Hitler ran against Hindenburg, Germany's president, in the March 1932 election and won 30.1 percent to his 49.6 percent. Since Hindenburg took less than half the votes, a second round took place during which Hitler and Hindenburg respectively won 36.8 percent and 53.0 percent. When German Chancellor (prime minister) Paul von Papen resigned on January 28, 1933, Hindenburg replaced him with Hitler on January 30.

Hitler's next step was to create a crisis to justify him receiving emergency powers. He had his henchmen burn down the Reichstag but as they prepared to do so they caught a communist also committing arson on February 27. Hitler proclaimed the danger of a communist revolution that only the Nazis could thwart. Hindenburg granted him temporary emergency powers of decree on February 28. In the March 1933 election, the Nazis won 43.91 of the vote that with the allied Nationalist Party's 8.1 percent gave them a majority of seats. On March 23, the Reichstag passed the Enabling Act that granted Hitler the permanent power of decree. With that, he decreed the suspension of all parties but the Nazis. He ordered mass arrests of communists and other radicals to be indefinitely incarcerated in a growing system of concentration camps. His Nuremburg Decrees stripped Jews of German citizenship, barred them from military or civil service, and prevented them from marrying non-Jews. Hitler launched a massive mostly secret buildup of Germany's military, including tanks, submarines, warplanes, and troop numbers forbidden by the 1919 Versailles Treaty; within a year, the army expanded from 100,000 to 300,000 troops and would surpass 1,000,000 by 1939. When Hindenburg died on August 2, 1934, Hitler abolished the presidency and assumed its powers as chancellor to make himself Germany's all powerful "leader" (Fuehrer).

Japanese fascism differed from that of Italy and Germany in two crucial ways. One was that Japan had no charismatic all powerful dictator like Mussolini or Hitler. Japanese revered their demi-god Emperor Hirohito yet his powers were purely symbolic. The emperor presided over the Imperial War Council that included three military and three civilian ministers. Decisions came through consensus with everyone more or less in accord. Like Italy and Germany, a fascist dictatorship came to power in Japan that overwhelmed a budding liberal democracy, but through a series of incremental steps from 1925 that suspended more rights and amassed more powers. The other way that Japan's fascism differed was its power to inspire soldiers and civilians to sacrifice themselves for the glory of Japan and its emperor, especially when there was no chance of victory.

The first step toward the Second World War came a decade before Pearl Harbor with Japan's conquest of Manchuria in September 1931.[11] Japan won a war against Russia for supremacy over Manchuria, China's northeastern region, in 1905. Under the Treaty of Portsmouth, Japan's received title to lease of the South Manchurian Railroad included the right to defend it with troops. A coterie of Japanese officers plotted to conquer natural resource rich Manchuria for Japan's empire. On September 18, 1931, they exploded a bomb on the tracks, killed some Chinese "terrorists" near the site, and with that excuse Japan's army swiftly overran the region. China's government protested to the League of Nations which appointed a five-man commission led by Victor Bulwer-Lytton to investigate. The Lytton Report issued on October 2, 1932 revealed the details of Japanese aggression. In conquering Manchuria, Tokyo violated the League of Nations Covenant of 1919 that outlawed international aggression, the Four Power and Nine Power Pacts of 1922 that protected China's territorial integrity and sovereignty, and the Kellogg-Briand Pact of 1928 that outlawed war.

The League of Nations assembly and council debated what to do. Secretary of State Henry Stimson reacted to Japan's imperialism on January 7, 1932, by refusing to recognize any of its conquests and demanding that it restore Manchuria to China. Roosevelt embraced that "Stimson Doctrine." The pending vote to condemn Japan's imperialism led Tokyo to walk out of the League of Nations on March 27, 1933. The decision of the League of Nations and United States to protest but not punish that blatant imperialist act encouraged fascist powers Japan, Italy, and Germany to commit a series of aggressions culminating with Germany's invasion of Poland in September 1939. Only then did Britain and France declare war against Germany.

All along, President Roosevelt viewed those aggressions with increasing alarm. Tragically, the more they threatened American interests, the less he could do to thwart them. A Senate investigation bolstered isolationist sentiments. Senator Gerald Nye of North Dakota chaired the seven member Special Committee on Investigation of the Munitions Industry that convened from April 12, 1934 to February 24, 1935. Nye's committee conduced 93 hearings and examined over 200 witnesses to determine whether the related financial and munitions industries, later called the military industrial complex, pressured the United States to enter the First World War to protect and enhance its investments. The committee found that the finance industry lent Britain, France, and their other allies $2.3 billion and Germany only $27 million from August 1914 to January 1917, while the munitions industry made enormous profits selling to the allies. The financial and munitions industries thus had a compelling interest that the allies win the war and that was most likely if the United States joined that alliance to war against Germany and its allies. The financial and munitions industries colluded to keep profits high and win war contract bids. Those findings were a major reason that Congress passed a series of neutrality laws starting in 1935 that strait-jacketed the president's ability to send aid to one side in a war.

Meanwhile, Tokyo justified its takeover of Manchuria with the Amau Doctrine. On April 17, 1934, Eliji Amau, a foreign ministry spokesman, asserted that Japan had an exclusive sphere of influence over East Asia and the western Pacific, and thus the right unilaterally to protect its interests in that sphere. They argued that Japan's Amau Doctrine for Asia was the equivalent of America's Monroe Doctrine for Latin America. In doing so, the Japanese repudiated America's Open Door policy and the Four Power and Nine Power Pacts of 1922 that upheld it.

Hitler emulated Japan by withdrawing Germany from the League of Nations on October 19, 1933. He issued the world a disturbing message on March 16, 1935. He denounced the Versailles Treaty's disarmament clause and revealed that Germany's military had already surpassed those limits. Protest but not punishment was the official reaction from London, Paris, Geneva, and Washington.

A war with enormous consequences erupted in 1935. Ethiopia, then called Abyssinia, was the last independent African kingdom. Emperor Haile Selassie ruled a realm more medieval than modern. Not only did slavery persist but Selassie ordered slave expeditions into neighboring British Kenya and Italian Somaliland and Eritrea. The Ethiopians sold excess slaves to Saudi Arabia. Although Ethiopia was a League of Nations member, Selassie refused to pay its minimum dues. In August, a series of border clashes between Ethiopia and Italy's colony of Somaliland provoked debate in the League of Nations over how to respond. Mussolini reinforced with troops and supplies Italy's army in Somaliland and threatened to invade Ethiopia. The debate at the League intensified but without votes on any resolution that mandated peace talks. Mussolini ordered his army to invade Ethiopia on October 3, 1935.

Ethiopian Emperor Haile Selassie appeared before the League of Nations assembly on October 10, and pleaded that the world's governments force Mussolini to withdraw his army. The British and French governments forged a consensus in the League's Coordination Committee for imposing sanctions on Italy that embargoed armaments, loans, and credit to Italy, and boycotted Italian products on October 11, but the League did not vote for it until October 31 and it did not begin until November 18.

The League wanted to add oil to the list of forbidden sales. Italy had little petroleum production and severed from imports its army and navy operations would grind to a halt. The Coordination Committee asked the White House to join the embargo. With half the world's oil exports, American participation was crucial to the embargo's success.

Legally, President Roosevelt could not do so. Congress passed and Roosevelt reluctantly signed on August 31, 1935, the Neutrality Act that prohibited the United States from providing "arms, ammunition, or implements of war" to either side in a war; listed special weapons that were forbidden; and required licenses for arms dealers. Those restrictions took effect when a president declared that war existed between two or more countries. The law failed to distinguish aggressors from victims and so severely hobbled the president's power to deter or undercut an aggressive country by aiding the victim. The law would expire on March 1, 1936, unless Congress and the president reapproved it. Congress renewed the Neutrality Act by a House vote of 355 to 27 on February 17 and the Senate by acclamation on February 18, and Roosevelt dutifully signed it on February 28, 1936. The latest version expanded the list of forbidden goods to include financial grants and loans.

Roosevelt could not formally join America to the embargo because the Neutrality Act did not list oil on the list of forbidden exports to belligerents. Instead, on October 31, he called for a "moral embargo" of exports to Italy. No oil producer complied. Indeed, international sales of oil along with iron, steel, copper, and other strategic raw materials to Italy nearly tripled over the next year.

Roosevelt's refusal to join the embargo was actually not critical for its success. The key to stopping Mussolini's aggression was Britain's control of the Suez Canal, through which troops, weapons, and supplies steamed to Italy's Somaliland from which all that proceeded to Ethiopia. Whitehall could have stopped that flow by preventing those ships from transiting the canal. Instead, British Prime Minister Stanley Baldwin and French Premier Pierre Laval, who was also foreign minister, chose not to take that vital step, fearing that it would push Mussolini into Hitler's arms. Instead, on December 11, foreign ministers Samuel Hoare of Britain and Laval of France, signed a deal that essentially ceded eastern Ethiopia to Italy. Mussolini played along the British and French governments by demanding more territory. The Italian army overran more of Ethiopia and Halie Selassie fled into exile. The Italians captured the capital, Addis Ababa, on May 5, 1936, and Mussolini announced Ethiopia's annexation with King Victor Emanuel its new emperor on May 7. The League of Nations ended its embargo against Italy on July 4.

Thus did the League of Nations commit its second egregious act of appeasing aggression that encouraged worse imperialism. Straitjacketed legally and politically, Roosevelt could merely explain those implications. During his State of the Union address on January 3, 1936, he warned Americans to recognize "marked trends toward aggression, of increasing armaments, of shortening tempers – a situation which has in it many of the elements that lead to the tragedy of general war."[12]

Meanwhile, most of the world's naval powers met in London from December 9, 1935 to March 25, 1936. Ideally, the delegates would renew previous treaties about to expire and further reduce naval power. Roosevelt and Prime Minister Baldwin wanted to retain the five-five-three ratio for warships among America, Britain, and Japan established by treaty at the Washington Conference of 1921 to 1922. Tokyo, however, had given notice in December 1934 that it intended to withdraw from that treaty on December 31, 1936, unless the Americans and British accepted Japanese parity in warships. The American and British delegations, backed by France, rejected parity on January 15. The Japanese angrily stormed out of the conference. That signaled the end of naval restrictions and the beginning of a new naval arms race. The only treaty signed involved submarine warfare and required submarine commanders to let passengers and crews of enemy merchant ships embark in life boats before sinking them; thirty-five states including Japan eventually signed that treaty.

Hitler defied not just the Versailles Treaty's signatories but his own generals' advice on March 2, 1936. He ordered German troops to march into the Rhineland Ruhr and Saar industrial regions in blatant violation of the Versailles Treaty. Hitler later admitted how worried he was that act would trigger war with France and Britain. France's army then numbered a million troops, more than twice that of Germany's army. Had the French army, supported by a British contingent, invaded Germany, Hitler would have had to order a humiliating retreat and his generals most likely would have overthrown him. And that would have prevented the Second World War. But as usual, appeasement prevailed in Geneva, London, Paris, and Washington.

The latest international crisis erupted on July 17, 1936, when General Francisco Franco led a military revolt against Spain's leftist government. The result was an increasingly bloody and destructive civil war over the next two years. Germany and Italy backed Franco's "nationalists" while the Soviet Union backed the "republicans" with weapons, loans, and even troops. A group of mostly socialist and communist Americans formed the Abraham Lincoln brigade that fought with the republicans against the nationalists. The brigade numbered around 450 troops when it was nearly wiped out in the battle of Jarama Valley near Madrid in February 1937; in all, 120 were killed and 175 wounded.

The Neutrality Laws covered only wars between not within countries. Fearing that somehow the United States would get involved in Spain's civil war, isolationists in Congress introduced the Spanish Embargo Act that forbad arms sales to either side. The Senate passed that law by 81 to 0 and the House by 404 to one, and Roosevelt signed it on January 8, 1937. Congress then actually voted for "permanent neutrality" for the United States with the Senate by 63 to 6 and the

House by 376 to 12, and Roosevelt's signature on May 1. This law forced the president to ban exports to any warring countries, canceled any arms contracts for countries then at war; and prohibited merchant ships from arming themselves. There was a loophole called "cash and carry." Foreigners could buy arms from American factories if they paid cash and carried the arms away in their own ships.

Japan's easy conquest of Manchuria in September 1931 only whetted the fascist appetite for conquering the rest of China.[13] The excuse came on July 7, 1937, when Japanese and Chinese troops got in a firefight at the Marco Polo bridge near Beijing. Tokyo launched a three-pronged offensive. The one from Manchuria captured Beijing and the surrounding region; a second up the Yangtze River valley culminated with Nanjing's capture and the slaughter of tens of thousands of people in December. The third spread over southeastern China. Generalissimo Chiang Kai-shek, China's dictator, retreated with his army's remnants from Nanjing to Chungking, 860 miles up the Yangtse River, where he established his capital of "Nationalist China."

The League of Nations debated what to do about Japan's attempt to conquer China. On October 6, the Assembly approved a resolution that condemned Japan's imperialism and advocated a Nine-Power Conference to negotiate the war's end. The United States was a signatory along with Japan, China, Britain, France, Italy, Belgium, the Netherlands, and Portugal of the 1922 Nine-Power Pact that upheld China's territorial integrity and sovereignty.

Roosevelt approved the League's resolution and said the United States would participate in the conference. Japan denounced and boycotted the Conference at Brussels that lasted from November 3 to 24, 1937. Roosevelt did not declare neutrality in the Sino-Japanese war because neither government formally declared war. Technically that let Roosevelt approve sales to the victim, China. But for now he refrained from doing so to avoid enflaming isolationists in Congress and newspaper editorial board rooms.

Yet, Roosevelt inadvertently did just that in a speech that he delivered in Chicago on October 5, 1937. Without naming the aggressors Japan, Germany, and Italy, he warned that: "The peace, the freedom, and the security of 90 percent of the population of the world is being jeopardized by the remaining 10 percent, who are threatening a breakdown of all international order." He then asserted this analogy that got his words dubbed the Quarantine Speech: "When an epidemic of physical disease starts to spread, the community approves and joins in a quarantine of the patients in order to protect the health of the community against the spread of the disease...War is a contagion, whether it be declared or undeclared…The peace of the world is today being threatened…There is no escape through mere isolation or neutrality…We are determined to keep out of war, yet we cannot insure ourselves against the disastrous effects of war and the dangers of involvement….America hates war. America hopes for peace. Therefore, America actively engages in the search for peace." That provoked a firestorm of criticism led by the *Chicago Tribune* and other isolationist newspapers along with Congressmen.

Meanwhile, the three fascist powers forged an alliance. Germany and Japan signed the Anti-Comintern Pact on November 25, 1936. That alliance was directed against the Soviet Union whose Comintern infiltrated agents into foreign countries to organize communist parties and other leftist groups into revolutions against the governments. Italy joined the Anti-Comintern Pact on November 6, 1937.

That pact helped embolden Japan's imperialists. Japanese warplanes and cannons on shore sank the American gunboat, USS *Panay*, and three oil tankers owned by Standard Oil Company on the Yangtze River a dozen miles upriver from Nanjing on December 12, 1937; three Americans died and more than fifty suffered wounds including the *Panay*'s commander.[14] The *Panay* had protected Americans and their assets in the region since 1928. The Japanese attack was deliberate as the *Panay* flew two large American flags and the day was bright and clear.

Roosevelt convened his cabinet to discuss how best to respond. The unprovoked attack so enraged Navy Secretary Claude Swanson, Interior Secretary Harold Ickes, and Vice President John Garner that they called for war against Japan. Roosevelt and his other advisors argued that neither America's military nor public was prepared for war. Senators like Henry Ashurst of Arizona and Henrik Shipstead of Minnesota openly declared their opposition to war and called for withdrawing all American forces from China and the Far East.

Roosevelt had Secretary of State Hull demand an apology and compensation from Tokyo. He had Treasury Secretary Morgenthau prepare to seize all Japanese assets in the United States if Tokyo did not yield. Japanese Foreign Minister Kiki Hirota did apologize and promise reparations. On April 22, 1938, Tokyo transferred $2,214,007.14 to Washington. Meanwhile, Roosevelt issued an executive order that established an economic warfare section within the Treasury Department. Roosevelt called for a moral embargo on aircraft, aviation fuel, and finance by American businesses to Japan.

Meanwhile, Roosevelt faced an effort in Congress to radically change the federal government's power to declare and wage war. When Italy invaded Ethiopia in 1935, Representative Louis Ludlow of Indiana was so worried that the United States would get involved in a war that he drafted a constitutional amendment that made that nearly impossible. His Ludlow Amendment transferred the power to declare war from Congress to a national referendum unless the United States was directly invaded. A Gallup poll revealed that 73 percent of Americans backed the amendment. [15] It was not until January 1938, that Ludlow mustered enough support to get the House of Representatives to debate his proposal. The Ludlow amendment lost a discharge petition by 188 for and 209 against. Yet that relatively close vote on such a radical proposal revealed the power of isolationists.

A threat emerged against American interests in neighboring Mexico. President Lazaro Cardenas issued an executive order that nationalized American petroleum investments in March 1938. The White House demanded market-value compensation to the investors for their loss. Mexico's government offered a fraction of that. The dispute festered for years until 1941, when Roosevelt accepted $24 million or 5 percent of what Standard Oil insisted was the lost market value. Atop that, Roosevelt granted Mexico a $40 million low interest loan and $300 million in Lend-Lease credits for the token military forces Mexico contributed to the allied cause. Roosevelt's appeasement of Mexico encouraged Venezuela, Columbia, Bolivia, Paraguay, Chile to expropriate American investments with token compensation. Washington was no more successful in getting those governments to pay full market value. So much for America's Good Neighbor policy toward Latin America.

Among the 1919 Versailles Treaty's restrictions on Germany was forbidding Austria from joining it. In March 1938, Hitler engineered Germany's peaceful annexation of Austria. In doing so German agents worked closely with Austria's army and Nazi Party. Hitler demanded that Austrian Chancellor Kurt Schuschnigg hold a referendum over German annexation. Schuschnigg reluctantly scheduled the referendum for March 13 and made Nazi Arthur Seyss-Inquart his security minister. The day before, Hitler ordered his army to march into Austria. The Austrian army and immense crowds of civilians joyfully greeted the invaders. Hitler's motorcade drove triumphantly through Vienna's streets packed with adoring fans on March 14. In a plebiscite held on April 10, 99.75 percent of Austrians approved annexation.

Britain and France were the two key nations for upholding the Versailles Treaty. Instead, British Prime Minister Neville Chamberlain and Premier Edouard Daladier acquiesced in Hitler's blatant violations of the treaty. Their appeasement disgusted Roosevelt, who privately fumed that: "If a Chief of Police makes a deal with the leading gangsters and the deal results in no more holdups, that Chief of Police will be called a great man – but if the gangsters do not live up to their word the Chief of Police will go to jail."[16]

Hitler's next aggression came six months later. He demanded that Czechoslovakia transfer to Germany its western region the Sudetenland because it was predominately German-speaking, and threatened war if he did not get it. President Evard Benes adamantly rejected that demand and appealed to Britain and France to support him. Chamberlain rejected any notion of going to war to protect Czechoslovakia. He rhetorically asked Britons to consider: "How horrible, fantastic, incredible it is that we should be digging trenches and trying on masks because of a quarrel in a far away country between people of whom we know nothing."[17] Chamberlain flew to Germany to meet with Hitler at his mountaintop villa at Berchtesgaden on September 15. Although Hitler browbeat Chamberlain into agreeing to the annexation, Benes still refused to surrender any territory.

Roosevelt acted on September 26, by appealing to the heads of Germany, Britain, France, and Czechoslovakia to peacefully resolve the crisis. The next day, he sent a message to Mussolini asking him to intercede with Hitler to compromise his demands. Mussolini got Hitler to postpone his invasion deadline and meet with Chamberlain, Daladier, and Mussolini in Munich on September 29. The four signed an agreement whereby Czechoslovakia transferred the Sudetenland to Germany and dismantled fortifications on its borders; Benes now had no choice but to accept that annexation. Upon returning to Britain, Chamberlain proclaimed that he had won "peace in our time." Winston Churchill condemned Chamberlain's appeasement: "The government had to choose between shame and war. They chose shame and will get war."[18]

A seventeen-year-old Jewish youth shot to death a German diplomat in Paris on November 7, 1938. Hitler used that as the excuse for his latest atrocities against Jews. On the night of November 9, German thugs vandalized, looted, and burned Jewish homes, 7,500 stores, and 200 synagogues, murdered several score Jews, and arrested over twenty-thousand. That terrorism was called Kristallnacht for all the broken glass. Over the following weeks, Berlin announced that the damage would be repaired by levying $400 million on Jews, closed all Jewish stores, confiscated Jewish financial assets, and forbade Jews from attending schools, universities, concerts, theaters, and even driving automobiles.

Roosevelt recalled Ambassador Hugh Wilson from Berlin and extended visas for foreign Jews living in the United States; Albert Einstein and his family were among the beneficiaries. During a press conference, Roosevelt expressed his astonishment that "such things could occur in a twentieth century civilization." Yet when asked whether the United States would accept more Jewish refugees, he replied, "That is not in contemplation. We have our quota system."[19]

The 1924 Immigration Act limited immigrants to 150,000 annually with nationality quotas of 2 percent of their number of legal residents in 1890. The quotas for Germany and Austria were respectively 25,957 and 1,413. Most Americans supported that system and opposed the Wagner-Rogers Bill that would admit 20,000 refugee German children. A 1938 Gallup Poll revealed that two-thirds wanted to retain the quotas and only five percent wanted to rescind them. Indeed, only 39 percent of Americans believed that Jews should have equal rights in the United States while 32 percent thought they should have economic restrictions, 11 percent favored social segregation, and 11 percent thought they should be deported.[20]

Nonetheless, Roosevelt was able to double the Jewish quota from 2,500 to 5,000 for 1935 then raise the number to 6,000 in 1936 and to 11,000 in 1937, but that was a tiny fraction of the millions suffering worsening prosecution. By merging the quotas of Germany and Austria and broadening visa requirements, he enabled around 50,000 Jews to immigrate to America by 1939.

Roosevelt feared that the public's thickening isolationism would result in a more isolationist Congress. Just before the 1938 midterm election, he warned in a radio broadcast that American national security was threatened by foreign "militarism and conquest, terrorism and intolerance," and that "democracy will save itself with the average man and woman by proving itself worth saving...[I]f American democracy ceases to move forward as a living force, seeking day and night by peaceful means to better the lot of our citizens, then Fascism and Communisms will grow in strength in our land."[21]

The Democrats lost significant ground in the 1938 midterm election, although they retained control of Congress. In the House of Representatives, Democrats won 17,715,560 votes or 48.7 percent of the total and their seats fell by 74 from 336 to 262; Republicans won 17,244,585 votes or 47.5 percent and their seats rose by 88 to 169. Two of three fringe parties also lost with the Progressive Party's seats falling from 8 to 2 and the Farmer-Labor from 5 to 1, while the American Labor Party won 1 seat. Republicans complained that Democrat control over statehouses let gerrymander congressional districts that robbed Republicans of a share of seats proportional to their voters. In the Senate, Democratic seats fell by eight to 69 while Republicans rose by eight to 23, while the Farmer-Labor Party,

Progressive Party, and an independent candidate held two, one, and one seats.

Roosevelt warned Americans of the worsening dangers they faced in his 1939 State of the Union address: "There can be no appeasement with ruthlessness. There can be no reasoning with an incendiary bomb. We know that a nation can have peace with the Nazis only at the price of total surrender." He then explained that, ironically, "We have learned that when we deliberately try to legislate neutrality, our neutrality laws may operate unevenly and unfairly – may actually give aid to an aggressor and deny it to the victim. The instinct of self-preservation should warn us that we ought not to let that happen anymore." He called on Congress to revise the Neutrality Law so that it promoted peace rather than war. [22]

In Congress and beyond, the political tide was shifting between isolationists and internationalists. Harry Price was the son of missionaries in China and had invested heavily in China. In 1938, he organized the American Committee for Non-Participation in Japanese Aggression to lobby Washington to sever trade with Japan to punish its imperialism in China. Henry Stimson, a former secretary of state, was the Committee's most prominent member. Price and other members met repeatedly with Stanley Hornbeck, the State Department's Asian expert, to discuss what more the United States could do to bolster China and weaken Japan. They also spoke with influential senators and representatives.

That lobbying paid off in 1939. In January, New York representative Hamilton Fish proposed that the United States sever its trade of scrap iron and other products to Japan that fed its war machine. Key Pittman of Nevada headed the Senate Foreign Relations Committee. The United States and Japan were among the signers of the 1922 Nine Power Pact that guaranteed China's territorial integrity and open trade. On April 27, Pittman introduced a resolution that would empower the president to impose economic sanctions on any Nine Power Pact signer that violated that treaty, a measure that clearly targeted Japan. In June, the State Department called on American businesses and consumers to impose a "moral embargo" against Japan, neither selling to nor buying from that country. Republican Senator Arthur Vandenberg of Michigan had been a stalwart isolationist until mid-1939 when he began changing his mind. The worsening imperialism of Japan, Germany, and Italy and the warnings by Roosevelt, Price, and other internationalists finally forced him to repudiate appeasement. On July 18, he introduced a resolution for the United States to give Japan a six-month notice that it would end their bilateral 1911 trade treaty. Once that was done, the United States legally could stop selling any product to Japan. The Senate approved that resolution by acclamation. Roosevelt authorized Secretary of State Hull to issue that notice to Tokyo on July 26.

Roosevelt's most enjoyable diplomacy during 1939 was with British leaders. In June, he hosted King George VI and Queen Mary at his Hyde Park estate, addressed them by their first names, and served them hot dogs and cocktails along with a formal dinner. He had long admired Winston Churchill and was relieved when Prime Minister Chamberlain summoned him from Parliament's back bench to head the naval ministry: "It is because you and I occupied similar positions in the World War that I want you to know how glad I am that you are once again back in the Admiralty...What I want you and the Prime Minister to know is that I shall at all times welcome it if you will keep me in touch personally with anything you want me to know about."[23]

Hitler ordered his army to take over the rest of Czechoslovakia on March 15, 1939. Having been stripped of much of their territory and fortifications with the Munich Pact, the Czechs did not resist. Chamberlain and Daladier acquiesced in Hitler's blatant violation of the Munich Pact. Chamberlain did commit Britain to Poland's defense and urged Daladier to join him.

That appeasement emboldened Mussolini to order his army to invade Albania on April 7, 1939. King Zog did not order his army to resist but instead fled with his entourage. The Italians overran the country by April 12. The League of Nations did nothing officially to protest let alone sanction Mussolini's blatant imperialism.

That provoked Roosevelt to appeal for peace to Hitler and Mussolini on April 15, 1939, with this key question: "Are you willing to give assurance that your armed forces will not attack or invade the territory of the following independent countries?" He then listed thirty-one countries including Poland, Russia, Belgium, the Netherlands, France, and Britain. On April 28, Hitler replied in a sarcastic and disdainful speech before the Reichstag: "Mr. Roosevelt! I fully understand that the vastness of your nation and the immense wealth of your country allow you to feel responsible for the history of the whole world...I, sir, am placed in a much more modest and smaller sphere...I...took over a State which was faced by complete ruin, thanks to its trust in the promises...and to the bad faith of democratic governments." He then boasted of transforming Germany from chaos and poverty into prosperity and power. He then pledged his support for "the justice, well-being, progress, and peace of the whole community."[24]

Poland was the next victim of imperialism, but this time as a joint venture between Nazi Germany and Communist Soviet Union. Foreign Ministers Joachim Ribbentrop and Vyacheslav Molotov signed a treaty on August 23 whereby they split Poland like a wishbone, with Germany taking the western two-thirds and Soviet Union the eastern third along with Baltic states Estonia, Latavia, and Lithuania. The Germans and Soviets invaded Poland respectively on September 1 and 17, and by the month's end each had conquered the territory their pact designated. The Soviets also overran the Baltic states.

Britain and France declared war against Germany but not the Soviet Union on September 3. As usual, they failed to back their declarations with power. With most of Germany's military might deployed in Poland, had the French army with a British contingent marched against Germany, they might well have won the war. Indeed, a German army intelligence report concluded that the "110 French and British divisions in the West were held completely inactive against the 23 German divisions." Had they attacked "they would have been able to cross the Rhine without our being able to prevent it."[25] But instead, they stayed put, the British in their island and the French behind their Maginot Line of defenses on the border with Germany. The Second World War had begun in Europe, but for the next seven months it was called the "phony war" because there was no fighting. Nonetheless, the Second World War was well under way.[26]

Roosevelt sought to free himself from the legal straitjacket that kept him from aiding aggression victims. In a fireside chat, he explained how the outbreak of war in Europe threatened American national security: "You must master at the outset a simple but unalterable fact in modern relations between nations. When peace has been broken anywhere, the peace of all countries everywhere is in danger." As for the war in Europe, he insisted that: "This nation will remain a neutral nation, but I cannot ask that every American remain neutral in thought as well. Even a neutral has a right to take account of facts. Even a neutral cannot be asked to close his mind or his conscience."[27] He publicly denounced the 1935 Neutrality Law on September 14: "I regret that Congress passed that Act. I regret equally that I signed that act."[28] He met with Congressional leaders on September 20, and asked them to repeal the law. They explained that they lacked the votes to do so. He asked them to find the votes. Over the next month they did. The Senate voted 63 to 30 on October 27 and the House 243 to 181 on November 2 to repeal the arms embargo act. Roosevelt gleefully signed it on November 4.

Nonetheless, nearly all Americans remained firmly isolationist. An October 1939 Gallup poll revealed that 95 percent did not want to join Britain and France in war against Germany for invading Poland, although 62 percent believed the United State must provide military aid to Britain and France. A November 1939 *Fortune* poll found only 20 percent favored aiding the democratic countries by any means short of war while 54 percent wanted to keep selling to both sides.[29]

The western front was tensely quiet from September 1939 to May 1940, while Hitler and Stalin expanded their empires elsewhere. The Soviets invaded Finland on November 30, but the Finns blunted their advance after a score of miles and inflicted heavy casualties; the Finns accepted an armistice that ceded the Karelian isthmus and borderlands on March 13, 1940. Hitler and Churchill simultaneously got the idea to invade Norway and seize the port of Narvik, the terminus of a railroad that conveyed iron ore from northern Sweden. Germany depended on that ore to feed its steel industry, the foundation for all its armaments. Since the war began, ships conveyed the ore to German ports by steaming within Norway's territorial waters. The Germans beat the British to the punch by landing and seizing Narvik and other key ports on April 9, and eventually repelled British attacks and crushed Norwegian resistance by June 10. On April 9, the Germans also marched unopposed into Denmark.

The "blitzkrieg" or "lightning war" against the western allies began on May 10, with attacks against France, Luxembourg, Belgium, and the Netherlands. The main offensive was by a tank corps dashing through the lightly defended Ardennes forest of eastern Belgium and eventually reaching the North Sea at Abbeville then barreling north to Dunkirk. Meanwhile other tank corps outflanked the Maginot Line and devastated the French army in northern France. The Netherlands and Belgium capitulated on May 15 and May 28, respectively. At Dunkirk, around 338,000 allied troops, two-thirds British and one-third French evacuated to Britain from May 26 to June 4. The French government fled Paris to Bordeaux on June 10, and the Germans marched unopposed into Paris on June 14. French Premier Reynaud resigned and Marshal Pierre Petain replaced him as premier on June 16. On June 22, Petain accepted an armistice with Germany that reduced France to a rump state in the center and south with its capital at Vichy and ceded the northern and western regions to Germany.

Germany's six week conquest of France and the Low Countries stunned Roosevelt and his advisors. All Roosevelt could do was condemn the invasion and have Treasury Secretary Morgenthau freeze the financial assets of the Netherlands, Belgium, and France in the United States to prevent the Germans from seizing and withdrawing them.

Meanwhile, Neville Chamberlain resigned and Winston Churchill took his place as prime minister on May 10, the day that blitzkrieg began. Churchill understood what becoming prime minister meant: "I felt as if I were walking with Destiny and that all my past life had been but a preparation for this hour and for this trial."[30] He cabled Roosevelt a request for aid on May 15. Although they had exchanged previous letters, this was the first key communication between Churchill and Roosevelt who would develop a profound partnership as allies and friends, arguably history's most consequential.[31] With typically vivid words, Churchill explained: "The scene has darkened swiftly...The small countries are simply smashed up, one by one, like matchwood... We expect to be attacked...both from the air and by parachute and air-borne troops in the near future, and are getting ready for that. If necessary we shall continue the war alone...But I trust you realize, Mr. President, that the voice and force of the United States may count for nothing if they are withheld too long."[32]

Roosevelt promised to do what he could. He appeared before Congress the next day and asked for a $1.2 billion supplementary defense budget. Congress complied not just with that request but subsequent ones until it approved an additional $37.3 billion in defense spending by May 1941 a year later.[33] He explained what protecting America demanded in a speech on June 10, 1940. First, Americans had to understand that to believe that their nation could survive as "a lone island in a world dominated by the philosophy of force was an obvious delusion." Instead, the United States must "extend to the opponents of force the material resources of this nation; and at the same time, we will harness and speed up the use of those resources in order that we ourselves may have equipment and training equal to the task."[34]

Churchill delivered a radio broadcast designed to inspire Americans and their leaders, especially Roosevelt as much as his fellow Britons: "We shall go on to the end....we shall never surrender, and even if, which I do not for a moment believe, this island ...were subjected and starving, then our empire beyond the seas, armed and guarded by the British fleet, would carry on the struggle until...the new world, with all its power and might, steps forth to the rescue and the liberation of the old."[35]

Roosevelt swiftly got Army Chief George Marshall to muster a list of "surplus" weapons and equipment to send to Britain that included "93 bomber planes, 500,000 Enfield rifles, 184 tanks, 76,000 machine guns, 25,000 Browning automatic rifles, 895 75mm guns, and 100 million rounds of ammunition." Marshall, a man of unquestionable moral rectitude, did so reluctantly because those were not surplus but essential army supplies. He later wrote that: "It was the only time that I recall that I did something that there was a certain amount of duplicity in it."[36]

The next critical battle was for the skies above Britain. If the Germans could win air supremacy, then they could invade Britain. The Battle of Britain lasted from July 10 to October 31, during which the Germans sent over waves of bombers escorted by fighter planes and the British tried to shoot them down with anti-aircraft guns and fighter planes. The Germans would have won had they persisted in attacking Britain's air fields but Hitler switched the strategy to bombing cities on August 24 after a British bombing attack on Berlin. The British shot down nearly two German planes for every plane they lost, 1,733 to 915, and eventually exhausting German air power.[37]

Meanwhile, the war's longest and most expensive battle raged for the Atlantic.[38] As they had in the First World War, the Germans sought to sever and starve Britain into submission by deploying submarines to sink ships carrying desperately needed supplies. German submarines eventually sank 4,786 merchant ships with 21 million gross tons along with 158 British and 29 American warships, and killed over 40,000 sailors. The allies destroyed 781 of 1,100 submarines with 32,000 sailors.[39] The allies countered German "wolf pack" or massed submarine tactics with convoys protected by flotillas of destroyers, destroyer escorts, and escort carriers along with long-range land-based B-24 Liberator bombers. The allies eventually won that grim battle of attrition by producing more ships and supplies than the Germans sank.

Meanwhile, Tokyo was increasingly bellicose. Prime Minister Fumimaro Konoye announced on November 3, 1938, Japan's assertion of a "New Order in Asia" whereby Tokyo would lead other Asian peoples. Foreign Minister Yosuke Matsuoka renamed that "New Order" the "Greater East Asia Co-Prosperity Sphere" on August 1, 1940. Tokyo took advantage of France's defeat by demanding that its Vichy regime cede three airfields and let Japan station 6,000 troops in northern Vietnam. The Vichy regime agreed on September 22, 1940, and Japan's military occupation began. The foreign ministers of Germany, Italy, and Japan signed in Berlin the Tripartite Pact that made them military allies on September 27, 1940. The Tripartite Pact was clearly aimed at deterring the United States from joining the war in Europe. Ambassador Joseph Grew wrote Roosevelt in December 1940 that: "Japan has become openly and unashamedly one of the predatory nations...which aims to wreck about everything that the United States stands for."[40]

Roosevelt did not mention Japan when he issued an executive order on July 2, 1940, that prohibited the export of forty products, although initially the most critical, high octane aviation fuel, petroleum, and scrap iron, were not on the list. Roosevelt included them in an executive order on July 25.

Roosevelt systematically prepared America for war from mid-1940.[41] His first step was to replace lackluster secretaries of war and navy, Harry Wooding and Charles Edison, with Henry Stimson and Frank Knox, both prominent Republican internationalists on June 20. Stimson was among America's most distinguished statesmen.[42] He had served as William Taft's secretary of war, Calvin Coolidge's governor-general of the Philippines, and Herbert Hoover's secretary of state. He had an impeccable education as a graduate of Philips Academy, Yale University, and Harvard Law School. Knox was a Spanish American War veteran, having charged up San Juan Hill with Lieutenant Colonel Theodore Roosevelt and his "Rough Riders" First Volunteer Cavalry regiment. He was a self-made millionaire who published the *Chicago Daily News* and became Alf Landon's running mate in the 1936 election.

Even more critical was Roosevelt's choice of General George Marshall to become army chief of staff on September 1, 1939, the day that Germany invaded Poland to precipitate the Second World War in Europe. Marshall proved to be a brilliant army chief of staff.[43] He graduated from Virginia Military Institute in 1901, received a second lieutenant's commission, and served in the Philippines. He was General John Pershing's chief operations planner during the First World War and his aide when he became army chief of staff after the war. While serving as Fort Benning's deputy commander, he revamped its Infantry School to emphasize cutting edge tactics, logistics, and training. He taught at the army's war College. He was promoted to brigadier general in 1936. He joined the War Plans Division and became deputy army chief of staff in 1938.

Roosevelt established the seven-member National Defense Advisory Commission (NDAC) and asked William Knudsen, General Motor's president, to head it in May 1940. NDAC's mission was to devise a plan for mobilizing America's economy for total war. He transformed NDAC into the Office of Production Management including Knudsen as chair along with War Secretary Stimson, Navy Secretary Knox, and Congress of Industrial Organization (C.I.O.) deputy chief Sidney Hillman.

Worsening fears about foreign spies, saboteurs, and provocateurs led Congress to pass the Alien Registration Act in April 1940, by acclamation in the Senate and 382 to 4 in the House. All foreign residents fourteen years or older had to register with the federal government, a process that included fingerprints and a photograph. Eventually 5 million foreigners registered. Roosevelt also bolstered America's counter-intelligence powers. On May 21, he authorized Attorney General Francis Biddle "to secure information by listening devices direct to the conversation or other communication of persons suspected of subversive activities against the Government of the United States, including suspected spies."[44]

Roosevelt conceived a plan to enhance British and American security. He would swap fifty destroyers to Britain in return for ninety-nine year leases for American troops to occupy eight British bases in the Western Hemisphere at Newfoundland, Bermuda, the Bahamas, Jamaica, Antigua, Trinidad, Saint Lucia, and Guiana. American and British diplomats got to work and signed an agreement on September 2. Roosevelt announced that agreement and implemented it as an executive agreement rather than treaty to bypass votes by the Senate on ratification and both houses on appropriations. He shrugged off the subsequent harsh criticism by isolationists in and beyond Congress.

America was unprepared for war. Amidst a spreading world war, America's 269,000-man army was the world's eighteenth largest in manpower. To alleviate that, the Burke-Wadsworth Bill authorized the first peacetime draft of men for the army. On September 14, the Senate passed it by 47 to 25 and the House by 232 to 124. The first step in realizing that draft came on October 16, when all men from twenty-one to thirty-six years had to register at one of 6,442 draft boards; those drafted would serve for one year. On October 28, President Roosevelt and War Secretary Stimson stood before a large glass bowl filled with 365 blue capsules, each containing a different number. Stimson was blindfolded. He reached in the bowl, extracted a capsule, and handed it to Roosevelt. The commander in chief opened it and announced, "One hundred fifty-eight."

Roosevelt disingenuously tried to sooth anguished parents of drafted sons with these words: "I can give assurance to the mothers and to the fathers of America that...their boys in training will be well housed and well fed...Your boys are not going to be sent into foreign wars... "When his speechwriter suggested adding "except in cases of attack," Roosevelt replied, "It's not necessary...If we're attacked it's no longer a foreign war."[45]

Amidst the worsening world war, 1940 was a presidential year. Roosevelt genuinely agonized over whether to run for a third term, something no other president had done.[46] Eleanor recalled that "my husband was torn. He would often talk about the reasons against a third term," but "there was a great sense of responsibility for what was happening. And the great feeling that possibly he was the only one who was equipped and trained and cognizant not only of the people who were involved in the future but of every phase of the situation." Perhaps most vital was Roosevelt's "feeling of not wanting to leave the center of history...When you are in the center of world affairs, there is something so fascinating about it that you can hardly see how you are going to live in any other way."[47] He actually prepared for leaving the White House by signing a secret contract with *Collier Magazine* in January 1940, whereby he would become a contributing editor with twenty-six yearly essays for $75,000. The contract would be void if Roosevelt ran for and won re-election.

Roosevelt decided to let the Democratic Party's delegates decide during the convention at Chicago from July 15 to 19. He won on the first ballot with 946 votes and 150 others scattered among four other candidates. He picked Agriculture Secretary Henry Wallace as his vice president. In his acceptance speech, Roosevelt explained the crucial challenge facing America: "The fact which dominates our world is the fact of armed aggression...aimed at the form of Government...that we in the United States have chosen and established for ourselves... It is not an ordinary war. It is a revolution imposed by force of arms, which threatens all men everywhere. It is a revolution which proposes not to set men free but to reduce them to slavery...in the interest of a dictatorship...Those, my friends, are the reasons why...my conscience will not let me turn my back upon a return to service."[48]

The Republicans convened at Philadelphia from June 24 to 28. The leading contenders were Wendall Willkie, the president of Commonwealth and Southern, the nation's largest utility holding company; Thomas Dewey, New York's district attorney; Senator Arthur Vandenburg of Michigan; and Senator Robert Taft of Ohio. The businessman beat the professional politicians on the sixth ballot. His running mate was Senator Charles McNary of Massachusetts. Willkie launched a serious campaign by traveling 18,785 miles through 31 states and delivering 560 speeches.[49] As the "peace candidate," he promised crowds that, "We will not undertake to fight anybody else's war. Our boys shall stay out of European Wars."[50]

In Roosevelt's campaign speeches, he echoed Willkie's line about staying out of the war but added "except in case of attack." In the election on November 5, Roosevelt trounced Willkie, but by a lesser amount than his two previous challengers. With all the votes counted, Roosevelt emerged with 27,313,945 or 54.7 percent and 449 Electoral College votes to Willkie's 22,347,744 or 44.8 percent and 82. In the House, Democrats won two net seats bringing their total to 267 while Republicans fell to 162 with seven net losses, while the Progressive Party, American Labor Party, Farmer-Labor Party, and an independent won three, one, one and one respective seats. In the Senate, Democrats lost three net seats falling to 66 while Republicans gained four to rise to 28 while the Progressive Party and Independent senators retained their seats.

Roosevelt conceived the idea of Lend-Lease that gave war equipment and weapons to Britain and other victims of fascist aggression, and called on Congress to enact it.[51] To justify that policy, he expressed perhaps his best analogy during a speech on December 17, 1940: "Suppose my neighbor's home catches fire, and I have a length of garden hose four or five hundred feet away. If he can take my garden hose and connect it with his hydrant, I may help him to put out the fire. Now what do I do? I don't say to him, "Neighbor, my garden hose cost me fifteen dollars; you have to pay me fifteen dollars for it." No! I don't want fifteen dollars. I want my garden hose back after the fire is over."[52]

In a fireside chat on December 29, Roosevelt warned the American people about enemies within the United States: "Their secret emissaries are active in our own and in neighboring countries. They seek to stir up suspicion and dissension to cause internal strife…These trouble-breeders have but one purpose. It is to divide our people, to divide them into hostile groups and to destroy our unity and shatter our will to defend ourselves. There are also American citizens, many of them in high places, who, unwittingly in most cases, are aiding and abetting the work of these agents." He ended his talk with these inspiring words: "The people of Europe who are defending themselves do not ask us to do their fighting. They ask us for the implements of war, the planes, the tanks, and the guns which will enable them to fight for their liberty and our security…We must be the great arsenal of democracy."[53]

Roosevelt sent Harry Hopkins to London to talk with Churchill and assess Britain's strategy and needs. Hopkins wrote Roosevelt that "Churchill is the gov't in every sense of the word – he controls the grand strategy and often the details…I cannot emphasis too strongly that he is the one and only person over here with whom you need to have a full meeting of minds...Churchill wants to see you...This island needs our help now Mr. President with everything we can give them."[54]

Roosevelt delivered yet another great speech in his State of Union before Congress on January 6, 1941. He asserted that: "Let us say to the democracies, 'We Americans are vitally concerned in your defense of freedom. We are putting forth our energies, our resources, and our organizing powers to give you the strength to regain and maintain a free world...In future days, which we seek to make secure, we look forward to a world founded upon four essential human freedoms: The first is freedom of speech and expression...The second is freedom of every person to worship God in his own way...The third is freedom of want....The fourth is freedom from fear."[55]

Congress acted decisively on Roosevelt's Lend-Lease proposal. Senate Majority Leader Alben Barkley and House Speaker John McCormack released the Lend-Lease Bill into their respective chambers on January 10, 1941. The bill empowered the president to "sell, transfer title to, exchange, lease, lend, or otherwise dispose of" any "defense article" to "the government of any country whose defense the President deems vital to the defense of the United States." The House voted 250 to 165 in favor on February 8, the Senate by 60 to 31 on March 8, and Roosevelt triumphantly signed it on March 11. On March 12, Congress appropriated $7 billion for Lend-Lease, the first of a series that eventually reached $51 billion. Of the total, Britain received the largest amount with $36.4 billion, then the Soviet Union with $11.2 billion, France with $3.2 billion, and China with $1.6 billion, with the remaining $2.6 billion dispersed among 32 minor allies. Churchill declared before Parliament that Lend-Lease was "the most unsordid act in the history of any nation."[56]

China was the first Lend Lease recipient. In April, the White House announced a $100 million loan to China and authorized Claire Chennault to head the Fourteenth American Volunteer Air Force, soon called the Flying Tigers, in China. Lend-Lease aid to China went from America's west coast ports to the port of Rangoon, Burma, Britain's colony. There the supplies were packed in train cars for the 550 miles of tracks to Lashio, where they were transferred to trucks for the 700-mile series of mostly dirt roads called the Burma Road that led over the mountains to Kunming, China.

Lend-Lease was a very public policy of aiding victims of Axis aggression. For now, Roosevelt kept secret a parallel act of collaboration. After his re-election, he sent to London a high-ranking team of army and navy officers to meet with their counterparts to understand their needs and plans, and what America could do to help. The American and

British teams were the Combined Chiefs of Staff's precursor. During their sojourn from January to March, they reached the key decision that, if America went to war against the Axis alliance, Washington would contain Japan's advances in the Pacific while working with Whitehall to dominate the Atlantic basin and defeat Germany and Italy first. On April 11, Roosevelt informed Churchill that he had extended America's naval and air defense of shipping in the Atlantic eastward to twenty-five west longitude, more than halfway across, and would protect Greenland and the Azore Islands, the respective provinces of Denmark and Portugal; he publicly announced those steps on April 25.

Roosevelt's calls for America to aid imperiled democracies overseas provoked critics to lambast American democracy's hypocrises and deficiencies, especially toward blacks. The most powerful black labor union was the Brotherhood of Sleeping Car Porters, founded by Philip Randolph in 1925, and since led by him. Randolph announced that on July 1, blacks would protest in Washington the refusal of defense contractors to use black labor or businesses.

Walter White, who headed the National Association for the Advancement of Colored People (NAACP), endorsed that march. Roosevelt and many others feared that protest could turn violent. He asked Eleanor and New York Mayor Fiorella LaGuardia to meet with Randolph and White to dissuade them from marching. When Randolph refused to cancel the march, Roosevelt invited Randolph, White, and other black leaders to the White House on June 18. Randolph demanded that Roosevelt issue an executive order forcing contractors to use black workers and businesses, and warned him that if he refused, a hundred thousand blacks would march through Washington. On June 25, Roosevelt issued Executive Order 8802 that banned discrimination on the basis of "race, creed, color, or national origin" in the federal government and defense industry, and established the five-member Fair Employment Practice Committee (FEPC) to enforce that rule. Randolph declared victory and called off the march.

Then in November, John Lewis, the United Mine Workers (UMW) president led his 53,000 members on strike because the National Defense Mediation Board rejected his demand to let the UMW form a closed shop that forced all miners to join. Roosevelt refused to negotiate and sought an injunction to force the miners back to work in return for arbitrary negotiations between the union and mine owners. Lewis accepted. They cut a deal just as America went to war.

Roosevelt and Churchill received stunning news in late June. Unable to conquer Britain, Hitler turned east and planned the conquest of the

Soviet Union. To that end, he massed 3.8 million troops and 3,500 tanks against the Soviet front line's 3 million troops and 11,000 tanks. The blitzkrieg began on June 22 and over the next half year the Germans repeatedly circled and destroyed Soviet armies, inflicting over 4 million dead, wounded, and captured while suffering 1 million casualties. But two forces eventually stopped the Germans – winter and American Lend Lease. The Germans besieged but never captured Leningrad and spluttered to a halt a dozen miles short of Moscow. During the war, the Americans gave the Soviets 17,499,861 tons of aid worth $11.3 billion that included 13,303 combat vehicles, 1,911 steam locomotives, 11,400 aircraft, and 427,284 among countless other vital items. Without that, the Germans would have conquered the Soviet Union at least as far as the Urals, and possibly enticed the Japanese to attack the surviving Soviet regime with a capital somewhere in Siberia.[57] And had that happened, the Second World War would have destroyed both Nazism and Communism. Instead, guided by that venerable political maxim, "the enemy of my enemy is my friend," Roosevelt and Churchill eventually allied with Stalin.

Throughout 1941, Secretary of State Cordell Hull and Japanese Ambassador Kichisaburo Nomura met over fifty times to talk past each other. Hull insisted that Japan withdraw from all its conquests since Manchuria in 1931 and Nomura was just as adamant that the United States must recognize those conquests.

Tokyo demanded that Vichy let Japan's military troops occupy eight air and two naval bases in southern Indochina on July 18. Faced with outright conquest, Vichy conceded. Japanese military forces including 25,000 troops began to take over those bases on July 23. Roosevelt reacted on July 26, with an executive order that froze Japan's assets in the United States and required the federal government to review and either approve or deny any Japanese purchases. On August 1, the White House suspended all licenses to export oil to Japan.

Japan's army completed its takeover of southern Indochina on September 23. Roosevelt announced on September 26, that the United States would embargo high octane aviation fuel and high grade iron and steel to Japan while the Export-Import Bank would issue China a $100 million loan. Most Americans backed the president's policies. Public opinion had steadily shifted toward a tougher stand against Japanese aggression. An early August Gallup poll found that 51 percent of Americans backed warring against Japan before it became overwhelmingly powerful. That number rose to 67 percent by late September.

When the United States imposed its embargo, Japan had eighteen months of oil stored. Japan's Imperial War Council agreed on September 6 to attack if the United States did not accept Japan's conquests by late November. They had Admiral Isoroku Yamamoto plan an offensive against American, British, and Dutch colonies in the Pacific Ocean. Yamamoto was an outstanding choice. No Japanese military leader better understood aircraft carrier warfare and America. He was a Harvard graduate student, had hitchhiked across the nation, and served as Japan's naval attaché at the embassy in Washington from 1926 to 1928. He championed and pioneered aircraft carrier warfare as commander of Japan's First Carrier Division, director of the Navy's Aeronautical Division, and as the Navy's vice minister.

The first summit between Roosevelt and Churchill was dramatic.[58] On August 3, Roosevelt boarded the presidential yacht *Potomac* at New London, Connecticut for what was called a week long fishing trip along New England's coast. Instead, he transferred to the USS *Augusta*, a heavy cruiser, that steamed north escorted by another heavy cruiser and four destroyers to anchor off Argentia, Newfoundland. Meanwhile, Churchill headed west from Scapa Flow, Scotland across the German submarine infested Atlantic aboard the HMS *Prince of Wales*, a battleship, accompanied by smaller warships.

Roosevelt and Churchill forged a partnership and friendship from August 9 to 12 that deepened over the next four years.[59] With Roosevelt were Army Chief George Marshall, Navy Chief Admiral Herold Stark, Army Air Chief General Henry "Hap" Arnold, and Admiral Ernest King, the Atlantic fleet commander, who held initial talks with their British equivalents, Admiral Dudley Pound, Field Marshal John Dill, Air Vice Marshal Wilfred Freeman, and Foreign Office deputy Alexander Cadogan. Roosevelt forbade his advisors from making any specific plans with the British, but instead should garner as much information as possible on their challenges and needs.

Roosevelt and Churchill both had the confidence, extroversion, and upper class social breeding that let each cheerfully hold his own against the other. Churchill's intellect, however, vastly surpassed that of Roosevelt and nearly everyone else.[60] He eventually wrote nearly forty books in between serving as an army officer on various campaigns when he was a young man and thereafter as a politician. He had a prodigious memory that let him recite epic poems he learned in his boyhood. Their daily routines differed. Roosevelt followed a standard nine-to-five workday followed by cocktails then dinner each evening. He enjoyed a martini and a glass or two of wine but never drank to excess. Churchill rose around mid-morning and had the first of a series of glasses of cognac, rum, champagne, wine, and cocktails that fueled him until late at night as he entertained guests with stories, quips, poetry recitations, and discourses on politics, history, or art until one or two in the morning. His body somehow absorbed vast amounts of alcohol without becoming incapacitated. Churchill usually had a one or two hour nap each afternoon that gave him a powerful second wind that kept him up till the wee hours. Both men were tobacco addicts, Roosevelt to Camel cigarettes and Churchill to Cuban cigars. Churchill later wrote that: "I formed a very strong affection, which grew with our years of comradeship, for this formidable politician who had imposed his will for nearly ten years upon the American scene, and whose heart seemed to respond to many of the impulses that stirred my own."[61]

Roosevelt and Churchill reached three critical decisions. One was to split the Atlantic Ocean for defending convoys, with American warships defending them to a line east of Greenland, Iceland, and the Azores where Britain's defense began. Another was for the United States to give Britain another $5 billion of Lend-Lease aid. Finally, Roosevelt and Churchill issued the Atlantic Charter, a declaration of principles that they dedicated themselves to upholding, including no territorial expansion, no changes in territory without the permission of the people involved, letting people determine their own form of government, equal terms of international trade for all countries, better working and living conditions for all people in every country, arms reduction, and a system of collective security.

A raucous debate preceded the Atlantic Charter. Roosevelt insisted that America could only ally with Britain if they shared common values in free trade and self-determination for all nations. He argued that: "I can't believe that we can fight a war against fascist slavery and at the same time not work to free people all over the world from a backward colonial policy." He condemned imperialism "which takes wealth in raw materials out of a colonial country, but which returns nothing to the people of that county." He called on Britain to transform its colonies into dominions, starting with India. Churchill angrily replied that if Britain embraced those principles it would have to give up its empire. He resented that Roosevelt had trapped him into a dilemma. Britain's survival depended on America yet the price was giving up the empire that had enriched Britain: "I believe you are trying to do away with the British empire...But in spite of that, we know that you constitute our only hope. And...you know that we know...that without America, the empire will not stand."[62]

Roosevelt's immediate priority was getting Congress to renew the conscription law. He got his way but by a razor-thin margin. On August 7, a solid majority of senators voted 37 to 19 for the draft's extension for a year. However, the vote in the House of Representatives could not have been closer – 203 for and 202 against on August 14. The opposition in Congress reflected and shaped the public's view with a Gallup poll on August 6 revealing that 45 percent opposed extending the draft.[63] Despite that victory, Churchill believed that Roosevelt followed rather than led public opinion. On September 30, he issued this pointed declaration in Parliament: "Nothing is more dangerous in wartime than to live in the temperamental atmosphere of a Gallup poll, always feeling one's pulse and taking one's temperature."[64]

War with Germany rather than Japan seemed more likely as its submarine fleet became increasingly aggressive against American war and merchant ships in 1941. A German submarine sank the American freighter *Robin Moor* on May 21, although no lives were lost. On September 4, the destroyer USS *Greer* tracked a German submarine and reported its position to a patrolling British bomber. After the bomber dropped depth charges, the submarine fired two torpedoes but missed the *Greer*. In response, the *Greer* dropped nineteen depth charges but those also missed. On September 11, Roosevelt issued the navy a "shoot on sight" order and publicly declared that "if German or Italian submarines enter the waters, the protection of which is necessary for American defense, they do so at their own peril." He justified that policy to the public with a typically vivid and simple analogy: "When you see a rattlesnake poised to strike, you do not wait until he struck you before you crush him."[65]

A submarine damaged the destroyer USS *Kearny* and killed eleven sailors on October 17. Roosevelt responded by declaring that, "America has been attacked. The USS *Kearny* is not just a Navy ship. She belongs to every man, woman, and child in this Nation."[66] A submarine sank the destroyer USS *Reuben James*, killing 115 sailors on October 27.

Despite these German atrocities against the United States, Roosevelt did not ask Congress for a war declaration. Although he knew he could win majorities in each house, powerful minorities would oppose the war. He wanted Americans to be united when they went to war. What he did was ask Congress to revise the Neutrality Act to let merchant ships arm and defend themselves. Congress complied with votes in the Senate by 50 to 37 on November 7 and the House by 212 to 194 on November 13; Roosevelt signed the law on November 17.

America enjoyed an increasingly powerful secret weapon against Japan.[67] The Research Bureau was a joint operation by the army's Signals Intelligence Service and the navy's Communications Special Unit whose cryptographers cracked a series of Japanese codes from the 1920s to the 1940s. The Research Bureau color coded their operations. The first breakthrough – Red – came in 1923 when a naval attaché acquired the Japanese navy's First World War code. Although the navy had since upgraded, having the original let cryptographers break the naval code – Blue – in 1932. The 1939 alliance between Tokyo and Berlin led to an upgraded Japanese code based on Germany's Enigma machine that the Research Bureau called "Purple." In July 1941, the Research Bureau cracked Japan's diplomatic code, called "Magic" and over the half year before Pearl Harbor, they deciphered over 7,000 diplomatic messages.[68] Listening posts on American islands in the Pacific let codebreakers record Japanese naval, army, and diplomatic communications, although they could only understand the latter until March 1942 when codebreakers cracked Purple.

Britain's codebreaking organization was the Government Code and Cypher School at Bletchley Park, a mansion eighty miles north of London midway between the universities of Oxford and Cambridge. Their cryptanalysts concentrated on cracking Germany's Enigma code, an effort by eighteen-hundred mathematicians and technicians that they codenamed Ultra. In January 1941, Roosevelt had two Magic decoding machines sent to Bletchley so that they could read Japan's diplomatic messages.

General Hideki Tojo replaced Fumimaro Konoye as prime minister on October 16. On November 5, the Imperial War Council asserted a November 25 deadline, later extended to November 29, for American acquiescences, and sent diplomat Saburo Kurusu to Washington to work with Ambassador Nomura to pressure Hull. On November 20, Nomura and Kurusu informed Hull that Japan would not advance further in Southeast Asia and would withdraw from Indochina if the United States accepted Japan's conquest of China and ended its trade embargo. On November 26, Hull replied with a ten-point elaboration of America's position that called on Tokyo to abandon all its conquests since Manchuria in return for which trade would resume.

Meanwhile, Magic intercepts revealed that Tokyo had a November 29 deadline although what happened then was opaque. A Japanese task force with eight cruisers, twenty destroyers, and thirty-five transport ships packed with 35,000 troops of five army divisions was steaming toward Southeast Asia with its destination and purpose unknown. Roosevelt assumed that, "We are likely to be attacked perhaps as soon as next Monday because the Japanese are notorious for attacking without warning. The question is how to manuever them into firing the first shot without too much danger to ourselves."[69] On November 24, the Navy Department warned all Pacific headquarters that "surprise aggressive movement in any direction including attack on the Philippines or Guam is a possibility."[70] On November 27, the White House warned America's Pacific commanders, General Douglas MacArthur at the Philippines and General Walter Short and Admiral Husband Kimmel at Hawaii to prepare for a pending Japanese attack: "This dispatch is to be considered a war warning. Negotiations with Japan appear to be terminated... Japanese future action unpredictable but hostile action possible at any moment. If hostilities cannot...be avoided the United States desires that Japan commit the first overt act. This policy should not be construed as restricting you to a course of action that might jeopardize your defenses."[71] MacArthur ignored the warming. Short and Kimball assumed that the threat was saboteurs lurking among Oahu's 150,000 Japanese population so the general parked warplanes closer together on the airfield; although reconnaissance flights scoured the seas, they did so in an arc from northwest to southwest of Hawaii as the Japanese fleet approached from the north. On December 6, Roosevelt sent Emperor Hirohito a plea for peace.

Admiral Isoroku Yamamoto masterminded the attack on Pearl Harbor as the key to eight separate but related offensives designed to conquer the southwestern Pacific Islands and Southeast Asia including America's colonies the Philippines, Guam, Wake, and Midway; Britain's Malaya, Singapore, and Burma; the Dutch East Indies; and Thailand. He initiated his plan in December 1940 and over the next year developed its details and had units train for their missions. To Prime Minister Konoye, he explained that if the Pearl Harbor attack succeeded, "we can run wild for six months or a year, but after that I have utterly no confidence. I hope you will avoid war."[72]

Yamamoto assigned Admiral Chuichi Nagumo to command the Pearl Harbor assault. Nagumo's fleet included six aircraft carriers with 414 aircraft, two battleships, three cruisers, nine destroyers, eight refueling tankers, twenty-three submarines, and five piggybacking midget submarines that gathered at Hitokappu Bay, off Etorofu Island in the Kurile Islands north of Hokkaido. In strict radio silence, the fleet began its voyage on November 25 and halted 220 miles north of Oahu on the morning of December 7. Nagumo launched the first wave of 140 bombers and 45 fighters at 6:20 and the second wave of 134 bombers and 34 fighters an hour later. The Japanese sank four battleships, damaged four battleships and fourteen other warships, destroyed 189 aircraft, damaged 159 aircraft, killed 2,335 servicemen and 68 civilians, and wounded 1,178 others. The Japanese suffered only 29 planes destroyed, 74 damaged, four midget submarines sunk, and 64 men killed.[73]

Japan's victory was at once overwhelming and incomplete. Fortunately, America's three aircraft carriers in the Pacific were not at Pearl Harbor. Two ferried Marine fighter squadrons to Wake and Midway islands; the other was at San Diego. Fearing that they lurked nearby and would attack, Nomura canceled a third wave that targeted oil storage and repair facilities. Had the Japanese destroyed the oil and repair resources, the navy would have had to withdraw to the West Coast, leaving Hawaii vulnerable to an invasion. Had those events happened, the Pacific war might have lasted years longer with far more horrific American casualties.

The next day, Roosevelt appeared before Congress to issue a terse war declaration: "Yesterday, December 7, 1941, a day that will live in infamy...I ask that the Congress declare that since the unprovoked and dastardly attack by Japan on Sunday, December 7, 1941, a state of war has existed between the United States and Japan." He pledged that: "No matter how long it may take us to overcome this premeditated invasion, the American people in their righteous might will win through to absolute victory." Congress almost unanimously approved that declaration with the Senate vote of 82 to 0 and the House vote of 388 to 1.[74]

Hitler and Mussolini declared war against the United States on December 11. Roosevelt sent a message to Congress asking it to reciprocate which the Senate did by 88 to 0 and the House by 393 to 0. As for the isolationists, the American First Committee dissolved itself on December 11 and Charles Lindberg never again publicly called for neutrality.

In a Fireside talk on December 9, Roosevelt presented Americans a sober yet inspiring vision of the incredible challenge they faced: "We are now in this war...Every single man, woman, and child is a partner in the most tremendous undertaking in our American history. We must share together the bad news and the good news, the defeats and the victories – the changing fortunes of war...It will not only be a long war, it will be a hard war...we must begin the great task that is before us by abandoning once and for all the illusion that we can ever again isolate us from the rest of humanity...the United States can accept no result except victory, final and complete...So we are going to win the war and we are going to win the peace that follows."[75]

Chapter 8

THE OPENING CAMPAIGNS

"The elimination of German, Japanese and Italian war power means the unconditional surrender by Germany, Italy, and Japan. That means a reasonable assurance of future world peace. It does not mean the destruction of the population of Germany, Italy, or Japan, but it does mean the destruction of the philosophies in those countries which are based on conquest and the subjection of other people." (Franklin Roosevelt)

America's entrance into the war was a dream come true for Prime Minister Winston Churchill: "To have the United States on our side was to me the greatest joy. England would live, the Commonwealth of Nations and the Empire would live."[1] He asked Franklin Roosevelt if he and his advisors could come to Washington, meet with the president and his advisors, and begin planning how to win a world war.

Roosevelt greeted Churchill at the White House on December 22. Churchill lingered off and on for three weeks. The president, prime minister, and their advisors celebrated Christmas together. Churchill addressed a joint session of Congress on December 26. After suffering a mild heart attack, Churchill recovered at Lend-Lease chief Edward Stettinius's mansion at Pompano, Florida from January 6 to 10. Churchill then returned to the White House, staying from January 11 to 14, before departing to Ottawa, Canada.

During their latest times together, the friendship between Roosevelt and Churchill deepened to a kind of intimate brotherhood. Churchill joyfully noted that: "We live here as a big family in the greatest intimacy and informality, and I have formed the very highest regard and admiration for the President. His breadth of view, resolution and his loyalty to the common cause are beyond all praise."[2] At one point, Roosevelt exuberantly declared to Churchill that: "It is fun to be in the same decade as you."[3] They spent their days in serious talks with their advisors then dined and afterward drank and smoked together through the evening until early morning, regaling each other with stories and quips. Churchill's bedroom was just down the hall from Roosevelt's. One morning Roosevelt was eager to share his idea to call the alliance the United Nations and wheeled himself into Churchill's bathroom just as he rose naked and wet from the tub. Roosevelt apologized and Churchill quipped, "Think nothing of it. The Prime Minister of Great Britain has nothing to conceal from the President of the United States."[4] Eleanor typically was the killjoy, belittling their relationship: "They looked like two little boys playing soldier. They seemed to be having a wonderful time, too wonderful in fact. It made me a little sad somehow."[5]

Four vital decisions emerged from this summit. One was to establish the Combined Chiefs of Staff of each nation's Joint Chiefs of Staff who would remain in Washington and oversee planning. Second was to defeat Germany first while blunting Japan's advances. Third was for one supreme commander to preside over each war theater. Fourth was for a statement of principles to guide the alliance that now numbered twenty-six governments in power or in exile fighting Axis imperialism. For that Roosevelt proposed and Churchill readily agreed that they avoid the word alliances and instead call themselves the United Nations. On January 1, 1942, representatives of those countries signed a "Declaration by the United Nations" whereby they would fight until victory guided by the Atlantic Charter's principles. The alliance's core were relations among America, Britain, Russia, China, and France that needed constant diplomacy to overcome their mutual suspicions and conflicting interest.[6]

Meanwhile, the Americans and British failed to agree on where to target their first invasion. The Americans wanted to land in northern France, the British in France's colonies of Morocco and Algeria. A disastrous British defeat that summer determined that decision. Then until the war's end, they would disagree on a series of other possible invasions and related strategies before eventually reaching compromises on each after often rancorous debates.[7]

The prolonged visit of Churchill and his entourage was a critical step in forging a working alliance. After their departure, Roosevelt resumed organizing his administration for war.[8] He had already amassed considerable power as commander-in-chief in the years leading to Pearl Harbor. On July 5, 1939, he issued an executive order that let him bypass the secretaries of war and navy to directly command generals and admirals. On September 8, 1941, a week after Germany's invasion of Poland, he proclaimed a limited national emergency under which he could wield limited emergency national defense powers. On May 27, 1941, he declared unlimited national emergency powers.

Roosevelt's war bureaucracy was naturally an organizational pyramid of pyramids like that of any other nation-state. His immediate advisors were his Top Policy Group that included Vice President Henry Wallace, Secretary of War Henry Stimson, Army Chief of Staff George Marshall, Office of Scientific Research and Development Director Vannevar Bush, and National Defense Research Committee chair James Conant.

The Combined Chiefs of Staff provided detailed planning for campaigns. The key people included Americans Chair Admiral William Leahy, Army Chief George Marshall, Admiral Ernest King, and Air General Harold "Hap" Arnold and Britons Chair General John Dill, Army General Alan Brooke, Admiral Dudley Pound, and Air General Charles Portal.[9] Despite their common cause in winning the war against their enemies, tensions of conflicting interests and national character permeated relations between the allies. General Dwight Eisenhower explained that "Britishers approach every military problem from the viewpoint of the Empire, just as we approach them from the viewpoint of American interest. One of the constant sources of danger to us in this war is the temptation to regard as our first enemy the partner that we must work with in defeating the real enemy."[10] The British tended to look down their noses at the Americans, who they considered ignorant and unsophisticated. The Americans, of course, knew and resented that. Marshall recalled that the Americans cooperated with the British to a point: "We discussed political things more than anything else...But were careful, exceedingly careful, never to discuss them with the British, and from that they took the count that we didn't observe these things at all."[11] Indeed, Marshal along with Roosevelt, Eisenhower, and many other chiefs were astute poker and bridge players who knew how to play their cards while misleading with banter and gestures.

One severe American weakness was its lack of a national intelligence agency. Instead the State, War, and Navy Departments had sections that gathered and analyzed information vital to their respective duties but rarely shared it with each other or even the president. The code-cracking operations by the Office of Naval Intelligence and the Military Intelligence Division established during and after the First World War were the most systematic attempts to gather secret information. The Federal Bureau of Investigation's Special Intelligence Service was charged with counter-espionage, or catching spies in the United

States although FBI agents often operated out of embassies in foreign countries against their espionage organizations.

Roosevelt understood how vital intelligence was to crafting the strategies, policies, and institutions that enhanced American national security.[12] He took the first step toward a national intelligence system on June 26, 1939, when he assigned George Messersmith, the undersecretary of state for administration, to coordinate the efforts of those four organizations. Messersmith made little progress in overcoming each organization's reluctance to share its intelligence sources, methods, and results with its rivals. Typically, instead of strengthening Messersmith, Roosevelt established a rival organization. On February 13, 1940, he had John Carter, a journalist and advisor create and head a small group within the State Department to gather intelligence on foreign countries, financed by $10,000 and overseen by his advisor Adolf Berle.

Roosevelt's decisive step toward a national intelligence agency came on July 11, 1941, when he established the Coordinator of Information (COI), renamed it the Office of Strategic Services and attached it to the Joint Chiefs of Staff on June 13 1942.[13] William "Wild Bill" Donovan was his choice to head it.[14] Few Americans then had more foreign espionage experience. Donovan had attended Columbia University as an undergraduate, then its law school. After passing the bar exam, he worked for a prestigious Wall Street law firm. In 1912, he formed and captained a cavalry troop within the National Guard. His troop was called to serve with General "Black Jack" Pershing's expedition to fight guerillas in Mexico in 1916. In 1917, he was promoted to major and received command of an infantry battalion that fought in France during the First World War. He led from the front, winning a Medal of Honor and Distinguished Service Cross, and was promoted to colonel. During the inter-war years, he held various Justice Department attorney positions while conducting numerous intelligence gathering missions in Russia, Europe, and Asia for various presidents with the most from Roosevelt. In June 1941, Donovan wrote and gave Roosevelt the "Memorandum of Establishment of Service of Strategic Information" that prompted the president to create ONI and have Donovan head it.

OSS received a charter that empowered it to conduct both espionage and unconventional warfare including sabotage and guerilla in December 1942. In foreign countries, OSS agents did what they could to gather vital information by any means, including the "three Bs" – bribery, blackmail, and burglary – while doing what they could to not get caught. As for unconventional warfare, OSS agents parachuted behind enemy lines to supply resistance groups, gather intelligence, blow up bridges, factories, and warehouses, assassinate enemy officers and officials, and attack isolated small groups of enemy soldiers. Donovan recognized how critical soft or psychological power was to politics, especially war. He established a psychological warfare section called the Foreign Information Service with 1,630 personnel that tailor-made and delivered propaganda to boost allied morale and undercut enemy morale, and disinformation that obscured just where allied attacks would appear. Britain's Secret Intelligence Service (SIS) or MI-6 and Special Operations Executive (SOE) provided critical training for OSS. Donovan worked closely with the heads of MI-6 operations in America, first James Padgett then William Stephenson; Padgett's assistant was Ian Fleming, who later authored the James Bond novels. Donovan also spent time in London learning from MI-6 chief Stewart Menzies. FBI director Hoover was able to crimp the organization's operational expanse; he got Roosevelt to issue an executive order on January 16, 1942, that kept OSS out of the United States and Latin America where only the FBI could operate.

Among Roosevelt's most vital acts that developed America's military and economic came on June 27, 1940, when he established the National Defense Research Committee (NDRC) and named Vannevar Bush to head it. Bush had been an MIT professor and dean of its engineering school, before becoming the Carnegie Foundation's director and chair of the National Advisory Committee on Aeronautics.[15] At NDRC, Bush established departments of patents and inventions, instruments and controls, communications and transportation, armor and ordnance, and chemistry and explosive, each with a brilliant collection of scientific and engineering minds. Bush's deputies were scientists James Conant of Harvard University and Karl Compton of MIT. They worked with industry to develop an array of cutting edge technologies. In 1942, Bush created the Office of Scientific Research and Development (OSRD) that actually created and tested prototypes, with the Joint Committee on New Weapons a key component. By 1944, that research network employed over 6,000 scientists, engineers, and technicians.[16] One among those scores of projects surpassed all others in cost, scale, and destructive power.

During the Second World War, five nations raced to develop a nuclear bomb – Germany, Japan, the Soviet Union, Britain, and the United States.[17] The idea for America's program originated with a letter that Roosevelt received from Albert Einstein that he wrote on August 2, 1942, and was hand delivered by economist Alexander Sachs to the White House on October 11. Einstein explained that a controlled splitting of a nuclear atom could produce a bomb powerful enough to destroy an entire city. He advised Roosevelt that the United States should develop a nuclear bomb before Germany or some other country did.

Roosevelt established a nine-man Advisory Committee on Uranium on October 21, whose most brilliant members initially included Sachs and physicists Edward Teller and Leo Szilard, and later Ernest Lawrence, Erico Fermi, and Neils Bohr. The Committee was first overseen by the National Defense Research Council led by James Conant and then the Office of Scientific Research and Development led by Vannevar Bush. On October 9, 1941, Bush advised Roosevelt to develop a nuclear bomb. Roosevelt approved that request on January 19, 1942. War Secretary Henry Stimson got Sam Rayburn, who chaired the House Appropriations Committee, to hide the program's funding in various parts of the annual War Department budget.

Roosevelt appointed General Leslie Groves to head what was code-named the Manhattan Project. Groves established a network of dozens of secret research and production facilities with the keys at Oak Ridge, Tennessee, Hanford, Washington, Livermore, California, the University of Chicago, Columbia University, and Los Alamos, New Mexico. Robert Oppenheimer headed the Los Alamos complex that eventually assembled the bomb. A scientific team led by Fermi achieved the first controlled nuclear chain reaction in a University of Chicago laboratory. The Manhattan Project eventually cost $2 billion and employed over 125,000 people. Roosevelt and Churchill agreed to merge their separate nuclear projects during their summit at Quebec in October 1942. Tragically, that was how Soviet spy Klaus Fuchs penetrated the Manhattan Project and sent critical information back to Moscow. Theodore Hall was another leading physicist spy for Moscow at Los Alamos; Hall passed on the blueprint for the device that triggered the bomb, saving the Soviets the years and enormous expense of developing it themselves.

The Joint Board of the War and Navy Departments had planned for war with Japan since 1906 along with other possible enemies. Each potential foe had a color code. Plan Orange against Japan evolved over time as Japan's empire grew and weapons evolved, especially aircraft carriers. In 1939, the Joint Board changed the code from Orange to Rainbow but kept refining and adjusting the plan's essence. The assumption was that the Japanese would conquer America's colonies of the Philippines and Guam but then would defend its vast Pacific empire with a hedgehog strategy. The Americans would mass land, air, and sea power for a drive northwest across the Pacific from one strategic island to the next directly to Japan, culminating with an invasion. That strategy would take years to realize.

The Japanese had several first-rate weapons. Their submarines and Nell 95 torpedo bombers had respective ranges of 10,000 and 1,300 miles, and fired a deadly twenty-four inch oxygen-fueled torpedo. The Mitsubishi A6M-Zero fighter plane was fast and maneuverable but lightly armored and lacked self-sealing fuel tanks; its pilots usually outfought American fighters until Hellcats and Mustangs appeared. Their warships had special equipment for night-fighting. Like the Germans, the Japanese developed some weapons that proved to be liabilities rather that assets, squandering resources that could have been better developed elsewhere. Their two super-battleships, the *Yamato* and *Musashi*, were the world's largest but never fought a significant battle and were sunk by American planes.

The Americans never before faced an enemy like the Japanese. Ambassador Joseph Grew, who served a decade in Tokyo, explained: "The Japanese will not crack...Only by utter physical destruction or utter exhaustion of their men and materials can they be defeated."[18] Japan's emperor held only symbolic political power but overwhelming cultural power. Japanese revered the emperor as a demi-god for whom their greatest duty was to sacrifice themselves to honor him. Surrender was the worst disgrace and forbidden by the military code. During the war, Tokyo promoted the idea of "a hundred million Japanese hearts beating as one" in devotion, service, and death for the emperor and his empire. That led nearly all Japanese troops to die fighting or by suicide rather than surrender. Their surrender rate varied from one to five percent on various islands. Even Japanese civilians killed themselves rather than yield to approaching enemy troops. On Saipan, mothers gripped their children's hands and leapt off cliffs while school girls in caves held grenades to their breasts and pulled the pins. That fanaticism actually helped the Americans as they mowed down mass charges of Japanese troops shouting "Banzai!" or "Live Ten Thousand Years!"

The Japanese believed their spirit could defeat American physical might. Indeed, they anticipated that devastating the Pearl Harbor fleet followed by conquering the Philippines would so devastate American morale that they would succumb to a peace treaty. The Americans proved that both those Japanese beliefs were utter delusions. American troops killed ten Japanese for every man they lost. However, Japanese troops were adept at slaughtering civilians, at least 20 million. Historian Victor Hansen observed that "no army in the Second World

War killed so many civilians while being inept at killing its better-armed enemies."[19]

America's war against Japan passed through two strategic phases, one defensive, the other offensive.[20] The first phase involved staving off Japan's offensives that six months after Pearl Harbor carved out an empire across the central and western Pacific, and Southeast Asia. A vital element of that strategy was defending the sea-lanes between America's West Coast and Australia. The Americans blunted a Japanese naval offensive at Coral Sea in May 1942 then devastated another, sinking four carriers, at Midway the next month. Midway was the decisive Pacific battle. Thereafter strategically the United States was always on the offensive until atomic bombs abruptly ended the war in August 1945.

America's worst defeat during the first phase was in the Philippines where Douglas MacArthur was in command. MacArthur is among America's most controversial generals.[21] He was first in his 1903 class at West Point and served his first two years as a lieutenant in the Philippines. During the First World War he rose swiftly as a regimental colonel, a brigade general, first the 42nd Division's chief of staff and then its commander as a major general. Along the way, he won seven silver stars, a record. He served in various posts including West Point's superintendent during the 1920s. In 1930, President Herbert Hoover named him army chief of staff. In 1935, he retired to serve as Philippine President Manuel Quezon's highly paid military advisor. He was eloquent, charismatic, and highly intelligent but his narcissism was even more powerful. He was a publicity hound who shamelessly promoted himself and undercut any rivals. For instance, of the 150 communiques his headquarters issued after the Japanese invasion, 109 mentioned and celebrated only him.[22] Although he displayed courage on the front line in the First World War, he visited the Bataan Peninsula front only once while staying safely at his Corregidor Island headquarters; soldiers bitterly condemned him as "Dugout Doug."

Roosevelt restored MacArthur to active duty and gave him command of American and Philippines forces on July 28, 1941. MacArthur's army numbered 100,000 troops, including 20,000 Americans and 80,000 Filipinos, although the latter were mostly ill-trained, inadequately equipped, and poorly motivated militia. Also under his command were 100 tanks, 277 aircraft, three cruisers, thirteen destroyers, and eighteen submarines.[23] His plan was to delay an invasion while concentrating his army in the Bataan Peninsula on Manila Bay's west side. His field commanders included General Jonathan Wainwright for the army,

Admiral Thomas Hart for the fleet, and General Lewis Brereton for the air force.

MacArthur's leadership was utterly inept as he committed one disastrous mistake after another. For instance, he failed to have supplies concentrated at the Bataan Peninsula for its defenders, including a depot filled with four years' worth of rice at Cabanaturan that the Japanese captured.[24] Although Washington ordered MacArthur on November 27, to prepare for an imminent Japanese attack, and on December 7, he learned of the Pearl Harbor attack seven hours before the Japanese assaulted the Philippines, the general did nothing. He refused Brereton's request to send his B-17s against Japan's air base on Taiwan. Had he done so, the raid might have spoiled the pending Japanese air attack from that base. Instead, 54 Japanese bombers escorted by 36 Zero fighters devastated the 35 B-17s and 100 P-40s parked wing-tip to wing-tip at Clark Air Force base; Brereton ordered the remnants flown south to safety at a base on Mindanao Island. Likewise, Hart steamed south with his fleet to avoid being wiped out.

Having achieved air superiority, General Masaharu Homma began landing 43,000 and 98 tanks, assisted by 541 bombers and fighter planes, at beaches on northern Luzon, the main island, on December 10. The Japanese routed the scattered Filipino regiments and pushed south toward Manila. MacArthur withdrew his troops into the Bataan Peninsula and placed his headquarters on Corregidor Island in Manila Bay where President Quezon and his family and entourage joined him.

The Japanese besieged the allied army. During the siege, the Japanese sent Quezon a message promising to grant the Philippines independence if he surrendered. MacArthur actually backed that deal but Roosevelt rejected it. On February 23, Roosevelt ordered MacArthur to escape, not wanting the Japanese to capture such a prestigious general who was the army's former chief of staff. On March 11, 1942, MacArthur turned over command to Wainwright, boarded a patrol boat with his wife, son, and staff, and fled to Mindanao where a B-17 flew them to Australia. Before leaving, he got Quezon to wire $500,000 to his bank account in New York for his "distinguished service."[25]

Bataan's 12,000 American and 64,000 Filipino defenders surrendered on April 9, and Wainwright surrendered his 13,000 troops on Corregidor island on May 6. Homma's army, which eventually numbered 130,000 troops, conquered the Philippines and inflicted 146,000 casualties, including 100,000 prisoners, while suffering only 11,225 casualties. The Japanese shot, bayoneted, or beheaded with Samurai swords as many as 650 Americans and 18,000 Filipinos on the "Bataan Death March" to prisoner of war camps followed by the deaths mostly by disease of another 16,000 men in the camps.[26] Meanwhile, Japanese task forces captured American held Guam on December 10 and Wake Island on December 23.

Britain's defense of its Southeast Asian colonies crumbled under Japan's assaults. A Japanese army besieged Hong Kong's 14,000 defenders from December 8 until Christmas Day, when Governor Mark Young surrendered. The regional key to Britain's defense was Singapore as a port and island straddling the Pacific and Indian Oceans and the strait between mainland southeast Asia and the Dutch East Indies. Japan's airfields in southern Indochina were in bombing distance of Singapore. General Tomoyuki Yamashita commanded 125,000 troops in the army to conquer Malaya and Singapore island. Facing them was the British army with 130,000 mostly colonial troops under General Arthur Percival. Yamashita's advanced corps of 30,000 troops and 200 tanks invaded Malaya on December 8, 1941, routed British-Indian forces before them, and advanced rapidly down the peninsula, eventually capturing over 50,000 troops. Meanwhile, Japanese aircraft sank Britain's unescorted battleships the HMS *Prince of Wales* and HMS *Repulse* off Malaya on December 11. The siege of Singapore lasted from February 8 to 15, when Percival surrendered 85,000 British and imperial troops after fierce bombardments and severed water pipes from the mainland. Meanwhile Japanese armies invaded a series of islands in the Dutch East Indies, and the Dutch surrendered the East Indies along with 93,000 troops on March 12.

The Japanese launched an air offensive and limited invasion of Burma from neighboring Thailand on December 20, and a massive invasion on January 20, 1942. General Hisaichi Terachi commanded the 95,000 Japanese troops. Defending southern and central Burma were 45,000 British troops, although mostly Indian colonials, while 95,000 Chinese troops defended northern Burma.

At the time, 79,000 tons of Lend-Lease goods bound for China were in warehouses in Rangoon and another 30,000 tons were at the railroad's northern terminus at Lashio.[27] Also on an airfield near Rangoon was the first contingent of Colonel Claire Chennault's American Volunteer Group, better known as the Flying Tigers.[28] Chennault initially recruited around 300 men including mechanics and 100 pilots, which he split into three squadrons; pilots received $600 a month and a $500 bonus for every Japanese plane they destroyed. One hundred Curtis P-40 Tomahawks were crated and shipped to Rangoon where they were reassembled and painted with a shark's face on the front and Chinese colors. The Flying Tigers first fought the Japanese when they invaded

Burma. As the Japanese advanced, the Flying Tigers withdrew along a series of airfields that eventually led to Kunming, China.

No American commander faced a more daunting challenge than General Joseph "Vinegar Joe" Stilwell.[29] In February 1942, Roosevelt dispatched him to the Nationalist Chinese headquarters at Chungking where he immediately assumed two duties, commander of American forces in China and chief of staff to Generalissimo Chiang Kai-shek, and from August 1943, deputy to Admiral Louis Mountbatten for the China-India-Burma region. Stilwell was an excellent choice for a near impossible mission. He was a first-rate professional who understood China, having been a military attaché at America's legation in Beijing from 1935 to 1939 during which he learned Chinese. He knew that he could do nothing to reform the corrupt, inept, and brutal regime led by Chiang and his Nationalist (Kuomintang, KMT) Party. Instead, he focused his efforts on leading the Chinese army in northern Burma and fighting with the British against the Japanese invaders.

The Japanese captured Rangoon on March 10, and overran most of Burma by May 28, with surviving allied forces retreating to India's northeastern region of Assam or into the Himalaya mountains of northern Burma. That victory cost the Japanese about 7,000 casualties and 117 lost warplanes while they inflicted 40,000 and 30,000 casualties, mostly prisoners, respectively on the Chinese and British, and shot down or captured 95 warplanes, mostly Flying Tigers.

Eventually Chennault received more P-40s crated and shipped to Calcutta, where they were flown "over the hump" or Himalaya Mountains to Kunming along with thousands of tons of supplies packed in P-47 transport planes. On July 4, 1942, Chennault transformed the Flying Tigers into the 23rd American Fighter Squadron repainted with the American white star in a circle. Over time, Chennault received enough men and various warplanes to command the 14th Air Force which also included a squadron of B-24 bombers.

The series of disastrous losses across the Pacific from Pearl Harbor to Singapore angered and frustrated Roosevelt. Eager to retaliate, he conceived a plan with Admiral Ernest King and Pacific naval chief Chester Nimitz to attack Japan that even if successful would inflict more symbolic than substantive damage. Lieutenant Colonel James Doolittle would lead a squadron of sixteen B-25s launched from the aircraft carrier USS *Hornet* to bomb Japanese cities and then fly to safety behind Chinese army lines in China. Initially, most of his other military advisors opposed that plan as too risky but eventually they reluctantly accepted, developed, and implemented it.

Unfortunately the launch occurred earlier than planned. Anticipating just such a raid, Admiral Yamamoto established a picket line of trawlers with radios in a semicircle 700 miles east of Japan. On April 18, after the *Hornet* encountered and sank one of the trawlers, Doolittle and his squadron took off fearing Japanese warships could converge and destroy the carriers. Thirteen of the sixteen bombers dropped their loads on industrial sites in Tokyo and the other three made separate attacks on Kobe, Nagoya, and Osaka, then flew on to China. Most ran out of fuel and the crew had to bail out. Others managed to land safely. Seventy-one of the eighty men including Doolittle reached Chinese lines. The Doolittle raid's physical bomb damage to Tokyo was negligible but had a powerful psychological impact. The imperial government had promised the population that the Americans posed no threat to Japan.

Admiral Shigeyoshi Inoue led a fleet with two carriers to sever the American supply line to Australia. Nimitz dispatched a fleet led by Admiral Frank Fletcher with the USS *Lexington* and USS *Yorktown* to intercept the Japanese. The battle of Coral Sea raged from May 4 to 8. Tactically the battle was a draw as each side suffered losses then steamed away. Japanese planes sank the *Lexington* and a destroyer, and damaged the *Yorktown*'s flight deck while American pilots sank a light carrier and a destroyer and damaged a large carrier. The Americans lost 69 planes and 656 sailors; the Japanese lost 97 planes and 966 sailors. Yet, strategically, Coral Sea was an American victory because the fleet turned back the Japanese attempt to sever that vital supply line.

In their Magic operation, the Research Bureau's cryptographers cracked Japan's naval code in May 1942. They learned of a Japanese fleet led by Yamamoto with six aircraft carriers, eleven battleships, sixteen cruisers and dozens of support warships steaming toward Midway Island, defended by a marine regiment. Nimitz and Fletcher conceived a brilliant strategy of positioning three carriers – the *Hornet*, *Enterprise*, and *Yorktown* – north of their route and ambushing them. During the battle of Midway from June 4 to 7, the Americans sank four carriers and a cruiser, shot down 248 planes, and killed 3,087 sailors while suffering a carrier and destroyer sunk, 150 planes shot down, and 307 killed. Midway was the Pacific War's strategic turning point. From then, the Japanese were nearly always on defense in a diminishing empire.[30]

Tragically, America's offensives involved two separate thrusts across the Pacific, one led by Nimitz island-hopping directly toward Japan, and the other by MacArthur toward the Philippines. Politics, not reason, determined that twin-thrust strategy. MacArthur demanded that command and mission to uphold the honor of himself and the army. The Japanese had inflicted a humiliating defeat on MacArthur when he commanded the Philippines and he wanted to avenge that. Thus did Roosevelt surrender strategic logic to MacArthur's ego and the army-navy rivalry. The sensible strategy was to have MacArthur or some other general hold the Southwest Pacific while Nimitz advanced steadily toward Japan, capturing islands where first bombers and then fighter escorts would devastate Japanese cities followed by an eventual invasion.

Throughout the war, Army Chief George Marshall's attempts to reason with MacArthur failed. For instance, MacArthur insisted on fulfilling his promise to the Filipino people that "I shall return," after his inept generalship lost the Philippines to the Japanese. Marshall argued that "bypassing the Philippines is not synonymous with abandoning them." MacArthur declared doing so would be "a blot on American honor."[31] That strategy led to tens of thousands of unnecessary American casualties and tens of billions of dollars of war products that were desperately needed elsewhere.

The first campaign to take a Japanese held island, that of Guadalcanal at the south end of the Solomon Islands was in MacArthur's bailiwick.[32] The regional Japanese headquarters was 1,200 miles north of Guadalcanal at Rabaul. Strategically, Guadalcanal was worthless along with the rest of the Solomon Islands in the southwest Pacific. The nearest deepwater allied supply port was 900 miles away at Noumea, New Caledonia while the harbor at Guadalcanal was so small and shallow that only one ship could unload at a time. The sensible strategy would have been for MacArthur simply to protect the direct shipping line between America and Australia. Instead, with General Robert Ghormley the theater commander, General Archer Vandegrift led the expedition that captured Guadalcanal on August 7 then fought off repeated Japanese attempts to retake the island and drive the American fleet from the surrounding seas. Admirals Fletcher, William "Bull" Halsey, and Richmond Turner commanded fleets that battled Japanese fleets. The campaign lasted six months until February 9, when Yamamoto withdrew his remaining forces. During that time the Americans committed 60,000 marines and soldiers, suffered 7,100 dead and 7,789 wounded, and lost 615 planes and 29 ships, including two heavy carriers, while the Japanese sent 32,000 troops, suffered 19,200 dead and 1,000 captured, and lost 683 planes and 38 ships including two battleships and a light carrier.

New Guinea was literally and figuratively a worse dead-end.[33] The Japanese invaded that Australian colony on January 23, 1942, and captured the north side while the Australians, reinforced by the Americans held the south side with their headquarters at Port Moresby. Each side poured in reinforcements and the fighting persisted until the war's end. MacArthur launched a series of campaigns that captured small ports westward on the north shore and neighboring islands. During that time, the allies suffered 42,000 casualties, including 12,291 American and 7,000 Australian dead, while the Japanese lost 200,000 troops, mostly from disease.

Throughout the war, Roosevelt and his advisors debated just how much to trust and fear Joseph Stalin and his brutal, genocidal communist regime.[34] The consensus shifted little from Ambassador Laurence Steinhardt's 1941 assessment: "My observation of the psychology of the individuals who are conducting Soviet foreign policy...has convinced me...that it is not possible to create 'international good will' with them...and that they are not affected by ethical or moral considerations, nor guided by relationships which are customary between individuals of culture and breeding. Their psychology recognizes only firmness, power, and force, and reflects primitive instincts and reactions that are entirely devoid of the restraints of civilization...Concessions... have been received...with marked suspicion and...as evidence of weakness."[35] As early as May 1943, William Bullitt conceived and justified the policy later called "containment": "the first step toward preventing the Soviet domination of Europe is the creation of a British-American line in Eastern Europe. The second is the setting up of democratic governments behind our lines and the prevention of communist revolt."[36]

Roosevelt's first wartime diplomacy with the Soviets occurred on May 29, 1942, when he greeted Foreign Minister Vyacheslav Molotov at the White House. Molotov's mission was to pressure Roosevelt to give Moscow massive aid and open a second front in Europe later that year. Roosevelt readily agreed, recognizing how vital the Soviet Union was in diverting German power. He explained to Marshall and King that: "Our principal objective is to help Russia...Russian armies are killing more Germans and destroying more Axis material than all 25 United Nations put together."[37] On June 11, the American and Soviet governments issued a joint declaration that the United States was committed to a second front in 1942.

Churchill returned for another summit that began at Roosevelt's Hyde Park mansion on June 19 and 20, then moved to the White House from June 21 to 25. The key decision reached came after heated debate. The American high command wanted to invade northern France as soon as possible while the British advocated an American army landing in French Morocco and Algeria then fighting its way east to link with a British army fighting west from Egypt. Amidst the debate horrible news arrived on June 21. In North Africa, German General Erin von Rommel's Afrika Korps had routed Britain's Eighth Army and captured Tobruk with 25,000 British soldiers. Churchill convinced Roosevelt to commit to an American invasion of Morocco and Algeria in November.

Roosevelt informed his Chiefs of Staff to make that happen. When they expressed their reluctance, he explained the strategic and practical rationale. America's military from the lowest private and sailor to the highest general and admiral needed combat experience against a relatively easy foe before taking on the battle-hardened German army in Europe. A disastrous "raid" by 10,000 Canadian troops against 1,500 German troops defending Dieppe, France on August 19, 1942, showed how difficult an invasion would be; the defenders killed, wounded, and captured about half the invaders before the survivors re-embarked and steamed back to Britain.

In contrast, the 125,000 French troops in Morocco and Algeria were mostly second-rate with wavering loyalties. Secret diplomacy might flip them from Germany's puppet Vichy regime into the alliance. Roosevelt sent Admiral William Leahy on a diplomatic mission to Vichy, the capital of the rump French state led by Marshal Philippe Petain that the Germans had established. Admiral Francois Darlan, Vichy's military commander, had secretly told Leahy that if the Americans invaded "with sufficient force in North Africa to be successful against the Nazis, he would not oppose us."[38] And If the French fought, the Americans would swiftly overwhelm them. That done, the American army would drive east against the rear of the German and Italian army fighting the British army in Egypt, and crush it. That victory and the hard experiences that realized it would be priceless for invading northern France in 1943. Those arguments and Churchill's plea in July resolved the debate. Roosevelt ordered his military staff to plan the invasion and subsequent campaign.[39] War Secretary Stimson remained pessimistic: "We have turned our back on the path of what I consider sound and correct strategy, and are taking a course which I feel will lead to a dangerous diversion and possible disaster."[40]

Meanwhile, a victorious battle at North Africa's far end made a successful invasion likelier.[41] General Bernard Montgomery commanded the Eighth Army's 195,000 troops and 1,029 tanks defending Egypt at El Alamein just 70 miles from Alexandria. Facing him was the Afrika Korps, a German and Italian army with 116,000 troops and 435 tanks; although General Erin Rommel was the commander, he had turned command over to General Georg Sturmer while he recovered from an illness in Germany. Montgomery launched his army against the Afrika Korps on October 23, and the British finally routed the enemy on November 11. Rommel flew back to lead Afrika Korps' remnants all the way back to the Mareth Line on the border between Tunisia and Libya. Montgomery slowly pursued with Eighth Army.

Roosevelt picked General Dwight Eisenhower to lead the invasion. He later explained why he eventually named Eisenhower supreme commander for Europe: "Eisenhower is the best politician of the military men. He is a natural leader who can convince men to follow him and that was what we need in this position more than any other quality."[42] Eisenhower was more than an amiable conciliator. He was highly intelligent and first in his class at Leavenworth's command school. He never led men in battle but instead steadily if slowly rose through the ranks as an administrator.[43]

The invasion of Morocco and Algeria involved three corps starting from two countries and hitting those beaches simultaneously on the morning of November 8. General George Patton's all American 35,000-man corps began in Hampton Roads, Virginia and was conveyed across the Atlantic by a fleet commanded by Admiral Henry Hewitt to land at widely dispersed Mehdia near Rabat, Fedala near Casablanca, and Saif. The other two corps steamed from British ports. General Lloyd Fredendall's all-American 33,000-man corps would land on either side of Oran, Algeria. General Charles Ryder's 39,000 mixed American and British corps would land on either side of Algiers. British General Kenneth Anderson commanded those three corps that composed the First Army. Tragically, the general who would be the war's greatest American combat leader was assigned sites the furthest from the German and Italian army.

A daring diplomatic mission preceded the invasion. A British submarine carried American General Mark Clark to surface offshore a beach seventy-five miles west of Algiers after midnight on October 22. He and four marines piled into a rubber boat and paddled ashore. There he met Robert Murphy, who headed America's diplomatic mission, and General Charles Mast, the French chief of staff for France's army in North Africa. Clark informed Mast of the pending invasion and asked him to order his troops to embrace, not fight, the Americans when they landed. Mast tentatively agreed and Clark and the marines returned to the submarine and steamed away. Murphy solicited a similar understanding from General Maxime Weygand, Vichy's high commissioner for French North Africa.

Despite these efforts, the French resisted each landing. The invaders overwhelmed the defenders with sheer numbers. France's troops were scattered and the relatively small numbers near the beaches were soon overrun. By chance, Admiral Darlan, the Vichy regime's military chief, was in Algiers to visit his sick son. Eisenhower had General Clark negotiate with him a cease-fire in return for heading the civil government for Morocco and Algeria. The final resistance ended on November 16. The allied army conquered Morocco and Algeria at the cost of 526 dead Americans, 574 dead British, and combined 756 wounded along with an escort carrier and four destroyers sunk while inflicting 1,396 dead and 1,997 wounded along with a light cruiser, five destroyers, and six submarines sunk. That was a relatively light price for the prize of not just a vast territory but experience against a second-rate foe. The Americans learned valuable lessons from the serious mistakes they made in combined operations, tactics, logistics, and communications.

With Morocco and Algeria secure, the next step was to pivot east. Five-hundred and sixty miles of wretched road separated Algiers and Tunis. Anderson ordered Ryder's corps followed by Fredendall's to advance along the coast. Meanwhile, Hitler had troops overrun Vichy France and poured reinforcements into Tunisia. First Army's lead troops reached Tunisia's border in late November then bogged down from German resistance, winter rains, and lack of supplies. Each side slowly built up its forces. Eventually there were 250,000 German and Italian troops split between General Hans-Jurgen Arnim's Fifth Panzer Army fighting Anderson's First Army westward and General Erin Rommel's Afrika Korps fighting Montgomery's Eighth Army southward. Anderson's army included a British corps on the northern front, a French corps on the central front, and Fredendall's American II Corps on the southern front.

Rommel repelled an attack by Montgomery on his heavily fortified Mareth Line, then massed his armored divisions and routed Fredendall at Kasserine Pass from February 18 to 24. The Germans inflicted 10,000 casualties including 3,300 dead and 3,000 prisoners along with destroying 183 tanks, 616 vehicles, and 208 cannon while suffering one-tenth the casualties, 989 killed and wounded and 608 captured, and losing 20 tanks, 67 vehicles, and 14 cannon. In the first major battle between them, the Germans inflicted a humiliating defeat on the Americans.[44]

The British were appalled by the American performance. General Harold Alexander, the senior commander for the Mediterranean, lamented "the poor fighting value of the Americans. They simply do not know their job as soldiers and this is the case from the highest to

Roosevelt and his Mother Sara

As a pampered only child, Franklin Roosevelt was devoted to his domineering mother who, even after he married Eleanor, insisted on sitting opposite him at the dinner table's other end and beside him while receiving guests at their Hyde Park mansion. Sara relegated Eleanor to side seats and secondary guests.

Wedding Photo of Roosevelt and Eleanor

The relationship between Roosevelt and Eleanor eventually failed as a marriage but succeeded during his presidency when she became a trusted advisor and envoy to various constituencies. Eleanor refused to have any more conjugal relations with Roosevelt after learning of his affair with her secretary Lucy Mercer.

Roosevelt as Assistant Naval Secretary

As Assistant Naval Secretary in Woodrow Wilson's presidency, Roosevelt gained valuable wartime experience in administration and diplomacy.

Newly elected New York Governor Roosevelt with predecessor Al Smith

Newly elected New York Governor Roosevelt shakes hands with his predecessor and patron Al Smith. Roosevelt's programs to battle the Great Depression as governor became prototypes for his New Deal policies as president.

Jobless and Homeless during the Great Depression

From the stock market's collapse in October 1929 until Roosevelt's presidential inauguration in March 1933, the Great Depression cut America's economy in half and left one of four workers jobless and millions of people poverty-stricken and homeless. Here a local Chamber of Commerce warns homeless, jobless men to get out of town.

Newly elected Roosevelt and his predecessor Hoover drive to the inauguration.

Franklin Roosevelt defeated Herbert Hoover with landslide results for himself and the Democratic Party in Congress and statehouses in the 1932 election. Most voters blamed Hoover's policies for worsening rather alleviating the Great Depression. Here the rivals drive to Roosevelt's inauguration at the Capitol, the first of his four victories in presidential elections.

Civilian Conservation Corps Workers

The Civilian Conservation Corps is the best known of dozens of Roosevelt's New Deal programs that boosted employment and developed the economy.

Hitler and Mussolini

Amidst the Great Depression from 1931 to 1939, the fascist governments of Japan, Italy, and Germany invaded a series of countries that culminated with the outbreak of war in Europe after Hitler had his army invade Poland, and Britain and France declared war against Germany. Here Adolf Hitler and Benito Mussolini are driven amidst exuberant crowds in one of their many summits.

Pearl Harbor

Japan's attack on America's fleet at Pearl Harbor was the first in a series of offensives over the next half year that conquered American, British, and Dutch colonies in Southeast Asia and the southwest Pacific. Congress overwhelmingly voted for Roosevelt's war declaration the day after the attack on December 7, 1941.

Roosevelt, Churchill, and the Combined Chiefs of Staff

Roosevelt and Winston Churchill quickly bonded in a deep friendship as they led their countries in alliance against the fascist powers in a world war. The American and British chiefs of staff combined in Washington to advise the president and prime minister then implement their decisions. There were numerous disputes between the Americans and British leaders and their staff members over which strategies to follow. Yet overall the alliance was a stunning success, largely due to the special relationship between the two leaders.

Roosevelt, Nimitz, and MacArthur

Although most of his decisions as commander in chief were strategically sound, Roosevelt at times yielded to pressure from powerful charismatic leaders. Here Roosevelt, General Douglas MacArthur, and Admiral Chester Nimitz meet at Honolulu. The sensible strategy to defeat Japan would have had MacArthur defend the Southwest Pacific with minimal forces while Nimitz island-hopped his armada toward Japan across the central Pacific. Roosevelt yielded to MacArthur's demand that his force be as powerful as Nimitz's and advance through the Solomon islands, New Guinea, and Philippines, even those were strategic dead ends.

Marshall and Eisenhower

Roosevelt selected General Dwight Eisenhower for command of American and eventually allied forces in Europe, and General George Marshall to serve as the Army Chief of Staff. Marshall was brilliant in organizing the army for a world war and working closely with the other services. Eisenhower was best at soothing relations and forging consensus among the American and British land, sea, and air commanders. Many American generals like Omar Bradley and George Patton privately bristled that he favored British plans over their own, especially those of General Bernard Montgomery.

Roosevelt and Truman

Roosevelt selected Senator Harry Truman of Missouri as his running mate in the 1944 election. Truman was renowned for his pragmatism, probity, and diligence, and came from an important midwest state. Yet Roosevelt kept Truman out of his inner policymaking circle. When Roosevelt died on April 12, 1945, Truman was uninformed about many critical issues, most importantly the atomic bomb program. Fortunately, he proved too be a quick study and decisive leader.

Yalta Summit with Roosevelt, Churchill, and Stalin

A seriously ill Roosevelt is seated between Churchill and Stalin at Yalta, with their advisors behind them. The concessions Roosevelt and Churchill made to Stalin's demands over the Soviet occupation of eastern European countries and German reparations provoked controversy then and since.

Hiroshima

Atomic bombs did what conventional bombs failed to do. The atomic bombings of Hiroshima on August 6 and Nagasaki on August 9 forced Japan's government to announce on August 14 that it would surrender. Conventional bombing of German and Japanese cities killed hundreds of thousands of people, wounded hundreds of thousands, and rendered hundreds of thousands homeless. Germany's regime surrendered on May 8, 1945, only after Hitler committed suicide and allied armies overran the country. Japan's surrender prevented an American invasion of the islands that would have resulted in millions of Japanese and hundreds of thousands of American casualties.

MacArthur presides over Japanese surrender

MacArthur stands before the American and allied delegation that observed Japan's surrender aboad the USS Missouri in Tokyo Bay on September 2, 1945. Unfortunately, Franklin Roosevelt did not live to see this final victory that he had done so much to win.

the lowest...Perhaps the weakest link...is the junior leader, who does not lead, with the result that their men do not fight." Chief of Staff Alan Brooke dismissed "Eisenhower as a general is hopeless! He submerges himself in politics and neglects his military duties, partly, I am afraid, because he knows little if anything about military matters."[45] The British talked the Americans into a command structure whereby Eisenhower presided while three Britons actually commanded allied forces, General Harold Alexander, Admiral Andrew Cunningham, and Air Marshal Arthur Tedder.

Eisenhower replaced Fredendall with Patton.[46] After arriving at II Corps headquarters on March 6, Patton did what he could to restore morale, fill depleted ranks, and mass supplies. Reinforcements swelled II Corps to 88,000 troops. Patton devised a plan for a two pronged offensive east to the sea to cut off Afrika Korps, now commanded by Italian General Giovanni Messe after an ill Rommel flew back to Germany for therapy. In a series of carefully planned attacks from March 16 to April 7, one prong fought its way to Maknassy Pass and the other to El Guettar, each about 75 miles short of their respective objectives, the ports of Sfax and Gabes. The Americans inflicted more damage than they endured, 6,000 casualties and 37 destroyed tanks to 5,000 casualties and 22 destroyed tanks.

Montgomery's Eighth Army defeated the enemy and captured those ports. Patton then shifted his forces and they fought their way to Fondouk Pass in central Tunisia. The allied armies joined forces and their 550,000 troops pushed 225,000 axis troops toward a pocket around Tunis and Bizerte. Patton was not present for the final victory. Eisenhower recalled him to command Seventh Army and plan the invasion of Sicily and named General Omar Bradley the II Corps commander. General Arnim surrendered on May 13. The entire Tunisian campaign cost the axis at least 300,000 troops and 450 tanks while the allies suffered 76,000 casualties including 2,715 American dead, 8,978 wounded, and 6,528 wounded, and 340 tanks. American soldiers and their commanders from the lowest officers to Eisenhower had experienced a bloody prolonged transformation from inept amateurs into skilled hardened veterans.[47]

Four months before that decisive victory, Roosevelt and Churchill held their first wartime foreign summit at Casablanca from January 14 to 24, 1943. The key issue that they and their chiefs of staff debated was where to attack the rest of that year and into the next. After conquering North Africa, the Americans wanted the next landing to be from England in northern France. The British vociferously opposed that as too risky and instead insisted on a Mediterranean strategy against Sicily, Italy, and Yugoslavia, Europe's "soft underbelly" as Churchill put it. In that debate, British Chief of Staff Alan Brooke bested a poorly prepared Eisenhower in clarity, confidence, and content. The Americans and British eventually agreed on a compromise. They would attack in the Mediterranean in 1943 and invade northern France in 1944.[48]

Meanwhile, Roosevelt and Churchill had to convince two rivals for command of the Free French movement to join forces. Darlan's assassination on December 24 left a political vacuum. Generals Charles de Gaulle and Henri Giraud had massive egos, ambitions, and hated each other. Of the two, de Gaulle was more resistant to acknowledging his rival, let alone conceding anything of substance. In a prolonged private talk, Roosevelt finally charmed de Gaulle first into signing a cooperation agreement with Giraud and then shaking hands with him before photographers. De Gaulle later wrote that he accorded Roosevelt "the loftiest of ambitions" and that "his intelligence, his knowledge, and his audacity gave him the ability…to realize them."[49]

Among the vital issues that Roosevelt and Churchill discussed was whether to end the war by a negotiated or unconditional surrender with the axis powers. They agreed that a lasting peace depended on destroying the fascist ideology and leaders who had launched their wars of conquest. Yet they worried that declaring that goal would provoke the fascist powers to fight all out to the bitter end. Churchill leaned toward making unconditional surrender a secret goal to be unveiled when the enemy verged on collapse. The trouble was that they would likely defeat each country separately. Imposing unconditional surrender on the first defeated fascist regime would clearly warn the survivors to hold out to the last cartridge. Then again, perhaps explaining that they were warring to liberate the peoples from their fanatical ideology and leaders might inspire resistance to those regimes. A related worry was that Stalin might cut a separate peace with Hitler. An official unconditional surrender policy might restrain him from doing that.

During a press conference on January 24, 1943, Roosevelt declared: "The elimination of German, Japanese and Italian war power means the unconditional surrender by Germany, Italy, and Japan. That means a reasonable assurance of future world peace. It does not mean the destruction of the population of Germany, Italy, or Japan, but it does mean the destruction of the philosophies in those countries which are based on conquest and the subjection of other people."[50]

Historian Rick Atkinson calls the North African campaign capped by Roosevelt's summit with Churchill in Casablanca, "a pivot point in American history, the place where the United States began to act like a great power – militarily, diplomatically, strategically, tactically. Along with Stalingrad and Midway, North Africa is where the Axis enemy forever lost the initiative in World War II. It is where Great Britain slipped into the role of junior partner in the Anglo-American alliance, and where the United States first emerged as the dominant force it would remain into the next millennium...None of it was inevitable – not the individual deaths, not the ultimate Allied victory, nor eventual American hegemony. History, like particular fates, hung in the balance, waiting to be tipped."[51]

Chapter 9

THE HOME FRONT

"It is our duty now to begin to lay plans...for the winning of lasting peace...We cannot be content, no matter how high the general standard of our living may be, if some fraction of our people...is ill-fed, ill-housed, and insecure... People who are hungry and out of a job are the stuff of which dictatorships are made." (Franklin Roosevelt)

Fighting a global war depended on mobilizing the nation's vast human and material resources.[1] That mobilization alleviated many people's lives with better jobs and pay, but exacerbated some long-standing inequities and animosities. Conflicts on the home front could affect distant military fronts by undermining production and morale. President Franklin Roosevelt did what he could to bolster production and morale.

The war eliminated the depression. The economy grew 8.5 percent in 1940, 16.1 percent in 1942, 12.9 percent in 1943, and 7.2 percent in 1944, before contracting 1.7 percent in 1945 as the government sharply cut back spending for personnel and products. The jobless rate fell from 14.6 percent in 1940 to 8.8 percent in 1941, 4.7 percent in 1942, 1.9 percent in 1943, 1.2 percent in 1944, and 1.9 percent in 1945. Government spending fueled that expansion as the federal budget soared from $9,055,269,000 in 1940 to $98,302,937,000 in 1945, military spending from $1,504,000,000 to $81,585,000,000, while the national debt skyrocketed six-fold from $42,967,531,000 to $258,682,187,000.

One critical issue was how to pay for the war. World War II cost America around $350,000,000,000. Bonds underwrote about half that and various taxes the rest. The Treasury launched an advertising campaign that encouraged Americans to buy "Victory Bonds" to express their patriotism and invest in their future. Hollywood stars like Betty Grable, Marlene Dietrich, Loretta Young, and Laren Bacall

144

appeared at "buy bonds" rallies. The 1942 Revenue Act established twenty tax rate categories that began with a combined regular tax and surplus tax of 19 percent on incomes from $624 to $1,999 and ended with 88 percent on incomes from $200,000. The excess profit tax had been graduated from 35 percent to 60 percent, but was now 90 percent. The results from 1940 to 1945 were astonishing as total revenues increased from $6,879,000,000 to $50,162,000,000, including income taxes from $1,110,000,000 to $18,396,000,000, corporate taxes from $978,000,000 to $16,360,000,000, and the rest from other sources.[2]

America had an enormous amount of hard power, including a vast mostly middle-class population; the world's largest economy; vast financial, manufacturing, and mining industries; and scientific networks. In 1941, the population numbered 131,669,275 people, including 118,214,870 whites and 12,865,518 blacks.[3]

After Congress declared war, hundreds of thousands of men volunteered for military service. That patriotic surge was millions of men short of what America's military needed to win a global conflict. Congress amended the 1940 Selective Training and Service Act to require all men from 18 to 65 to register, of whom those from 19 to 45 could immediately be drafted, and the draft would continue until six months after the war officially ended. The House voted by acclamation on December 17 and the Senate by 79 to 2 on December 18, 1941. Eventually, 49 million men registered, 36 million were classified, and 10 million were drafted. Around 373,000 or 4 percent dodged the draft, of which 16,000 received prison terms. Around 72,000 applied for conscientious objector (pacifist) status, and 52,000 of them received it while 11,950 worked in civilian public service jobs. The 6,442 draft boards rejected four of ten men they examined for physical or psychological reasons or because they were fathers or felons. The Marine Corps was purely voluntary and accepted all able-bodied unmarried men from seventeen to thirty, although one could serve in the ranks until age thirty-five. Civilians volunteered their time to aid the military through organizations like the United Service Organization (U.S.O.), Red Cross, Salvation Army, Knights of Columbus, and Boy Scouts.

To their credit, all four Roosevelt sons fought in the war. James was a marine at Guadalcanal, Tawara, and the Solomon Islands, won a Navy Cross and Silver Star, and rose to colonel of a battalion. Elliot flew over 300 photoreconnaissance missions in the Army Air Corps, was twice wounded, and rose to colonel. Frank junior captained the destroyer USS *Ulvert Moore,* and won the Navy Cross, Legion of Merit, and Purple Heart. John served on the aircraft carrier USS Wasp, won a Bronze Star, and rose to lieutenant. At times, Elliot and Frank served as military aides for their father.

One organizational priority was putting all the services under one roof. The result was the Pentagon just across the Potomac River from Washington. George Bergstrom designed the five-sided building with five floors above and two floors below ground. Colonel Leslie Grove and the Army Corps of Engineers supervised the construction that began on September 11, 1941, cost $83 million, and was mostly completed when the Pentagon was dedicated on January 15, 1943.

Roosevelt valued the power of propaganda. He established the Office of Facts and Figures (OFF) to provide the public with positive information about the war effort on October 24, 1941, and named Archibald MacLeish, the Librarian of Congress, to head it. He bolstered the nation's counter-espionage powers by forming the Office of Censorship on December 19, 1941, with Byron Price the director. On January 27, 1942, he instructed Price "to coordinate the efforts of the domestic press and radio in voluntarily withholding from publication military and other information which should not be released in the interest of the effective prosecution of the war."[4] OFF's Intelligence Bureau employed 126 people to measure public opinion through its own surveys and those of other organizations. On March 27, 1942, Congress passed the War Powers Act that bolstered the president's powers to conduct the war as he thought necessary.

At OFF, MacLeish faithfully provided literal facts that might cause many people to question the war effort rather than figurative facts that emotionally connected them. MacLeish explained that: "A democratic government is more concerned with the provision of information to the people than it is with the communication of dreams and aspirations... The duty of government is to provide a basis for judgment; and when it goes beyond that, it goes beyond the prime scope of its duty."[5] But that was exactly where Roosevelt wanted that organization to go. On June 13, 1942, he transformed the Office of Facts and Figures into the Office of Wartime Information (OWI), and replaced MacLeish with Elmer Davis a popular journalist and radio broadcaster. Davis was adept at promoting public information favorable and countering public information unfavorable to the United States and its war effort to keep morale high among Americans.

Mobilizing the economy for war required a partnership between government and businesses, whereby the former organized and subsidized the latter. As War Secretary Stimson explained: "If you are going to try to go to war, or to prepare for war in a capitalist country, you have got to let business make money out of the process or business won't work."[6]

In the White House, Roosevelt presided over and tried to coordinate mobilization through the Office of Emergency Management and the National Defense Advisory Commission, each led by teams of businessmen and bureaucrats. The Office of Production Management was co-chaired by William Knudsen and Sidney Hillman, the respective presidents of General Motors' president and the CIO affiliate, Amalgamated Clothing Workers of America. The Supply Priorities and Allocation Board dated to 1939, when assistant war secretary Louis Johnson convinced Roosevelt to create it to prepare plans for mobilizing America's economy and population if it went to war. Roosevelt combined it with the Office of Production Management to make the War Production Board, and named Donald Nelson, a Sears Roebuck board member, its chief on January 13, 1942.

As Washington mobilized the economy for war, Americans faced shortages of ever more products that they relied on. The War Production Board tried to alleviate shortages of war goods and soaring prices with rationing. The Office of Price Administration (OPA) oversaw the ration system through 5,500 ration boards. Each household received a monthly ration book of coupons to be redeemed at stores. Automobiles received an A, B, or C sticker, with A's allowed only three weekly gallons, B's eight gallons, and C's unlimited gallons for doctors and others who provided vital services. Only a few people like doctors were allowed to buy new cars. Virtually everyone was stuck with their existing car for the war's duration with a limited weekly strictly rationed gasoline and no available new tires. To save material, the War Production Board devised a "victory suit" for men that included narrow lapels and cuffless trousers, and pleatless skirts and two-piece bathing suits for women to save material better used for military uniforms. Washington encouraged Americans to nurture "victory gardens" with vegetables for the family table, thus reducing the demand and thus prices.

Washington launched a series of recycling drives to collect critical materials like steel, aluminum, and, especially, rubber. Japan's capture of Southeast Asia's rubber plantation caused a worsening shortage in the United States. Washington forbade the production of new cars and tires along with gasoline were strictly rationed. To alleviate the shortage, Roosevelt called on June 12, 1942, for Americans to contribute "old tires, old caps, gloves – whatever you have that is made of rubber" for a penny a pound to service stations, and the government bought that rubber for $25 a ton. By that program, the government collected 450,000 tons of scrap rubber in just a month.[7]

The most important way Washington alleviated shortages was underwriting production costs for industries. For instance, the War Production Board subsidized the synthetic rubber industry by investing $700 million to build fifty-five factories then leased them to rubber companies. By 1944, synthetic rubber production surpassed one million tons and accounted for 87 percent of all rubber. The War Production Board oversaw and underwrote the construction of a twenty-four inch diameter, 1,250 mile long pipeline from the oil fields of Texas to a refinery complex in New Jersey that pumped 335,000 barrels daily.[8]

When the War Production Board's performance fell short of Roosevelt's expectations, typically he did not fire Nelson or reorganize the bureaucracy but created a new rival organization, the Office of War Mobilization with its director James Byrnes, a supreme court justice. To diminish supply bottlenecks, Roosevelt established the Controlled Material Plan (CMP) with Ferdinand Eberstadt the supply traffic cop. Eberstadt sorted out and allocated critical supplies, especially steel, copper, and aluminum. The Board of Economic Warfare, headed by Vice President Wallace, was charged with securing vital national resources from overseas and refining them in American factories.

The soaring demand for a seemingly endless array of raw materials and refined products caused prices to soar. Roosevelt got Congress to pass the Emergency Price Control Bill that he signed on January 30, 1942. The law empowered the Office of Price Administration (OPA), directed by Leon Henderson, to impose price ceilings on products and rented properties, and to prosecute those who committed "profiteering, hoarding, manipulation, speculation, and other disruptive practices" with heavy fines and prison terms.

A serious obstacle to expanding war production was limited housing for rising numbers of workers. Roosevelt worked with Congress to devise and pass two laws, the 1940 National Defense Housing (Lanham) Act and 1941 Defense Public Works Act, along with establishment of the War Public Works agency to build housing and the Work Public Services agency to provide child care. For housing, the federal government spent $351 million and local governments $106 million. There were 3,102 child care centers that babysat, fed, and often educated over 130,000 young children. In February 1942, Roosevelt established the National Housing Agency that eventually spent $2.5 billion to build, renovate, or subsidize housing. The Office of Price Administration imposed rent controls and lowered rents for 86 million tenants.[9]

Manpower was also increasingly scare as demand by the military and industry skyrocketed and competed with each other. Unemployment fell from 14.6 percent in 1940 to 1.2 percent in 1944, the lowest rate in

American history. In October 1942, Paul McNutt, the War Manpower Commission's chief, asked Roosevelt to combine the Selective Service and Employment Service in his organization so that he could coordinate the supply and demand for military and civilian labor. Roosevelt did so by executive order on December 5.

Roosevelt established the National Defense Mediation Board in March 1941, to settle disputes between workers and managers. That Board proved incapable of keeping peace in some key mines and industries. In January 1942, Roosevelt transformed it into the War Labor Board, headed by William Davis, an acclaimed lawyer who specialized in labor issues. Yet, that new bureaucracy was no more effective than its predecessor. Union membership during the war increased by half from 10,500,000 in 1941 to 14,750,000 in 1945.[10]

The various bureaucracies naturally aided corporations with the most manufacturing and labor power. The one hundred largest corporations won 30 percent of government contracts in 1940 and 70 percent in March 1943. Fifty-six corporations won 75 percent of government military contracts.[11] Small business owners complained that they could not compete and faced bankruptcy from huge corporations with their subsidiaries and supply priorities. To alleviate that, Congress passed and the president signed the Small Business Act on May 26, 1942; the votes were 82 to 0 in the Senate and 244 to 0 in the House. The Act established the Smaller War Plants Corporation with $150 million to identify suppliers and help them transform their production for war goods. At best the program slowed the steady concentration of manufacturing.

Among the reasons why production soared and concentrated was Roosevelt's suspension of all anti-trust investigations on March 28, 1942. The document that Roosevelt approved explained: "In the present all-out effort to produce quickly and uninterruptedly a maximum amount of weapons of warfare...court investigations, suits, and prosecutions unavoidably consume the time of executives and employees... engaged in war work...contrary to the national interest and security... The deferment...shall not mean...the exoneration of the individual or corporation."[12]

The Defense Plants Corporation, led by Jesse Jones, was the most effective board. During the war, it contributed two-thirds of a business's investment plan to improve production. That amounted to $15 billion in public money to $11 billion in private money or $26 billion total investments that modernized America's industries.[13]

American military production was astonishing. From 1941 to 1945, factories manufactured 5,475 cargo ships, 87,620 warships, 107,351 tanks, 324,000 aircraft, 2.4 million trucks, 20 million rifles, and 44 billion ammunition rounds; many ended up in the hands of allies through Lend-Lease. Productivity steadily swelled. Ford's Willow Run complex produced a B-24 every 63 minutes and 8,685 aircraft. Boeing Plant 2 alone manufactured 6,981 B-17 bombers while Douglas and Lockheed produced another 5,745 B-17s.[14] From 1940 to 1945, the navy expanded from 1,099 vessels to 50,759 and personnel from 160,997 to 3,383,196; new warships included ten battleships, 92 aircraft carriers, 35 cruisers, 148 destroyers, 140 submarines, and 43,255 landing craft.[15]

The United States and its allies suffered an increasingly severe shortage of merchant ships as enemy submarines torpedoed them faster than new ones were launched. No one was more vital in overcoming that crisis than shipbuilder Henry Kaiser. Much as Henry Ford did for the automobile industry, Kaiser organized a standard simple design and production process for what were called Liberty Ships that steadily reduced construction times from 355 days in 1940 to 60 days in 1942. A Liberty Ship could carry as much as 440 light tanks, 2,840 jeeps, or three million C-rations.[16] Kaiser eventually had ten shipyards, with eight on the west coast, producing Liberty Ships and other warships.

Within the country, most military personnel, equipment, and supplies rode the rails. By one count: "American railroads furnished 97 percent of all domestic troop movements and about 90 percent of all domestic movements of Army and Navy equipment supplies. In the forty-five months of war, 113,891 special troop trains moved 43,700,000 members of the armed forces, or an average of nearly a million men a month."[17]

The Americans swiftly developed an array of increasingly sophisticated weapons, although some types emphasized reliable quantity rather than superiority over enemy versions. Tanks improved to a point, first light Stuarts with a 37-millimeter cannon, then medium Lees (known as Grants with a British style turret) with a 51-millimeter cannon, and, finally, Shermans with a short 75-millimeter cannon. The Sherman was comparable to Germany's Mark IV but inferior in firepower and armor to the Mark-V Panther with its long 75-millimeter and Mark VI Tiger with its 88-millimeter cannons. In battles, the American tactic was for a tank column to spread out and try to outflank the German tanks for shots into their more vulnerable sides and rear. Standard field artillery included 105-millimeter and 155-millimeter cannons.

As for aircraft, ground based fighters began with P-40s, then twin-engineered P-38s, fighter-bomber P-47 Thunderbolts, and finally P-51 Mustangs, the war's best fighter plane for speed, maneuverability, range with a belly-tank, and deadliness. Carrier fighter planes evolved from the F4F Wildcat to the superior F6F Hellcat. With three times more training hours and eventually better planes, American pilots were superior to enemy pilots. The Americans shot down three German planes for every one among them that was downed.[18] The worst warplane was the slow, easily shot down Douglas Devastator TBD torpedo plane that scored no hits during the battle of Midway; the military withdrew it from service. In contrast, the Dauntless SBD dive bombers with their thousand-pound bombs sank four carriers at Midway and remained in service. Heavy bombers included first B-17 Flying Fortresses, then B-24 Liberators, and finally B-29 Superfortresses with respective bomb loads of 4,800, 8,000, and 20,000 pounds. The Norden gyro bombsight was the world's most sophisticated device for hitting a target from as much as five miles above. The C-47 was an excellent transport plane for troops, paratroopers, or supplies.

As for warships, the war's most powerful was America's Essex class of seventeen aircraft carriers with each displacing 27,100 tons, holding a hundred aircraft, and cruising as fast as 35 knots. Altogether the Americans commissioned around 150 large fleet, smaller light, and smallest escort carriers during the war. The four Iowa class battleships exceeded all others in speed and firepower. American naval superiority became so overwhelming that, according to historian Victor Hansen, the United States "never lost a battleship after Pearl Harbor or a fleet carrier after 1942."[19]

American Tambor class submarines were first-rate; they displaced 1,500 tons, could cruise 10,000 miles, steamed twenty-one knots on the surface, and dove to periscope depth in thirty-five seconds. Their only weakness were the Mark-14 torpedoes that fired too low and mostly shot beneath targets and were often duds if they did hit something. Engineers did not correct those defects until 1943. While losing 53 vessels, American submarines sank 1,314 Japanese vessels with 5.3 million total tons; although the submarine force was only 2 percent of the navy it inflicted 55 percent of the sinkings of Japanese.[20]

Transport vessels were vital to victory. American shipyards launched over 2,700 Liberty ships and 500 larger Victory ships. As for vessels that conveyed invading troops to beaches, Landing Craft, Assault (LCA) vessels led the way. They were 41 feet long, 10 feet wide, and chugged around seven miles per hour with a maximum load of 36 troops. The hinged front dropped and troops dashed out into the shallow water. Once troops secured a landing, shallow draft Landing Ship, Tank (LST) vessels followed. They were 328 feet long and 50 feet wide with a bow that opened like a sideways mouth from which vehicles and troops disgorged onto a wharf or beach.

The tooth to tail ratio for America's military was long. Ground combat troops numbered only 16 percent of the 12.2 million men in uniform while 40 percent were in the rear mostly in the supply chain.[21] The army peaked at 8,276,958 troops in 1944.[22] The standard American rifle for soldiers and marines was the 30.06 caliber M-1 Garand with an eight bullet clip. A platoon usually had one or more of its strongest men carrying a M1918 Browning Automatic Rifle (BAR) with an eighteen bullet clip. Although troops shouldered packs that could weigh as much as sixty pounds, those in Europe got plenty of lifts; every infantry division was mechanized with 1,400 vehicles. Tactically the Americans were superior to Japanese by killing ten for every one of them killed, but inferior to Germans by losing a man and a half to every one they killed. One of ten soldiers suffered "combat fatigue, today called "post-traumatic stress disorder" (PTSD). Although thousands of men deserted or were absent without leave, only one was executed for that crime.[23]

As if fighting a world war was not burdensome enough for Roosevelt and his fellow Americans, a series of labor strikes plagued the nation during the summer of 1942. John Lewis, the United Mine Workers (UMW) chief, violated a national "no-strike" understanding for the war's duration when he led 400,000 miners to shut down production until they received two dollars a day, double-pay on Sundays, and pay from the time they reached the property until the time they left rather than their remote sites deep in the mine itself. That threatened to grind to a halt factories, trains, cities, and homes that depended on coal for fuel. The resulting production and transportation cutbacks as supplies dwindled damaged the economy and war effort. That inspired wildcat strikes by workers at other industries with the worst at Detroit's automobile plants that had been converted to making war weapons and equipment.

The War Labor Board failed to resolve the strikes. Roosevelt called on Lewis and other strike leaders to return to work. He explained that "every American coal miner who has stopping mining coal...directly and individually is obstructing our war effort...We will win this war only as we produce and deliver our total American effort on the high seas and on battle fronts. And that requires unrelenting, uninterrupted effort here on the home front...Therefore I say to all miners...the production of coal will not be stopped."[24]

When the strikes persisted, Congress responded with the Smith-Connally or War Labor Disputes Act that empowered the federal government to seize and run factories, mines, railroads, and other industries when workers went on strike. That bill passed the Senate by 65 to 16 on May 5 and the House by 233 to 141 on June 4. Roosevelt vetoed that bill on June 25, with this justification: "Let there be no misunderstanding of the reasons which prompt me to veto this bill at this time. I am unalterably opposed to strikes in wartime. I do not hesitate to use the powers of government to prevent them." But, for the first half of 1942, "99.95 percent of the work went forward without strikes and that only 5 one-hundredths of 1 percent of the work was delayed by strikes. That record was has never been equaled in this country."[25] So he rejected the bill both as a reward to most unions and workers for their cooperation and to prevent the federal government from expanding powers that might provoke strikes, violence, and economic disruptions. That argument did not prevent angry members of Congress from overriding his veto that same day by 56 to 25 in the Senate and 244 to 108 in the House.

Interior Secretary Harold Ickes negotiated a compromise between the union and the mine owners. Miners received a dollar fifty cent daily wage hike and work days would include 45 minutes arrival at and departure from the mine entrance rather than underground at their remote work sites.

A key question was how the Japanese got away with their Pearl Harbor attack. Roosevelt signed on December 18, 1941, an executive order establishing a special investigative commission for Pearl Harbor that included Supreme Court Chief Justice Owen Roberts, Generals Frank McCoy and Joseph McNarney, and Admirals Joseph Reeves and William Standby. The Roberts Commission issued a report on January 23, that accused Hawaii's Admiral Husband Kimmel and General Walter Short of "dereliction of duty." The Roberts Commission did not investigate General Douglas MacArthur who was just as inept in defending the Philippines. A joint congressional committee that reexamined the Pearl Harbor disaster in 1945 and 1946 with much for information available accused Kimmel and Short of "errors of judgment." In all, there were eight Pearl Harbor investigations that accumulated fifteen thousand pages of testimonies and reports.

Conspiracy theorists claim that Roosevelt knew about the pending attack but cynically chose not to inform Stark and Kimmel so that the resulting catastrophe would shock Congress into overwhelming support for war against Japan.[26] The facts decisively refute that notion. Washington's first warning about an imminent attack somewhere in the Pacific to Kimmel and Short at Honolulu along with MacArthur at Manila was on November 24 followed by a more detailed warning three days later. The warning did not specify attacks on Hawaii and the Philippines because military intelligence had no information about that. None of the 239 decoded diplomatic messages from Tokyo to the Washington embassy in the half year before the attack mentioned Pearl Harbor. The army-navy intelligence board had cracked the diplomatic code but not the military code.

Two authors, Roberta Wohlstetter John Costello, separately examined the information available to military intelligence at the time and reached the same conclusion. Amidst the scree, military intelligence overlooked some key information nuggets that might have identified Pearl Harbor for attack, but by mistake rather than design.[27] In the intelligence bureaucratic pyramid, each section at the lowest level gathers and assesses available information then sends that report to the next level, which makes one report from those it receives, then sends that report to the next level. Each section and level involves choices of what is important and how it fits together. Some trimmings did not appear important at the time but in hindsight were vital. Beyond that, the volume of intercepts overwhelmed the number of decriptors, and they piled up unread. Another problem was Admiral Raymond Turner, the martinet and micromanager in charge of war plans; Turner did not understand the intelligence yet often interfered in the analytical process, delaying, diverting, and warping it.

As usual, ironies abounded. Admiral Chester Nimitz acknowledged that: "If we had been warned, our fleet would have gone out to sea, and...all our ships would have been destroyed...in deep water... We would have lost the entire Pacific Fleet and eighteen to nineteen thousand men, instead of the ships and 3,300 men we did lose."[28]

A great fear was subversion within the United States. Roosevelt first explained that threat in a speech on May 26, 1940: "We know the new methods...The Trojan Horse. The Fifth Column that betrays a nation unprepared for treachery. Spies, saboteurs, and traitors are the actors in this new strategy...But there is an added technique for weakening a nation at its very roots...It is first, a dissemination of discord... [by] a group that may be sectional or racial or political...to exploit its prejudices through false slogans and emotional appeals. The aim is...to create confusion...political paralysis and eventually a state of panic... The unity of the state can be so sapped that its strength is destroyed."[29]

When America went to war in December 1941, over 5 million foreigners had complied with the 1940 Foreign Registration Act to register with the federal government by filling out a form and submitting a photograph and fingerprints. The federal government designated 315,000 German, 895,000 Italian, and 92,000 Japanese residents as enemy aliens who were forbidden from designated military zones or possessing firearms, cameras, shortwave radios, secret codes, and other sabotage or espionage equipment, and were subject to deportation or internment.

Roosevelt issued an executive order on December 8, 1941, the day after Pearl Harbor, that designated all German, Italian, and Japanese non-citizens as enemy aliens. Within seventy-two hours, Attorney General Francis Biddle had arrested 2,303 suspected spies and saboteurs, including 1,291 Japanese, 857 Germans, and 147 Italians. Eventually, Washington interned 11,000 German, 11,600 Italian, and 119,000 Japanese foreign residents and American citizens. Most Germans were interned at Fort Lincoln, North Dakota, most Italians at Florence, Alabama, and the Japanese among ten remote "relocation centers" in seven western states for most of the war. [30]

For Japanese American internees, the crucial act was Roosevelt's issuance on February 19, 1942, of Executive Order 9066 that authorized the army to "prescribe military areas...from which any and all persons may be excluded." That vague statement did not mention Japanese Americans or any other group. General John De Witt commanded the West Coast region that included California, Oregon, Washington, and part of Arizona. He used that order as the excuse first to give Japanese Americans living there the deadline of March 27 to leave or else be interned. War Secretary Stimson asked Congress to authorize that internment with a law. On March 21, Congress passed a bill empowering the War Department to remove Japanese Americans from the West Coast and established the War Relocation Authority to implement that. Roosevelt named Milton Eisenhower, the general's brother, the War Relocation Authority's director.

The decision to intern all remaining West Coast Japanese Americans emerged from ever more prominent voices that demanded it. The Robison Commission that investigated the Pearl Harbor disaster claimed without citing any evidence let alone arrests that Japanese Americans had aided the attack. California Governor Culbert Olsen, Attorney General Earl Warren, and the state's delegation in Congress demanded internment. General De Witt, the West Coast commander, called on Roosevelt to intern all Japanese American, claiming they posed a danger of espionage and sabotage. When confronted with the fact that no Japanese Americans had been caught committing either crime, De Witt bizarrely replied, "the very fact that no sabotage has taken place is a disturbing and confirming indication that such action will be taken." He also insisted that: "A Jap is a Jap...It makes no difference whether he is a citizen or not...I don't want any of them... There is no way to determine their loyalty."[31]

Mingled fear, greed, jealously, vengeance, and racism motivated advocates. Many people genuinely worried that many among 120,000 Japanese American secretly worked for Tokyo as spies and saboteurs that aided the Pearl Harbor attack and prepared for a future Japanese invasion. Industrious Japanese Americans had developed $400 million worth of flourishing businesses, farms, and homes that jealous, avarious rivals hoped to acquire if they were confiscated. Japanese Americans were astonishingly productive; although they owned only 1 percent of California's farm land they produced 40 percent of the crops. Japanese Americans were an immediate easy target for vengeance and a different and despised race for white Americans.[32]

The internment process began on March 27. The order permitted each Japanese American to take only one suitcase of things to the camp. That forced Japanese Americans to sell their property at fractions of its worth. They made the most of their internment by establishing businesses, hobby clubs, sports teams, garden plots, and schools. When the roundup ended on August 7, 1942, 119,803 Japanese Americans were interned among ten camps. There most stayed until the order was lifted in January 1945, and they could leave. Around 12,000 young men escaped the camps by joining special military units. Another 17,000 mostly young people left to attend schools. Twenty-eight percent refused to swear allegiance to the United States; many of them protested and rioted, and eventually 18,500 dissidents were interned at the Tule Lake camp. Internees included 33,000 first generation Japanese immigrants (issei) without citizenship, and 79,000 second (nisei) and 7,000 third (sansei) generation who were born in America and so were citizens. Under international law, a nation can intern enemy foreign nationals but not its own citizens. Three wartime Supreme Court rulings split on the internment's constitutionality, with *Hirabayashi versus United States* (1943) and *Korematsu versus United States* (1944) upholding and *Ex Parte Endo* (1944) denying that citizens could be interned without due process.

Japanese-Americans won extraordinary combat laurels when Nisei were allowed to fight. Over 12,000 Japanese Americans volunteered and over 10,000 served in the 442nd Regiment, a segregated unit. The 442nd "Go For Broke" Regiment fought in Italy, southern France, the Rhineland, and southern Germany. Along the way, the troops earned 18,143 medals including 21 Medals of Honor and seven Presidential Unit Citations while suffering 9,486 casualties.[33]

The internment of German, Italian, and Japanese foreign residents and Americans was not the first violation of civil rights for American citizens and residents. During World War I, Congress passed the Espionage Act of 1917 that empowered President Wilson to order German-Americans to register at local police stations and post offices. Of 482,000 who registered, the government interned 4,000 German Americans feared to be security risks. The 1918 Alien Act empowered the federal government to deport foreign anarchists, communist, and other dangerous subversives. The 1918 Sedition Act outlawed anyone who advocated treason or denounced the war effort, armed forces, or federal government.[34]

Roosevelt officially rescinded the internment order on January 20, 1945, freeing the remaining residents to leave the camps. By that time, one-third had already departed, either by joining the military or moving east to states without restricted military zones. In all, the interned Japanese Americans lost over $400 million worth of wealth and endured horrific emotional suffering.

The Germans had a spy and sabotage network in American and at times infiltrated agents by submarine at deserted beaches. In June 1942, two four-man teams landed, one near Amagansett on Long Island, New York, and the other at Ponte Vedra, Florida. Authorities eventually caught both teams with their explosives and timing devices. Roosevelt ordered them tried by a military commission, which found them guilty, with six sentenced to death, one to life, and the other to thirty years in prison. That well-publicized swift apprehension and elimination of the saboteurs intimidated other spies and saboteurs.

Sedition or overthrowing America's political system was a fear during World War II and the Cold War that followed. In July 1942, Attorney General Francis Biddle had twenty-nine members of the Socialist Workers Party arrested and charged with violating the 1917 Espionage Act, 1940 Smith Act, and other laws against sedition. In the jury trial, five received acquittals, eleven one year, and twelve sixteen month sentences, while one committed suicide. The 1939 Hatch Act made it illegal for federal officials to use their offices for political purposes or belonging to a group that advocated sedition like the Communist Party, Socialist Workers Pary, Silver Shirt League, and German-American Bund. The Civil Service Commission investigated 273,500 people and found 1,180 guilty of violating the Hatch Act and they were either fired or not hired.[35]

The Soviets developed an extensive spy network in the United States, mostly among Communist Party members or sympathizers.[36]

One of their best placed agents within the Roosevelt administration was Harry Dexter White, the assistant treasury secretary. White met with Ambassador Andrei Gromyko at the Soviet embassy and several times with his NKVD handler in various places in Washington or driving around in an automobile, and with American communist agent Whitaker Chambers. White influenced American policy in Moscow's power by convincing his boss, Treasury Secretary Morgenthau, to increase aid to Stalin's regime; providing copies of the currency printing plate for postwar Germany so the Soviets could make their own version; cutting aid to Chiang Kai-shek's National Party regime headquartered at Chungking, China, thus strengthening the Chinese Communist Party; and putting communist sympathizers in important Treasury Department positions. White also enthusiastically backed Morgenthau's plan to deindustrialize and breakup Germany; the communists would greatly benefit from the resulting chaos, poverty, and despair.[37] Another was Alger Hiss, who in 1944 became director of the State Department's Office of Political Affairs and executive secretary for the Dumbarton Oaks Conference that designed the United Nations, then was part of Roosevelt's entourage to the Yalta summit in February 1945. A possible agent was Harry Hopkins, Roosevelt's closest advisor during the war. Roosevelt sent Hopkins on several diplomatic missions to Moscow during which he had long talks with Stalin and other key officials. In Washington, he spent time with NKVD officer Iskhak Akhmerov who recruited and handled Hiss. Hopkins was outspoken in backing appeasement for Soviet advances in eastern Europe and Germany.[38]

Countless people within and beyond the United States grimly noted the irony that Roosevelt repeatedly called for a democratic crusade against the fascist powers when racism permeated America. The mass internment of Japanese-American citizens was the most blatant violation of a group's constitutional rights. Blacks suffered varying restrictions on jobs, schools, and housing across the nation, and across the southern states "Jim Crow" laws imposed segregation for restaurants, hotels, public transportation, restrooms, recreation facilities, and even drinking fountains. Racism was worst in the South where state and local governments imposed laws that limited the rights by blacks to vote and run for office.

The Supreme Court in *Smith versus Allwright* (1944) struck down one especially egregious law that prevented blacks from voting in the Texas Democratic Party's primary. That reversed the decision of *Grovey versus Townsend* (1935) that the Democratic Party could legally bar blacks from its primary because it was a private organization. The 1944 ruling encouraged black voter registrations to rise steadily in Texas and elsewhere.

Of the services, the marines and air force barred blacks from serving, the army segregated blacks in their own units with white officers, and the navy mostly confined blacks to kitchen duties and sanitation. In 1940, blacks numbered only 4,700 of the army's 270,000 troops and only 4,000 of the navy's 161,000 sailors. On army and navy bases alike, blacks were restricted to a few seats in theaters or on transport when whites were present. Blacks at southern bases faced even worse restrictions when they tried to visit, shop, eat, or drink in nearby towns.

The military justified its policy with official studies. The Army War College's 1925 "Report on Negro Manpower" presented findings highly critical of black soldiers and people: "the American negro has not progressed as far as other sub species of the human family...The cranial cavity of the negro is smaller than white...The psychology of the negro, based on heredity derived from mediocre African ancestors, cultivated by generations of slavery, is one from which we cannot expect to draw leadership...In general the negro is jolly, docile, tractable, and lively but with harsh or unkind treatment can become stubborn, sullen, and unruly. In physical courage, he falls well back of whites...Negro troops are efficient and dependable only so long as led by capable white officers."[39]

During the war, the NAACP led by Walter White and the Committee on Racial Equality (CORE), founded in March 1942 and led by James Farmer, lobbied Washington to end discrimination against blacks in the armed forces. After learning of these inequities and injustices, Eleanor did what she could to end them. First, she implored her husband to issue an executive order that abolished military racial discrimination and provided equal benefits and opportunities for promotion. She wrote a series of letters calling for reforms to War Secretary Stimson and Army Chief Marshall.

That campaign of Eleanor and other influential black and white spokespeople eventually won some limited victories. On March 10, 1943, the War Department issued a directive that banned racial discrimination at base shops (post exchanges), theaters, officer clubs, and other facilities. The army and navy opened more job categories to blacks. Yet most blacks remained behind the lines as stevedores, truck drivers, cooks, and garbage haulers.

Despite the persistent discrimination, black ranks in the army soared from 5,000 to 920,000, and the number of officers from five to 7,000, while what they did expanded from support to combat. When the war began, they were mostly restricted to cooking, cleaning, hauling, and digging; before the war ended, they fought on land, sea, and in the air. In Europe, blacks numbered half the troops in transportation units hauling supplies and men, and twenty-two combat units.

One black combat unit earned accolades for its fighting abilities. The army's 99th Pursuit Squadron was known as the Tuskegee Airmen because it was based at Tuskegee, Alabama. In 1944, the army deployed the Tuskegee Airmen in Italy. Lieutenant Colonel Benjamin Davis was the 99th's brilliant commander. He was West Point's fourth black graduate, enduring four years of isolation by his fellow cadets. He graduated 35th of 275 cadets then underwent advanced infantry and eventually fighter plane training. In 1943, the 99th was first deployed at Tunis in time to provide air cover for the allied invasion of Sicily in July then Italy in September. They flew P-40 Warhawks, then P-47 Thunderbolts, and finally P-51 Mustangs mostly escorting bombers to distant targets. The Tuskegee Airmen received three Distinguished Unit Citations, flew 1,578 missions, shot down 112 enemy craft, destroyed or damaged 273 enemy planes on the ground, suffered 63 planes shot down by the enemy, and never lost a bomber to enemy gunfire. Davis flew 67 missions and won a Silver Star.[40]

Racial tensions between whites and blacks over jobs, housing, and parks erupted into fights and riots in 1943. The worst came in June at Detroit where twenty-five blacks and nine whites died and 433 were injured, while rioters looted and burned scores of businesses. Roosevelt authorized the dispatch of 3,800 troops to restore order. Riots in New York City's mostly black Harlem district in August resulted in six dead and 400 wounded.[41] There were other race riots at Beaumont, Texas, Greenville, Pennsylvania, Mobile, Alabama, Indianapolis and Indiana.

Riots and fights erupted between Anglos and Hispanics in Los Angeles in May and June 1943. Many Mexican American youth joined gangs that fought each other for "turf," and dressed in "zoot suits," or baggy pants and jackets. At a night club near the Chavez Ravine military base, some zoot suiters beat two sailors who made passes at some Hispanic girls. Over the following weeks gangs of sailors and soldiers battled gangs of zoot suiters. The police eventually restored order with mass arrests of mostly zoot suiters.

As they had in World War I, women made economic gains during World War II by filling many jobs vacated by men who joined the military. At the peak in 1944, women were one of three civilian workers or 19 million, with 5 million newly employed. Of them, three of four were married and six of ten were over thirty-five years old, and one of three had children under fourteen years old. The poster called "Rosie the Riveter" exemplified those women.[42] Rosie was a confident young women dressed in work clothes with her arm raised with a clenched fist and saying, "We can do it!"

Eleanor recognized the difficulties that working women faced for shopping, cleaning their homes, cooking for their families, and caring for their children. She proposed a list of reforms to alleviate those challenges including "staggering the opening and closing times of factories, keeping bank and department stores open at night, encouraging butchers to hold back part of their meat supply until 6 p.m., asking war plants to hire personal shoppers for the women, to take the orders in the morning and have the filled grocery bags waiting at the door at the end of the shift."[43] Above all, Eleanor recognized child care as the greatest need. Neither her husband nor anyone in Congress sponsored a bill to realize those ideas. Instead, it was up to families and businesses to do what they could. Many corporations with large female work forces did provide day care. By 1945, programs cared for a million and a half children while their mothers worked.[44]

Then there were the women who served in uniform. Eventually around 350,000 women joined auxiliary groups for the army and navy, the respective Women's Army Corps (WACs) and Women Accepted for Voluntary Emergency Service (WAVES). They performed vital rear echelon tasks that freed more men to fight at the front.

A sex scandal occurred that the press did not investigate let alone report. State Department Secretary Cordell Hull and undersecretary Sumner Welles bickered over policy and protocol. Roosevelt liked and depended on both men to carry out missions. Hull got the upper hand over Welles when FBI director J. Edgar Hoover shared a secret report with him that Welles was a closet homosexual who had solicited a Pullman Car railroad porter for sex. Hull revealed that to Roosevelt on July 16, 1943. Roosevelt got Welles to resign on September 30. He was so disgusted by both Welles' sexual deviance and Hull's political deviance that he relegated the State Department to a secondary role in the war's diplomacy. Hull never again attended a summit between Roosevelt and Churchill. Roosevelt replaced Welles with Edward Stettinius, who had been an executive for General Motors then U.S. Steel before accepting a top post with the Lend Lease Agency and then became undersecretary of state.

Other key positions opened. A heart attack killed Navy Secretary Frank Knox on April 28, 1944. Roosevelt replaced him with James

Forrestal, a Wall Street financier who had served as the navy undersecretary since August 22, 1940. Ill health forced Hull to resign on November 27, 1944. Roosevelt replaced him with Stettinius.

Despite the patriotic support of most American for the war, the Democratic grip on Congress weakened sharply in the 1942 midterm election. In the House, Democratic seats fell 45 to 222 while Republicans soared by 47 to 209, while the Progressive Party, Farmer-Labor Party, and American Labor Party won respectively two, one, and one seats. In the Senate, Democrats lost eight seats to retain 57 while Republicans won nine seats to hold 38; a Progressive Party and an independent each held a seat.

Roosevelt increasingly thought of postwar America and whether prosperity or poverty would prevail. To help forestall another economic collapse, he called for an economic bill of rights during his State of the Union address on January 11, 1944. After celebrating the tremendous progress that America and its allies had made against the Axis powers, he asserted that: "It is our duty now to begin to lay plans...for the winning of lasting peace...We cannot be content, no matter how high the general standard of our living may be, if some fraction of our people... is ill-fed, ill-housed, and insecure...This Republic had at its beginning under the protection of certain inalienable political rights...As our nation has grown in size and...our industrial economy expanded... these political rights proved inadequate to assure us equality in the pursuit of happiness...[T]rue individual freedom cannot exist without economic security and independence. Necessitous men are not free men. People who are hungry and out of a job are the stuff of which dictatorships are made."[45]

He was especially concerned that home-coming veterans "must not be demobilized into an environment of inflation and unemployment, to a place in a bread line, or on a corner selling apples." To prevent that, Roosevelt conceived what became the General Infantry (G.I.) Bill of Rights whereby the federal government paid for college or vocational training for veterans for up to four years. In calling for Congress to enact such a bill, he argued that: "Lack of money should not prevent any veteran of this war from equipping himself for the most useful employment for which his aptitudes and willingness qualify him...I believe the Nation is morally obligated to provide this training and education and the necessary financial assistance by which they can be secured."[46]

The Senate and House voted unanimously for the G.I. Bill of Rights and Roosevelt signed it into law on June 22, 1944. The G.I. Bill guaranteed every veteran a loan of up to $2,000; provided those unable to find work with $20 a week for fifty-two weeks; and provided those who enrolled in college up to $500 in annual tuition and $75 a month for living expenses.

Nineteen-forty-four was a presidential election year.[47] Roosevelt had played coy in 1940 when asked if he would run for re-election, saying he would leave that question to the delegates at the Democratic Party convention. For the 1944 election, he replied that he would accept the nomination because he had "as little right to withdraw as the soldier has to leave his post in the line. All that is within me cries out to go back to my home on the Hudson River, but the future existence of the nation and the future existence of our chosen form of government are at stake."[48]

The Democrats held their convention at Chicago from July 19 to 21. Roosevelt won on the first ballot with 1,089 votes to 89 for Senator Harry Byrd of Virginia and one for James Farley, Roosevelt's former campaign manager and postmaster general. Roosevelt agreed to pressure by Democratic Party chair Robert Hannegan and other insiders to dump his controversial leftist vice president Henry Wallace and instead take as his running mate Senator Harry Truman of Missouri, an honest, hardworking, loyal pragmatist. Truman won the nomination on the first ballot with 626 votes to Wallace's 329 votes.[49]

The Republican Party convened three weeks earlier at Chicago from June 26 to 28. New York Governor Thomas Dewey won the nomination on the first ballot with 1,056 to one votes. Ohio Governor John Bricker became his running mate with 1,057 votes to two.

Roosevelt decisively won his fourth presidential election with 25,612,916 or 53.4 percent and 432 Electoral College votes to Dewey's 22,017,929 or 45.9 percent and 99. In the House, Democrats gained 22 seats to hold 244 while Republicans lost 29 to retain 189 while the Farmer-Labor Party, American Labor Party, and Progressive Party won respectively two, one, and one seats. In the Senate, the Democrats lost a seat to retain 57 while the Republicans one to rise to 38 and the Progressive Party senator kept his seat.

Roosevelt and his supporters rejoiced in his victory. Now he could devote himself solely to doing what must be done to win the global war.

Chapter 10

THE CONQUESTS

"There is going to be a race for Berlin and the United States should
have Berlin." (Franklin Roosevelt)

Prime Minister Winston Churchill arrived at the White House on
May 11, 1943, for another prolonged sojourn. When he left for home
on May 27, he did not go home empty-handed. President Franklin
Roosevelt agreed to a partnership with Britain on the nuclear bomb
project. Yet Churchill was deeply disappointed. He had an overriding
goal that Roosevelt and his military advisors rejected, invading the
Italian peninsula after capturing Sicily. Churchill explained that: "He
is not in favor of landing in Italy. It is most discouraging. I only crossed
the Atlantic for this purpose. I cannot let the matter rest where it is."[1]

Army Chief of Staff George Marshall and General Dwight Eisenhower
had reluctantly agreed to invading Sicily and adamantly opposed
invading the Italian peninsula as a diversion from an invasion of
northern France and drive east toward Berlin. For such a brilliant man
to advocate such an absurd strategy is among Churchill's paradoxes.
The mostly flat lands of northern France, the Low Countries, and
Germany are perfect tank country for rapid advances while most of the
northern Mediterranean is mountainous and so easily defended. The
allied invasion of mountainous Italy became a debacle. Yet Churchill
clung to his belief that his Mediterranean strategy was the best way
to defeat Germany. He was haunted by the hundreds of thousands
of Britons killed and maimed during four years of trench warfare a
generation before, and feared that any invasion of France would lead
to another blood-soaked stalemate. Instead, he continually pressured
Roosevelt to commit to attacking Europe's "soft underbelly" in
the Mediterranean.

That was not the only issue that split the allies. Britain's empire clearly was crumbling as ever more colonials yearned to govern themselves. After Singapore's surrender, 40,000 of the 45,000 captured Indian troops turned coats to join the Indian National Army that Tokyo established.[2] Roosevelt urged Churchill to rally Indian loyalty by giving them and other colonies home rule now with the promise of postwar independence. Churchill angrily rejected that notion.

The third prolonged summit between Roosevelt and Churchill began at the president's Hyde Park estate from August 12 to 14, moved to Quebec from August 17 to 24, shifted to the White House from September 1 to 6 and September 7 to 10, then ended at Hyde Park from September 11 and 12. The big decisions were for an American to lead the campaign in France, for Lord Louis Mountbatten to command the southeast Asian front, and how to manage the Italian government's transition from enemy to ally.

During the Casablanca conference in January 1943, Roosevelt and his staff had conceded to Winston Churchill and his staff their insistence that capturing Sicily should be the next campaign against Germany and Italy. The Americans had wanted to invade northern France and drive east toward Berlin in 1943. The British argued that massing enough troops and supplies for that campaign would take until 1944. The sensible strategy was to overrun Sicily, just ninety sea miles from Tunisia, and then other parts of the southern Mediterranean basin that Churchill insisted was Europe's "soft underbelly."[3]

Actually, both sides were wrong. The best strategy would have been to capture lightly defended Sardinia and Corsica. That would have given allied troops the perfect jump offs for a landing in southern France in spring 1944, the same time as a cross-channel invasion of northern France; those armies would crush the Germans between them. Meanwhile, bombers and escort fighters based in Corsica could attack enemy positions in most of France and Italy. In contrast, taking Sicily would be a jump off solely for landing in southern Italy. Fighting up the mountainous easily defended Italian peninsula was strategically a literal and figurative dead-end. Tragically, that was what happened.

After yielding to the British on Sicily, the Americans had wanted George Patton's Seventh Army to land on the north coast near Palermo then drive east to Messina where they would join Bernard Montgomery's army that had landed near Syracuse and drove north. Instead, the British prevailed in getting Patton's Seventh Army to land in southern Sicily to protect Montgomery's left flank even though there were no good ports, just fishing villages, along that stretch of coast. That would crimp Seventh Army's supplies.

For Sicily, General Dwight Eisenhower, the theater commander, was ultimately responsible for caving in to the British plan, largely conceived by Montgomery. Eisenhower's strength as a commander was his political skill at forging a team and strategy among rival prima donnas. As will be seen, that came at an enormous cost in blood and treasure. Time after time, he sacrificed superior strategies on the altar of "allied unity." That, of course, was a false choice. Catering to one domineering personality or group meant alienating others. A leader is as great as the plans conceived and implemented under his command that win one's goals at the least cost.

Montgomery was ecstatic at relegating the Americans to a secondary role. Like Patton, Montgomery was a vainglorious scene-stealer and showboat.[4] The similarities ended there. Patton was a brilliant former cavalry officer now tank commander, who excelled at rapid thrusts and encirclements of the enemy. Montgomery was a plodding general who only attacked after building up overwhelming forces and firepower that pulverized the enemy. The Sicily campaign revealed those stark differences.

The Seventh and Eighth Armies each initially numbered around 80,000 troops when they landed on July 9, preceded by air and naval bombardments and parachute drops behind enemy lines.[5] Eventually, those numbers swelled to around 467,000 ground forces, 600 tanks, 14,000 vehicles, and 1,800 cannon. Over the next five weeks they faced around 60,000 German and 250,000 Italian troops commanded by General Alfredo Guzzoni. Montgomery's army bogged down in southeastern Sicily while Patton's swiftly drove northwest toward Palermo and other ports. Patton's strategy was for massed armor to spearhead advances on multiple roads, repel counterattacks, and "bypass resistance" that infantry mopped up. After capturing Palermo on July 23, Patton pivoted eastward for parallel advances along the coast and roads inland. Twice when the Axis massed in strongholds, he outflanked and routed them with seaborne landings in their rear. His advanced guard captured Messina on August 16, and the next day he triumphantly welcomed a chagrined Montgomery into the city.

The allies inflicted a decisive defeat on the Axis in Sicily. As for casualties, they killed 4,325 Germans, wounded 13,500, and captured 10,100, and killed around 4,678 Italians, wounded 35,404, and captured 116,861, while suffering 2,811 Americans dead, 6,971 wounded, and 686 captured or missing, and 2,938 British killed, 9,212 wounded, and 2,782 captured or missing.

Yet the allies could have bagged nearly all the 60,000 Germans and 250,000 Italians committed to the island had Montgomery used landings to outflank the enemy on Sicily's east coast or, much better, landed at Reggio on the Italian peninsula's toe to cut off their retreat. Had Patton been allowed to land near Palermo rather than fight his way north from southern beaches without a good port for supplies, he would have captured Messina weeks sooner and cut off nearly all the Axis troops.

The Sicilian campaign's greatest strategic result was to provoke a coup d'état in Rome.[6] Benito Mussolini, Il Duce or "The Leader," was the Fascist Party's flamboyantly charismatic leader who had bullied weak-willed King Victor Emmaneul III into naming him prime minister in 1922, and thereafter established a dictatorship. He wanted to create a new Roman Empire, but his leadership abilities along with Italy's military and economic power fell far short of his ambitions. The results were disastrous military campaigns in the Balkans, North Africa, and now Sicily. That increasingly embittered and eventually emboldened ever more of his Fascist Grand Council and the population against him. On July 25, Victor Emmanuel summoned Mussolini, announced that he was replacing him with General Pietro Badoglio, and had him arrested and sent under guard to a resort hotel in the central Apennine Mountains.

Tragically, the king and prime minister did not immediately announce that Italy would withdraw from the war into neutrality, order the relatively few German troops then in Italy out of the country, and seal off with Italian troops the border behind them. Instead, they debated for six weeks what to do while Hitler poured reinforcements into Italy, fearing he would lose his ally, and sent a commando team to rescue Mussolini and fly him to Germany.

Compounding the tragedy, Roosevelt and Churchill also dithered. Rather than immediately open secret negotiations with Italian embassies in neutral Lisbon, Portugal or Berne, Switzerland, they adopted a wait and see stance for the Italians to make the first diplomatic move. During a press conference on July 30, a reporter asked President Rosevelt if he would negotiate with the new Italian government. Roosevelt replied that, "I don't care who we deal with in Italy so long as it isn't a member of the Fascist government, so long as they get them to lay down their arms, and so long as we don't have anarchy. Now his name may be king, or a prime minister, or a mayor of a town or village."[7]

Roosevelt then committed the worst allied strategic blunder of the European theater. He rejected his advisors' advice and bowed to the insistence by Churchill and his advisors that they invade southern Italy and fight their way north.[8] The British argued that the peninsula was just a couple of miles across the Messina Straits from their massive army in Sicily and the accompanying massive air and naval forces there and across North Africa. There were just 8,000 German troops in southern Italy while the Italian army was split between pro- and anti-German leaders. The allies would rapidly overrun Italy.

The strategy was for America's Fifth Army led by General Mark Clark and Britain's Eighth Army led by Montgomery to fight side-by side up the peninsula's respective west and east halves, with British General Harold Alexander in overall command. On September 3, Montgomery led the way by invading the toe and seizing Reggio, an act that would have decisively won the Sicilian campaign had he committed it seven weeks earlier. On September 9, Clark's army landed near Salerno while General George Hopkinson's British airborne division landed near and captured Taranto.[9] Over the next several weeks Montgomery's army advanced up the toe to support Clark and link with Hopkinson. By late September, the Fifth and Eighth armies had captured southern Italy below Naples and Bari but stalled before the German army commanded by General Heinrich von Vietinghoff, a skilled commander who exploited the mountainous terrain ideal for defense. General Albert Kesselring was in overall command of German troops throughout the Italian peninsula.

Meanwhile, tentative diplomatic gestures by the Italian government and allies led to Victor Emannuel's radio broadcast that Italy would unconditionally surrender on September 8. In doing so, the Italian government rejected two other possibilities. The king did not announce that Italy would be neutral and give both German and allied troops a deadline to withdraw nor did he announce that Italy had joined the allies and the Italian army would fight the Germans. The king, prime minister, and their entourage then fled Rome and eventually flew to safety behind allied lines at Brindisi. A German paratrooper division seized power in Rome while German troops poured into the peninsula to dismantle and intern the Italian army whose commanders, without orders to resist and mostly Fascist and sympathetic, acquiesced rather than resisted.

Italy would be the graveyard for the reputations of allied generals and literally for a hundred thousand or so of their soldiers, airmen, and sailors. Clark proved to be an utterly unimaginative plodder.[10] The Italian peninsula campaign lasted from September 3, 1943 until May 2, 1945. During those eighteen months the allied troops slowly, sporadically ground their way north with each mile costing vast blood and treasure in a literal and figurative strategic deadend. The Germans held out for months at a series of defensive lines that spanned the peninsula from east to west, most notably the Gustav Line in southern and Gothic Line in northern central Italy. The one attempt to outflank the Germans with a landing ineptly led by General John Lucas at Anzio on January 22, 1944, was a disaster. The Germans swiftly hemmed and nearly overran the beachhead. As Churchill vividly put it to Eisenhower: "We hoped to land a wildcat that would tear out the bowels of the Boche. Instead, we have stranded a vast whale with its tail flopping about in the water."[11] Eventually, 135,000 Germans fought 150,000 Americans until the final breakout on June 5, with each side suffering around 40,000 casualties.[12]

Clark remained Fifth Army's commander while first Montgomery, then Oliver Leslie and finally Richard McCreevy headed Eighth Army. The allies captured Naples on October 1, 1943, Rome on June 4, 1944, and Bologna on April 21, 1945. Clark admitted that Kesselring "is quicker than we are, quicker at regrouping his forces, quicker at thinning out a defensive front to provide troops to close gaps at decisive points...quicker at reaching decisions on the battlefield. By comparison, our methods are often slow and cumbersome."[13]

Roosevelt embarked with his chief military advisors, Marshall, King, and Arnold, aboard the battleship USS *Iowa* at the Potomac River mouth on November 11, 1943. They steamed across the Atlantic on the first leg of a 17,224 mile round trip to Tehran where Roosevelt would summit with Stalin and Churchill.[14] Along the way, Roosevelt explained to his advisors that, "There is going to be a race for Berlin and the United States should have Berlin."[15] He wanted America's zone to include Berlin and northwest Germany with its ports of Hamburg, Lubeck, Rostock, and Bremerhaven. He anticipated a million American troops occupying Germany for at least a year or two after the war. At Oran, Algeria, Eisenhower boarded to discuss strategy with Roosevelt and the other military chiefs.

The *Iowa* steamed on to Tunis where Roosevelt flew to Cairo for a four day summit with Churchill and Chang Kai-shek, China's generalissimo. Among Roosevelt's postwar visions was anchoring China as an ally and stabilizing force in East Asia. He explained that "I really feel that it is a triumph to have got the four hundred and twenty-five million Chinese in on the allied side. This will be very useful 25 or 50 years hence, even though China cannot contribute much military or naval support for the moment."[16] Meanwhile, Roosevelt made two significant concessions to Chiang and Chinese nationalism. In a bilateral treaty signed on January 11, 1943, the United States gave up its power of extraterritoriality in China that included trials of American criminal suspects in American courts. Then, on December 17, 1943, Congress passed the Magnusson Act that repealed the 1882 Chinese Exclusion

Act. For Roosevelt and Churchill, the summit's emotional height was motoring out to gaze in wonder at the pyramids.

Roosevelt flew from Cairo to Tehran on November 27. His delegation at the talks included Averill Harriman, ambassador to the Soviet Union, Charles Bohlen who headed the State Department's East European Division, and troubleshooter Harry Hopkins. Rather than stay at the secure but remote American embassy, Roosevelt accepted Stalin's invitation for them to reside at the Soviet embassy's compound. Two reasons explain that decision. One was security. The American embassy was a long way through crowded streets to the Soviet embassy where the summit would take place. Avoiding that potential gauntlet for assassins certainly seemed to be a sensible precaution. Also, Roosevelt was determined to show Stalin that he trusted and wanted to work closely with him despite the listening devices imbedded in the residence. To that end, he refused to meet alone with Churchill and teased the prime minister in Stalin's presence and was silent when Stalin blistered him on various issues. Nonetheless, the three of them amiably celebrated Churchill's sixty-nineth birthday with a grand banquet on November 30.

Roosevelt believed that Stalin was just another political boss amenable to friendly reason, mutual interests, and compromise. He boasted to Churchill that "I can personally handle Stalin better than either your Foreign Office or my State Department. Stalin hates the guts of all your top people. He thinks he likes me better, and I hope he will continue to do so."[17]

Instead, Stalin played Roosevelt like a hooked fish. In reality, Stalin was a ruthless tyrant who had consolidated his power and completed communism imposition on the Soviet Union by having ten million or more people shot or starved to death and another ten million or so enslaved in Siberian labor camps. Harry Hopkins vividly described Stalin as: "an austere, rugged determined figure in boots that shone like mirrors, stout baggy trousers and snug fitting blouse. He wore no ornaments, military or civilian. He's built close to the ground like a football coach's dream of a tackle. He's about five foot six, about a hundred and ninety pounds. His hands are huge, as hard as his mind. His voice is harsh but ever under control. He's a chain smoker…He laughs often enough, but it's a short laugh, somewhat sardonic… There's no small talk in him."[18]

Most of the talks concerned Europe's postwar fate, with Germany's future central.[19] The three leaders agreed that destroying the Nazi regime and its leaders was crucial. The question was whether also to destroy Germany by demolishing its heavy industries and breaking it up into smaller states. They agreed to split Germany into three occupation zones but could not agree where to draw the lines or whether they should be permanent.

Stalin insisted on moving Poland's borders westward, with the Soviet Union taking what was currently eastern Poland while Poland's western frontier would anchor on the Oder and Neisse Rivers. Roosevelt and Churchill accepted the shift but the prime minister tried to get the president to insist that the London exiled Polish government have equal status with the communist Lublin exiled Polish government. Roosevelt demurred from pressuring Stalin on this.

Stalin then demanded the three Baltic states of Estonia, Latvia, and Lithuania. Roosevelt suggested that plebiscites could best determine where the loyalties of those peoples lay. Stalin was noncommittal to that. He pressured Roosevelt and Churchill to commit to an invasion of northern France in 1944. Roosevelt eagerly and Churchill reluctantly backed that invasion time and place. Roosevelt got Churchill to accept an invasion of southern France later in 1944. Roosevelt asked Stalin to join the war against Japan after Germany was defeated. Stalin agreed. The three leaders signed a document committing them to war against Germany until it unconditionally surrendered, and to prosecute any war crimes committed by Germans.

Tragically, Roosevelt failed to insist with Stalin that American troops would occupy Berlin and northern Germany, and then inform the State Department. As a result, that vision disappeared at a critical conference of the European Advisory Commission that opened in London on January 14, 1944. America's ambassador to Britain, John Winant and his deputy George Kennan represented the United States. They acquiesced to British envoy William Strang's proposal that British troops occupy northwest Germany, American troops southwest Germany, and Soviet troops eastern Germany as far westward as parts of the Elbe River. They also agreed to split Berlin into three occupation zones.

The Oder River that runs from south to north around forty miles east of Berlin would have been the best line to realize Roosevelt's vision. That, of course, depended on two things. Roosevelt and Churchill insisting on it and then American and British armies beating the Soviets to that line. Tragically, Roosevelt and Churchill failed to do either.

Among the war's controversies was Roosevelt's policy toward the Holocaust.[20] The decision for Hitler's "Final Solution" to exterminate all Jews and other "undesirables" came at the Wannsee Conference of high-ranking Nazi officials on January 20, 1942. Word of that "holocaust" trickled out. Rabbi Stephen Wise was Roosevelt's friend and headed the American Jewish Congress. In December 1942, Wise met Roosevelt, informed him of the worsening Holocaust, and asked him publicly "to warn the Nazis that they will be held to strict accountability for their crimes." Roosevelt acknowledged that, "We have received confirmation from sources." The problem was, "We are dealing with an insane man" impervious to morality or reason. "Hitler and the group around him represent...a national psychopathic case. We cannot act toward them by normal means," but "we will do all in our power to be of service to your people in this tragic moment."[21]

Roosevelt sent word to Churchill and Stalin calling for a united "Declaration on Jewish Massacres" that condemned "in the strongest possible terms this bestial policy of cold-blooded extermination" and their determination to prosecute all those responsible for war crimes. Neither wanted to do so since each faced a "Jewish problem," Churchill in Palestine and Stalin in the Soviet Union. Public calls would embolden Jews to assert their interests. Instead, on December 17, 1942, the allied governments issued a condemnation of German atrocities including mass starvation and murder of innocent people but did not mention Jews.

Actually, the allies were powerless to do anything to reduce let alone halt the slaughter. A public warning about war crimes would be fruitless. Calls for bombing the extermination camps would have aided the Nazis. Calls for bombing the railroad tracks leading to the camps would have missed the targets from several miles up but subjected the bombing crews flying beyond fighter escorts to extermination by German fighter planes. The only way to end the holocaust was to destroy Hitler's regime by allied armies fighting their way to Berlin from the east and west, and liberating the survivors from the camps they overran.

Chaim Weizmann, the Zionist movement's chief, met with Roosevelt in June 1943, and pressed him to call for a Jewish homeland in Palestine, a British mandate since 1920. Roosevelt embraced the idea but explained the timing for such an announcement was wrong because it would incite Palestine's Arabs to attack Jews living there and divert British troops from fighting the Germans to crush the uprising. Yet, Roosevelt not only favored a national Jewish homeland but proposed resettling the Arabs elsewhere in the Middle East and leaving Palestine for joint occupation and governance by Jews and Christians. He asked Jewish Rabbi leaders Wise and Abba Silver to announce the president's promise that "full justice will be done to those who seek a Jewish home" and he "was happy that the doors of Palestine are today open to Jewish refugees." Tragically, the latter assertion was false as British authorities limited immigration to Palestine.[22]

Roosevelt established a War Refugee Board on January 22, 1944, and named Treasury Secretary Morgenthau, Secretary of State Hull, and War Secretary Stimson to oversee it and Treasury undersecretary John Pehle to direct it. Through the War Refugee Board, Washington's policy was "to take all measures within its power to rescue victims of enemy oppression in imminent danger of death" and provide them "relief and assistance consistent with the successful prosecution of the war."[23]

What Roosevelt could do was pledge that justice would prevail against war criminals. In October 1942, he announced that: "The United Nations have decided to establish the identity of those...who are responsible for the innumerable acts of savagery. As each of these criminal deeds is committed, it is being carefully investigated, and the evidence is being relentlessly piled up for the future purpose of justice. We have made it clear that the United Nations seek no mass reprisals against the populations of Germany or Italy or Japan but the ringleaders and their brutal henchmen must be named and apprehended and tried in accordance with the judicial processes of criminal law."[24]

Roosevelt's decision to pursue twin offensives in the Pacific undermined each. The two commanders, Admiral Chester Nimitz in the central Pacific and General Douglas MacArthur in the southwest Pacific, competed for warships, warplanes, troops, and supplies. Their commands overlapped in the Solomon Islands. Navy Chief of Staff Ernest King and Army Chief of Staff George Marshall worked with Nimitz and MacArthur to devise a coordinated plan to take the Solomons, with Rabaul, Japan's headquarters, the ultimate objective. Operation Cartwheel eventually involved thirteen separate related campaigns that began in March 1943 and ended with Rabaul's neutralization in February 1944; although the Japanese held Rabaul, their air and naval power was destroyed so they posed no threat. Admiral William "Bull" Halsey and MacArthur respectively commanded the operations in the northern and southern Solomons and New Guinea. The most prominent Japanese death was that of Admiral Yamamoto; the Americans partly avenged Pearl Harbor when eighteen P-38 Lightnings shot down the plane carrying him on April 18, 1943.

Nimitz was as low key and humble as MacArthur was narcissistic and melodramatic.[25] He directed operations in his central Pacific theater from his headquarters at Pearl Harbor. His first campaign did not begin until November 20, 1943, with twin landings at Tarawa and Makin in the Gilbert Islands. For Tarawa, Admiral Raymond Spruance and General Holland Smith respectively commanded the fleet and 18,000 marines. Tarawa's 2,600 troops and 2,200 armed laborers were deeply dug in and devastated the marines as they surged ashore. The marines suffered 1,009 dead and 2,101 wounded while killing 4,690 fighters and capturing only 17 soldiers and 169 laborers during the three day battle; many marine casualties came from their landing at low tide which forced them to cross hundreds of yards of coral reef and shallow waters under constant fire. For Makin, Admiral Raymond Turner and General Ralph Smith respectively commanded the fleet and 6,470 soldiers. Only 400 Japanese defended Makin but they held out four days and killed 763 Americans and wounded 185 before they were wiped out.

The next steps were the two nearby islands of Kwajalein and Roi-Namur. Turner and Holland Smith led that expedition. Tactical lessons learned from previous campaigns led to far fewer losses. The fighting lasted from January 31 to February 3, 1944. The marines killed all but 166 of Kwajalein's 5,000 defenders and all but 87 of Roi-Namur's 3,000 defenders, while suffering 142 dead and 845 wounded to take Kwajalein and 206 dead and 617 wounded to take Roi-Namur.

Truk was to the Caroline islands what Rabaul had been for the Solomons, a regional headquarters with an airfield and deep port. Admiral Marc Mitscher led a fleet whose air strikes and bombardment devastated the defenders on February 17 and 18, destroying 250 warplanes, sinking 15 war and 32 merchant ships, and killing over 4,500 airmen, sailors, and soldiers while losing 25 planes and 45 dead. Then came the battle for Eniwetok from February 17 to 23, in which the soldiers and marines killed all but 144 of the 3,500 defenders while suffering 313 dead and 874 wounded.

Meanwhile, MacArthur conducted a series of offensives in the southwest Pacific. The first target was the Admiralty Islands where the capture of Los Negros Island took from February 29 to May 19, 1944, that cost 326 dead and 1,190 wounded of 35,000 soldiers and marines led by General William Chase and killed all but 75 of the 4,000 Japanese defenders. That completed the isolation and neutralization of Rabaul, Japan's regional headquarters. Meanwhile, 30,000 marines and soldiers led by General Robert Eichelberger captured New Guinea's north coast port of Hollandia between April 22 and 27; the Americans suffered 152 dead and 1,057 wounded while killing all but 300 of the 3,300 defenders. The battle for Biak island lasted from May 27 to August 17. The Japanese conducted a skilled defense, sending in reinforcements then withdrawing most of the troops when defeat was inevitable. Eichelberger commanded the expedition that suffered

438 killed and 2,361 wounded in combat along with 7,234 casualties from disease. The Japanese lost around 4,000 dead and 300 capture. Biak's airfield was within range of Japanese targets on the southern Philippine island of Mindanao.

Development of a state-of-the-art heavy bomber and fighter plane determined Nimitz's next two key targets. The B-29 Superfortress had a 3,000 mile range and 20,000 pound bombload. The P-51 Mustang with a disposable belly fuel tank had a 1,600 mile range and could outmaneuver any enemy fighter. The islands of Tinian and Iwo Jima, 1,500 and 800 respective miles from Japan, would serve as the respective bases for B-29s and P-51s.

Thirty-two thousand Japanese defended Saipan and another 10,000 Japanese civilians lived there.[26] Admiral Richmond Turner and General Holland Smith commanded the respective sea and land forces. Seventy-one thousand marines and soldiers fought the Japanese from June 15 to July 9, before securing most of the island. During that time they suffered 3,225 dead and 13,099 wounded while killing 25,155 soldiers and capturing 1,810; around 5,000 civilians died either in cross-fires and bombardments or from suicide. Saipan's capture was essential for the capture of nearby Tinian with a smaller 8,000-man garrison. Forty-thousand marines eventually surged ashore to battle Tinian's defenders from July 24 to August 1. The marines suffered 368 dead and 1,921 wounded while capturing only 404 Japanese and killing the rest. With that island secure, engineers began constructing an airfield with runways long enough for the B-29s.

Meanwhile, converging fleets led by Admirals Jisaburo Ozawa and Kakuji Karita that totaled three heavy and six light carriers packed with 222 fighters and 200 dive- and torpedo-bombers and five battleships attacked the American fleets covering Saipan. On June 19, the Japanese admirals unleashed their carrier warplanes accompanied by around 300 warplanes based on the Philippines against Admiral Marc Mitscher's Task Force 58 with seven heavy and eight light carriers with 900 warplanes and seven battleships. The Battle of the East Philippines Sea, also dubbed the Great Marianas Turkey Shoot, was the largest carrier battle. On June 19 and 20, the Americans shot down 645 warplanes and sank two heavy and one light carriers and a battleship while losing 123 warplanes before the Japanese withdrew.

After capturing Tinian for a B-29 base, Nimitz and his staff targeted Iwo Jima for the escort P-51 base followed by Okinawa or Taiwan (Formosa) as a base for invading Japan itself. Strategically, those were the sole logical objectives. Offensives elsewhere would divert and squander precious lives and treasure. That meant canceling

MacArthur's planned invasion of the Philippines. Roosevelt met with Nimitz and MacArthur at Pearl Harbor where Nimitz made that case and MacArthur vehemently contested it. Roosevelt later complained that "nobody has ever talked to me the way MacArthur did."[27] What the general said was: "Mr. President, if your decision be to bypass the Philippines and leave it millions of wards of the United States and thousands of internees and prisoners of war to languish in their agony and despair – I dare to say that the American people would be so aroused that they would register most complete resentment against you at the polls this fall."[28] Once again, Roosevelt caved into MacArthur's powerful charisma, authority, and political argument that masked a strategy that severely harmed America's war effort by diverting critical human and material resources into a dead end.

Roosevelt had Nimitz support MacArthur's Philippines campaign. Nimitz's first step was to invade the Palau islands whose central island was Peleliu starting on September 15. The belief was that Peleliu was vital for an air base for the Philippines campaign. Forty-seven thousand mostly marines took more than two months to destroy resistance on those islands, with the last eliminated on November 27. That victory proved to be pyrrhic with 2,143 American dead and 8,514 wounded while only 360 of the 12,000 defenders surrendered. The air base proved to be inadequate.

The Philippines campaign lasted ten months, beginning with the landing on Leyte island.[29] For that, MacArthur committed General Walter Kruger's army and Admiral Thomas Kinkaid's Seventh fleet, while Nimitz supplied "Bull" Halsey's Third Fleet. The carrier warplanes of both fleets conducted bombing attacks against Japanese positions in Leyte, Luzon, and other Philippine islands along with Taiwan and Okinawa in the weeks leading up to the landing. The Americans destroyed around 500 Japanese warplanes while losing around 100. The first wave of Kruger's 164,000 troops hit Leyte's beaches on October 17. Facing them were 70,000 Japanese commanded by General Tomoyuki Yamashita. The Americans hit the beach against light resistance and pushed inland. The fighting lasted two and a half months until December 29. The Americans suffered 4,501 dead and 11,991 wounded while killing over 65,000 Japanese before Yamashita withdrew the remnants to other islands.

Admiral Soemu Toyoda, the Pacific fleet commander, sought to isolate the Americans by destroying their supply fleet.[30] From October 22 to 26, four Japanese fleets with combined forces of one heavy and two light carriers, seven battleships, 10 cruisers, and 300 warplanes converged on the landing. Fending off those attacks were the Third and Seventh Fleets led respectively by Admirals William "Bull" Halsey and Thomas Kinkaid and three task forces with combined warships of eight heavy and nine light carriers, eighteen escort carriers, twelve battleships, twenty-four cruisers, 116 destroyers, and 1,500 warplanes. The Americans sank all four carriers and seven battleships along with ten cruisers, and shot down over 300 warplanes while the Japanese sank a light carrier, two escort carriers, and three destroyers, and shot down 255 warplanes during the battle of Leyte Gulf.

During the Philippines campaign the Japanese introduced a new weapon – the Kamikaze or "Divine Wind" – "smart bombs" of pilots flying planes packed with explosives into American warships were highly destructive and deadly over eleven months until the war's end.[31] By one count, "2,800 Kamikaze attackers sank 34 navy ships, damaged 368 others, killed 4,900 sailors, and wounded over 4,800. Despite radar detection…airborne interception, attrition, and massive anti-aircraft barrages, 14 percent of kamikazes survived to score a hit on a ship; nearly 8.5 percent of all ships hit by kamikazes sank."[32]

Meanwhile, American submarines became increasingly deadly from improved torpedoes and intelligence. The initial Mark-14 torpedo fired low under the target or failed to explode when it hit. By 1943, engineers corrected those flaws. Cryptanalysts cracked a series of naval codes that let them provide submarine captains precise voyages of Japanese war and merchant ships. In 1943 alone, they sent word of around 800 voyages of which American submarines intercepted and spotted around 350, were able to fire at around one-third, of which they sank 34 and damaged 56. In 1944, American submarines sank around 600 ships with 2.7 million tons displacement, more than the 2.2 million sunk the two previous years. The final total was 1,300 sinkings including a battleship, eight aircraft carriers, and eleven cruisers. The submarine service was only 2 percent of the navy's personnel but inflicted 55 percent of Japan's naval losses.[33]

Stalemate prevailed on the mainland Asian fronts from June 1942 until March 1944. Chinese Generalissimo Chiang Kai-shek rejected pressure by General Joe Stilwell, his advisor and commander of American troops on that front, to attack the Japanese in China. Chiang sought to retain his best divisions to fight the communists in northern China after Japan was defeated. Chiang did let Stilwell train, equip, and deploy two Chinese armies, effectively the size of divisions, against the Japanese in northern Burma as British forces attacked from India. The Japanese blunted those offensives. A major reason for Stilwell's failed offensives was a shortage of weapons, equipment, and supplies.

Japan's severance of the Burma Road forced the allies to develop two alternative routes to convey supplies to China. A stream of C-47 transports flew supplies "over the Hump" or Himalayan Mountains to air bases in Yunnan, China. Stilwell had the Ledo road constructed from India's Assam province to China's Yunnan province. The land and air routes caused Lend-Lease supplies to rise from 3,700 tons in 1942 to 61,000 tons in 1943, although that still fell far short of the need.[34] That need was especially acute because gangs stole and sold on the black market many of the goods. Chiang's Nationalist Party cadres got kickbacks up the hierarchy to the generalissimo himself.

Stilwell's clearest military success was appointing General Frank Merrill to lead the 5307 Provisional Unit, a thousand-man battalion of veteran volunteers from Pacific campaigns to conduct long range raids behind Japanese lines to gather intelligence and destroy supply bases. "Merrill's Marauders" was inspired and trained by British General Orde Wingate and his "Chindit" raiders.

General William Slim commanded the British army, mostly composed of colonial Indian troops. that first repelled a series of Japanese attacks at Imphal and Kohima near the border from March 3 to July 3, 1944, then counterattacked to devastate and rout the enemy from northern and central Burma. Stilwell's troops and Merrill's Marauders played an important secondary role by diverting Japanese forces and recapturing the strategic crossroads city of Myitkyina on the Ledo Road in August 1944.

During those same months, the Japanese routed thirty-four Chinese divisions in Honan and Henan provinces between the Yangtze and Yellow Rivers in central China. Stilwell urged Chiang to commit his best divisions that he kept in reserve and coordinate defense with the communist army northward. An alarmed Roosevelt wrote Chiang probably his most damning letter to a foreign leader. He warned that "if you fail to send reinforcements...we will lose all chance of opening land communications with China and immediately jeopardize the air route over the Hump. For this you must yourself be prepared to accept the consequences and assume the personal responsibility... Only drastic and immediate action on your part alone can be in time to preserve the fruits of your long struggle and the efforts we have made to support you. Otherwise political and military considerations alike are going to be swallowed in military disaster." Chiang claimed that he "understood," but stubbornly refused to act.[35]

Roosevelt sent General Patrick Hurley to Chiang at his Chunking capital, to get him to appoint Stilwell to head the Chinese army and reduce his regime's corruption, incompetence, and brutality.

Chiang angrily rejected those requests and instead demanded that he recall Stilwell. Roosevelt reluctantly had American General Albert Wedemeyer, then British Admiral Louis Mountbatten's chief of staff, replace Stilwell on October 27, 1944. Although Wedemeyer was more diplomatic than "Vinegar Joe" Stilwell, he was just as unsuccessful in getting Chiang to vigorously fight the Japanese. He complained to Army Chief of Staff Marshall that the "Chinese have no conception of organization, logistics, or modern warfare," of "vacillating" Chiang and "the chicanery of his advisors who have selfish, mercurial motives" with "self-sacrifice and patriotism...unknown," and a "starving" army.[36]

The Chinese Communist Party's capital was Yanan, in northern China. Under Mao Zedong's leadership, the communist guerrilla war against the Japanese had driven them from four provinces. Roosevelt sent Vice President Henry Wallace to Chungking to reinforce Hurley in urging Chiang to coordinate strategy with the communists. Chiang rejected the notion. Hurley sent Colonel David Barrett with OSS and foreign service officers to Yanan to assess the communist regime, then flew there on November 7, 1944, to meet Mao and his deputy Chou Enlai. The contrast between the Chungking and Yanan regimes was stark as the communists appeared to be a model of political and military efficiency and austerity. Yet the Americans could extend little aid to the communists and could not reform the nationalists.

The only effective joint warfare effort was the Sino-American Co-Operative Special Technical Organization (SACO) established by treaty in 1942. Captain Milton Miles led a team of naval and OSS officers that worked with General Tai Li, who headed the Nationalist government's intelligence organization called the Bureau of Investigation and Statistics. SACO trained, equipped, and dispatched operatives to infiltrate Japanese lines on espionage, sabotage, assassination, and subversion missions, and form the Loyal Patriotic Army (LPA) to wage guerilla war. Tai insisted that OSS not operate independently in China but only as his advisors.

The most effective OSS guerrilla warfare effort was Detachment 101 led by Major Carl Eifler in northern Burma. According to Historian Ronald Spector, by "late 1944, Detachment 101 had a strength of 599 Americans and almost 10,000 Kachin tribesmen. By war's end, they had inflicted an estimated 5,500 casualties on the enemy and rescued over 200 allied airmen. Only 15 Americans and less than 200 rangers were killed in action."[37] OSS agents allied with Ho Chi Minh's Viet Minh coalition of communists and nationalists fighting the Japanese in Indochina in July 1945.

The Joint Chiefs conceived a plan to bomb Japan by the Twentieth Bomber Command's B-29s based in China. By April 1944, Chiang's regime had built an airfield near Chengdu and the first squadron of seven B-29s flew from India over the Hump to land there. The trouble was that all the aviation fuel and spare parts also had to be flown to the Chengdu base. The first strike came on June 15, when sixty B-29s attacked the Yawata iron and steel complex. The vast distance to and from Japan with limited fuel forced the mission to shift to bombing Japanese positions in China and Southeast Asia.

The Japanese responded with an offensive that overran those bases and forced Chennault to relocate his air force to bases westward far beyond range of Japan.

The invasion of France took two years to prepare.[38] Over a million men and millions of tons of supplies had to be shipped across the Atlantic to British ports and then dispersed among scores of bases and depots. Historian Rick Atkinson documented the astonishing logistical demands for just the American army after it landed. Each soldier required 41.268 pounds worth of supplies daily. The Americans collected in twenty-two British ports, 301,000 vehicles 1,800 train locomotives, 20,000 rail cars, 2.6 million small arms, 2,700 artillery pieces, 300,000 telephone poles, and 7 million tons of gasoline, oil, and lubricants, and 60 million K rations.[39]

General Dwight Eisenhower commanded the invasion. The plan was for 156,000 troops and 2,000 tanks of two armies, the American First and the British Second with two corps each, to land at five separate beaches along a fifty mile stretch of Normandy's coast, with a division on each in the first wave. Generals Omar Bradley and Miles Dempsey respectively commanded the First and Second Armies of the Twenty-First Army Group headed by General Bernard Montgomery.

Deception was critical for the invasion's success. The allies wanted the Germans to mass most of their forces along the narrowest stretch of the English Channel between Calais, France and Dover, England. To that end they leaked word that General George Patton's Third Army based in eastern England would land there. They displayed hundreds of inflatable tanks and trucks in fields for German reconnaissance planes to spot. They had scores of radio units send fake coded messages to each other similar to any large army as it prepared for an invasion. Meanwhile, they kept the actual invader armies under as much camouflage and radio silence as possible. To avoid mistaken identity for anti-aircraft crews and fighter pilots, all 13,000 allied planes had three white stripes on the rear fuselage and each wing.

The landing's success also depended on high tides to carry landing craft over implanted obstacles and mines, and good flying weather for the bombers, strafers, and paratroopers. The landing, called D-Day, was scheduled for June 5, 1944, but stormy weather that day forced its postponement to the next day, June 6. The armada numbered 6,939 vessels including 1,217 warships, 864 cargo and troop ships, 4,126 landing craft, and the rest various auxiliary ships. Two hundred and fifty-five mine sweepers led the other ships to anchorages seven miles from the British beaches and eleven miles from the American beaches. As the first wave of 50,000 troops climbed down rope nets from their ships to landing craft, two airborne divisions dropped west of the American beaches and one airborne division dropped east of the British beaches to secure those flanks while the warships and thousands of airplanes bombarded 50,000 German troops deployed in bunkers and pill boxes along the coast. After the first wave fought its way ashore and advanced inland, the second wave then third waves of 50,000 troops each followed. That first day the allies suffered around 10,000 casualties including 4,414 dead, and may have killed, wounded, and captured as many Germans.

For the next two months, the allies slowly fought their way further inland while landing more troops and supplies. Normandy's terrain was broken up among bocage or farms surrounded by thick hedges atop earthen mounds which were easily defended by ever more German troops hurried there from elsewhere in France and beyond. The allies suffered a severe supply cutback when a storm from June 19 to 21, destroyed one artificial harbor and damaged another off the Normandy coast. Although the Americans captured the port of Cherbourg, the Germans had so heavily mined and sunk ships in it that it took the troops months to clear and use it.

Meanwhile, the allies conducted round-the-clock strategic bombing of Germany and other countries, with the British Bomber Command led by Air Marshal Arthur Harris by night and the American 8th Air Force led by General Carl Spatz by day.[40] The targets varied but the emphasis was on enemy air bases, industrial complexes, and V-1 and V-2 missiles sites. Yet bombing by British Lancasters and American Flying Fortresses from several miles above ground, especially at night, was extremely inaccurate at relatively small sites like factories. The reality was that the allies carpet-bombed German cities into rubble and killed 353,000 civilians. Yet the bombing campaign did destroy about a quarter of Germany's industry and 57,405 aircraft while tying down 1.1 million troops in fighter squadrons and anti-aircraft batteries. The allies suffered enormous losses to inflict that damage, with the Americans alone suffering 18,400 lost planes, 51,000 dead, and 30,000 captured.

While strategic bombing was and remains controversial, tactical air power was critical to the allied victory. From the landing in Normandy on June 6, 1944 until Germany's surrender on May 8, 1945, American fighters and fighter-bombers flew 212,731 sorties and fired 24 million rounds against German planes, troops, trucks, trains, tanks, and other targets.[41]

The Germans began firing two types of missiles at British cities. V-1s were a 27-foot long missile with a 1,970 pound warhead that when fired flew 400 miles per hour in a 160 mile arc. Of the 10,492 V-1s fired, British planes and anti-aircraft guns shot down around 4,000, around 4,000 hit the countryside, but around 2,419 exploded in London to kill 6,189 people and wound 17,981. V-2s were a forty-five foot long missile with a 2,200 pound warhead that when fired flew 55 miles high at 1,790 miles per hour then plunged to its target. Unlike the noisy V-1s dubbed "buzz bombs," V-2s could not be detected until they exploded. Of 3,172 fired at sixteen cities in Britain, France, Belgium, the Netherlands and Germany, 1,358 hit London to kill 2,759 people and wound 6,523 others. V-1s and V-2s were weapons of terror and diversion. They diverted enormous amounts of German money, minds, and manpower to build, protect, and fire. They diverted enormous amounts of allied money, minds, and manpower to capture their elusive launch sites. A major goal for the Americans and Soviets was to capture as many of the missile program's scientists, technicians, and facilities as possible.[42]

Two armies, Patton's Third and Harry Crerar's First Canadian massed behind the First and Second Armies. Eisenhower formed two army groups, the Twelfth American commanded by Bradley with General Courtney Hodges heading First along with Patton's Third, and the Twenty-first British commanded by Montgomery with Demsey's Second and Crerar's First Armies.

The breakout came in two stages, first by Hodge's First Army at St. Lo from July 24 to 27, followed by Patton's Third Army at Avranches on August 1. From Avranches, Patton sent one corps west to wipe out Germans in Brittany, a second corps south to the Loire and then east, and the third arching northeast toward the German Seventh Army's headquarters at Le Mans. The outflanked Germans fled to escape encirclement. Patton then fought north to cut off the Germans at Argentan where Crerar's army fighting south was supposed to join him. But Crerar stalled at Falaise and Eisenhower rejected Patton's request to keep driving north to Falaise because that was within Montgomery's designated territory. As a result over 100,000 Germans managed to flee through the dozen mile gap. That was the first of three critical times during the fighting in France and beyond when Eisenhower put Montgomery's ego before Patton's strategy to inflict a decisive defeat on the Germans.

Patton raced his two corps east and by late August they had crossed the Seine. He requested permission to turn north and cut off the retreating Germans. Eisenhower rejected this request. A French division followed by an American division liberated Paris on August 25. Those advances came at a high cost. From June 6 to August 31, the Americans suffered 134,000 casualtiess, and the British, Canadians, and other contingents suffered 91,000 casualties. The allies inflicted at least 250,000 casualties on the Germans.[43]

Amidst the allied advance east across France, a cabal nearly assassinated Hitler. On July 20, Hitler convened a staff conference at his Wolf's Lair headquarters in East Prussia. Colonel Claus Stauffenberg was the key member of a plot to kill Hitler and seize power in Berlin. He left his briefcase with a time bomb beneath the large table, excused himself, and left for Berlin where he would join other plotters to take power. A heavy table leg shielded Hitler from the blast that killed three officers and wounded most others in the room. Hitler had the Gestapo track down and eliminate the plotters. The Gestapo arrested over 7,000 suspects and executed 4,980. Among plotters was brilliant General Erin Rommel; Hitler had him commit suicide.

General Alexander Patch's Seventh Army invaded the French Riveria around St. Tropez on August 15 against light resistance.[44] Patch sent two divisions west to capture Toulon and Marseilles then advance up the Rhone River Valley and three divisions northeast to cut off as many Germans as possible. Patch's advanced forces captured Grenoble and Lyon by September 2 and linked with Patton's Third Army in eastern Burgundy by September 15.

That critical offensive almost never happened. Churchill and his staff adamantly opposed it, and instead insisted that Seventh Army land in Trieste, Italy for an advance north though that mountainous region toward Ljubljana and then toward Vienna. Fortunately, Roosevelt followed his joint chiefs' advice to reject that plan as a strategic deadend like Italy's peninsula, and back Patch's invasion of southern France whose broad Rhone Valley offered good tank country.

By mid-September, the allied armies occupied a four hundred mile front from the North Sea near Ostend across most of Belgium and eastern France to Belfort near the Swiss border. And there they stalled for lack of gasoline along with countless other supplies. Fuel and other supplies had to be carried by truck convoys – "the Red Ball Express" – from Normandy's beaches and eventually Cherbourg to each army's increasingly distant depots where they were divvied among the divisions. Third Army, for instance, was down to 32,000 daily gallons, one-tenth its needs.[45] Patton pleaded with Eisenhower for more gas so he could smash through Germany's undermanned Seigfried Line and reach the Rhine within a week or so. Eisenhower replied that supplies had to be divvied to each army. That stall enabled the Germans to occupy the Siegfried Line they had constructed of concrete bunkers and pillboxes behind minefields and "dragon's teeth" concrete pillars to impede tanks and other vehicles.

All along, Montgomery complained that Eisenhower's broad front strategy of overwhelming the Germans everywhere was a mistake because logistically it was unsustainable. He argued that all available fuel and other supplies be given to his Twenty-first Army Group for a special operation designed to smash through German defenses and cross the Rhine River at Arnhem. Eisenhower approved his Operation Market Garden plan for three airborne divisions to land along a sixty-four mile stretch of road and capture bridges while armored divisions fought their way up that road. That campaign lasted from September 17 to 22, during which the Second Army did capture Eindhoven and Nijmegen but was repelled at Arnhem. That narrow front strategy was vulnerable to German counterattacks on its flanks and suffered constant traffic jams.[46] But the plan's worst flaw was that it led north to the lower Rhine and the Netherlands rather than east to the central Rhine and industrial Ruhrland with Germany's heart beyond, and thus was the latest strategic deadend. Once again, to appease Montgomery and "allied unity," Eisenhower approved a campaign that squandered power and delayed final victory, while rejecting Patton's that would have done the opposite.

Meanwhile, the Soviet Red army ground down the Germans on the eastern front. Like Roosevelt, Stalin's strategies involved winning the war and winning the peace. He intended to conquer eastern Europe and incorporate it into the Soviet empire. To that end, he imposed communist regimes on each country that the Soviets overran.

In Poland, the communist government was in Lublin, in the east not far from the Soviet border. In London, a group of exiled Poles had established a democratic government with an underground in Warsaw, the capital. On August 1, the Soviet army was just six miles from Warsaw. The underground Poles revolted against the Germans hoping that the Soviets would soon join them in liberating the city. Stalin saw this as a great chance to let two enemies, the Germans and democratic Poles to kill each other. He ordered his army to halt its advance and refused to send any supplies to the Poles in Warsaw. By October 4, the Germans finally crushed the revolt after slaughtering over 250,000 people.

Churchill was so upset by Soviet conquests that he flew to Moscow and confronted Stalin on October 9. Churchill proposed a power-sharing deal for each country whereby the Soviets were 90 percent dominant in Romania, 75 percent in Bulgaria, while the Soviets and British would be 50–50 in Hungary and Yugoslavia, and the British would be 90 percent in Greece. He did not mention the three Baltic states, Estonia, Latvia, and Lithuania, nor Poland, thus tacitly conceding them. He wrote down those percentages on a piece of paper and presented it to Stalin, who, smiled cynically and drew a blue check on it and handed it back. Churchill then worried: "Might it not be thought rather cynical if it seemed we had disposed of these issues, so fateful to millions of people, in such an offhand manner? Let us burn the paper." Stalin replied, "No, you keep it."[47] Roosevelt accepted that deal when Churchill told him about it after he returned to London. Here is yet another puzzling example of naivete trumping the prevailing realism of Roosevelt and Churchill. Those words and percentages were meaningless. The only thing that mattered was boots on the ground. Several million Soviet boots on the ground in eastern Europe would determine the fate of those countries.

All along, Roosevelt fought his own battles, political with congressmen, bureaucrats, businessmen, and union leaders at home and diplomatic with allies. His most unpleasant diplomatic conflict was with Charles de Gaulle, who pressured him to recognize his French Committee on National Liberation (FCNL) or Free French movement as France's legitimate government in exile that would take over France after it was liberated. Roosevelt disliked and distrusted de Gaulle, whom he found arrogant, humorless, unreliable, and power-hungry. He had Eisenhower not tell de Gaulle about the pending D-Day landings until two days before, worried that the mercurial Frenchmen would try to interfere or leak the plan.

De Gaulle visited Washington from July 6 to 9, 1944, to directly demand that the president and key department heads embrace the FCNL as France's legitimate government. Roosevelt met him twice at the White House, and de Gaulle also talked separately with Secretary of State Hull, War Secretary Stimson, and Treasury Secretary

Morgenthau. Roosevelt assured de Gaulle that France would be among the "policemen" that would cooperate in managing international relations after the war. On July 11, Roosevelt announced that the Free French movement "is qualified to exercise the administration of France." When Hull pressed him for a full recognition, Roosevelt explained that, "the Provisional Government has no direct authority from the people" so it was "best to let things go along as they are." Roosevelt finally agreed to a joint declaration by the allies recognizing the FCNL on October 25, 1944, two months after the liberation of Paris and de Gaulle's installation of his organization in power there.

Throughout the war, the allied leaders and their advisors debated Germany's postwar fate. Treasury Secretary Morgenthau asserted the harshest plan. He called for stripping Germany of its heavy industries, breaking it up into smaller states, and grounding the economy on producing crops and livestock. War Secretary Henry Stimson denounced Morgenthau's plan as a "Carthaginian peace" and "Semitism gone wild for vengeance and" that "will lay the seeds for another war in the next generation."[48] He argued that Germany should be reconstructed and integrated within Europe as an economic engine of growth and prosperity that reduced the chances for war. Typically, rather than choose between the two, Roosevelt gave the impression separately to Morgenthau and Stimson that he favored his plan.

During a meeting with Roosevelt on January 16, 1944, Morgenthau pressured him to accept his plan and do anything possible to save the surviving Jews from the Holocaust. Roosevelt reassured Morgenthau that Germany would suffer a harsh fate but explained that militarily the allies could only liberate the concentration camps after defeating Germany's armies. Six days later as a consolation prize, Roosevelt established the War Refugee Board, chaired by Assistant Secretary of State John McCloy, to provide shelter, food, medicine, and other aid to Jews and others that fled the Nazis. The War Refugee Board issued a report in June 1944 that bombing railroad tracks leading to concentration camps would likely miss or be swiftly repaired while diverting crucial air power from destroying German industries, while bombing the camps themselves would help the Nazis murder the prisoners. The only way to save the survivors was for allied armies to overrun the camps and defeat Germany as swiftly and decisively as possible.[49]

Meanwhile, Roosevelt released this statement to reporters on March 24: "In one of the blackest crimes of all history – begun by the Nazis in the days of peace and multiplied by them a hundred times in the time of war – the wholesale, systematic murder of the Jews of Europe goes on unabated every hour...None who participate in these acts of savagery shall go unpunished...Hitler is committing these crimes against humanity in the name of the German people. I am asking every German and every person...everywhere under German domination to show the world by his action that...he does not share these insane criminal desires. Let him hide these pursued victims, help them to get over their borders and do what he can to save them from the Nazi hangmen."[50]

Stimson's War Department issued an occupation plan called the Handbook for Military Government in Germany that emphasized practical ways to provide short-term humanitarian aid with food, medicine, and shelter for the needy and long-term financial aid that revived the economy, put people to work, and rebuilt infrastructure like railroads, stations, bridges, roads, and electricity grids.

Roosevelt's latest summit with Churchill was at Quebec from September 12 to 16, 1944. He had Treasury Secretary Morgenthau accompany him to present his plan to strip Germany of its industries and break it up into agrarian states. That plan appalled Churchill who insisted that: "I am all for disarming Germany, but we ought not prevent her living decently...You cannot indict a whole nation."[51] Morgenthau's Plan was leaked to the press which prompted the *Washington Post, New York Times*, and *Wall Street Journal* to report and denounce the plan. That carried the debate over Germany's fate from behind firmly closed doors among high allied leaders and officials to the public.

Thomas Dewey, the Republican presidential candidate, denounced Morgenthau's plan on the campaign trail as "so clumsy that Mr. Roosevelt himself finally dropped it. But the damage was done" and for bolstering Nazi Germany with the equivalent of "ten fresh German divisions. It put fight back into the German army. It stiffened the will of the German nation to resist. Almost overnight the headlong retreat of the Germans stopped. They stood and fought fanatically."[52]

Roosevelt received protests from his inner circle. Army Chief of Staff Marshall denounced Morgenthau's Plan for stiffening German resistance. OSS Chief William Donovan presented a report from Allen Dulles, in Bern, who warned that Morgenthau's Plan was backfiring by enhancing the Nazi regime's determination to fight ruthlessly without surrendering. Roosevelt peddled back from the plan.

One vital issue that the president and his key advisors agreed on was how to reconstruct the global economy. Secretary of State Hull explained how freer trade and greater interdependence among countries boosted the national prosperity and security of each: "I know that without expansion of international trade, based upon fair dealing and equal treatment for all, there can be no stability and security either within or among nations...I know the withdrawal by a nation from orderly trade relations with the rest of the world inevitably leads to regimentation of all phases of national life, to the suppression of human rights, and all too frequently to preparations for war and a provocative attitude toward other nations."[53]

The Roosevelt administration hosted a conference attended by 730 delegates from 44 countries at the Mount Washington Hotel at Bretton Woods, New Hampshire from July 1 to 22, 1944.[54] The delegates agreed that postwar economic expansion depended on stable currency exchange rates and financial investments. To that end, they established two global financial organizations that received money from and dispensed money to their nation-state members. Countries that joined the International Monetary Fund (IMF) agreed to fix their currencies to the price of gold at $32 an ounce could borrow money to make short-term investments to maintain their currency's value. The International Bank for Reconstruction and Development (IRBD) or World Bank lent money to members for investments that reconstructed their war-shattered cities and infrastructure like roads, railroads, ports, electricity grids, and water and sewage systems then other projects that further developed their economies.

Roosevelt's vision for the Four Policemen managing international relations was first realized during the preliminary negotiations for designing the United Nations at Dumbarton Oaks, a mansion and estate in Georgetown, a Washington neighborhood from August 21 to October 7.[55] Undersecretary of State Edward Stettinius chaired the committee with Ambassadors Alexander Cadogan of Britain, Wellington Koo of China, and Andrei Gromyko of the Soviet Union. There were actually separate sessions for Koo and Gromyko because Stalin had not yet recognized Chiang Kai-shek's regime as China's legitimate government. Stettinius and Cadogan had to fend off Gromyko's demand that all sixteen Soviet "republics" be members; they agreed to defer that dispute to a future meeting. Nonetheless, the four envoys eventually agreed to a rough draft that included a Security Council with the four as permanent members and other states with temporary two-year memberships, a general assembly where each state would have an equal vote, and a secretariat headed by a secretary-general. That plan would be submitted to a conference of all existing or would-be United Nations members at San Franciso from April to June 1945.

Chapter 11

THE DENOUEMENT

"This time we are not making the mistake of waiting until the end of the war to set up the machinery of peace. This time, as we fight together to win the war, we work together to keep it from happening again." (Franklin Roosevelt)

"I didn't say the result was good. I said it was the best I could do." (Franklin Roosevelt)

By December 1944, Franklin Roosevelt was confident that the final defeat of Germany and Japan was inevitable, although just when and at what cost was impossible to predict. In the Pacific, parallel thrusts by Admiral Chester Nimitz and General Douglas MacArthur had fought their way across swaths of that vast ocean but were still far from Japan. Although MacArthur was bogged down in the Philippines, Nimitz was preparing to invade Okinawa in the Ryukyu Island chain extending from Japan itself. In Europe, the Soviets were on the Oder River just forty miles east of Berlin, while in northwest Europe the now seven armies, four American and one each British, Canadian, and French, appeared stalled in the snowy, frozen winter.

Hitler and his staff secretly massed the Fifth and Sixth Panzer armies for a massive attack on the thinly defended fifty-mile stretch of the allied line held by First Army in the Ardennes Forest of southeastern Belgium.[1] The plan was to punch through that line and race to Antwerp, the allied supply center. The German offensive began on December 16, 1944, and after a week had pushed a huge bulge westward in the allied line. Within that bulge was the strategic crossroads town of Bastogne, where the Americans repulsed repeated attacks.

After learning of the offensive, General Dwight Eisenhower assigned Generals Omar Bradley and Bernard Montgomery, the respective commanders of Army Groups Twelve and Twenty-one, to organize counteroffensives by troops respectively south and north of the bulge. Bradley rankled at having temporarily to cede command of his First Army to Montgomery, but retained authority over General George Patton's Third Army. Typically Montgomery needed two weeks to devise an elaborate set-piece offensive against the bulge's north side. Patton promised Eisenhower that he would attack with three divisions on December 22.[2] He was good to his word. He had anticipated the German blitzkrieg and had his staff devise a flank attack plan. Third Army troops fought their way through German lines to join forces with Bastogne's defenders on December 26. But Eisenhower rejected Patton's plan to attack the bulge's base and cut off and destroy the German forces westward.

Instead, Eisenhower insisted that they flatten the bulge from its westward tip eastward. That strategy cost the allies vast unnecessary death and destruction. By the time the Americans eliminated the bulge on January 28, they had suffered 105,000 casualties, including 19,246 dead and 23,000 prisoners as well as lost 800 tanks and 1,000 aircraft while inflicting 82,000 casualties and destroying 550 tanks and 800 aircraft.[3] The allies could replace their loses, the Germans could not. Hitler's gamble was a crippling defeat. He would have prolonged the war had he kept those forces in reserve to blunt allied spring offensives.

The war's most controversial summit unrolled among Franklin Roosevelt, Winston Churchill, and Joseph Stalin at Livadiya Palace in Yalta from February 4 to 11, 1945.[4] Roosevelt and Churchill rendezvoused at Malta before and then took separate flights to Yalta. Each day, the three leaders met for formal talks for several hours then reconvened each evening for dinner and drinking that ended hours later. With Roosevelt were Harry Hopkins, Admiral William Leahy, War Secretary Edward Stettinius, and Charles Bohlen, the State Department translator. Accompanying Churchill were Foreign Secretary Anthony Eden, Foreign Office Undersecretary Alexander Cadogan, Secretary to the Cabinet Edward Bridges, Clark Kerr, ambassador to the Soviet Union. Hovering near Stalin were Foreign Minister Molotov, Deputy Foreign Minister Andrei Vyshinsky, and Andrei Gromyko, ambassador to the United States.

Three crucial forces shaped the summit's decisions. One was the hard power of boots on the ground. When the summit opened, Soviet forces were on the Oder River forty miles east of Berlin while American and British forces were west of the Rhine River with Berlin around three hundred miles away. Another was the president's health. Roosevelt was literally at death's door and looked it. He was haggard, emaciated, listless, at best could focus two to four hours daily, and dozed off during long meetings. His heart was enlarged and his blood pressure soared as high as 240/130. Yet, at times, he rallied and displayed some of his charm, knowledge, and intelligence. The third was that Roosevelt, in his lucid moments, did what he had done at Tehran, currying favor with Stalin by denigrating and disputing Churchill. In doing so, he again played into Stalin's hands. Stalin sought to split Roosevelt and Churchill, and the president was doing that for him.

The result was that Roosevelt and Churchill struggled to stave off a series of Stalin's demands. Stalin demanded reparations. The allies agreed on $20 billion of which the Soviets would receive half. A tripartite commission would determine how to extract and distribute the money.

Stalin insisted on a free hand in Poland. Roosevelt amiably and Churchill adamantly wanted free elections in which the London exile government led by Stanislaw Mikolajczyk would compete with the communist Lublin exile government that the Red army had put in power in Warsaw. Roosevelt was actually indifferent to the London Polish government to whom he had not bothered appointing an ambassador. His chief concern was that Stalin give him a political fig-leaf that he could display to Polish-American voters in the next election. Stalin granted him that with his promise to conduct "free elections" in Poland. Of course, what he meant was a communist-style election with the results pre-determined. After the summit, when Stalin continued to bar the London Poles from their homeland, Churchill erupted in fury to Roosevelt: "Poland has lost her frontier. Is she now to lose her freedom?...We are in the presence of a great failure and an utter breakdown of what was settled at Yalta."[5]

Roosevelt asked Stalin to reiterate and elaborate his previous promise to war against Japan within three months of Germany's surrender. Stalin offered some new details while having Roosevelt repeat his pledge to accept the Soviet takeover of the Kurile Islands and Sakhalin Island's southern half from Japan, and special rights and Port Arthur as a naval base in Manchuria from China in return for Stalin recognizing Chiang Kai-shek's regime as China's legitimate government.

Stalin made one "concession." He had previously demanded that all fifteen so-called "republics" of the Soviet Union be given separate seats in the United Nation along with the Soviet Union, or sixteen altogether. Now he was willing to settle for three extra, Ukraine, Lithuania, and Belarus with the Soviet Union, for four seats altogether.

How did Roosevelt's miserable health affect his performance at Yalta. Leahy later observed "that Roosevelt conducted the Crimean

Conference with great skill and...his personality... dominated the discussions," while Harriman felt that although the proceedings fatigued him, the president "had blocked out definite objectives which he had clearly in his mind and he carried on the negotiations with his usual skill and perception."[6]

Roosevelt later privately offered a fair evaluation of the conference: "I didn't say the result was good. I said it was the best I could do."[7] To Congress on March 1, he presented an ideal version that subsequent history would belie: "The Crimea Conference was a successful effort by the three leading Nations to find a common ground for peace. It sought to spell the end of the system of unilateral action, the exclusive alliances...the balance of power, and all other expedients that have been tried for centuries – and have always failed. This time we are not making the mistake of waiting until the end of the war to set up the machinery of peace. This time, as we fight together to win the war, we work together to keep it from happening again." He then went on to say: "The conference...was a turning point, I hope, in our history and therefore in the history of the world...We shall have to take the responsibility for world collaboration or we shall have to bear the responsibility for another world conflict...Twenty-five years ago, American fighting men looked to the statesmen of the world to finish the work of peace for which they fought and suffered. We failed them then. We cannot fail them again."[8]

That soon proved to be his last address to Congress. His most startling gesture was sitting in a chair rather than standing at the podium, and admitting that he was crippled: "I hope you will pardon me for the unusual posture of sitting down during the presentation of what I want to say, but...it makes it a lot easier for me in not having to carry about ten pounds of steel around on the bottom of my legs, and also because I have just completed a fourteen thousand mile trip."[9] Until that time reporters, photographers, and others aware of his disability that required a wheelchair, being lifted, and painfully standing and walking had kept the secret.

Roosevelt went to his "Little White House" at Warm Springs, Georgia on March 28 for several weeks of relaxing therapy. He was accompanied by his daughter Anna and soon joined by Lucy Mercer Rutherfurd with whom he had resumed his affair after her husband died in March 1944.

A diplomatic dispute with Moscow erupted while he was there. In March, Allen Dulles, the OSS station chief for Switzerland, met twice in Zurich with General Karl Wolff who sought on behalf of Italian front commander General Albert Kesselring to unconditionally surrender his army. Roosevelt and Churchill dutifully informed Stalin of that diplomatic channel. Stalin first demanded that several Soviet generals join any subsequent formal talks then, fearing Roosevelt and Churchill sought a separate peace with Germany, demanded that the talks end. On April 4, Roosevelt wrote Stalin that his message "astounded" him, and that: "It would be one of the great tragedies of history if, at the very moment of victory now within our grasp, such distrust, such lack of faith should prejudice the entire undertaking after the colossal losses of life, material, and treasure involved. I cannot avoid a feeling of bitter resentment toward your informers for such a vile misrepresentation of my actions or those of my trusted subordinates."[10] Stalin replied with a conciliatory message.

That was Roosevelt's last diplomatic act. A cerebral hemorrhage killed him on April 12. Lucy hurried away as Eleanor and an entourage arrived by plane. A train conveyed Roosevelt's body to Washington where it appeared at the White House for a brief funeral ceremony, then was taken to Hyde Park, where he was buried in his estate's garden on April 15.

Before leaving for Warm Springs, Eleanor had summoned Vice President Harry Truman to the White House. She stunned him by announcing that, "Harry, the president is dead." Truman offered his deep condolence and asked if there was anything he could do. Eleanor replied, "Is there anything we can do for you? For you are the one in trouble now."[11]

Harry Truman had the character and political experience to be a successful president.[12] He was renowned for his honesty, modesty, plain-speech, hard work, and common sense. He was born in the small farm town of Lamar, Missouri In 1884, but grew up in the neighboring large town of Independence. After graduating from high school, he failed to get his congressman to sponsor him for West Point. Instead, he held a series of jobs including bank clerk in Independence and for a decade returned to the family farm although he detested farming. He served in the National Guard from 1905 to 1911, and rose to corporal of the artillery company. During the First World War, he rejoined his regiment and eventually became the artillery company's captain. After the war, he and a partner invested in a men's clothing store but they eventually filed for bankruptcy. After a courtship lasting half a dozen years, he married Bess Wallace in 1919, and they soon had Margaret, their only child.

Tom Pendergast was the boss of the Kansas City Democratic Party machine.[13] He backed Truman's candidacy for a series of political posts first for judge of eastern Jackson County in 1922, then chief judge of Jackson County in 1928, and finally Missouri's open Senate seat in 1934. Throughout those years, Truman managed to benefit from Pendergast's machine without directly palming bribes or anything else illegal. He did, however, turn a blind eye to the machine's ballot stuffing, and, when asked, appointed Pendergast flunkies to administrative posts and gave contracts to Pendergast business cronies regardless of their merits.

As senator, Truman served on the Appropriations and Interstate Commerce Committees and acquired fame chairing the wartime Special Committee to Investigate the National Defense Program and expose waste, red-tape, graft, price-gouging, and excessive profits. He was a realist. His response to the German invasion of the Soviet Union in June 1941, was: "If we see that Germany is winning, we ought to help Russia, and if Russia is winning we ought to help Germany, and that way let them kill as many as possible – although I don't want to see Hitler victorious under any circumstances."[14]

Truman enthusiastically backed Roosevelt's New Deal and war policies. That along with his pragmatism and home in a key midwest state prompted Roosevelt to drop his controversial leftist vice president Henry Wallace and tap him as his running mate in 1944. But thereafter, Roosevelt had little to do with Truman and kept him from his inner circle. After taking the oath of office, Truman received briefings on an array of vital issues of which the atomic bomb project was the most critical. Fortunately, he was a quick study and soon understood the essence of each challenge.

As president, Truman listened carefully to his advisors and forged agreements on policies. Biographer Alonzo Hamby explained that: "every major decision of his presidency…was the product of careful political or diplomatic planning and group consensus, not individual whim. The man who liked to present himself as a quick decision maker was actually slow and cautious on big things."[15] He kept most of Roosevelt's cabinet except for one key post. He asked Secretary of State Edward Stettinius to resign and replaced him with his friend James Brynes, a former senator from South Carolina.[16]

Franklin Roosevelt died when the war's end in Europe was literally just beyond the horizon and that in the Pacific was inevitable if hazy.[17] Truman essentially presided over the related economic, military, and diplomatic strategies developed by his predecessor to win the war and then win the peace. While his administration was unified on those policies, it split bitterly over how to deal with Stalin, Soviet expansion, and communism's revolutionary ideology. The most prominent hardliners included former ambassador William Bullitt, War Secretary Henry Stimson, Navy Secretary James Forrestal, and Army Chief of Staff George Marshall versus the most prominent appeasers Harry Hopkins and former ambassador Joseph Davies.

Throughout early 1945, the allies massed troops and supplies for a final set of offensives designed first to clear German troops west of the Rhine then cross that river and surge east to crush the Germans against the Soviet army fighting westward. By early March, the Germans had retreated east of the Rhine, dynamiting every bridge behind them but one. General Courtney Hodges's First Army captured at Remagen the only intact bridge on March 7; the Germans tried to blow it up as the Americans attacked, but the explosion was too weak. Hodges reinforced the bridgehead to repel repeated German attacks over the next two weeks.

Typically, Patton beat Montgomery across the Rhine. On March 23, he packed six battalions in boats and sent them over to secure a beachhead near Oppenheim and build a pontoon bridge behind them. Within days, he had other pontoon bridges span the river up- and down-stream across which his divisions rumbled then fanned out to overrun German forces. Typically, Montgomery built up overwhelming forces for a carefully planned battle by his Twenty-First Army Group with 1.2 million troops in the British Second, Canadian First, and American Nineth armies that crossed against light opposition, preceded by massive artillery and air bombardments then paratroopers from two divisions from March 24 to 28. Up the Rhine, the American Seventh and French First Armies seized their own crossings. Fighting was limited as hundreds of thousands of Germans surrendered knowing their nation had lost the war. Among the allied troops driving eastward were two especially trained units with specific missions, one to find and intern leading German scientists, engineers, and technicians, and the other to find and secure looted works of art, the "Monuments Men."[18] Over March and April, around 440,000 Germans fought 1,338,500 allied troops, a one to three ratio, and inflicted 312,000 casualties, including 119,000 Americans along with destroying 3,377 aircraft and 8,011 tanks and other armored vehicles while suffering around 200,000 casualties before the final surrender.

Meanwhile, the Red Army steamrolled the German army's remnants in eastern Germany. The Soviets outnumbered and outgunned the Germans with eleven times more infantry, seven times more tanks, and twenty times more artillery; 180 Soviet divisions battled 80 severely depleted German divisions.[19]

Churchill urged Truman to race the American and British armies eastward and liberate as much of Germany as possible, ideally as far as Berlin, to prevent the Soviets from taking over. Meanwhile, Patton begged Eisenhower to let him drive toward Berlin or Prague. Eisenhower, backed by Army Chief of Staff George Marshall, rejected that notion. They worried that advancing western allied troops might inadvertently clash with Soviet troops. Eisenhower dismissed Berlin as a "political object."[20]

Truman reluctantly accepted the advice of Marshall and Eisenhower, but like Churchill he worried about the Soviets advancing to the heart of Europe. At the White House, he met Foreign Minister Vyacheslav Molotov on April 23. Molotov came with a list of demands that he assumed he could intimidate the neophyte president into accepting. After Truman bluntly rejected those demands, Molotov complained that, "I have never been talked to like that in my life." Truman replied, "Carry out your agreements and you won't get talked to like that."[21]

The Soviets launched a massive offensive in late March that punched through and routed the Germans with an army surrounding Berlin in late April and Russian and Americans troops joyfully shaking hands at Torgau on the Elbe River on April 25. Hitler transferred General Albert Kesselring to command the western front in late April 1945, and replaced him as Italy's commander with General Heinrich von Vietinghoff. Vietinghoff signed a surrender document on April 29 that took effect on May 2, 1945. After naming Admiral Karl Donitz his successor, Hitler thrust a pistol in his mouth and pulled the trigger on April 30. Over the next week, Donitz and several subordinates tried to arrange an armistice. Eisenhower agreed to receive a German ambassador at his headquarters in Rheims, France. Donitz sent General Alfred Jodl, who signed a document for Germany's unconditional surrender on May 7, 1945 that took effect at midnight, May 8. The war in Europe was finally over.

A merciless war continued to rage in the Pacific. General Haywood Hansell's Twenty-First Bomber Command began bombing Japan from bases at Tinian, Saipan, and Guam on November 24, 1944. His strategy was to fly 30,000 feet high in daylight with high explosives to hit industrial targets far below. That strategy inflicted little damage. On January 20, 1945, the Joint Chiefs replaced Hansell with General Curtis Lemay, who shifted the strategy to low-level night attacks that dropped incendiary bombs.[22]

LeMay insisted that Iwo Jima be captured to provide an airfield for P-51 Mustang fighter escorts and for emergency landings for B-29s crippled by Japanese warplanes or flak during their missions. Iwo Jima was four and a half miles long and two and a half miles wide with extinct volcano Mount Suribachi looming above the mostly flat sandy terrain.[23] The Japanese turned that small island into a warren of deep interconnected bunkers and tunnels that could withstand bombs and shells. It took 110,000 marines commanded by General Harry Schmidt five weeks to capture Iwo Jima from their landing on February 19 until March 26, 1945. American casualties surpassed that of the defenders, 26,571 including 6,821 dead; they killed all but 216 of the 21,000 defenders. The Japanese also destroyed 127 American tanks and 153 warplanes. That terrible cost in American blood to seize Iwo Jima was partly offset by the number of lives saved as 2,400 planes made emergency landings there before the war's end. The photo of the five marines raising the American flag atop Mount Suribachi became a national icon.[24]

LeMay's mass flights of B-29s dropping incendiary bombs systematically destroyed Japanese cities, with sixty-four mostly charred ruins, 400,000 dead, hundreds of thousands of wounded, and millions of homeless refugees by the war's end. The worst attack devastated Tokyo on March 9 and 10, when 334 B-29s destroyed 267,171 buildings and killed at least 83,793 and wounded 40,918.[25]

As for ground combat, in the Philippines after securing Leyte, General Douglas MacArthur had General Walter Krueger's Sixth army first invade Mindoro island on December 15, then the main island of Luzon on January 9. The Japanese fought fiercely. The Americans did not capture the devastated capital of Manila until March 4. Meanwhile, MacArthur had General Robert Eichelberger's Eighth Army overrun other Philippine islands including Palawan, Zamboanga, Panay, Mindanao, and Cebu. All along, Filipino guerrillas aided the American advance. The death and destruction persisted until Tokyo announced on August 15 that Japan would surrender. The entire campaign for the Philippines cost the Americans around 145,000 casualties, including 10,380 dead, 35,550 wounded, and 93,400 illnesses, 33 warships sunk, 95 warships damaged, and 485 warplanes destroyed while killing as many as 220,000 Japanese, sinking 95 warships, and destroying 1,300 warplanes. As for Filipinos, around 100,000 died just in the battle for Manila and perhaps 500,000 during the fighting from September 1944 to August 1945.[26] Strategically and morally that was a horrendous waste of blood and treasure since Japan's defeat depended on who held Okinawa, the key island in the Ryukyu Island chain, not the Philippines.

The invasion of Okinawa began on April 1, 1945, with 180,000 marines and soldiers conveyed, supported, and protected by 1,200 ships including forty fleet, light, and escort carriers with 3,000 warplanes and eighteen battleships, and. General Simon Buckner commanded the Tenth Army of two army and two marine divisions in the initial landing with one marine and two army divisions eventually landing elsewhere. Admiral Richmond Turner commanded the amphibious phase after which Admiral Raymond Spruance took over the fleet. Defending Okinawa were 80,000 Japanese troops, 40,000 Okinawan conscripts commanded by General Mitsuru Ushijima. The Japanese fought the invaders virtually every foot of the way until the Americans wiped out the last serious resistance on June 22. During the 82-day campaign, over 700 kamikazes flew against the Americans, with over 200 striking targets. That victory cost the Americans 50,000 casualties, including 12,500 dead and 36,122 wounded along with 763 warplanes, 153 tanks, and 21 sunk and 386 damaged ships; Buckner was among the dead and the highest ranking American officer killed during the war. The Japanese suffered 77,166 dead soldiers, perhaps 15,000 conscripts and 80,000 civilians, 1,430 destroyed warplanes and a sunk battleship and fourteen other warships.

Japan's four main islands include Honshu the largest where Tokyo is located, Hokkaido to the north, Kyushu southwest and Shikoku south. All four islands are mountainous terrain that aids defenders. Kyushu's south tip is only 400 miles from Okinawa. The Pacific War's next stage was the invasion of Kyushu, scheduled for November 1, followed by the invasion of Honshu on March 1, 1946. Estimated American casualties for capturing just Kyushu ranged as high as 268,000 of 767,000 invaders, while perhaps a million or more Americans would be killed or maimed before Honshu was secured. Defending Japan were over 2 million soldiers and tens of millions of civilian men, women, and children over twelve years old who were given spears and grenades to use against the Americans. Millions of Japanese soldiers and civilians would die fighting or from carpet bombings and crossfires. Then a horrendous secret weapon kept those horrors from happening.[27]

President Truman established the Interim Committee to debate ways to encourage the Japanese to surrender before the invasion, how to use the atomic bomb if it worked, and what to do with the technology after the war. The Committee's most prominent members included War Secretary Stimson, Navy Secretary Forrestal, Secretary of State Brynes, Under-secretary of State Joseph Grew, the former ambassador to Japan, and Manhattan Project director Robert Oppenheimer. In a series of meetings that began on May 9, they reached key decisions.

They agreed to retain Emperor Hirohito as a constitutional monarch in a democratic political system while abolishing the military. They would not invite an international group of observers to witness the atomic bomb's test and then convey that news to Tokyo, fearing that a dud would encourage the Japanese to never give up. If the test succeeded, they decided not to inform the Japanese fearing that they would put American war prisoners as hostages in unbombed cities. They concluded that only the shock of an entire city destroyed with one bomb might force Japan's government to surrender. They also opposed sharing the technology with the Soviet Union. On July 4, the Combined Policy Committee approved the use of atomic bombs against Japan. Truman would make the final decisions of when and where to drop the bombs.

Meanwhile, diplomats realized Roosevelt's vision for the United Nations. Eight hundred and fifty delegates from 50 countries attended the United Nations Conference on International Organization from April 25 to June 26, 1945. They debated and negotiated details of the United Nations Charter or constitution that the Big Four had devised during the Dumbarton Oaks conference the previous October. They signed the United Nations Charter on June 26. The Senate ratified the United Nations Charter by 89 to 2 on July 28, 1945.

Truman sought a summit with Stalin and Churchill to forge understandings on increasingly divisive issues, especially the fate of eastern Europe. They met at the Cecilianhof Palace in Potsdam, a Berlin suburb from July 17 to August 2.[28] Accompanying Truman were Secretary of State Brynes and advisor Harry Hopkins. Accompanying Churchill and Foreign Minister Anthony Eden were opposition leaders Clement Atlee and Ernest Bevin, who replaced them on August 1, after the Labor Party beat the Conservative Party in an election on July 5, with the results announced on July 26.

Truman, Churchill, and Stalin mostly rehashed issues and agreements forged at the earlier Tehran and Yalta summits. They agreed generally on German reparations, denazification, war crimes trials, and four allied occupation zones; the communist-dominated Lublin government for Poland with frontiers shifted westward to the Oder-Neisse Rivers and Curzon line; Soviet war against Japan within a month; and free elections for eastern European countries.

Truman received stunning news on July 16. The Manhattan Project had successfully tested an atomic bomb at the Trinity Site in New Mexico's desert near Alamogordo. On July 24, Truman told Stalin that scientists had created a "new weapon of unusual destructive force." Stalin replied that "he was glad to hear it and hoped we would make good use of it against the Japanese."[29] Stalin already knew about the atomic bomb project through spies embedded at Los Alamos. On July 26, Truman, Churchill, and Chiang Kai-shek with a proxy issued the Potsdam Declaration demanding that Tokyo "proclaim now... unconditional surrender" or else suffer "prompt and utter destruction" in return for an allied occupation that demilitarized and democratized Japan, conducted war crimes trials, and established "in accordance with the freely expressed will of the Japanese people...a peacefully inclined and responsible government." Although the declaration did not mention the emperor, the framers assumed that the Japanese would understand that they could retain the imperial institution if it upheld international peace and responsibility.

Japan's Imperial War Council met and unanimously agreed to reject the peace offering. Prime Minister Kantaro Suzuki's public response on July 28 had one key word – *Mokusatsu* – which means to treat something with utter silent contempt and loathing.

Truman authorized the military to drop the first atomic bomb on a Japanese city.[30] That mission was the duty of the 509th Composite Group of fifteen modified B-29s with specially trained crews to drop atomic bombs commanded by General Paul Tibbets from the base on Tinian Island. Tibbets piloted the B-29 that dropped an atomic bomb that destroyed Hiroshima on August 6; the explosion immediately killed 70,000 people and perhaps another 70,000 died from radiation poisoning over the next few months. The White House issued a statement that if the Japanese did not immediately surrender "they may expect a rain of ruin from the air, the like of which has never been seen on this earth." Moscow declared war against Japan on August 8, and launched a massive offensive against Japanese forces in China and Korea the next day. With no word from Tokyo, Truman authorized a second bombing that destroyed Nagasaki on August 9, killing 40,000 people and thereafter perhaps 30,000 more.

Even after suffering two vaporized cities, Japan's Supreme War Council of three military and three civilian leaders presided over by Hirohito debated what to do, with the civilians favoring surrender and the military insisting that all Japanese die fighting. Finally, on August 10, the emperor resolved the stalemate by agreeing to surrender. Later that day, Tokyo announced that it would accept the Potsdam Declaration as the basis for surrender providing "it does not compromise...the prerogatives of His Majesty as a sovereign ruler." The White House issued on August 11 this reply: "From the moment of surrender, the authority of the emperor and the Japanese government to rule the State shall be subject to the Supreme Commander of the Allied Powers who will take such steps as he deems proper to effectuate the surrender terms." When Tokyo signaled its acceptance, Truman ordered all military operations against Japan halted but nearly had to resume them. Japan's government thwarted two attempted military coups to prevent the capitulation. On August 14, Hirohito issued a radio broadcast that informed Japan's military and civilians that Japan would surrender.

Truman appointed Douglas MacArthur to be the Supreme Commander for Allied Powers who would oversee Japan's surrender and occupation until the country had been demilitarized and democratized. A massive American fleet anchored in Tokyo Bay on September 2. Aboard the battleship USS *Missouri*, MacArthur headed the allied delegation that received Japan's delegation led by Foreign Minister Mamoru Shigemitsu. After the Japanese officials signed the surrender document, MacArthur signed on the alliance's behalf followed by each ally's envoy. The Second World War officially ended that day.

The number of people who died directly and indirectly from the Second World War will never be known. The general estimate is around 25 million military deaths and 50 million civilian deaths, including 27 million Soviets, 20 million Chinese, 7.4 million Germans, 6 million Poles, 3.1 million Japanese, 600,000 French, 500 Italians, 450,000 British, and the rest from around fifty other countries and colonies. The cost of the destruction and lost economic potential is incalculable.[31]

The United States suffered a total of 405,399 military deaths including 291,557 from combat and 113,842 from other causes like accidents, disease, and mortal wounds, and 670,826 non-mortal wounded along with 12,100 civilian deaths. Although twelve million or one in ten Americans served in the military during the Second World War, the million who were killed and wounded was less than one percent of the nation's population. The war cost America $288 billion at the time but with interest payments on loans and veterans' benefits including health care and education the eventual price was $664 billion.[32]

Chapter 12

THE LEGACY

"Every single man, woman, and child is a partner in the most tremendous undertaking of our American history. When we resort to force, we are determined that this force will be directed toward ultimate good as well as immediate evil. We Americans are not destroyers – we are builders. We are now in the midst of a war, not for conquest, not for vengeance, but for a world in which this Nation, and all this Nation represents, will be safe for our children." (Franklin Roosevelt)

"Victory in this war is the first and greatest goal before us. Victory in peace is the next." (Franklin Roosevelt)

Leadership is the art of getting others willingly to follow one's choices for a common purpose.[1] Leadership can come from formally heading a government, army, corporation, or some other organization or group as well as from behind the scenes through intermediaries. A leader must be a salesperson, marketing a vision and the way to attain it to followers. Leaders appeal not just to people's reason but more vitally to their hopes and fears. Above all, leaders must be masters of power, getting others to do things they might not otherwise do and acquiring the means for them to succeed. Ultimately, leaders are judged by their accomplishments, by the threats they thwart and the opportunities they seize or create. Great national leaders make their realms more prosperous, powerful, and secure.

Franklin Roosevelt excelled at leadership by any measure. He was elected four times to the presidency by solid majorities while no other president has served more than two terms. As president he faced the unprecedented challenges of first the Great Depression and then imperialism by Japan, Germany, and Italy. The policies he devised and implemented through Congress led America out of the Great Depression. The policies he devised and implemented through

Congress in alliance with Britain, the Soviet Union, and China crushed the fascist powers in the Second World War.

Roosevelt's leadership abilities were rooted in his personality and character. His ebullient, confident personality inspired his immediate advisors, key political, business, labor, and other leaders, and the public. Just as vital was his character of mingled courage, probity, self-discipline, toughness, compassion, and open-mindedness. Eleanor explained that: "He never talked about his doubts...I never knew him to face life, or any problem that came up, with fear, and I have often wondered if that courageous attitude was communicated to the people of the country. It may well be what helped them to pull themselves out of the depression in the first years of his administration as president."[2]

Among Roosevelt's greatest strengths was his skill at explaining complex problems and possible solutions in simple language that nearly anyone could understand. "Fireside chat" perfectly described his radio broadcast technique of speaking in an intimate tone and words that gave listeners the impression he was beside them in their living rooms sharing their concerns and desires. He knew how to appeal to people's deepest emotions, encouraging their hopes, soothing their fears, and inspiring and unifying them with a progressive vision of their collective future. For instance, shortly after Pearl Harbor, he declared: "Every single man, woman, and child is a partner in the most tremendous undertaking of our American history. When we resort to force, we are determined that this force will be directed toward ultimate good as well as immediate evil. We Americans are not destroyers – we are builders. We are now in the midst of a war, not for conquest, not for vengeance, but for a world in which this Nation, and all this Nation represents, will be safe for our children."[3]

Roosevelt understood that being a politician involved playing roles with none more exalted than playing the president. Each president interpreted and acted that role differently according to his own character, principles, experiences, and aspirations. Although people expected and accepted that variety, they wanted any president to display mingled attributes of gravitas, wisdom, generosity, toughness, open-mindedness, and humor greater than that of other men. For most Americans, Roosevelt exemplified that image.

Roosevelt was hyper-conscious that he constantly played the president whether it was with an audience of one in the Oval Office or tens of millions listening to one of his radio broadcasts. For Roosevelt, playing president came naturally because he had consciously acted a series of roles all his life, but his skills expanded after polio crippled him when he was thirty-nine years old. His most challenging role was not the presidency, a role that he relished naturally playing, but was pretending and getting others to believe that he was not crippled.[4]

During Roosevelt's presidency, the Democratic and Republican parties overlapped ideologically with progressive Republicans and conservative Democrats.[5] That allowed for bipartisan pragmatic domestic and foreign policies. Roosevelt was adept at reaching across the aisle to progressive Republicans on domestic issues and internationalist Republicans on foreign issues. He forged political partnerships and friendships with Senators Robert Norris of Nebraska and New York mayor Fiorella LaGuardia. He welcomed into his inner policy circle Republicans Henry Stimson as war secretary and Frank Knox as naval secretary.

Roosevelt established the modern Democratic Party as a coalition among workers, farmers, women, blacks, Catholics, Jews, and big city bosses. Women and blacks were the most vital defectors he enticed from the Republican to the Democratic Party. The Democratic Party had a Women's Division affiliated with the League of Women Voters, the National Consumers League, and the Women's Trade Union League. For blacks, the Democratic Party forged ties with the National Association for the Advancement of Colored People (NAACP) and Urban League.

Roosevelt established the modern presidency. Historian William Leuchtenburg concluded that: "Under Roosevelt, the White House became the focus of all government – the fountainhead of ideas, the initiator of action, the representative of the national interest. He took an office which had lost much of its prestige and power in the previous twelve years and gave it an importance which even Theodore Roosevelt and Woodrow Wilson had not done. [H]e re-created the modern presidency."[6] He believed that government had to be as powerful as the problems facing the nation. He captured his political philosophy's essence during his 1932 presidential campaign in a speech before the Commonwealth Club in San Francisco: "The age of enlightened administration has come." The 1933 Economy Act empowered Roosevelt to reorganize the federal government to cut waste and boost efficiency. To that end, Roosevelt issued scores of executive orders that created or transformed organizations designed to overcome specific problems.

Ultimately Roosevelt's leadership legacy rests on how his policies transformed the United States into an economic and military superpower. His New Deal policies saved America's market system from itself.[7] Four forces shape markets – supply, demand, greed, and fear. Historically, the freer a market, the sooner it self-destructs in two ways. The larger more dynamic businesses first devour smaller, less dynamic businesses then each other until oligopolies and monopolies destroy the free market with price fixing, profit-gouging, and shoddy goods and services. Speculators drive up stock and property prices far beyond their genuine value then dump those assets when they believe the frenzy has peaked, precipitating a market meltdown as sellers desperately search for buyers.

Roosevelt's first hundred days as president were critical to reviving the economy. Each of the fifteen bills that he proposed or embraced created institutions that transformed the economy from a vicious cycle of worsening bankruptcies, joblessness, poverty, and despair into a virtuous cycle of expanding businesses, jobs, income, and confidence. Over the next half dozen years he worked closely with congressional leaders to refine or establish new programs that further developed the economy.

Financial and banking programs like Glass-Steagall, the Federal Bank Deposit Insurance Corporation, and the Securities and Exchange Commission established a stable system that prevented another financial collapse for another five decades until a series of deregulations provoked severe contractions. The contrast before and after 1933 was stunning. Bank failures plummeted from 4,004 in 1933 to around ten a year thereafter. By one count, "from 1921 to 1933 depositors had lost on average $156 million or $0.45 per $100 in commercial banks. From the establishment of deposit insurance to 1960, losses averaged only $706,000 a year or less than $0.002 per $100, with little more than half those losses occurring during 1934."[8]

The array of New Deal institutions, laws, and regulations that required businesses to disclose their operations, rewarded compliance, punished rule-breakers, and gave entrepreneurs and homeowners the confidence to invest in new businesses and homes that, in turn, stimulated greater and more prolonged growth. The Home Owner Loan Corporation and the Federal National Mortgage Association encouraged home ownership with low interest, long-term loans. Over the next four decades, home ownership swelled steadily from four in ten families to seven in ten.

The New Deal boosted work conditions and wages for most blue-collar laborers. Thanks mostly to the 1935 Wagner Act, the portion of workers in unions rose from 9 percent to 34 percent, and of miners from 21 percent to 72 percent from 1930 to 1940. Legalized unions and minimum wages uplifted blue-collar workers with more income and security.

Several New Deal policies alleviated poverty. The Federal Emergency Relief Administration provided loans and grants to needy people. By one count in 1933 alone, three New Deal organizations, the Federal Emergency Relief Administration (FERA), the Civilian Conservation Corps (CCC), and the Civil Works Administration (CWA) provided income for 8 million families that included 28 million people or 22 percent of the population. Around 15 percent of the population received some form of relief as late as 1939. Recipients received about $350 a year, a fraction of the $1,200 considered essential for a family of five.[9] Social Security was the New Deal's most enduring anti-poverty program as it provided pensions to elderly and handicapped people. Before social security, nine in ten elderly people living alone were poor but with pensions eventually four in five were middle class or wealthy.

Only the farm and ranching sectors failed to revive during the New Deal. Farmers faced a vicious cycle dilemma – the more productive they were, the poorer they became because crop prices dropped as supply exceeded demand. Desperate farmers planted more crops to earn more money but that worsened prices. Banks foreclosed on ever more bankrupt farms. New Deal agriculture policies alleviated the plight of many farmers and ranchers by distributing $4.5 billion in various subsidies along with crop price floors, subsidies, and provision of electricity from 1933 to 1939. Net farm income more than doubled from $2 billion in 1932 to $4.6 billion in 1939. From 1930 to 1940, total farm production value changed little from $10 billion to $11.4 billion, the farm population from 30,529,000 to 30,547,000, the number of farms from 6,295,00 to 6,102,000, acreage from 990,112,000 to 1,065,114, average farm acreage from 157 to 175, and cost for fertilizer and lime from $297,000,000 to $306,000,000. Nonetheless, that decade's significant drops were average farm total value from $47,994 to $33,758, production value from $7,624 to $5,532, and farm income from $12,497 to $10,979. Meanwhile, the number of tractors nearly doubled from 920,000 to 1,567,000 increasing production and productivity, and rendering ever more farm hands redundant.[10]

New Deal agriculture policies exacerbated other problems. One was to widen the gap between rich and poor farmers. The wealthiest 1 percent of farmers received 21 percent of benefits.[11] Rich farmers got around the $50,000 subsidy cap by dividing their land among different legal but related owners like one's wife and children. Policies that helped farmers with higher crops hurt consumers who paid higher prices for them. Another downside of higher crop prices was fewer American sales in foreign markets. Roosevelt hoped the Agricultural Adjustment Administration (AAA) established in May 1933, would break that vicious cycle with programs that raised farm income with relief checks, floor prices for commodities, and payments for farmers not to plant some crops or raise some livestock. After the Supreme Court struck down the AAA as unconstitutional in 1935, Roosevelt and Congress wrote four separate laws that propped up the farm economy while evading successful legal challenges.

Conservation programs, led by the CCC, restored millions of acres of forests, grasslands, and watersheds, while Washington expanded the national park system with 12 million acres that included Olympic, Everglades, Isle Royale, and King's Canyon. Complexes of dams, hydroelectricity plants, power lines, roads, and bridges developed the Tennessee, Columbia, Colorado, and Missouri River valleys. The Soil Conservation Service and Taylor Grazing Act began to restore lands ravaged by overgrazing, overcropping, and clearcutting compounded by drought, wind storms, and deluges.

For Roosevelt, the New Deal legacy's most vital success was emotional rather than monetary, political rather than economic. In his June 1935 fireside chat, he explained: "But it is more than the recovery of the material basis of our individual lives. It is the recovery of confidence in our democratic processes, our republican institutions. We have survived all of the arduous burdens of a great economic calamity...Confidence is growing on every side, renewed faith in the vast possibilities of human beings to improve their material and spiritual status through the instrumentality of the democratic form of government."[12]

Each New Deal policy and institution attracted critics. Many of those organizations overlapped and competed with one another. The result was not quite a "tower of Babel," but certainly wasteful and inefficient. Of Roosevelt's bureaucracies, the National Recovery Administration (NRA) was widely reviled for its red tape that entangled businesses while doing little to enforce the deals it struck with them to provide minimum wages and permit union for their workers. The Supreme Court declared the NRA unconstitutional for regulating commerce within states on May 27, 1935.

Perhaps Roosevelt's most criticized policy was his attempt to "pack the Supreme Court." In a series of decisions in 1935, the Supreme Court struck down as unconstitutional several key New Deal programs including the Railroad Retirement Act, the National Industrial Recovery Act, and the Agricultural Adjustment Act. He feared that eventually the justices would eliminate all his administration's efforts to alleviate the depression, joblessness, and poverty. In January 1937, he presented

Congress a plan to add a new justice to the Supreme Court for every one over seventy years old who refused to retire. That provoked a firestorm of criticism and Congress overwhelmingly rejected his proposal. However, that attempt did cause one conservative justice, to reverse his stance on subsequent New Deal cases, thus upholding the programs with 5 to 4 votes. Then one conservative justice died and another retired, which let Roosevelt replace them with justices that shared his political outlook. In all, Roosevelt appointed eight new justices and shifted the Supreme Court's outlook from conservative to liberal.

The New Deal alleviated but did not end America's Great Depression, the Second World War did. The economy expanded from $55 billion in 1933 to $124 billion in 1941, then skyrocketed to $211 billion by 1945. Meanwhile, the jobless rate fell slowly from 24.9 percent when he took office in 1933, to 9.9 percent in 1941, then during the war years plummeted to 4.7 percent in 1942, 1.9 percent in 1943, 1.2 percent in 1944, and 1.9 percent in 1945. Meanwhile, per capita income more than doubled from $432 to $934 over eight years then reached $1,515 over the next three years. The Second World War benefited farmers and ranchers with greater demand and higher prices for their crops and livestock. From 1940 to 1945, the farm population fell from 30,547,000 to 24,420,000 and from 23.2 percent to 17.5 percent of the total population but farm acreage expanded from 1,065,114 to 1,141,615, and farm value from $41,829,000 to $69,369,000 which meant average farm income expanded nearly 40 percent in five years.

12.1 National and Personal Income in Dollar and Jobless Rates, 1929, 1932–1945[13]

	Gross National Income	Per Capita Income	Jobless Rate
1929	103,100,000,000	847	3.2
1932	58,000,000,000	465	23.6
1933	55,600,000,000	442	24.9
1934	65,100,000,000	514	21.7
1935	72,200,000,000	567	20.1
1936	82,500,000,000	643	16.9
1937	90,400,000,000	701	14.3
1938	84,700,000,000	651	19.0
1939	90,500,000,000	691	17.2

1940	99,700,000,000	754	14.6
1941	124,500,000,000	934	9.9
1942	157,900,000,000	1,171	4.7
1943	191,600,000,000	1,401	1.9
1944	210,100,000,000	1,518	1.2
1945	211,900,000,000	1,515	1.9

12.2 Changes in Gross National Product, 1929–45[14]

Year	Percentage Change
1929	6.7
1930	-9.8
1931	-7.0
1932	-14.7
1933	-1.8
1934	9.1
1935	9.9
1936	13.9
1937	5.3
1938	-5.0
1939	8.6
1940	8.5
1941	16.1
1942	12.9
1943	13.2
1944	7.2
1945	-1.7

12.3 Federal Budget, Federal Civilian Workforce, National Debt, 1929, 1933–1945[15]

	Federal Budget	Federal Civilian Workforce	National Debt
1929	3,127,199,000	579,559	19,931,088,000
1932	4,659,182,000	605,496	19,487,088,000
1933	4,598,496,000	603,587	22,538,673,000
1934	6,644,602,000	698,649	27,053,141,000

1935	6,497,008,000	780,582	28,700,893,000
1936	8,421,608,000	867,432	33,778,543,000
1937	7,733,033,000	895,993	36,424,614,000
1938	6,764,628,000	882,226	37,164,740,000
1939	8,841,224,000	953,891	40,439,532,000
1940	9,055,269,000	1,042,420	42,967,531,000
1941	13,254,948,000	1,437,682	48,961,444,000
1942	34,036,861,000	2,296,384	72,442,445,000
1943	79,367,714,000	3,299,414	136,696,090,000
1944	94,986,002,000	3,332,356	201,003,387,000
1945	98,302,937,000	3,816,310	258,682,187,000

| 12.4 Farm Population, Land, and Wealth[16] | | | | |
	Farm Population	Share of Total Population	Number of Farms	Total Acres	Total Value of all Farm Property
1933	32,393,000	25.9%	6,741,000	1,027,415	$36,249,000,000
1940	30,547,000	23.2%	6,102,000	1,065114	$41,829,000,000
1945	24,420,000	17.5%	5,859,000	1,141,615	$69,369,000,000

Over a dozen years, most Americans transformed from poverty to prosperity, with most Americans solidly middle class. Meanwhile, the concentration of wealth lessened. The richest one and five percent of people enjoyed 14.50 percent and 26.09 percent of all national income in 1929, 12.48 percent and 25.34 percent in 1933, and 8.81 percent and 17.39 percent in 1945.

Life expectancy is another way to determine whether peoples' lives are improving. Life expectancy rose from 57.1 years in 1929 to 63.3 in 1933 to 65.9 in 1945 despite the war losses. From 1930 to 1940, the average lifetime rose from 59.7 to 62.9, for white men from 58.7 to 62.1, for white women from 63.5 to 66.6, for black men from 47.3 to 51.5, and for black women from 49.2 to 54.9, then rose further to 64.4 for white men, 69.5 for white women, 56.1 for black men and 59.6 for black women by 1945.[17]

America's entry into the Second World War fulfilled what the New Deal began. Washington's mobilization of the nation's people, industries, and natural resources for total war finally ended the Great Depression by putting virtually all able-bodied and minded people to work. Congress eliminated the Civilian Conservation Corps, the National Youth Administration, and the Works Progress Administration to free all those laborers for factories and military units. The war caused the greatest mobility in American history. Over 12 million left their homes to join the military and another 15.3 million moved to jobs mostly in the defense industry. In all, one of five Americans moved to join the military or for a better paying job. As in the First World War, the biggest civilian flow was from southern farms to northern factories although western factories were nearly as alluring in the Second World War.

	Budget	Total	Army	Navy	Marine
1940	1,504,000,000	458,365	269,023	160,997	28,345
1941	6,062,000,000	1,801,101	1,462,315	284,427	54,359
1942	23,987,000,000	3,858,791	3,075,608	640,570	142,613
1943	63,212,000,000	9,044,745	6,994,472	1,741,750	308,523
1944	76,874,000,000	11,451,719	7,994,750	2,981,365	475,604
1945	81,585,000,000	12,123,455	8,267,958	3,380,817	474,680
1946	44,731,000,000	3,030,088	1,891,011	983,398	155,679

12.5 Defense Budget, Total, Army, and Navy Personnel, 1929, 1933, 1940–46[18]

Roosevelt's record is most mixed for civil rights. He took some measures that slightly alleviated opportunities for blacks in the economy and military. Yet he presided over the worst violation of constitutional protection for civil rights in American history with the internment of 120,000 west coast Japanese-Americans, including 80,000 citizens, during the Second World War. Overall, Roosevelt had excellent relations with Jews who were only 3 percent of America's population but occupied 15 percent of his top administration posts.[19] Yet, critics condemned Roosevelt for not allowing more Jewish refugees into the United States. As for women, their job opportunities improved during the Roosevelt years, but the war not the New Deal caused that.

As for blacks, Roosevelt most notoriously refused to endorse an anti-lynching law fearing it would alienate southern Democratic senators and representatives whose votes he needed for his other New Deal policies. Overall, the New Deal benefited blacks less than whites. Programs like the CCC, PWA, and WPA employed both races and paid them the same. The rural electricity programs illuminated white and black farmhouses alike. Yet the housing programs tended to subsidize white flight to the suburbs.

Discrimination against blacks was a major reason for their worse poverty and longevity. Blacks had fewer opportunities to become high paying professionals like doctors, lawyers and engineers, or well-paid factory workers. Bright young people had fewer universities that accepted them as students. Many blacks were trapped in neighborhoods with vicious cycles of poverty, joblessness, bad schools, crime, despair, and corrupt and inept officials. Another reason for worse poverty was that blacks had more children and more children out of wedlock than whites. The number of births per thousand for white and black women were 17.6 and 25.5 in 1933 and 19.7 and 26.5 in 1945. The percentage of births out of wedlock was 3.6 percent for white and 35.6 percent for blacks in 1940.[20] Although longevity increased, blacks lagged whites. Worse poverty, unhealthy diets, deficient medical care, and violence explain why blacks generally did not live as long as whites.

12.6 Longevity by Race and Gender, 1929, 1933, 1940, 1945 [21]				
	White Men	White Women	Black Men	Black Women
1929	57.2	63.5	45.7	47.6
1933	62.7	66.3	53.5	56.0
1940	62.1	66.6	51.5	54.9
1945	64.4	69.5	56.1	59.6

Conditions for blacks improved during the Second World War. On June 25, 1941, Roosevelt signed Executive Order 8802 that forbade discrimination "by race, creed, color, or national origin" in government or defense industries. From 1940 to 1944, the number of employed blacks expanded from 4.4 million to 5.5 million, black family income rose from 40 percent to 60 percent of white families, the share of defense workers climbed from 3 percent to 8.3 percent, the share of black women in the female industrial workforce rose from 6.5 percent to 18 percent.[22] Military discrimination against blacks also lightened during the war. Black duties expanded from mostly rear echelon support jobs like cooking, cleaning, hauling, and driving to fighting on the front line in separate infantry, tank, and air regiments and alongside white sailors at sea. It was not until 1948, when President Truman issued Executive Order 9981, that blacks and whites served in the same army and marine units.

Roosevelt paid a political price for his reforms as southern conservative Democrats increasingly criticized and opposed his measures. Among them the most prominent were Senators Harry Byrd of Virginia, Carter Glass of Virginia, Millard Tydings of Maryland, Josiah Bailey of North Carolina, Ellison Smith of South Carolina, and Walter George of Georgia. Four southern senators – Claude Pepper of Florida, Lister Hill of Alabama, Theodore Bilbo of Mississippi, and John Rankin of Mississippi – remained stalwart New Dealers although they opposed black civil rights.

Job opportunities for women improved from 1930 to 1950, with 10,752,000 in the workforce or 23.6 percent of the total in 1930, 12,113,400 or 30.9 percent in 1940, and 16,522,600 or 33.9 percent in 1950. The number of married female workers eventually surpassed those that were single, with 3,071,000 to 5,725,000 in 1930, 4,675,000 to 6,377,000 in 1940, and 8,635,000 to 5,274,000 in 1950, revealing that the traditional restriction that respectable married women did not work and respectable men solely provided income for their families was weakening.[23] The trouble was that women mostly worked in low wage jobs and were paid less than men for the same jobs while few professional careers were open to women.

Among the working women was Eleanor Roosevelt. The relationship between Roosevelt and Eleanor failed as a marriage but eventually succeeded as a political partnership. Historian Doris Kearns Goodwin compared their temperaments, interests, priorities, and styles: "She was more earnest, less devious, less patient, less fun, more uncompromisingly moral; he possessed the more trustworthy political talent, the more finely tuned sense of timing, the better feel for the citizenry, the smarter understanding of how to get things done. She could travel the country when he could not; she could speak her mind without the constraints of public office. She was the agitator, he was the politician."[24]

During the White House years, Eleanor steadily strengthened her advisory role with her husband. As she developed her career she acquired the knowledge, skills, and confidence to share information and ideas with him on a broadening range of issues. She acted as his conscience on issues of poverty, joblessness, homelessness, neglected children, refugees, and racial discrimination. Goodwin insightfully explained the difference between them: "While Eleanor thought in terms of what should be done, Franklin thought in terms of what could be done."[25] She was careful not to pressure him too often and only on issues that she believed were critical. She avoided discussing some things with him. For instance, she explained that: "I never questioned Franklin about his political intentions. The fact that I myself never wanted him to be in Washington made me doubly careful not to intimate that I had the slightest preference."[26]

Roosevelt mastered political skills early in his career and eventually became just as masterful a statesman. For foreign policy, Roosevelt was a principled realist. He took a long view of politics, domestic and international. He understood that a just peace among belligerents made a future war among them less likely. He explained that in his 1943 State of the Union address: "Victory in this war is the first and greatest goal before us. Victory in peace is the next."[27] He understood that American peace and prosperity depended on global peace and prosperity, explaining that: "Our civilization cannot endure unless we, as individuals, realize our responsibility to and dependence on the rest of the world. For it is literally true that the 'self-supporting' man or woman has become as extinct as the man of the stone age."[28]

Roosevelt's greatest foreign policy conception was the related Four Policemen and United Nations. The Four Policemen included America, Britain, China, and the Soviet Union which would manage international relations within their respective regional sphere of influence while cooperating in resolving global problems through the United Nations Security Council, with the General Assembly for members to debate but not decide issues. The spheres included America and the western hemisphere, Britain and its soon to be former empire, China and the Far East, and the Soviet Union and eastern Europe. Roosevelt's vision was essentially a more sophisticated and world-wide version of the Concert of Europe devised by the great powers Britain, Russia, Prussia, Austria, and France during the Congress of Vienna from October 1814 to June 1815, to collectively manage European relations after Napoleon's defeat. Yet deep flaws lay within Roosevelt's plan. The Soviet Union was too imperialistic and China was too weak to serve as constructive policemen in their spheres.

Pragmatism preceded principle if a conflict rose between them. For instance, Roosevelt approved a deal whereby Francois Darlan, the Vichy regime's military commander, surrendered French North Africa in return for governing it. When Charles de Gaulles's envoy criticized him for doing so, he angrily replied, "Of course I'm dealing with Darlan since Darlan's giving me Algiers! Tomorrow I'd deal with Laval if Laval were to offer me Paris!"[29] Pierre Laval was the Vichy regime's foreign minister who the French government later tried and executed for collaborating with Nazi Germany.

When Roosevelt became president in March 1933, American policy toward Latin America was grounded on two related principles. The 1823 Monroe Doctrine asserted an American sphere of interest over the entire Western Hemisphere but especially the Caribbean basin, Mexico, and central America. That meant preventing any European state or states from expanding existing or establishing new power within that realm. The 1903 Theodore Roosevelt Corollary asserted America's right to intervene and restore order in any Latin American country suffering war or radicalism that threatened American economic and strategic interests.

Roosevelt retained the Monroe Doctrine but repudiated the Roosevelt Corollary in 1934 with his Good Neighbor Policy whereby he withdrew an American contingent in Haiti and pledged no more military interventions. He sought first to relieve Latin Americans of their "fear of American aggression – territorial or financial – and, second to take them in a kind of hemispheric partnership in which no Republic would obtain undue advantage."[30]

During Roosevelt's dozen year presidency, Washington gave Latin American countries over two billion dollars in low interest loans and Lend Lease aid. The Good Neighbor policy toward Latin America removed the fear of retaliation but inspired contempt, not love, and that was disastrous for American investors. During the late 1930s into the 1940s, the governments of Mexico, Bolivia, Chile, Venezuela, Columbia, Argentina, Ecuador, Peru, and Paraguay nationalized American investments and paid either no or token compensation at fractions of the market value. Nearly all the regimes were dictatorships leaning either communist or fascist but sharing vicious cycles of corruption, incompetence, brutality, and poverty.

That was not the only example of a Roosevelt's foreign policy with contradictory principles that harmed American and western interests. For instance, in principle, Roosevelt passionately hated imperialism and colonialism. He pressured Churchill and de Gaulle to promise to transform their colonies into trusteeships that nurtured them toward eventual independence, by using America's policy toward the Philippines as a model. To that Churchill defiantly declared, "I have not become the King's First Minister in order to preside over the liquidation of the British Empire."[31] Yet, Roosevelt tolerated and appeased Stalin's brutal conquest and colonization of eastern Europe. After OSS chief William Donovan acquired Soviet codebooks, Roosevelt actually had them returned to Stalin.[32]

Roosevelt failed to understand Stalin, the Soviet empire, or communism. He naively believed that Stalin was just another politician that he could win over with charm and compromises. He wrote Churchill that "I can personally handle Stalin better than either your Foreign Office or my State Department. Stalin hates the guts of all your top people. He thinks he likes me better, and I hope he will continue to do so."[33] Charles Bohlen, the State Department's Russian expert and translator for Roosevelt during his summits, found him ignorant "of the great gulf that separated the thinking of a Bolshevik from a non-Bolshevik, and particularly from an American. He felt that Stalin viewed the world somewhat in the same light as he did, and that Stalin's hostility and distrust…were due to the neglect that Soviet Russia had suffered at the hands of other countries for years after the Revolution. What he did not understand was that Stalin's enmity was based on profound ideological convictions."[34] Nor did Roosevelt comprehend that Stalin's genocide exceeded Hitler's in numbers of victims. Stalin's pathologies were as masked as Hitler's were flamboyant, but they were just as ruthless.

Roosevelt asserted and reveled in his role as commander-in-chief. He respected his military and civilian advisors, and listened carefully to their perspectives, but ultimately he decided what to do. Historian Kent Greenfield found twenty-two major military decisions that Roosevelt made contrary to his inner circle's prevailing advice.[35]

How could Roosevelt confidently, decisively do that? He had never served in the military and was not a student of military history. Yet he instinctively grasped grand strategy that often cut through the military bureaucracy, rival services and personalities, and standard operating procedures that warp and stunt thinking. Alfred Mahan's 1890 book, *The Influence of Seapower upon History* critically shaped Roosevelt's worldview for its lessons on how a nation gets, keeps, and enhances global economic and military power against rivals. His love of stamp-collecting gave him an excellent understanding of world geography as he learned where all those stamps came from and their histories, governments, and cultures. Nonetheless, he made mistakes, some catastrophic.

Roosevelt fought the Second World War the same way he did the Great Depression, with a plethora of organizations. He established most of them with executive orders. Many had overlapping powers and duties that led to supply bottlenecks, conflicting missions, squandered resources, and fierce political infighting.

Politics inevitably warps grand strategy. That is bad enough when just one nation's political and military leaders are involved. The military services elbow each other for the most missions, men, and material resources while, if the nation is a democracy, its leader worries how his decisions will affect the next election. A charismatic domineering civilian or military leader can browbeat others in the inner circle into following his strategy and shunning a superior strategy promoted by a self-effacing colleague. Politics magnify when two prominent democratic nations are allied.

During the Second World War, Roosevelt committed two strategic blunders that squandered enormous numbers of American lives and billions of dollars' worth of supplies, weapons, and ships. He did so by yielding to the demands of two charismatic leaders, General Douglas MacArthur and Prime Minister Winston Churchill.

One strategic deadend was in the Pacific. Ideally, MacArthur's command should have received the bare minimum for holding the line in the southwest Pacific while Admiral Chester Nimitz got all he needed for his island-hopping strategy across the central Pacific toward Tokyo. Instead, Roosevelt yielded to MacArthur's demand for simultaneous equally powerful thrusts, with his capturing the Solomon Islands, New Guinea, and the Philippines. The result was tens of thousands of American dead and a hundred thousand or so wounded along with tens of billions of dollars' worth of warships, supplies, aircraft, and weapons diverted and squandered from critical fronts in the Pacific and Europe.

The other strategic deadend was in Europe. Roosevelt bowed to Churchill's insistence that invading and fighting up the Italian peninsula from the toe to the Alps was Europe's "soft underbelly." Instead, the mountainous and hilly peninsula proved to be perfect for defense. By the war's end the allies had battled their way no further than the Po valley's southern rim, and, as in the Philippines left devastated cities, and countless dead and wounded soldiers and civilians behind.

The systematic destruction of cities by waves of aircraft dropping high explosive or incendiary bombs was at once legally a war crime and a moral and strategic dilemma.[36] The round the clock bombing by America's air force by day and Britain's by night of German and other European cities destroyed them along with perhaps 400,000 lives and wounded hundreds of thousands of people and rendered millions homeless. In Japan, the Americans destroyed 64 cities with conventional bombs and two with atomic bombs, killing over 600,000 people. General George Patton wrote that: "We all feel that indiscriminate bombing has no military value and is cruel and wasteful, and that all such efforts should always be on purely military targets and on selected commodities which are scarce."[37] Overall, the Americans suffered

43,000 dead, 6,000 destroyed aircraft, and expended $43 billion in their air campaigns during the Second World War.[38]

The atomic bombs brought the war to an abrupt halt, thereby saving millions of lives that would have been lost during an invasion of Japan's home islands over the next several years. But what about the carpet bombing of European and Japanese cities with conventional bombs? The Germans and Japanese fought on despite the horrendous losses. Unfortunately, the federal government's Strategic Bombing Survey conducted during and after the war suffered a deeply flawed methodology that rendered its information and conclusions unreliable. The Survey's worst conclusion was that Japan was poised to surrender and the atomic bombings were unjustified. Historians have systematically demolished that report point-by-point.[39]

Among Roosevelt's worst diplomatic failures was with Italy's government after King Victor Emmanuel deposed Benito Mussolini and replaced him with General Pietro Badoglio on July 25, 1943. Ideally, American diplomats in Lisbon, Berne, and other neutral capitals would have secretly informed their Italian counterparts that the allies would welcome Italy's repudiation of its alliance with Germany into neutrality or, even better, United Nations membership. Tragically, that did not happen until several weeks passed, during which Hitler poured German troops into Italy to prevent either possibility. Victor Emmaneul did not sign a surrender document until September 3, then he and his inner circle had to flee into exile behind allied lines on September 8, after the Germans took over Rome. Without orders to resist the Germans, Italy's army largely surrendered to Germany's. Thus did Roosevelt and Churchill fumble a chance to get a viable ally then compounded that blunder with the catastrophic decision to invade Italy which over the next eighteen months inflicted devastating losses to the allies and population and destruction of many of its beautiful cities.

Some diplomatic problems defy solutions. Roosevelt included China as one of the "four policemen" that would manage postwar international relations. He knew that China was a poverty-stricken country torn apart by a civil war between the Nationalist and Communist Parties, and an international war between them and the invading Japanese. Yet he saw China's potential to be a global power if a far-sighted leader and efficient government took power and developed China's economy. Tragically, that leader did not exist.

Chiang Kai-shek's Nationalist Chinese regime posed conundrums for Roosevelt. Chiang was a brutal, corrupt, and inept warlord and his Nationalist Party was essentially a rapacious mob organization that exploited and alienated the population, pushing them into the hands of Mao Zedong's Communist Party. Yet Roosevelt feared that pressuring Chiang to reform might collapse his regime and give the Japanese the chance to conquer China. General Joseph Stilwell accompanied Chiang to the Cairo summit with Roosevelt and Churchill in November 1943. At one point, Roosevelt was so disgusted with Chiang's obduracy and imperiousness that he told Stilwell to "get rid of him once and for all. You know what I mean. Put in someone you can manage." The idea of having Chiang assassinated appalled Stilwell who angrily replied, "this is not the solution for the China problem...the United States doesn't go in for this sort of thing."[40]

Roosevelt also despised Charles de Gaulle for his arrogance, mendacity, and double-dealing. Yet he also recognized that de Gaulle was a powerful symbol of French nationalism and as such had the potential to create and lead a stable postwar democratic government. Eventually, he accepted de Gaulle as the head of a French government in exile.

Roosevelt provoked legions of critics for his policies and personality. George Kennan had very mixed feelings about him. He praised Roosevelt for his strategic skills: "I have the impression that in major instances he influenced public opinion less through the power of his words than through the quiet shaping, in a manner conducive to his purposes, of the environmental factors, the external factors, in which the formulation of wartime policy had to proceed." Yet, he dismissed his mind and manner as featherweight, "a very superficial man, ignorant, dilettantish...in intellectual horizon."[41] Harry Truman kept mum about Roosevelt's deficiencies until after he retired from public service. He called Roosevelt "the coldest man I ever met. He didn't give a damn personally for me or you or anyone else in the world." Even worse, "Roosevelt wasn't an administrator. Oh he liked to play one outfit against another....He was always careful to see that no credit went to anyone else for accomplishments.[42] Roosevelt did not impress British Air Marshal Charles Portal who accompanied Churchill to several summits: "I am sure that FDR is completely unable to think hard about anything. He is tremendously perceptive of an atmosphere, and the most wonderful politician, but on these occasions when he meets... [Churchill and Stalin]...he is absolutely pathetic. It is such a pity, but I suppose everyone fails in one way or another."[43] Roosevelt sometimes took pleasure in the pain of others. After observing Roosevelt's bullying of Churchill at the Tehran summit with Stalin, Averill Harriman, the ambassador to the Soviet Union, observed that: "He always enjoyed other people's discomfort. I think it is fair to say that it never bothered him very much when other people were unhappy."[44]

Franklin Roosevelt's role model as a man, politician, and statesman was his fifth cousin, Theodore Roosevelt who preceded him on earth by twenty-three years and in the White House by thirty-two years. Franklin was naturally inspired by his cousin's dazzling career and adventures that eventually landed him the presidency. Franklin tried to emulate Theodore in his own political and family life. Like Theodore, Franklin served as a state assemblyman, assistant naval secretary, and New York governor on the way to the White House. He also wanted to have six children just like his cousin. Like Theodore, Franklin was a progressive and pragmatic problem-solver who cultivated his political skills to enact an array of reforms as governor and president that were approved by legislatures and implemented by bureaucracies that bettered people's lives and economically bolstered the nation. Both fought corruption and defied political bosses and their machines. Both were realistic internationalists who recognized that American wealth and security depended on corporations selling and investing in markets around the world protected by a powerful navy. Alfred Mahan's *The Influence of Sea Power Upon History* (1890) and *The Interest of America in Sea Power, Present and Future* (1897) critically shaped their outlooks.

The similarities end there. Theodore was intellectually brilliant, Franklin merely bright. Theodore was a death-defying adventurer, explorer, hunter, police commissioner, lieutenant colonel, and fighter who suffered many injuries and dodged death many times. Franklin carefully avoided all that. Theodore was a devoted and passionate husband. Franklin cheated on Eleanor with at least one mistress. Theodore genuinely enjoyed romping with his children. Franklin's limited time with his offspring was more from duty than pleasure. The least important difference between them was political affiliation with Theodore a Republican and Franklin a Democrat.

The most vital difference was their presidencies. Theodore faced no national crisis during his eight years in the White House; he achieved a lot, especially in conservation, but at a steady unhurried pace. In twelve years, Franklin faced and his policies overcame America's two worst crises after the Civil War, the Great Depression and the Second World War. For that Franklin's presidency was far more consequential than his cousin's.

For presidencies, Franklin Roosevelt is better compared to Abraham Lincoln. They were commander in chiefs during the nation's two bloodiest conflicts, the Civil War and the Second World War with at least 612,000 and 405,000 respective dead. The Civil War was truly existential for the United States; without Lincoln's leadership the Confederates probably would have won independence and if so the history of America and the world would have changed decisively and mostly for the worse, with a truncated United States, Confederate slavocracy, and during the twentieth century possibly enduring fascist and communist regimes in Europe. The Second World War did not pose an existential threat to the United States, especially after the Americans developed nuclear bombs, although just when and how the allies defeated the axis powers depended on key decisions ultimately made by Roosevelt. Neither Lincoln nor Roosevelt had training as military officers nor experienced combat. Yet both confidently asserted their commander in chief roles and made numerous critical strategic decisions often at odds with and better than their military advisors recommended. Each had conflicts with some of his prima donna generals, most notably Lincoln with George McClellan and Roosevelt with Douglas MacArthur. Each composed brilliant speeches that captured the essence of the challenges that Americans faced and how to overcome them, Lincoln from his own genius and Roosevelt with several writers. Both devised and implemented progressive reforms that crucially developed the economy, Roosevelt during nine years preceding and three years of war and Lincoln during four years of war. Neither lived to see his war's end. Although both wars were essentially won when they died, the question was what each would have done differently from his successor for vital postwar challenges, Lincoln instead of Andrew Johnson for Reconstruction and Roosevelt instead of Harry Truman for the Cold War. Would Lincoln's policies have sustained political and economic progress by southern blacks liberated by slavery's abolition but repressed and exploited by Jim Crow and Black Code laws? Would Roosevelt's policies either prevented or mitigated the Cold War?

Another key comparison is Franklin Roosevelt and Winston Churchill. They formed a deep partnership and friendship as the wartime leaders of America and Britain during the Second World War. In all, they spent 113 days together and exchanged over 2,000 letters. Roosevelt's speechwriter Robert Sherwood observed that they "established an easy intimacy, a joking informality, and a moratorium on pomposity and cant – and also a frankness in intercourse."[45] Churchill delighted in being with Roosevelt "with all his buoyant sparkle, his iridescence" was like "opening a bottle of champagne."[46] Although Roosevelt valued Churchill's friendship, he put politics first. For instance, during both the Tehran and Yalta summits, he at times snubbed or denigrated Churchill to ingratiate himself with communist tyrant Joseph Stalin.

Overall, both were brilliant politicians and statesmen. Each pushed through his legislature key economic and political reforms that improved most people's lives and during the Second World War provided inspiring leadership for his nation. Yet, Churchill far surpassed Roosevelt in his career and character.[47] Churchill's public service as a soldier and parliamentarian lasted 79 years (1895–1964), three times longer than Roosevelt's twenty-five years (1911–20, 1929–45). Roosevelt never served in the military. Churchill was a genuine hero who came under fire in Cuba, India, South Africa, Sudan, and the trenches of France in the First World War. As for high culture, Roosevelt was a dilettante who displayed little interest in the fine arts, literature, or philosophy. Churchill was truly a Renaissance man who wrote more than forty wonderful books, painted several hundred mostly good paintings, and understood and discoursed with other brilliant minds on literature, art, history, and science. As for personality, both were extroverts who loved being the center of attention. Indeed, that was the worst challenge to their friendship as each at times tried hogging the spotlight from the other. Yet, Roosevelt controlled his emotions better so that he always appeared upbeat and ebullient no matter what he felt or thought. Churchill was an emotional rollercoaster mostly with exhilarating highs, but with grumpy interludes and at times dark sojourns near the existential abyss. Churchill's eyes often welled with tears when he was deeply moved. Roosevelt publicly shed tears only once, during his mother's burial.[48] In sum, Churchill was more profound and complex than Roosevelt.

Yet the president may have exceeded the prime minister as a subtle and sophisticated politician and statesman. Sherwood made this comparison: "when an American statesman and a British statesmen meet, the former will be plain, blunt, down to earth, ingenuous to a fault, while the latter will be sly, subtle, devious, and eventually triumphant. In the case of Roosevelt and Churchill, this formula was somewhat confused. If either of them could be called a student of Machiavelli, it was Roosevelt; if either was the bull in a china shop, it was Churchill...the word 'stubborn'...may be flattering or derogatory. In any case, it was this quality which, at times, made him extremely tiresome to deal with and at other times – and especially times of most awful adversity – made him great."[49]

Like any friends, they had their spates, mostly over strategy. Here Roosevelt was mostly a pragmatist while Churchill was more visionary. For Churchill's proposals, Roosevelt quipped that: "He has a hundred ideas a day and about four of them are good."[50] Although the leaders agreed that the American army's first invasion should be in North Africa to trap the Axis army against the British army fighting westward, thereafter Roosevelt and his military advisors insisted that a massive invasion in northern France and then drive east was the only way to defeat Germany. Yet, Roosevelt gave in to Churchill's insistence on landings first in Sicily and then Italy's mainland, thus delaying D-Day in Normandy for a year. He did so after firmly rejecting Churchill's calls for landings across the eastern Mediterranean basin in Yugoslavia and Greece that would dilute allied power in literal as well as figurative strategic dead ends.

Amidst a world war, Roosevelt severely strained relations with Churchill by insisting that he publicly promise India, the British Empire's "jewel in the crown," eventual independence. At the Quebec conference, Churchill tried to get Roosevelt to understand his naivete and ignorance about India and other colonies with a mock proposal to "give the United States half of India to administer and we will take the other half and we will see who does better." Later, when Roosevelt sent envoy William Philips with his anti-colonial message, Churchill erupted, declaring "Take India if that is what you want!...But I warn you that if I open the door a crack there will be the greatest blood-bath in all history."[51] Indeed, over a million people died from murder, starvation, and disease after Britain granted freedom to India and Pakistan in 1947, and they immediately warred against each other. In the House of Commons, Churchill promised: "We mean to hold our own. I have not become the King's first minister in order to preside over the liquidation of the British Empire."[52]

Ultimately, Churchill's respect and friendship for Roosevelt was unshakeable. He explained that "I formed a very strong affection which grew over our years of comradeship for this formidable politician who had imposed his will for nearly ten years upon the American scene, and whose heart seemed to respond to many of the impulses that stirred my own."[53] After they parted ways at the end of their Casablanca conference, Churchill confessed to an aide that: "If anything happened to that man, I couldn't stand it. He is the truest friend; he has the farthest vision; he is the greatest man I have ever known."[54]

A leader is great to the degree and array of ways he or she changes history for better or worse. Despite his character flaws and policy mistakes, Franklin Roosevelt's towering place in American and world history is assured.

ACKNOWLEDGEMENTS

As always, I am so grateful for Frontline's team of John Grehan, Martin Mace, and Lisa Hooson to produce my book. They are as kind as they are professional.

BIBLIOGRAPHY

Agarossi, Elena, *A Nation Collapses: The Italian Surrender of 1943*, New York: Cambridge University Press, 2000.

Albion, Robert, and Robert Connery, *Forrestal and the Navy*, New York: Columbia University Press, 1962.

Allen, Frederick, *Only Yesterday: An Informal History of the 1920s*, New York: Harper and Row, 1957.

Alperovitz, Gar, *Atomic Diplomacy: Hiroshima and Potsdam – the Use of the Atomic Bomb and the American Confrontation with the Soviet Union*, New York: Penguin, 1985.

Alperovitz, Gar, *The Decision to Use the Atomic Bomb and the Architecture of an American Myth*, New York: Knopf, 1995.

Alter, Jonathan, *The Defining Moment: FDR's Hundred Days and the Triumph of Hope*, New York: Simon and Schuster, 2006.

Alvarez, David, *Secret Messages: Codebreaking and American Diplomacy, 1930–1945*, Lawrence: University Press of Kansas, 2000.

Ambrose, Stephen, *Eisenhower and Berlin, 1945: The Decision to Halt at the Elbe*, New York: W.W. Norton, 1967.

Ambrose, Stephen, *The Supreme Commander: The War Years of Dwight D. Eisenhower*, New York: Anchor, 2012.

Ambrose, Stephen, *D-Day, June 6, 1944: The Climatic Battle of World War II*, New York: Simon and Schuster, 2013.

Anderson, Terry, *The United States, Great Britain, and the Cold War, 1944–1947*, Columbia: University of Missouri Press, 1981.

Andrew, Christopher, and Oleg Gordievsky, *KGB: The Inside Story of Its Foreign Operations from Lenin to Gorbachev*, New York: Harper Collins, 1995.

Armor, John, and Peter Wright, *Manzanar*, New York: Times Books, 1988.

Arnold, Michael, *Hollow Heroes: An Unvarnished Look at the Wartime Careers of Churchill, Montgomery, and Mountbatten*, Philadelphia: Casemate, 2015.

Astor, Gerald, *The Greatest War: Americans in Combat, 1941–1945*, Novato, Calif.: Presidio, 1999.

Astor, Gerald, *The Bloody Forest: The Battle for the Hurtgen, September 1944 to January 1945*, Novato, Calif.: Presidio Press, 2000.

Atkinson, Rick, *An Army at Dawn: The War in North Africa, 1942–1943*, New York: Henry Holt, 2002.

Atkinson, Rick, *The Day of Battle: The War in Sicily and Italy, 1943–1944*, New York: Henry Holt, 2007.

Axelrod, Alan, *Nothing to Fear: Lessons in Leadership from FDR, President of the Greatest Generation*, Paramus, N.J.: Prentice Hall Press, 2003.

Badger, Anthony, *The New Deal: The Depression Years, 1933–1940*, Chicago: Ivan Dee, 2002.

Barnes, Harry, *Pearl Harbor After a Quarter of a Century*, New York: Arno Press, 1972.

Barron, Leo, *Patton's First Victory: How General George Patton Turned the Tide in North Africa and Defeated the Africa Korps at El Guettar*, Mechanicsville, Penn.: Stackpole Books, 2017.

Beard, Charles, *President Roosevelt and the Coming of the War, 1941*, New York: Transaction Publishers, 1948.

Bellush, Bernard, *Franklin D. Roosevelt as Governor of New York*, New York: AMS Press, 1968.

Bennett, Edward, *Franklin D. Roosevelt and the Search for Victory: American-Soviet Relations, 1939–1945*, Wilmington, Del.: Scholarly Resources, 1990.

Bennett, Edward, *Franklin D. Roosevelt and the Search for Security: American-Soviet Relations, 1933–1939*, Wilmington, Del.: Scholarly Resources, 1997.

Bergman, Andrew, *We're in the Money: Depression America and Its Films*, Chicago: Ivan R. Dee, 1992.

Bergstrom, Christer, *The Ardennes: Hitler's Winter Offensive, 1944–45*, New York: Casemate, 2014.

Berlin, Ira, et al., eds., *Remembering Slavery: African Americans Talk About Their Personal Experiences of Slavery and Freedom*, New York: New Press, 1998.

Bernstein, Irving, *The Turbulent Years: A History of the American Worker, 1933–1941*, Boston: Houghton Mifflin, 1970.

Berthon, Simon, and Joanna Potts, *Warlords: An Extraordinary Recreation of World War II through the Eyes and Minds of Hitler, Roosevelt, Churchill, and Stalin*, New York: Da Capo, 2006.

Beschloss, Michael, *The Conquerors: Roosevelt, Truman, and the Destruction of Hitler's Germany, 1941–1945*, New York: Simon and Schuster, 2002.

Bethon, Simon, *Allies at War: The Bitter Rivalry among Churchill, Roosevelt, and de Gaulle*, London: HarperCollins, 2002.

Bird, Kai and Martin Sherwin, *American Prometheus: The Triumph and Tragedy of Robert Oppenheimer*, New York: Alfred Knopf, 2005.

Blinkhorn, Martin, *Fascism and the Right in Europe, 1919–1945*, New York: Routledge, 2000.

Bloomfield, Gary, *George S. Patton: On Guts, Glory, and Winning*, New York: Globe Pequot, 2017.

Blum, John, *V Was or Victory: Politics and American Culture during World War II*, New York: Harcourt, Brace, and Company, 1976.

Blum, Robert, *Drawing the Line: The Origins of the American Containment Policy in East Asia*, New York: W.W. Norton, 1982.

Blumenson, Martin, ed., *The Patton Papers: 1940–1945*, Boston: Houghton Mifflin, 1974.

Blumenson, Martin, *Patton: The Man behind the Legend, 1885–1945*, New York: William Morrow, 1985.

Blumenson, Martin, *Kasserine Pass: Rommel's Bloody, Climatic Battle for Tunisia*, New York: Cooper Square, 2000.

Bohlen, Charles, *Witness to History, 1929–1969*, New York: W.W. Norton, 1969.

Booth, Owen, and John Walton, *World War II: Primary Sources in World Warfare*, New York: Amber Books, 2017.

Borg, Dorothy, and Shumpei Okamoto, eds., *Pearl Harbor as History: Japanese-American Relations, 1931–1941*, New York: Columbia University Press, 1973.

Botjer, George, *Sideshow War: The Italian Campaign, 1943–45*, College Station: Texas A and M University Press, 1996.

Boyer, Paul, et al., *The Enduring Vision: A History of the American People*, Lexington, Mass.: D.C. Heath and Company, 1993.

Boyer, Paul, *By the Bomb's Early Light: American Thought and Culture at the Dawn of the Atomic Age*, Chapel Hill: University of North Carolina Press, 1994.

Brands, H.W., *Traitor to His Class: The Privileged Life and Radical Presidency of Franklin Delano Roosevelt*, New York: Anchor Books, 2008.

Bremer, C.D., *American Bank Failures*, New York: Columbia University Press, 2020.

Brewer, William, *Operation Torch: The Allied Gamble to Invade North Africa*, New York: St. Martin's, 1988,

Brinkley, Alan, *Voices of Protest: Huey Long, Father Coughlin, and the Great Depression*, New York: Vintage, 1983.

Brinkley, Alan, *Franklin Delano Roosevelt*, New York: Oxford University Press, 2009.

Brinkley, Alan, *The End of Reform: New Deal Liberalism in Recession and War*, New York: Vintage, 2011.

Brinkley, David, *America Goes to War: The Extraordinary Story of the Transformation of a City and a Nation*, New York: Knopf, 1988.

Buhite, Russell, *Decisions at Yalta: An Appraisal of Summit Diplomacy*, Wilmington, Del.: SR Books, 1986.

Buhite, Russell, and David Levy, eds., *FDR's Fireside Chats*, Norman: University of Oklahoma Press, 1992.

Burg, David, ed., *The Great Depression*, New York: Facts on file, 2005.

Burner, David, *Herbert Hoover: A Public Life*, New York: Alfred Knopf, 1978.

Bunker, John, *Liberty Ships: Ugly Ducklings of World War II*, Annapolis: Naval Institute Press, 1972.

Caddick-Adams, Peter, *Snow and Steel: The Battle of the Bulge, 1944–45*, New York: Oxford University Press, 2014.

Capozzolla, Christopher, *Uncle Sam Wants You: World War I and the Making of the Modern American Citizen*, New York: Oxford University Press, 2008.

Carlson, Earland, *Franklin D. Roosevelt's Fight for the Presidential Nomination, 1928–1932*, Ann Arbor, Mich.: University of Michigan Press, 1956.

Caro, Robert, *The Power Broker: Robert Moses and the Fall of New York*, New York: Vintage, 1975.

Carver, Joseph, Jerome Ennels, and Daniel Haulman, *The Tuskegee Airmen: An Illustrated History, 1939–1949*, Athens, Georgia: New South Press, 2011.

Casey, Steven, *Cautious Crusade: Franklin D. Roosevelt, American Public Opinion, and the War against Nazi Germany*, New York: Oxford University Press, 2001.

Cashman, Sean, *America in the Twenties and Thirties*, New York: New York University Press, 1989.

Chace, James, *1912: Wilson, Roosevelt, Taft, and Debs: The Election that Changed the Country*, New York: Simon and Schuster, 2005.

Chandler, William, *The Myth of TVA: Conservation and Development in Tennessee Valley, 1933–1983*, Cambridge, Mass.: Ballinger Publishing, 1984.

Chang, Iris, *The Rape of Nanking: The Forgotten Holocaust of World War II*, New York: Basic Books, 1997.

Churchill, Winston, *World War II: The Grand Alliance*, Boston: Houghton Mifflin, 1950.

Churchill, Winston, *Great War Speeches*, New York: Corgi Books, 1957.

Churchill, Winston, *Memoirs of the Second World War*, Boston: Houghton Mifflin, 1987.

Clark, Lloyd, *Anzio: The Friction of War, Italy and the Battle for Rome, 1944*, New York: Headline Publisher, 2007.

Clausen, Henry, and Bruce Lee, *Pearl Harbor: Final Judgment*, New York: Crown Publishers, 1992.

Clemens, Diane Shaver, *Yalta*, New York: Oxford University Press, 1971.

Coakley, Robert, and Richard Leighton, *Global Logistics and Strategy, 1943–1945, The United States Army in World War II*, Washington D.C.: U.S. Army, 1989.

Cohen, Adam, *Nothing to Fear: FDR's Inner Circle and the Hundred Days that Created Modern America*, New York: Penguin, 2009.

Cole, Wayne, *Charles A. Lindbergh and the Battle against American Intervention in World War II*, New York: Harcourt Brace, Jovanovich, 1974.

Cole, Wayne, *Roosevelt and the Isolationists, 1932–1945* (Lincoln: University of Nebraska Press, 1983.

Cole, Wayne, *Determinism and American Foreign Relations during Franklin D. Roosevelt Era*, Lanham, Maryland: University Press of America, 1994.

Cole, Wayne, *Roosevelt and the Isolationists, 1932–45*, Lincoln: University of Nebraska Press, 1983.

Congden, Don, ed., *The 30s: A Time to Remember*, New York: Simon and Schuster, 1962.

Conger, Jay, *The Charismatic Leader: Behind the Mystique of Exceptional Leadership*, San Francisco: Jossey-Bass, 1989.

Conn, Peter, *The American 1930s: A Literary History*, New York: Cambridge University Press, 2009.

Connaughton, Richard, *MacArthur's Defeat in the Philippines*, New York: Abrams, 2003.

Cook, Blanche Wiesen, *Eleanor: The Early Years, 1884–1933*, New York: Viking, 1992.

Cook, Blanche Wiesen, *Eleanor Roosevelt: The Defining Years, 1933–1948*, New York: Penguin, 2000.

Cook, Blanche Wiesen, *Eleanor Roosevelt: The War Years and After, 1939–62*, New York: Viking, 2016.

Costello, John, *Days of Infamy: MacArthur, Roosevelt, Churchill – the Shocking Truth Revealed*, New York: Pocket Books, 1994.

Costigliola, Frank, *Roosevelt's Lost Alliances: How Personal Politics Helped Start the Cold War*, Princeton, N.J.: Princeton University Press, 2013.

Cox, Alvin, and Hilary Conroy, eds., *China and Japan: The Search for Balance since World War I*, Santa Barbara, Calif.: ABC-CLIO, 1978.

Cray, Ed, *General of the Army: George C. Marshall, Soldier and Statesman*, New York: W.W. Norton, 1990.

Creese, Walter, *TVA's Public Planning: The Vision, the Reality*, Knoxville: University of Tennessee Press, 2003.

Cross, Robin, *Operation Dragoon: The Allied Liberation of the South of France, 1944*, New York: Pegasus, 2019.

Cutler, Thomas, *The Battle of Leyte Gulf, 23–26 October 1944*, New York: HarperCollins, 1994.

Dallek, Robert, *Franklin D. Roosevelt and American Foreign Policy, 1932–1945*, New York: Oxford University Press, 1979.

Dallek, Robert, *Franklin Delano Roosevelt: A Political Life*, New York: Viking, 2017.

Danchow, Alex, and Daniel Todman, eds., *Field Marshal Lord Alan Brooke: War Diaries, 1939–1945*, Berkeley: University of California Press, 2001.

Daniels, Josephus, *The Wilson Era: Years of Peace, 1912–1917*, Chapel Hill: University of North Carolina Press, 1944.

Daniel, Josephus, *The Wilson Era: Years of War and After, 1917–1821*, Chapel Hill: University of North Carolina Press, 1946.

Daniels, Jonathan, ed., *The Complete Presidential Press Conferences of Franklin D. Roosevelt*, New York: Da Capo, 1972, 22.

Daniels, Rogers, *Franklin D. Roosevelt and the New Deal, 1932–1940*, New York: Harper Perennial, 2009.

Daniels, Rogers, *Franklin D. Roosevelt: The War Years, 1939–1945*, Urbana: University of Illinois Press, 2016.

Daniels, Roger, *Franklin Delano Roosevelt: The Road to the New Deal, 1889 to 1939*, Urbana: University of Illinois Press, 2018.

Davis, Kenneth *Invincible Summer: An Intimate Portrait of the Roosevelts based on Recollections of Marion Dickerson*, New York: Atheneum, 1974.

Davis, Kenneth, *FDR: The Beckoning of Destiny, 1882–1928: A History*, New York: G.P. Putnam's Son, 1972.

Davis, Kenneth, *FDR: The New York Years, 1928–1932: A History*, New York: Random House, 1983.

Davis, Kenneth, *FDR: The New Deal Years, 1933–1937: A History*, New York: Random House, 1979.

Davis, Kenneth, *FDR: Into the Storm, 1937–1940: A History*, New York: Random House, 1993.

Davis, Kenneth, *FDR.: The War President, 1940–1943*, New York: Random House, 2000.

Davis, Lynn Etheridge, *The Cold War Begins: Soviet-American Conflict over East Europe*, Princeton, N.J.: Princeton University Press, 1974.

Davis, Michael, *Politics as Usual: Thomas Dewey, Franklin Roosevelt, and the Wartime Presidential Election of 1944*, Chicago: Northwestern University Press, 2014.

Davis, Richard, *Bombing the European Axis Powers* (Maxwell Air Force Base, Al: Air University Press, 2006.

De Gaulle, Charles, *The Complete War Memoirs*, New York: Simon and Schuster, 1964.

D'Este, Carlo, *The Fatal Decision: Anzio and the Battle for Rome*, New York: Harper Collins, 1991.

D'Este, Carlo, *Patton: A Genius for War*, New York: Perennial Harper, 1996.

D'Este, Carlo, *Eisenhower: A Soldier's Life*, New York: Henry Holt, 2002.

D'Este, Carlo, *Bitter War: The Battle for Sicily, July-August 1943*, New York: Perennial, 2008.

Dimbleby, Jonathan, *The Battle of the Atlantic: How the Allies Won the War*, New York: Oxford University Press, 2016.

Dinunzio, Mario, *Franklin D. Roosevelt and the Third American Revolution*, Santa Barbara, Calif.: ABC-Clio, 2011.

Dinunzio, Mario, ed., *The Great Depression and New Deal: Documents Decoded*, Santa Barbara, Calif.: ABC-Clio, 2014.

Divine, Robert, *The Reluctant Belligerent: American Entry into World War II*, New York: Wiley, 1979.

Dixon, Wheeler, *American Cinema of the 1940s: Themes and Variations*, New Brunswick, N.J.: Rutgers University Press, 2005.

Doenecke, Justus, and John Wilz, *From Isolation to War, 1931–41*, Arlington Heights, Ill.: Harlan Davidson, 1991.

Doenecke, Justus, and Mark Stoler, *Debating Franklin D. Roosevelt's Foreign Policies*, New York: Rowman and Littlefield, 2005.

Donovan, Robert, *Conflict and Crisis: The Presidency of Harry S. Truman, 1945–1948*, New York: W.W. Norton, 1977.

Donovan, Robert, *Tumultuous Years: The Presidency of Harry S. Truman,1949–1953*, New York: W.W. Norton, 1982.

Dower, John, *War without Mercy: Race and Power in the Pacific War*, New York: Random House, 1986.

Drowne, Kathleen, and Patrick Huber, *The 1920s: American Popular Culture through History*, Westport, Conn.: Greenwood Press, 2004.

Druks, Herbert, *Harry S. Truman and the Russians, 1945–1953*, New York: Robert Speller and Sons, 1966.

Dubofsky, Melvyn, and Warren Van Tine, *John L. Lewis: A Biography*, New York: Quadrangle Books, 1977.

Dubovsky, Melvin, Athan Theoharis, and Daniel Smith, *The United States in the Twentieth Century*, Englewood Cliffs, N.J.: Prentice Hall, 1978.

Duffy, James. *War at the End of the World: Douglas MacArthur and the Forgotten Fight for New Guinea, 1942–1945*, New York: Dutton Caliber, 2017.

Dumenil, Lynn, *The Modern Temper: American Culture and Society in the 1920s*, New York: Hill and Wang, 1995.

Duncan, Dayton, and Ken Burns, *The Dust Bowl: An Illustrated History* (New York: Chronicle Books, 2012).

Dunn, Susan, *1940: FDR, Willkie, Lindberg, Hitler – the Election amid the Storm*, New Haven, Conn.: Yale University Press, 2014.

Eckes, Elfred, *A Search for Solvency: Bretton Woods and the International Monetary System, 1941–1971*, Austin: University of Texas Press, 1975.

Eden, Robert, ed., *The New Deal and Its Legacy: Critique and Reappraisal*, New York: Greenwood, 1989.

Edmonds, Robin, *The Big Three: Churchill, Roosevelt, and Stalin in Peace and War*, New York: W.W. Norton, 1991.

Edsel, Robert, *The Monuments Men*, New York: Center Street, 2009.

Eisenberg, Carolyn, *Drawing the Line: The American Decision to Divide Germany, 1944–1949*, New York: Cambridge University Press, 1996.

Eisenhower, Dwight, *Crusade in Europe: A Personal Account of World War II*, New York: Vintage, 2021.

Ellis, Edward, *A Nation in Torment: The Great American Depression, 1929–1939*, New York: Kodansha, 1995.

Ellis, John, *World War II: A Statistical Survey for All the Combatants*, New York: Facts On File, 1993.

Ellis, John, *Cassino, the Hollow Victory: The Battle for Rome, January-June 1944*, New York: Arum, 2003.

Epstein, Daniel, *Sister Aimee: The Life of Aimee Semple McPherson*, New York: Mariner Books, 1994.

Eubank, Keith, *Summit at Teheran: The Untold Story*, New York: Morrow, 1985.

Evans, Hugh, *The Hidden Campaign: FDR's Health and the 1944 Election*, New York: Routledge, 2002.

Fausold, Martin, *The Presidency of Herbert Hoover*, Lawrence: University Press of Kansas, 1985.

Feingold, Henry, *The Politics of Rescue: The Roosevelt Administration and the Holocaust, 1938–1945*, New York: Holocaust Library, 1970.

Feis, Herbert, *The Road to Pearl Harbor*, New York: Atheneum, 1963.

Feis, Herbert, *From Trust to Terror: The Onset of the Cold War*, New York: W.W. Norton, 1970.

Fender, Julie, *FDR's Shadow: Louis Howe, the Force Behind Franklin and Eleanor Roosevelt,*New York: Palgrave Macmillan, 2009.

Ferrell, Robert, *Harry S. Truman: A Life*, Columbia: University of Missouri Press, 1994.

Ferrell, Robert, *Harry S. Truman and the Modern Presidency*, Boston: Little, Brown, 1983.

Ferrell, Roberts, *Truman and Pendergast*, Columbia: University of Missouri Press, 1999.

Ferrell, Robert, *Choosing Truman: The Democratic Convention of 1944*, Columbia: University of Missouri Press, 2000.

Fleming, Denna Frank, *The Cold War and Its Origins, 1917–1960*, 2 vols., Garden City, Doubleday, 1961.

Foot, John, *Blood and Power: The Rise and Fall of Italian Fascism*, New York: Bloomsbury, 2022.

Forty, Simon, and Leo Marriott, *Operation Market Garden, September 1944*, New York: Casemate, 2018.

Fox, Stephen, *Uncivil Liberties: Italian Americans under Siege during World War II*, Parkland, Fla.: Universal Publishers, 2000.

Fox, Stephen, *America's Invisible Gulag: A Biography of German American Internment and Exclusion in World War II*, New York: Peter Lang, 2000.

Frank, Richard, *Downfall: The End of the Imperial Japanese Empire*, New York: Random House, 1999.

Freidel, Frank, *Franklin D. Roosevelt: The Apprenticeship*, Boston: Little, Brown, 1952.

Freidel, Frank, *Franklin D. Roosevelt: The Ordeal*, Boston: Little, Brown, 1954.

Freidel, Frank, *Franklin D. Roosevelt: The Triumph*, Boston: Little, Brown, 1956.

Freidel, Frank, *Franklin D. Roosevelt: Launching the New Deal*, Little, Brown, 1973.

Freidel, Frank, *Franklin D. Roosevelt: A Rendezvous with Destiny*, Boston: Little, Brown, 1990.

French, Warren, ed., *The Forties: Fiction, Poetry, Drama,* Deland, Fla.: Everett/ Edwards Company, 1969.

Fromkin, David, *In the Time of the Americans: FDR, Truman, Eisenhower, Marshall, MacArthur – The Generation that Changed America's Role in the World,* New York: Alfred Knopf, 1995.

Funk, Arthur, *The Politics of Torch: The Allied Landings and the Putsch at Algiers,* Lawrence: University Press of Kansas, 1974.

Gaddis, John, *The United States and the Origins of the Cold War, 1941–1947,* New York: Columbia University Press, 1972.

Gaddis, John, *Strategies of Containment: A Critical Appraisal of Postwar American Security Policy,* New York: Oxford University Press, 1982.

Gaddis, John, *The Long Peace: Inquiries into the History of the Cold War,* New York: Oxford University Press, 1987.

Gaddis, John, *The United States and the End of the Cold War: Implications, Reconsiderations, Provocations,* New York: Oxford University Press, 1992.

Gaddis, John, *We Know Nothing: Rethinking Cold War History,* Oxford: Clarendon Press, 1997.

Gaddis, John, *The Landscape of History: How Historians Map the Past,* New York: Oxford University Press, 2002.

Gaddis, John et al., eds., *Cold War Statesmen Confront the Bomb: Nuclear Diplomacy since 1945,* New York: Oxford University Press, 1999.

Galbraith, John Kenneth, *The Great Crash: 1929,* Boston: Houghton Mifflin, 1955.

Gallagher, Hugh, *FDR's Splendid Deception: The Moving Story of Roosevelt's Massive Disability and the Intense Efforts to Conceal It from the Public,* New York: Dodd, Mead, 1985.

Gallup, George, *The Gallup Poll: Public Opinion, 1935–1971,* 2 vols., New York: Random House, 1972.

Garcia, Juan Vasquez, *Storm over Europe: Allied Bombing Missions in the Second World War,* London: Pen and Sword, 2020.

Gardner, Lloyd, *Spheres of Influence: The Great Powers Partition Europe, from Munich to Yalta,* Chicago: Ivan R. Dee, 1993.

Gardner, Richard, *Sterling-Dollar Diplomacy: The Origins and Prospects of Our international Economic Order,* New York: McGraw, 1969.

Gelb, Norman, *Desperate Venture: The Story of Operation Torch, the Allied Invasion of North Africa,* London: Hoddert and Stoughton, 1992.

Gilbert, Martin, *Churchill and America,* New York: Free Press, 2005.

Gimbel, John, The American Occupation of Germany: Politics and the Military, 1945–1949, Palo Alto, Calif.: Stanford University Press, 1968.

Gimbel, John, *The Origins of the Marshall Plan,* Palo Alto, Calif.: Stanford University Press, 1976.

Goginos, Manny, *The Panay Incident: Prelude to War,* Lafayette, Ind.: Purdue University Press, 1967.

Golay, Michael, *America 1933: The Great Depression, Lorena Hickok, Eleanor Roosevelt, and the Shaping of the New Deal,* New York: Simon and Schuster, 2016.

Goldberg, David, *Discontented America: The United States in the 1920s,* Baltimore: Johns Hopkins University Press, 1999.

Goldberg, Ronald, *America in the Twenties,* Syracuse: Syracuse University Press, 2003.

Golway, Terry, *Machine Made: Tammany Hall and the Creation of Modern American Politics*, New York: Liveright, 2014.

Goodwin, Doris Kearns, *No Ordinary Time: Franklin and Eleanor Roosevelt: The Home Front in World War II*, New York: Simon and Schuster, 1994.

Gormley, James, *The Collapse of the Grand Alliance, 1945–1948*, Baton Rouge: Louisiana State University Press, 1987.

Gormley, James, *From Potsdam to the Cold War: The Big Three Diplomacy, 1945–1947*, Wilmington, Del.: SR Books, 1990.

Grant, James, *Bernard Baruch, The Adventures of a Wall Street Legend*, New York: Axios Press, 2012.

Greenfield, Kent, *American Strategy in World War II: A Reconsideration*, Baltimore: Johns Hopkins University Press, 1963.

Gregory, James, *American Exodus: The Dust Bowl Migration and Okie Culture in California*, New York: Oxford University Press, 1991.

Grint, Keith, *Leadership: Limits and Possibilities*, New York: Palgrave, 2005.

Grogin, Robert, *Natural Enemies: The United States and Soviet Union in the Cold War, 1917–1991*, New York: Rowman and Littlefield, 2001.

Gropman, Alan, ed., *The Big L: American Logistics in World War II*, Washington D.C.: National Defense University Press, 1997.

Hallas, James, *Saipan: The Battle that Doomed Japan in World War II*, Mechanicsville, Pa.: Stackpole Books, 2019.

Hamby, Alonzo, *Beyond the New Deal: Harry S. Truman and American Liberalism*, New York: Columbia University Press, 1971.

Hamby, Alonzo, *Man of the People: A Life of Harry S. Truman*, New York: Oxford University Press, 1995.

Hamby, Alonzo, *Man of Destiny: FDR and the Making of the American Century*, New York: Basic Books, 2015.

Hamilton, Nigel, *Monty: The Battles of Field Marshal Bernard Montgomery*, New York: Random House, 1994.

Hamilton, Nigel, *The Mantle of Command: FDR at War, 1941–1942*, New York: Houghton Mifflin, 2014.

Hammond, Bryn, *El Alamein: The Battle that Turned the Tide in the Second World War*, London: Osprey, 2012.

Hanson, Victor, *The Second World Wars: How the First Global Conflict Was Fought and Won*, New York: Basic Books, 2020.

Harbutt, Frazer, *The Iron Curtain: Churchill, America, and the Origins of the Cold War*, New York: Oxford University Press, 1986.

Hark, Ina Rae, *American Cinema of the 1930s: Themes and Variations*, New Brunswick, N.J.: Rutgers University Press, 2007.

Harper, John, *America and the Reconstruction of Italy, 1945–1948*, Cambridge: Cambridge University Press, 1986.

Harper, *American Visions of Europe: Franklin D. Roosevelt, George F. Kennan, and Dean G. Acheson*, Cambridge: Cambridge University Press, 1994.

Harriman, Averill, and Elie Abel, *Special Envoy to Churchill and Stalin, 1941–1946*, New York: Random House, 1975.

Hart, David, *Forged Consensus: Science, Technology, and Economic Policy in the United States, 1921–1953*, Princeton, N.J.: Princeton University Press, 1998.

Hart, Liddell, *History of the Second World War*, Old Saybrook, Conn.: Konecky and Konecky, 1970.

Hasegawa, Tsuyoshi, *Racing the Enemy: Stalin, Truman, and the Surrender of Japan*, Cambridge, Mass.: Harvard University Press, 2005.

Hastings, Max, *Overlord: D-Day and the Battle for Normandy, 1944*, New York: Pan Books, 2005.

Hawley, Ellis, *The Great War and the Search for Modern Order: A History of the American People and Their Institutions, 1917–1933*, New York: St. Martin's Press, 1979.

Hathaway, Robert, *Ambiguous Partnership: Britain and America, 1944–1947*, New York: Columbia University Press, 1981.

Haynes, Richard, *The Awesome Power: Harry Truman as Commander in Chief*, Baton Rouge: Louisiana State University Press, 1973.

Heardon, Patrick, *The Architects of Globalism: Building a New World Order during World War II*, Fayetteville: University of Arkansas Press, 2002.

Herman, Arthur, *Douglas MacArthur: American Warrior*, New York: Random House, 2017.

Herring, George,, *Aid to Russia, 1941–1946: Strategy, Diplomacy, and the Origins of the Cold War*, New York: Columbia University Press, 1973.

Hershberg, James, *James B. Conant: Harvard to Hiroshima and the Making of the Nuclear Age*, Stanford, Calif.: Stanford University Press, 1993.

Hett, Benjamin, *The Death of Democracy: Hitler's Rise to Power and the Downfall of the Weimar Republic*, New York: St. Martin's Griffin, 2020.

Hett, Benjamin, *The Nazi Menace: Hitler, Churchill, Roosevelt, Stalin, and the Road to War*, New York: St. Martin's Griffin, 2021.

Hill, Robert, ed., *The FBI's RACON: Racial Conditions in the United States during World War II*, Boston: Northeastern University Press, 1995.

Hiltzik, Michael, *The New Deal: A Modern History*, New York: Free Press, 2011.

Hirshson, Stanley, *General Patton: A Soldiers' Life*, New York: Harper Collins, 2002,

Hodgson, Godfrey, *The Colonel: The Life and Wars of Henry L. Stimson, 1867–1950*, New York: Knopf, 1990.

Hofstadter, Richard, *The American Political Tradition and the Men Who Made It*, New York: Alfred Knopf, 1948.

Holmes, W.J., *Undersea Victory: The Influence of Submarine Operations on the War in the Pacific*, Garden City, N.Y.: Doubleday, 1963.

Holsker, Dieter, *V-Missiles of the Third Reich, the V-1 and V-2*, New York: Monogram Aviation Publishers, 1994.

Hone, Trent, *Mastering the Art of Command: Admiral Chester Nimitz and Victory in the Pacific*, Annapolis: Naval Institute Press, 2022.

Hoopes, Townsend, and Douglas Brinkley, *FDR and the Creation of the U.N.*, New Haven, Conn.: Yale University Press, 1997.

Howard, Michael, *The Mediterranean Strategy in World War II*, London: Greenhill Books, 1993.

Hoyt, Edwin, *Inferno: The Fire Bombing of Japan, March 9-August 15, 1945*, New York: Madison Books, 2000.

Hughes, Robert, *American Visions: The Epic History of Art in America* New York: Alfred Knopf, 1997.

James, Rita, ed., *As We Saw the Thirties: Essays on Political and Social Movements of the Decade*, Urbana: University of Illinois Press, 1967.

Jeffries, John, *A Third Term for FDR: The Election of 1940*, Lawrence: University Press of Kansas, 2017.

Johnsen, William, *The Origins of the Grand Alliance: Anglo-American Military Collaboration from the Panay to Pearl Harbo*, Lexington: University Press of Kentucky, 2016.

Jordan, David, *FDR, Dewey, and the Election of 1944*, Bloomington: University of Illinois Press, 2012.

Judge, Edward, and John Langdon, *A Hard and Bitter Peace: A Global History of the Cold War*, New York: Rowman and Littlefield, 2018.

Kato, Daniel, *Liberalizing Lynching: Building a New Racialized State*, New York: Oxford University Press, 2016.

Katznelson, Ira, *Fear Itself: The New Deal and the Origins of Our Time*, New York: Liveright Publishing, 2003.

Kaye, Harvey, *FDR on Democracy: The Greatest Speeches and Writings of President Franklin Roosevelt*, New York: Simon and Schuster, 2020.

Kelly, Cynthia, *The Manhattan Project: The Birth of the Atomic Bomb in the Words of Its Creators, Eyewitnesses, and Historians*, New York: Black Dog and Leventhal Publishers, 2020.

Kelly, Orr, *Meeting the Fox: The Allied Invasion of Africa from Operation Torch to Kasserine Pass to Victory in Tunisia*, New York: Wiley, 2002.

Kennedy, David, *Freedom from Fear: The American People in Depression and War, 1929–1945*, New York: Oxford University Press, 1999.

Kennedy, Susan Estabrook, *The Banking Crisis of 1933*, Lexington: University of Kentucky Press, 1973.

Kennett, Lee, *G.I.: The American Soldier in World War II*, New York: Scribner's, 1987.

Kimball, Warren, *The Most Unsordid Act: Lend Lease, 1938–1941*, Baltimore: Johns Hopkins, 1969.

Kimball, Warren, ed., *Churchill and Roosevelt: The Complete Correspondence*, 3 vols., Princeton, N.J.: Princeton University Press, 1984.

Kimball, Warren, *The Juggler: Franklin Roosevelt as Wartime Statesman*, Princeton, N.J.: Princeton University Press, 1991.

Kimball, Warren, *Churchill, Roosevelt, and the Second World War*, New York: Harper Collins, 1997.

Kitaoka, Shinichi, *From Party Politics to Militarism in Japan, 1923 to 1941*, New York: Lynne Rienner, 2020.

Klehr, Harvey, *The Heyday of American Communism: The Depression Decade*, New York: Basic Books, 1984.

Klehr, Harvey, and John Haynes, *The American Communist Movement: Storming Heaven Itself*, New York: Twayne, 1992.

Klein, Maury, *Rainbow's End: The Crash of 1929*, New York: Oxford University Press, 2001.

Kleiner, Sam, *The Flying Tigers: The Untold Story of the American Pilots Who Waged a Secret War against Japan*, New York: Viking, 2018.

Klingaman, William, *1929: The Year of the Great Crash*, New York: Houghton Mifflin, 1989.

Kluger, Michael, and Richard Evans, *Roosevelt and Churchill: The Atlantic Charter, A Risky Meeting at Sea that Saved Democracy*, London: Frontline, 2022.

Kolko, Gabriel, *The Politics of War: The World and United States Foreign Policy, 1943–1945*, New York: Harper and Row, 1969.

Konstam, Angus, *Salerno 1943: The Allied Invasion of Italy*, London: Pen and Sword, 2007.

Kourig, Bennett, *The Myth of Liberation: East-Central Europe in U.S. Diplomacy and Politics since 1941*, Baltimore: Johns Hopkins University Press, 1973.

Kuklich, Bruce, *American Policy and the Division of Germany: The Clash with Russia*, Ithica, N.Y.: Cornell University Press, 1972.

LaCerra, Charles, *Franklin Delano Roosevelt and Tammany Hall of New York*, Lanham, Maryland: University Press of America, 1997.

Lane, Ann, and Howard Temperley, eds., *The Rise and Fall of the Grand Alliance, 1941–1945*, New York: St. Martin's Press, 1995

Larrabee, Eric, *Commander in Chief: Franklin Delano Roosevelt, His Lieutenants, and Their War*, New York: Harper and Row, 1987.

Lash, Joseph, *Eleanor and Franklin: The Story of their Relationship*, New York: W.W. Norton, 1971.

Lash, Joseph, *Roosevelt and Churchill, 1939–1945: The Relations that Saved the West*, New York: W.W. Norton, 1976.

Lash, Joseph, *Love, Eleanor: Eleanor Roosevelt and Her Friends*, Garden City, N.Y.: Doubleday, 1982.

Lash, Joseph, *Dealers and Dreamers: A New Look at the New Deal*, New York: Doubleday, 1988.

Leahy, William, *I Was There*, New York: McGraw-Hill, 1950.

Lebo, Harlan, *Citizen Kane: A Film-maker's Journey*, Los Angeles: Angel City Press, 2022.

Leff, Mark, *The Limits of Symbolic Reform: The New Deal and Taxation, 1933–1939*, New York: Cambridge University Press, 1984.

Leighninger, Robert, *Long-range Public Investment: The Forgotten Legacy of the New Deal*, Columbia: University of South Carolina Press, 2007.

Lerner, William, ed., *Historical Statistics of the United States: Colonial Times to 1970*, 2 vols., Washington D.C.: Government Printing Office, 1975.

Leuchtenburg, William, *The Perils of Prosperity: 1914–1932*, Chicago: University of Chicago Press, 1993.

Leuchtenberg, William, *The Supreme Court Reborn: The Constitutional Revolution in the Age of Roosevelt*, New York: Oxford University Press, 1995.

Leuchtenburg, William, *Herbert Hoover: The 31st President, 1929–1933*, New York: Times Books, 2009.

Leuchtenburg, William, *Franklin Delano Roosevelt and the New Deal: 1932–1940*, New York: Harper Perennial, 2009.

Levering, David, *The Improbable Wendell Willkie: The Businessman Who Saved the Republican Party and the Country, and Conceived a New World Order*, New York: Liveright, 2018.

Levering, Ralph, *American Opinion and the Russian Alliance, 1939–1945*, Chapel Hill: University of North Carolina Press, 1976.

Levy, Herbert, *Henry Morgenthau, Jr.: The Remarkable Life of FDR's Secretary of the Treasury*, New York: Skyhorse Publishing, 2010.

Lewin, Ronald, *The American Magic: Codes, Ciphers, and the Defeat of Japan*, New York: Farrar, Straus, and Giroux, 1982.

Lichtman, Allan, *Prejudice and the Old Politics: The Presidential Election of 1928*, Chapel Hill: University of North Carolina Press, 1979.

Lifton, Robert, and Greg Mitchell, *Hiroshima in America: Fifty Years of Denial*, New York: Putnam's Sons, 1995.

Linderman, Gerald, *The World within War: America's Combat Experience in World War I*, New York: Free Press, 1997.

Lingeman, Richard, *Don't You Know There's a War On?: The American Home Front, 1941–1945*, New York: G.P. Putnam's Sons, 1971.

Longworth, Alice Roosevelt, *Crowded Hours: Reminiscences of Alice Roosevelt Longworth*, New York: Charles Scribner's Sons, 1933.

Louchheim, Katie, ed., *The Making of the New Deal: The Insiders Speak*, Cambridge, Mass.: Harvard University Press, 1983.

Lowitt, Richard, *The New Deal and the West*, Bloomington: University of Indiana Press, 1984.

Lowitt, Richard, and Maurine Beasley, eds., *One Third of a Nation: Lorena Hickok Reports on the Great Depression*, Urbana: University of Illinois Press, 1981.

MacDonald, Charles, *A Time for Trumpets: The Untold Story of the Battle of the Bulge*, New York: William Morrow, 1997.

MacEachin, Douglas, *The Final Months of the War with Japan: Signals Intelligence, U.S. Invasion Planning, and the A-Bomb Decision*, Langley, Vir.: Center for the Study of Intelligence, 1998.

MacIssac, David, *Strategic Bombing in World War Two: The Story of the United States Strategic Bombing Survey*, New York: Garland, 1976.

Maddox, Robert, *Weapons for Victory: The Hiroshima Decision Fifty Years Later*, Columbia: University of Missouri Press, 1995.

Maher, Neil, *Nature's New Deal: The Civilian Conservation Corps and the Roots of the American Environmental Movement*, New York: Oxford University Press, 2009.

Manchester, William, *American Caesar: Douglas MacArthur, 1880–1964*, Boston: Little, Brown, 1978.

Mangione, Jerre, *The Dream and the Deal: The Federal Writers Project, 1935–1943*, Boston: Little, Brown, 1972.

Marks, Frederick, *Wind Over Sand: The Diplomacy of Franklin Roosevelt*, Athens: University of Georgia Press, 1990.

Martelle, Scott, *1932: FDR, Hoover, and the Dawn of a New America*, New York: Citadel, 2023.

Martin, Robert, *Hero of the Heartland: Billy Sunday and the Transformation of American Society, 1862–1935*, Bloomington: University of Indiana Press, 2002.

Matloff, Maurice, *Strategic Planning for Coalition Warfare, 1943–1944*, Washington D.C.: Government Printing Office, 1959.

McCaffrey, James, *Going for Broke: Japanese Americans Soldiers in the War against Nazi Germany*, Norman: University of Oklahoma Press, 2017.

McCoy, Donald, *Coming of Age: The United States during the 1920s and 1930s*, New York: Penguin, 1973.

McCullough, David, *Truman*, New York: Simon and Schuster, 1992.

McElvaine, Robert, *The Great Depression: America, 1929–1941*, New York: Three Rivers, 2009.

McGovern, James, *And a Time for Hope: Americans in the Great Depression*, Westport, Conn.: Praeger, 2000.

McJimsey, George, *Harry Hopkins: Ally of the Poor and Defender of Democracy*, Cambridge, Mass.: Harvard University Press, 1987.

McJimsey, George, *The Presidency of Franklin Delano Roosevelt*, Lawrence: University Press of Kansas, 2000.

McKenna, Marian, *Franklin Roosevelt and the Great Constitutional War: The Court Packing Crisis of 1937*, New York: Fordham University Press, 2002.

McMahon, Kevin, *Reconsidering Roosevelt on Race: How the President Paved the Way to Brown*, Chicago: University of Chicago Press, 2002.

Meacham, Jon, *Franklin and Winston: An Intimate Portrait of an Epic Friendship*, New York: Random House, 2003.

Mee, Charles, *The Meeting at Potsdam*, New York: M. Evans and Company, 1975.

Mee, Charles, *The Marshall Plan*, New York: Simon and Schuster, 1984.

Mikolashek, Jon, *General Mark Clark: Commander of America's Fifth Army in World War II and Liberator of Rome*, New York: Casemate, 2020.

Miller, Nathan, *New World Coming: The 1920s and the Making of Modern America*, New York: Scribner, 2003.

Miscamble, Wilson, *From Roosevelt to Truman: Potsdam, Hiroshima, and the Cold War*, New York: Cambridge University Press, 2007.

Mitchell, Gregg, *The Campaign of the Century: Upton Sinclair's Race for Governor of California and the Birth of Modern Politics*, New York: Random House, 1992.

Mitter, Rana, *China's War with Japan, 1937–1945: The Struggle for Survival*, New York: Penguin, 2014.

Moe, Richard, *Roosevelt's Second Act: The Election of 1940 and the Politics of War*, New York: Oxford University Press, 2013.

Morgan, Ted, *FDR: A Biography*, New York: Simon and Schuster, 1985.

Morgan, Iwan, and Philip Davies, *Hollywood and the Great Depression: Film, Politics, and Society in the 1930s*, Edinburgh: Edinburgh University Press, 2018.

Morgan, Iwan, *FDR: Transforming the Presidency and Renewing America*, New York: Bloomsbury, 2022.

Morgenstern, George, *Pearl Harbor: The Story of the Secret War*, New York: Devin-Adair Company, 1947.

Morse, Arthur, *While Six Million Died: A Chronicle of American Apathy*, New York: Random House, 1968.

Moskin, Robert, *Truman's War: The Final Victories of World War II and the Birth of the Postwar World*, New York: Random House, 1996.

Musher, Sharon Ann, *Democratic Art: The New Deal's Influence on American Culture*, Chicago: University of Chicago Press, 2015.

Nadeau, Remi, *Stalin, Churchill, and Roosevelt Divide Europe*, New York: Praeger, 1990.

Nasaw, David, *The Patriarch: The Remarkable Life and Turbulent Times of Joseph P. Kennedy*, New York: Penguin, 2013.

Neal, Stephen, *Happy Days Are Here Again: The 1932 Democratic Convention, the Emergence of FDR, and How America Was Changed Forever*, New York: Harper, 2005.

Neiberg, Michael, *Potsdam: The End of World War II and the Remaking of Europe*, New York: Basic Books, 2015.

Nelson, Craig, *Pearl Harbor: From Infamy to Greatness*, New York: Scribners, 2016.

Nester, William, *Winston Churchill and the Art of Leadership: How Winston Changed the World*, London: Frontline Books, 2020.

Newcomb, Richard, *Iwo Jima: The Dramatic Account of the Epic Battle that Turned the Tide of World War II*, New York: Henry Holt, 2002.

Newman, Robert, *Truman and the Hiroshima Cult*, East Lansing: Michigan State University Press, 1995.

Nixon, Edgar, ed., *Franklin D. Roosevelt and Foreign Affairs*, 2 vols., Cambridge, Mass.: Harvard University Press, 1969.

Norman, Michael, and Elizabeth Norman, *Tears in the Darkness: The Story of the Bataan Death March and Its Aftermath*, New York: Farrar, Straus, and Giroux, 2009.

Northouse, Peter, *Leadership: Theory and Practice*, New York: Sage, 2021.

O'Brien, Philip, *How the War Was Won: Air-Sea Power and Allied Victory in World War II*, New York: Cambridge University Press, 2019.

O'Donnell, Patrick, *Operatives, Spies, and Saboteurs: The Unknown Story of the Men and Women of World War II's OSS*, New York: New Press, 2014.

Offner, Arnold, and Theodore Wilson, eds., *Victory in Europe, 1945: From World War to Cold War*, Lawrence: University Press of Kansas, 2000.

Ottanelli, Frazer, *The Communist Party of the United States: From the Depression to World War II*, New Brunswick, N.J.: Rutgers University Press, 1991.

Padgett, Philip, *Advocating Overlord: The D-Day Strategy and Atomic Bomb*, Lincoln: University of Nebraska Press, 2018.

Palmer, Niall, *The Twenties in America: Politics and History*, Edinburgh: University of Edinburgh Press, 2006.

Parrish, Michael, *Anxious Decades: America in Prosperity and Depression, 1920–1941*, New York: W.W. Norton, 1992.

Patterson, *Congressional Conservatism and the New Deal: The Growth of the Conservative Coalition in Congress, 1933–1939*, Lexington: University of Kentucky Press, 1967.

Pearlmutter, Amos, *FDR & Stalin: A Not So Grand Alliance, 1943–1945*, Columbia: University of Missouri Press, 1993.

Pederson, William, *The FDR Years*, New York: Facts on File, 2006.

Pendar, Kenneth, *Adventures in Diplomacy: Our French Dilemma*, New York: Dodd, Mead, 1945.

Perkins, Frances, *The Roosevelt I Knew*, New York: Viking, 1946.

Perrett, Geoffrey, *America in the Twenties: A History*, New York: Simon and Schuster, 1982.

Persico, Joseph *Roosevelt's Secret War: FDR and World War II Espionage*, New York: Random House, 2001.

Persico, Joseph, *Roosevelt's Centurions: FDR and the Commanders He Led to Victory in World War II*, New York: Random House, 2013.

Peters, Charles, *Five Days in Philadelphia: The Amazing "We Want Willkie!" Convention of 1940 and How It Freed FDR to Save the Western World*, New York: Public Affairs, 2005.

Petersen, Michael, *Missiles for the Fatherland: Peenemunde, National Socialism, and the V-2 Missile*, New York: Cambridge University Press, 2011.

Picchi, Blaise, *Five Weeks of Giuseppe Zangara: The Man Who Would Assassinate FDR*, Chicago: Academy Chicago Publishers, 1998.

Pietrusza, David, *1920: The Year of Six Presidents*, New York: Carroll and Graf, 2006.

Pietrusza, David, *Roosevelt Sweeps Nation: FDR's 1936 Landslide and the Triumph of the Liberal Ideal*, New York: Diversion Books, 2022.

Pike, Frederick, *FDR's Good Neighbor Policy: Sixty Years of Generally Gentle Chaos*, Austin: University of Texas Press, 1995.

Plesur, Milton, *The 1920s: Problems and Paradoxes*, Boston: Allyn and Bacon, 1969.

Plokhy, S.M., *Yalta: The Price of Peace* New York: Viking, 2010.

Polenberg, Richard, ed., *America at War: Homefront, 1915–1945*, Englewood Cliffs, N.J.: Prentice Hall, 1968.

Polenberg, Richard, *War and Society: The United States, 1941–1945*, New York: J.B. Lippincott Company, 1972.

Poppendieck, Janet, *Breadlines Knee-deep in Wheat: Food Assistance in the Great Depression*, Berkeley: University of California Press, 2014.

Preston, Diane, *Eight Days at Yalta: How Churchill, Roosevelt, and Stalin Shaped the Postwar World*, New York: Atlantic Monthly Press, 2022.

Preston, William, *Aliens and Dissenters: Federal Suppression of Radicals, 1903–1933*, Cambridge, Mass.: Harvard University Press, 1963.

Potter, E.B., *Nimitz*, Annapolis, Maryland: Naval Institute Press, 2013.

Prange, Gordon, *At Dawn We Slept: The Untold Story of Pearl Harbor*, New York: Penguin, 1982.

Raack, R.C., *Stalin's Drive to the West, 1938–1945: The Origins of the Cold War*, Palo Alto, Calif.: Stanford University Press, 1995.

Raper, Arthur, *The Tragedy of Lynching*, Chapel Hill: University of North Carolina Press, 1933.

Reeves, Richard, *Infamy: The Shocking Story of the Japanese American Internment in World War II*, New York: Picador, 2016.

Riccards, Michael, and Cheryl Flagg, *Party Politics in the Age of Roosevelt: The Making of Modern America*, New York: Rowman and Littlefield, 2022.

Rickard, John, *Advance and Destroy: Patton as Commander in the Bulge*, Lexington: University Press of Kentucky, 2011.

Ritchie, Donald, *Electing FDR: The New Deal Campaign of 1932*, Lawrence: University of Kansas Press, 2007.

Robertson, David, *Sly and Able: A Political Biography of James F. Byrnes*, New York: W.W. Norton, 1994.

Robinson, Greg, *By Order of the President: FDR and the Internment of Japanese Americans*, Cambridge, Mass.: Harvard University Press, 2001.

Rochester, Anna, *Why Farmers Are Poor*, New York: International Publishers, 1940.

Rhodes, Richard, *The Making of the Atomic Bomb*, New York: Simon and Schuster, 1986.

Rolf, David, *The Bloody Road to Tunis: Destruction of the Axis Forces in North Africa, November 1942-May 1943*, London: Frontline, 2015.

Roll, David, *The Hopkins Touch: Harry Hopkins and the Forging of the Alliance to Defeat Hitler*, New York: Oxford University Press, 2013.

Roll, David, *George Marshall: Defender of the Republic*, New York: Dutton Caliber, 2019.

Rollins, Alfred, *Roosevelt and Howe*, New York: Knopf, 1962.

Romanus, Charles, and Riley Sunderland, *Stilwell's Mission to China*, Washington D.C.: Army Military History Department, 1953.

Romanus, Charles, and Riley Sunderland, *Stilwell's Command Problems*, Washington D.C.: Army Military History Department, 1956.

Romanus, Charles, and Riley Sunderland, *Time Runs Out in the CBI*, Washington D.C.: Army Military History Department, 1959.

Rook, William, *Chamberlain and Roosevelt: British Foreign Policy and the United States, 1937–1940*, Columbus: Ohio State University Press, 1988.

Rooney, David, *Stilwell the Patriot: Vinegar Joe, the Brits, and Chiang Kai-shek*, London: Greenhill, 2005.

Roosevelt, Eleanor, *This I remember*, New York: Harper and Brothers, 1949.

Roosevelt, Eleanor, *The Autobiography of Eleanor Roosevelt*, New York: Harper and Brothers, 1961.

Roosevelt, Elliot, ed., *FDR: His Personal Letters, 1905–1928*, New York: Duell, Sloan, and Pearce, 1947.

Roosevelt, Elliot, ed., *FDR: His Personal Letters, 1928–1945*, New York: Duell, Sloan, and Pearce, 1950.

Roosevelt, James, *My Parents: A Differing View*, Chicago: Playboy Press, 1976.

Rosen, Robert, *Saving the Jews: Franklin D. Roosevelt and the Holocaust*, New York: Thunder Mouth's Press, 2008.

Rosenman, Samuel, *Working with Roosevelt*, New York: Harper and Brothers, 1952.

Roskill, Stephen, *The Art of Leadership*, Hamden, Conn.: Archon Books, 1965.

Rossi, Elena Aga, *The Origins of the Bipolar World: Roosevelt's Policy toward Europe and the Soviet Union: A Reevaluation*, Berkeley: University of California Press, 1993.

Ryan, Cornelius, *The Longest Day: June 6, 1944*, New York: Simon and Schuster, 1994.

Ryan, Cornelius, *A Bridge Too Far*, New York: Simon and Schuster, 1974.

Sainsbury, Keith, *Churchill and Roosevelt at War: The War They Fought and the Peace They Hoped to Make*, New York: New York University Press, 1994.

Sainsbury, Keith, *The Turning Point: Roosevelt, Stalin, Churchill, and Chiang Kai-shek, 1943: the Moscow, Cairo, and Teheran Conferences*, New York: Oxford University Press, 1985.

Saloutos, Theodore, *The American Farmer and the New Deal*, Ames: Iowa State University Press, 1982.

Schaffer, Ronald, *Wings of Judgment: American Bombing in World War II*, New York: Oxford University Press, 1995.

Schaller, Michael, *Douglas MacArthur*, New York: Oxford University Press, 1989.

Scharz, Thomas, *The Genius of the System: Hollywood Filmmaking in the Studio Era*, New York: Pantheon, 1989.

Schild, Georg, *Bretton Woods and Dumbarton Oaks: American Economic and Political Postwar Planning in the Summer of 1944*, New York: St. Martin's, 1995.

Schlesinger, Arthur, *The Coming of the New Deal, 1933–1935*, New York: Mariner Books, 2003.

Schlesinger, Stephen, *Act of Creation: The Founding of the United Nations, A Story of Superpowers, Secret Agents, Wartime Allies and Enemies, and Their Quest for a Peacefull World*, Boulder, Colo.: Westview Press, 2003.

Schom, Alan, *The Eagle and the Rising Sun: The Japanese-American War, 1941–1942: Pearl Harbor through Guadalcanal*, New York: W.W. Norton, 2004.

Schwabe, Daniel, *Burning Japan: Air Force Bombing Strategic Change in the Pacific*, Lincoln, Ne.: Potomac Books, 2015.

Schweitzer, Authur, *The Age of Charisma*, Chicago: Nelson-Hall, 1984.

Shannon, David, *Between the Wars: America, 1919–1941*, Boston: Houghton Mifflin, 1965).

Sheppard, Si, *The Buying of the Presidency?: Franklin D. Roosevelt, the New Deal, and the Election of 1936*, New York: Praeger, 2014.

Sherry, Michael, *The Rise of American Air Power: The Creation of Armageddon*, New Haven, Conn.: Yale University Press, 1987.

Sherwood, Robert, *Roosevelt and Hopkins: An Intimate History*, New York: Harper and Brothers, 1948.

Shirer, William, *The Rise and Fall of the Third Reich: A History of Nazi Germany*, New York: Simon and Schuster, 2011.

Shivelbusch, Wolfgang, *Three New Deals: Reflections on Roosevelt's America, Mussolini's Italy, and Hitler's Germany*, New York: Picador, 2007.

Sickels, Robert, *American Popular Culture Through History: The 1940s*, New York: Greenwood, 2004.

Sitkoff, Harvard, *The Black Struggle for Equality*, New York: Hill and Wang, 2008.

Sixsmith, E.K.G., *Eisenhower as Military Commander*, New York: Da Capo, 1972.

Smith, Elberton, *The Army and Economic Mobilization*, Washington D.C.: Department of the Army, 1949.

Smith, Gaddis, *American Diplomacy during the Second World War*, New York: Knopf, 1985.

Smith, Jean, *FDR*, New York: Random House, 2007.

Smith, Jean, *Eisenhower in War and Peace*, New York: Random House, 2012.

Smith, Robert, *Triumph in the Philippines: The War in the Pacific*, Honolulu: University Press of the Pacific, 2005.

Snow, Richard, *A Measureless Peril: America in the Fight for the Atlantic, the Largest Land Battle of World War II*, New York: Scribner, 2011.

Solomon, William, *The Cambridge Companion to American Literature of the 1930s*, New York: Cambridge University Press, 2018.

Spector, Ronald, *Eagle against the Sun: The American War with Japan*, New York: Vintage, 1985.

Stafford, David, *Roosevelt and Churchill: Men of Secrets*, New York: Overlook Press, 2011.

Steele, Richard, *Propaganda in an Open Society: The Roosevelt Administration and the Media, 1933–1945*, New York: Bloomsbury Academic, 1985.

Steil, Benn, *The Battle for Bretton Woods: John Maynard Keynes, Harry Dexter White, and the Making of a New World Order*, Princeton, N.J.: Princeton University Press, 2014.

Steinfels, Margaret O'Brien, *Who's Minding the Children: The History and Politics of Day Care in America*, New York: Simon and Schuster, 1973.

Stevenson, Elizabeth, *Babbitts and Bohemians: From the Great War to the Great Depression*, New Brunswick, N.J.: Transaction Publishers, 1998.

Stewart, Adrian, *Kamikaze: Japan's Last Bid for Victory*, London: Pen and Sword, 2022.

Stoler, Mark, *The Politics of the Second Front: American Military Planning and Diplomacy in Coalition Warfare, 1941–1943*, Westport, Conn.: Greenwood, 1977.

Stoler, Mark, *Allies and Adversaries: The Joint Chiefs of Staff, the Grand Alliance, and United States Strategy in World War II*, Chapel Hill: University of North Carolina Press, 2000.

Stoler, Mark, *Allies at War: Britain and America against the Axis Powers, 1940–1945*, New York: Bloomsbury, 2007.

Stoler, Mark, and Molly Michelmore, eds., *The United States in World War II: A Documentary History*, Indianapolis: Hackett Publishing Company, 2018.

Stover, John, *The Life and Decline American Railroad*, New York: Oxford University Press, 1970.

Stowe, David, *Swing Changes: Big Band Jazz in New Deal America*, Cambridge, Mass.: Harvard University Press, 1996.

Streissguth, Thomas, *The Roaring Twenties*, New York: Facts on File, 2009.

Symonds, Craig, *The Battle of Midway*, New York: Oxford University Press, 2013.

Tansill, Charles, *Back Door to War: The Roosevelt Foreign Policy, 1933–1941*, Chicago: Regnery, 1952.

Takaki, Ronald, *Double Victory: A Multicultural History of America in World War II*, Boston: Little, Brown, 2000.

Taubman, William, *Stalin's American Policy: From Entente to Détente to Cold War*, New York: W.W. Norton, 1982.

Teague, Michael, *Mrs. L: Conversations with Alice Roosevelt Longworth*, New York: Doubleday, 1981.

Theobald, Robert, *The Final Secret of Pearl Harbor*, New York: Devin-Adair Company, 1954.

Theoharis, Anthan, *The Yalta Myths: An Issue in U.S. Politics, 1945–1955*, Columbia: University of Missouri Press, 1970.

Thomas, Gordon, *The Day the Bubble Burst: A Social History of the Wall Street Crash of 1929*, Garden City, N.Y.: Doubleday, 1979.

Thompson, Robert, *A Time for War: Franklin Delano Roosevelt and the Path to Pearl Harbor*, New York: Prentice-Hall, 1991.

Thorpe, Charles, *Oppenheimer: The Tragic Intellect*, Chicago: University of Chicago Press, 2008.

Toland, John, *Infamy: Pearl Harbor and Its Aftermath*, Garden City, N.J.: Doubleday, 1982.

Toland, John, *The Story of the Bulge*, New York: Meridian, 1985.

Toland, John, *The Last 100 Days: The Tumultuous and Controversial Story of the Final Days of World War II in Europe*, New York: Modern Library, 1994.

Toll, Ian, *Pacific Crucible: The War at Sea I the Pacific, 1941–1942*, New York: W.W. Norton, 2012.

Toll, Ian, *The Conquering Tide: The War in the Pacific, 1942–1944*, New York: W.W. Norton, 2016.

Toll, Ian, *Twilight of the Gods: War in the Western Pacific, 1944–1945*, New York: W.W. Norton, 2021.

Truman, Harry, *Memoirs: Year of Decisions*, New York: Doubleday, 1955.

Tucker, Gerrard, *The High Tide of American Conservatism: Davis, Coolidge, and the 1924 Election*, New York: Emerald Book Company, 2010.

Tucker-Jones, Antony, *Operation Dragoon: The Invasion of Southern France, 1944*, London: Pen and Sword, 2020.

Tugwell, Rexford, *The Democratic Roosevelt*, Garden City, N.Y.: Doubleday, 1957.

Tugwell, Rexford, *The Brains Trust*, New York: Viking, 1969.

Unger, Debi, and Irwin Unger, *George Marshall: A Biography*, New York: Harper Brothers, 2014.

Utley, Jonathan, *Going to War against Japan, 1937–1941* (Knoxville: University of Tennessee Press, 1984.

Vance, Rupert, *The Human Geography of the South: A Study in Regional Resources and Human Adequacy*, Chapel Hill: University of North Carolina Press, 1932.

Walker, Samuel, *Prompt and Utter Destruction: Truman and the Use of Atomic Bombs against Japan*, Chapel Hill: University of North Carolina Press, 1997.

Waller, Douglas, *Wild Bill Donovan*, New York: Free Press, 2011.

Ward, Geoffrey, *Before the Trumpet: Young Franklin Roosevelt, 1882–1905*, New York: Harper and Row, 1985.

Warren, Donald, *Radio Priest: Charles Coughlin, the Father of Hate Radio*, New York: Free Press, 1996.

Watkins, T.H., *The Hungry Years: America in an Age of Crisis*, New York: Henry Holt, 1999.

Watts, Steven, *The Magic Kingdom: Walt Disney and the American Way of Life*, Columbia: University of Missouri Press, 2001.

Weinstein, Allen, and Alexander Vassiliev, *The Haunted Wood: Soviet Espionage in America – the Stalin Era*, New York: Random House, 1999.

Weintraub, Stanley, *The Last Great Victory: The End of World War II, July-August 1945*, New York: Dutton, 1995.

Weiss, Nancy, *Charles Francis Murphy, 1858–1924: Respectability and Responsibility in Tammany Politics*, Northampton, Mass.: Smith College Press, 1968.

Weiss, Nancy, *Farewell to the Party of Lincoln: Black Voters in the Age of FDR*, Princeton, N.J.: Princeton University Press, 1983.

Welky, David, ed., *America between the Wars, 1919–1941: A Documentary Reader*, New York: John Wiley, 2012.

Western, Simon, *Leadership: A Critical Text*, New York: Sage, 2019.

Wheelan, Joseph, *Midnight in the Pacific: Guadalcanal – the World War II Battle that Turned the Tide of War*, New York: Da Capo Press, 2017.

Wheeler-Bennet, John, and Anthony Nicolls, *The Semblance of Peace: The Political Settlement after the Second World War*, London: Palgrave Macmillan, 1974.

White, Graham, *FDR and the Press*, Chicago: University of Chicago Press, 1979.

White, Richard, *Kingfish: The Reign of Huey P. Long*, New York: Random House, 2009.

Williams, Harry, *Huey Long*, New York: Vintage, 1981.

Willner, Ann Ruth, *The Spellbinder: Charismatic Political Leadership*, New Haven, Conn.: Yale University Press, 1984.

Winfield, Betty Houchin, *FDR and the News Media*, New York: Columbia University Press, 1994.

Winkler, Allan, *Home Front U.S.A.: America during World War II*, New York: Wiley Blackwell, 2012.

Wohlstetter, Roberta, *Pearl Harbor: Warning and Decision*, Palo Alto, Calif.: Stanford University Press, 1962.

Wood, Bryce, *The Making of the Good Neighbor Policy*, New York: W.W. Norton, 1967.

Worster, Donald, *The Dust Bowl: The Southern Plains in the 1930s*, New York: Oxford University Press, 2004.

Wright, Ellen, and Michael Fabre, eds., *The Richard Wright Reader*, New York: Harper and Row, 1978.

Wright, Frank Lloyd, *An Autobiography*, New York: Longman Greens and Company, 1936.

Wyman, David, *The Abandonment of the Jews: America and the Holocaust, 1941 to 1945*, (New York: Pantheon, 1984.

Yamamoto, Eric, Lorraine Bannai, and Margaret Chon, *Race, Rights, and Reparations: Law and the Japanese American Incarceration*, Frederick, Maryland: Aspen Publishing, 2021.

Young, William, *American Popular Culture Through History: The 1930s*, New York: Greenwood, 2002.

Zachary, Pascal, *Endless Frontiers: Vannevar Bush, Engineer of the American Century*, New York: Free Press, 1997.

CHAPTERS AND ARTICLES

Berstein, Barton, "Compelling Japan's Surrender without the A-Bomb, Soviet Entry, or Invasion: Reconsidering the US Bombing Survey's Early Surrender Conclusions," *Journal of Strategic Studies*, vol. 18, no. 3 (June 1995), 101–48.

Bix, Herbert, "Japan's Delayed Surrender: A Reinterpretation," *Diplomatic History*, vol. 19, no. 2 (Spring 1995), 197–225.

Frank, Richard, "Why Truman Dropped the Bomb," *Weekly Standard* (August 9, 2005), 20–25.

Hallion, Richard, "Precision Weapons, Power Projection, and the Revolution in Military Affairs," *Air Force Historical Studies Office*, website, May 29, 1999.

Hamby, Alonzo, "An American Democrat: A Reevaluation of the Personality of Harry S. Truman," *Political Science Quarterly*, vol. 106, no. 1 (Spring 1991), 33–55.

Kelly, Thomas, and Douglas Lonnstrom, "Political Science and Historians Poll," Betty Boyd Caroli, ed., *First Ladies: From Martha Washington to Michelle Obama*, New York: Oxford University Press, 1987.

Mark, Eduard, "Venona's Source 19 and the Trident Conference of 1943: Diplomacy or Espionage," *Intelligence and National Security*, vol. 13, no. 2 (Summer 1998), 1–31.

Newman, Robert, "Ending the War with Japan: Paul Nitze's 'Early Surrender' Counterfactual," *Pacific Historical Review*, vol. 64, no. 2 (May 1995), 167–94.

Nice, David, "The Influence of War and Party System Aging on the Ranking of a President," *Western Political Quarterly*, vol. 37, no. 3 (September 1984), 443–55.

Porter, David, "American Historians Rate Our Presidents," William Paterson and Ann McLaurin, eds., *The Rating Game in American Politics*, New York: Irvington Publishers, 1987.

Stimson, Henry, "The Decision to Use the Atomic Bomb," *Harper's Magazine*, vol. 194 (February 1947), 97–107.

Vila, Brian, and John Bonnett, "Understanding Indignation: Gar Alperovitz, Robert Maddox, and the Decision to Drop the Atomic Bomb," *Reviews in American History*, vol. 24, no. 3 (September 1996), 529–36.

Walker, Samuel, "The Decision to Use the Atomic Bomb: A Historiographical Update," Michael Hogan, ed., *America in the World: The Historiography of American Foreign Relations since 1941* (New York: Cambridge University Press, 1995), 83–104.

NOTES

Abbreviations

Gallup Poll George Gallup, *The Gallup Poll: Public Opinion, 1935–1971*, 2 vols., New York: Random House, 1972.

Lerner, *Historical Statistics* William Lerner, ed., *Historical Statistics of the United States: Colonial Times to 1970*, 2 vols. (Washington D.C.: Government Printing Office, 1975).

Introduction: Franklin Roosevelt and the Art of Leadership

1 David Porter, "American Historians Rate Our Presidents," William Paterson and Ann McLaurin, eds., The Rating Game in American Politics (New York: Irvington Publishers, 1987); Thomas Kelley and Douglas Lonnstrom, "Political Science and Historians Poll," Betty Boyd Caroli, ed., First Ladies: From Martha Washington to Michelle Obama (New York: Oxford University Press, 1987); David Nice, "The Influence of War and Party System Aging on the Ranking of a President," *Western Political Quarterly*, vol. 37, no. 3, (September 1984), 443–55.
2 Joseph Lash, *Eleanor and Franklin: The Story of their Relationship* (New York: W.W. Norton, 1971), 424.
3 Goodwin, *No Ordinary Time*, 306.
4 Kimball, *Juggler*, 14.
5 Rexford Tugwell, *The Brains Trust* (New York: Viking, 1969), 304.
6 Rexford Tugwell, *The Democratic Roosevelt* (New York: Harper Brothers, 1957), 44.
7 Smith, *FDR*, 263.
8 George McJimsey, *The Presidency of Franklin Delano Roosevelt* (Lawrence: University Press of Kansas, 2000), 25.
9 Kennedy, *Freedom from Fear*, 247.
10 Kennedy, *Freedom from Fear*, 249.
11 David Kennedy, *Freedom from Fear: The American People in Depression and War, 1929–1945* (New York: Oxford University Press, 1999), 99–100.
12 Buhite, *FDR's Fireside Chats*, 133.
13 Alan Brinkley, *The End of Reform: New Deal Liberalism in Recession and War* (New York: Alfred Knopf, 1995), 16.
14 Kennedy, *Freedom from Fear*, 250–51.
15 Franklin D. Roosevelt, *Whither Bound?* (Boston: Houghton Mifflin, 1926), 4–15.
16 Buhite, *FDR's Fireside Chats*, 118.
17 Warren Kimball, *The Juggler: Franklin Roosevelt as Wartime Commander* (Princeton, N.J.: Princeton University Press, 1991), 2.
18 Goodwin, *No Ordinary Time*, 24.

19 Goodwin, *No Ordinary Time*, 23.
20 Kimball, *Juggler*, 7.
21 Samuel Rosenman, *Working with Roosevelt* (New York: Harper and Brothers, 1952), 45.
22 Alfred Rollins, *Roosevelt and Howe* (New York: Knopf, 1962), 14–15.
23 Russell, Buhite, and David Levy, eds., *FDR's Fireside Chats* (Norman: University of Oklahoma Press, 1992).
24 Doris Kearns Goodwin, No Ordinary Time: Franklin and Eleanor Roosevelt: The Home Front in World War II (New York: Simon and Schuster, 1994), 308.
25 Winfield, *FDR and the News Media*, 104.
26 Frances Perkins, *The Roosevelt I Knew* (New York: Viking, 1946), 72.
27 Joseph Persico, *Roosevelt's Centurions: FDR and the Commanders He Led to Victory in World War II*, (New York: Random House, 2013), 248.
28 Samuel Rosenman, *Working with Roosevelt* (New York: Harper and Brothers, 1952), 11.
29 Frances Perkins, *The Roosevelt I Knew*, 385.
30 Graham White, *FDR and the Press* (Chicago: University of Chicago Press, 1979); Richard Steele, *Propaganda in an Open Society: The Roosevelt Administration and the Media, 1933–1945* (New York: Bloomsbury Academic, 1985); Betty Houchin Winfield, *FDR and the News Media* (New York: Columbia University Press, 1994).
31 Winfield, *FDR and the News Media*, 202; Buhite, *FDR's Fireside Chats*, xiii.
32 Winfield, *FDR and the News Media*, 66.
33 Eleanor Roosevelt, *This I Remember* (New York: Harper and Brothers, 1949), 346.

Chapter 1: The Making of a Leader

1 For the best multivolume biographies, see: Frank Freidel, *Franklin D. Roosevelt: The Apprenticeship* (Boston: Little, Brown, 1952); Frank Freidel, *Franklin D. Roosevelt: The Ordeal* (Boston: Little, Brown, 1954); Frank Freidel, *Franklin D. Roosevelt: The Triumph* (Boston: Little, Brown, 1956); Frank Freidel, *Franklin D. Roosevelt: Launching the New Deal* (Little, Brown, 1973); Frank Freidel, Frank, *Franklin D. Roosevelt: A Rendezvous with Destiny* (Boston: Little, Brown, 1990); and Kenneth Davis, *FDR: The Beckoning of Destiny, 1882–1928: A History* (New York: G.P. Putnam's Son, 1972); Kenneth Davis, *FDR: The New York Years, 1928–1932: A History* (New York: Random House, 1983); Kenneth Davis, *FDR: The New Deal Years, 1933–1937: A History* (New York: Random House, 1979); Kenneth Davis, *FDR: Into the Storm, 1937–1940: A History* (New York: Random House, 1993); Kenneth Davis, *FDR.: The War President, 1940–1943* (New York: Random House, 2000)

For the best one-volume biographies, see: Ted Morgan, *FDR: A Biography* (New York: Simon and Schuster, 1985); Jean Smith, *FDR* (New York: Random House, 2007); H.W. Brands, *Traitor to His Class: The Privileged Life and Radical Presidency of Franklin Delano Roosevelt* (New York: Anchor Books, 2008); Alan Brinkley, *Franklin Delano Roosevelt* (New York: Oxford University Press, 2009); Alonzo Hamby, *Man of Destiny: FDR and the Making of the American Century* (New York: Basic Books, 2015); Robert Dallek, *Franklin Delano Roosevelt: A Political Life* (New York: Viking, 2017).

For his presidency, see: George McJimsey, *The Presidency of Franklin Delano Roosevelt* (Lawrence: University Press of Kansas, 2000); Iwan Morgan, *FDR: Transforming the Presidency and Renewing America* (New York: Bloomsbury, 2022).

For primary sources, see: Elliott Roosevelt, ed., *FDR: His Personal Letters, 1905–1928* (New York: Duell, Sloan, and Pearce, 1947); Elliott Roosevelt, ed., *FDR: His Personal Letters, 1928–1945* (New York: Duell, Sloan, and Pearce, 1950);

William Pederson, *The FDR Years* (New York: Facts on File, 2006); Mario Dinunzio, *Franklin D. Roosevelt and the Third American Revolution* (Santa Barbara, Calif.: ABC-Clio, 2011); Harvey Kaye, *FDR on Democracy: The Greatest Speeches and Writings of President Franklin Roosevelt* (New York: Simon and Schuster, 2020).

2   For his childhood through college, see: Geoffrey Ward, *Before the Trumpet: Young Franklin Roosevelt, 1882–1905* (New York: Harper and Row, 1985).

3   Smith, *FDR*, 30.

4   Ward, *Young Roosevelt*, 253–55.

5   For the best biographies, see: Eleanor Roosevelt, *This I remember* (New York: Harper and Brothers, 1949); Eleanor Roosevelt, *The Autobiography of Eleanor Roosevelt* (New York: Harper and Brothers, 1961); Blanche Wiesen Cook, *Eleanor: The Early Years, 1884–1933* (New York: Viking, 1992); Blanche Wiesen Cook, *Eleanor Roosevelt: The Defining Years, 1933–1948* (New York: Penguin, 2000); Blanche Wiesen Cook, *Eleanor Roosevelt: The War Years and After, 1939–62* (New York: Viking, 2016).

For the relationship between Franklin and Eleanor, see: Joseph Lash, *Eleanor and Franklin: The Story of their Relationship* (New York: W.W. Norton, 1971); Doris Kearns Goodwin, *No Ordinary Time: Franklin and Eleanor Roosevelt: The Home Front in World War II* (New York: Simon and Schuster, 1994).

6   Michael Teague, *Mrs. L: Conversations with Alice Roosevelt Longworth* (New York: Doubleday, 1981), 151.

7   Goodwin, *No Ordinary Time*, 373.

8   Smith, *FDR*, 48.

9   Cook, *Eleanor Roosevelt*, 536.

10   Joseph Lash, *Love, Eleanor: Eleanor Roosevelt and Her Friends* (Garden City, N.Y.: Doubleday, 1982), 57.

11   Eleanor Roosevelt, *The Autobiography of Eleanor Roosevelt* (New York: Harper and Brothers, 1961), 57–60.

12   Goodwin, *No Ordinary Time*, 179.

13   Smith, *FDR*, 234.

14   Terry Golway, *Machine Made: Tammany Hall and the Creation of Modern American Politics* (New York: Liveright, 2014).

15   Nancy Weiss, *Charles Francis Murphy, 1858–1924: Respectability and Responsibility in Tammany Politics* (Northampton, Mass.: Smith College Press, 1968).

16   Charles LaCerra, *Franklin Delano Roosevelt and Tammany Hall of New York* (Lanham, Maryland: University Press of America, 1997).

17   Weiss, *Murphy*, 21.

18   Smith, *FDR*, 66.

19   Brands, *Traitor to His Class*, 58.

20   Frances Perkins, *The Roosevelt I Knew* (New York: Viking, 1946), 11.12.

21   Morgan, *FDR*, 127.

22   Smith, FDR, 82; Eleanor Roosevelt, *Autobiography*, 68.

23   Alfred Rollins, *Roosevelt and Howe* (New York: Knopf, 1962); Julie Fender, *FDR's Shadow: Louis Howe, the Force Behind Franklin and Eleanor Roosevelt* (New York: Palgrave Macmillan, 2009).

24   James Chace, *1912: Wilson, Roosevelt, Taft, and Debs: The Election that Changed the Country* (New York: Simon and Schuster, 2005).

25   Josephus Daniels, *The Wilson Era: Years of Peace, 1912–1917* (Chapel Hill: University of North Carolina Press, 1944), 124.

26   Josephus Daniels, *The Wilson Era: Years of War and After, 1917–1921* (Chapel Hill: University of North Carolina Press, 1946), 253.

27   Brands, *Traitor to His Class*, 75.

28   Smith, *FDR*, 124.
29   Lerner, *Historical Statistics*, 2: 1114, 1141.
30   Joseph Persico, *Roosevelt's Secret War: FDR and World War II Espionage* (New York: Random House, 2001), 9.
31   Smith, *FDR*, 153.
32   Brands, *Traitor to His Class*, 138.
33   Eleanor Roosevelt, Autobiography, 109–10.
34   David Pietrusza, *1920: The Year of Six Presidents* (New York: Carroll and Graf, 2006).
35   Goodwin, *No Ordinary Time*, 80.
36   Gerrard Tucker, *The High Tide of American Conservatism: Davis, Coolidge, and the 1924 Election* (New York: Emerald Book Company, 2010).

Chapter 2: The Governor

1   Robert Slayton, *Empire Statesman: The Rise and Redemption of Al Smith* (New York: Free Press, 2001); Christopher Finan, *Alfred E. Smith, The Happy Warrior* (New York: Hill and Wang, 2002).
2   Bernard Bellush, *Franklin D. Roosevelt as Governor of New York* (New York: AMS Press, 1968).
3   Bellush, *Roosevelt as Governor*, 9.
4   Allan Lichtman, *Prejudice and the Old Politics: The Presidential Election of 1928* (Chapel Hill: University of North Carolina Press, 1979).
5   Robert Caro, *The Power Broker: Robert Moses and the Fall of New York* (New York: Vintage, 1975).
6   Smith, *FDR*, 231.
7   Smith, *FDR*, 235.
8   Eleanor Roosevelt, *This I remember* (New York: Harper and Brothers, 1949), 46.
9   Smith, *FDR*, 246–47.
10   Bellush, *Roosevelt as Governor*, 220.
11   Bellush, *Roosevelt as Governor*, 79.
12   For the stock market crash, see: John Kenneth Galbraith, *The Great Crash: 1929* (Boston: Houghton Mifflin, 1955); Gordon Thomas, *The Day the Bubble Burst: A Social History of the Wall Street Crash of 1929* (Garden City, N.Y.: Doubleday, 1979); William Klingaman, *1929: The Year of the Great Crash* (New York: Houghton Mifflin, 1989); Maury Klein, *Rainbow's End: The Crash of 1929* (New York: Oxford University Press, 2001).
13   McElvaine, *Great Depression*, 38.
14   For the 1920–1933 era, see: David Shannon, *Between the Wars: America, 1919–1941* (Boston: Houghton Mifflin, 1965); Donald McCoy, *Coming of Age: The United States during the 1920s and 1930s* (New York: Penguin, 1973); Ellis Hawley, *The Great War and the Search for Modern Order: A History of the American People and Their Institutions, 1917–1933* (New York: St. Martin's Press, 1979); Sean, Cashman, Sean, *America in the Twenties and Thirties* (New York: New York University Press, 1989); Michael Parrish, *Anxious Decades: America in Prosperity and Depression, 1920–1941* (New York: W.W. Norton, 1992); William Leuchtenburg, *The Perils of Prosperity: 1914–1932* (Chicago: University of Chicago Press, 1993); Elizabeth Stevenson, *Babbitts and Bohemians: From the Great War to the Great Depression* (New Brunswick, N.J.: Transaction Publishers, 1998); David Welky, ed., *America Between the Wars, 1919–1941: A Documentary Reader* (New York: John Wiley, 2012).

For the Republican Party, see: Karl Schriftgiesser, *This Was Normalcy: An Account of Party Politics during Twelve Republican Years, 1920–1932* (Boston: Little, Brown, and Company, 1948); John Hicks, *Republican Ascendency: 1921–1933* (New York: Harper and Row, 1960); Ethan Ellis, *Republican Foreign Policy, 1921–1933* (New Brunswick, N.J.: Rutgers University Press, 1968); Robert Murray, *The Politics of Normalcy: Governmental Theory and Practice in the Harding-Coolidge Era* (New York: W.W. Norton, 1973); Katherine Sibley, ed., *A Companion to Warren G. Harding, Calvin Coolidge, and Herbert Hoover* (New York: Wiley-Blackwell, 2014).

15 David Burner, *Herbert Hoover: A Public Life* (New York: Alfred Knopf, 1978); Martin Fausold, *The Presidency of Herbert Hoover* (Lawrence: University Press of Kansas, 1985); William Leuchtenburg, *Herbert Hoover: The 31st President, 1929–1933* (New York: Times Books, 2009).

16 McElvaine, *Great Depression*, 65.

17 James McGovern, *And a Time for Hope: Americans in the Great Depression* (Westport, Conn.: Praeger, 2000), 3.

18 Martin Fausold, *The Presidency of Herbert Hoover* (Lawrence: University Press of Kansas, 1985), 73.

19 For the Great Depression, see: Edward Ellis, *A Nation in Torment: The Great American Depression, 1929–1939* (New York: Kodansha, 1995); David Kennedy, *Freedom from Fear: The American People in Depression and War, 1929–1945* (New York: Oxford University Press, 1999); T.H. Watkins, *The Hungry Years: America in an Age of Crisis* (New York: Henry Holt, 1999); Robert McElvaine, *The Great Depression: America, 1929–1941* (New York: Three Rivers, 2009); Mano Dinuzio, ed., *The Great Depression and New Deal: Documents Decoded* (Santa Barbara, Calif.: ABC-Clio, 2014).

20 Lerner, *Historical Statistics*, 1:177, 225, 135; 2:1038; Rik Hafer, *The Federal Reserve System: An Encyclopedia* (New York: Greenwood, 2005), 18; Kennedy, *Freedom from Fear*, 163–64.; C.D. Bremer, *American Bank Failures* (New York: Columbia University Press, 2020).

21 Eric Sevareid, "Not So Wild a Dream," in Don Congden, ed., *The 30s: A Time to Remember* (New York: Simon and Schuster, 1962), 109.

22 Smith, *FDR*, 250.

23 Bellush, *Roosevelt as Governor*, 123–34.

24 Betty Houchin Winfield, *FDR and the News Media* (Urbana: University of Illinois Press, 1990), 18.

25 Smith, *FDR*, 243–44.

26 Bellush, *Roosevelt as Governor*, 168.

27 Bellush, *Roosevelt as Governor*, 95, 98.

28 Bellush, *Roosevelt as Governor*, 146.

29 Bellush, *Roosevelt as Governor*, 187.

Chapter 3: The First Hundred Days

1 Earland Carlson, *Franklin D. Roosevelt's Fight for the Presidential Nomination, 1928–1932* (Ann Arbor, Mich.: University of Michigan Press, 1956); Donald Ritchie, *Electing FDR: The New Deal Campaign of 1932* (Lawrence: University of Kansas Press, 2007); Stephen Neal, *Happy Days Are Here Again: The 1932 Democratic Convention, the Emergence of FDR, and How America Was Changed Forever* (New York: Harper, 2005); Scott Martelle, *1932: FDR, Hoover, and the Dawn of a New America* (New York: Citadel, 2023).

2 Smith, *FDR*, 257–58.

3   Elliot Roosevelt, ed., *F.D.R.: His Personal Letters, 1928–1945* (New York: Duell, Sloan, and Pearce, 1950), 252.

4   Smith, *FDR*, 263.

5   Rexford Tugwell, *The Brains Trust* (New York: Viking, 1969), 357–59, 427–34.

6   Mario Dinunzio, *Franklin D. Roosevelt and the Third American Revolution* (Santa Barbara, Calif.: ABC-Clio, 2011), 94–95.

7   Eleanor Roosevelt, *This I Remember* (New York: Harper and Brothers, 1949), 69.

8   Mario Dinunzio, ed., *The Great Depression and New Deal: Documents Decoded* (Santa Barbara, Calif.: ABC-Clio, 2014), 41.

9   Alan Brinkley, *The End of Reform: New Deal Liberalism in Recession and War* (New York: Vintage, 2011), 70.

10 Smith, *FDR*, 282.

11 Eleanor Roosevelt, *This I Remember*, 74–75.

12 Rexford Tugwell, *The Democratic Roosevelt* (Garden City, N.Y.: Doubleday, 1957), 36.

13 Blaise Picchi, *Five Weeks of Giuseppe Zangara: The Man Who Would Assassinate FDR* (Chicago: Academy Chicago Publishers, 1998).

14 Alter, *Defining Moment*, 3.

15 Michael Teague, *Mrs. L.: Conversations with Alice Roosevelt Longworth* (New York: Doubleday, 1981), 171, 161.

16 Katie, Louchheim, ed., *The Making of the New Deal: The Insiders Speak* (Cambridge, Mass.: Harvard University Press, 1983); Joseph Lash, *Dealers and Dreamers: A New Look at the New Deal* (New York: Doubleday, 1988); Anthony Badger, *The New Deal: The Depression Years, 1933–1940* (Chicago: Ivan Dee, 2002); Arthur Schlesinger, *The Coming of the New Deal, 1933–1935* (New York: Mariner Books, 2003); Ira Katznelson, *Fear Itself: The New Deal and the Origins of Our Time* (New York: Liveright Publishing, 2003); William Leuchtenburg, *Franklin Delano Roosevelt and the New Deal: 1932–1940* (New York: Harper Perennial, 2009); Adam Cohen, *Nothing to Fear: FDR's Inner Circle and the Hundred Days that Created Modern America* (New York: Penguin, 2009); Roger Daniels, *Franklin D. Roosevelt and the New Deal, 1932–1940* (New York: Harper Perennial, 2009); Michael Hiltzik, *The New Deal: A Modern History* (New York: Free Press, 2011); Mario Dinuzio, ed., *The Great Depression and New Deal: Documents Decoded* (Santa Barbara, Calif.: ABC-Clio, 2014); Roger Daniels, *Franklin Delano Roosevelt: The Road to the New Deal, 1889 to 1939* (Urbana: University of Illinois Press, 2018).

17 For the best overview, see: Jonathan Alter, *The Defining Moment: FDR's Hundred Days and the Triumph of Hope* (New York: Simon and Schuster, 2006).

18 Susan Estabrook Kennedy, *The Banking Crisis of 1933* (Lexington: University of Kentucky Press, 1973).

19 Badger, *New Deal*, 71.

20 Buhite, *FDR's Fireside Chats*, 15, 17.

21 Theodore Saloutos, *The American Farmer and the New Deal* (Ames: Iowa State University Press, 1982).

22 Bernard Bellush, *Franklin D. Roosevelt as Governor of New York* (New York: AMS Press, 1968), 92.

23 Anna Rochester, *Why Farmers Are Poor* (New York: International Publishers, 1940), 11–13.

24 Neil Maher, *Nature's New Deal: The Civilian Conservation Corps and the Roots of the American Environmental Movement* (New York: Oxford University Press, 2009).

25 William Chandler, *The Myth of TVA: Conservation and Development in Tennessee Valley, 1933–1983* (Cambridge, Mass.: Ballinger Publishing, 1984); Walter Creese, *TVA's Public Planning: The Vision, the Reality* (Knoxville: University of Tennessee Press, 2003).

26   Badger, *New Deal*, 176.
27   Buhite, *FDR's Fireside Chats*, 29.
28   Smith, *FDR*, 354.
29   Adam Cohen, *Nothing to Fear: FDR's Inner Circle and the Hundred Days that Created Modern America* (New York: Penguin, 2009), 265.
30   Smith, *FDR*, 345.
31   Badger, *New Deal*, 199.
32   T.H. Watkins, *The Hungry Years: A Narrative History of the Great Depression in America* (New York: Henry Holt, 1999), 221.

Chapter 4: The Corrections

1   Herbert Levy, *Henry Morgenthau, Jr.: The Remarkable Life of FDR's Secretary of the Treasury* (New York: Skyhorse Publishing, 2010).
2   Graham White, *FDR and the Press* (Chicago: University of Chicago Press, 1979); Richard Steele, *Propaganda in an Open Society: The Roosevelt Administration and the Media, 1933–1945* (New York: Bloomsbury Academic, 1985); Betty Houchin Winfield, *FDR and the News Media* (New York: Columbia University Press, 1994).
3   Winfield, *FDR and the News Media*, 65.
4   Winfield, *FDR and the News Media*, 56, 112.
5   Kenneth Davis, *Invincible Summer: An Intimate Portrait of the Roosevelts based on Recollections of Marion Dickerson* (New York: Atheneum, 1974), 128–29.
6   Watkins, *Hungry Years*, 444.
7   James Gregory, *American Exodus: The Dust Bowl Migration and Okie Culture in California* (New York: Oxford University Press, 1991); Donald Worster, *The Dust Bowl: The Southern Plains in the 1930s* (New York: Oxford University Press, 2004); Timothy Egan, *The Worst Hard Time: The Untold Story of Those Who Survived the Great American Dust Bowl* (New York: Houghton Mifflin, 2006); Dayton Duncan and Ken Burns, *The Dust Bowl: An Illustrated History* (New York: Chronicle Books, 2012).
8   Badger, *New Deal*, 170.
9   Richard Lowitt, *The New Deal and the West* (Bloomington: University of Nebraska Press, 1984), 34, 35; Watkins, *Hungry Years*, 434.
10   Janet Poppendieck, *Breadlines Knee-deep in Wheat: Food Assistance in the Great Depression* (Berkeley: University of California Press, 2014), 144–45.
11   Badger, *New Deal*, 173.
12   Lowitt, *New Deal and the West*, 73–75.
13   Lowitt, *New Deal and the West*, 81.
14   Lowitt, *New Deal and the West*, 94.
15   David Welky, ed., *America Between the Wars, 1919–1941: A Documentary Reader* (New York: Wiley-Blackwell, 2012), 165.
16   Lowitt, *New Deal and the West*, 122, 127, 133.
17   Kennedy, *Freedom from Fear*, 252–53.
18   Kennedy, *Freedom from Fear*, 275.
19   Mark Leff, *The Limits of Symbolic Reform: The New Deal and Taxation, 1933–1939* (New York: Cambridge University Press, 1984).
20   Iwan Morgan, *FDR: Transforming the Presidency and Renewing America* (New York: Bloomsbury, 2022), 152.
21   McElvaine, *Great Depression*, 252.
22   Leuchtenburg, *Roosevelt and the New Deal*, 105.
23   Michael Riccards and Cheryl Flagg, *Party Politics in the Age of Roosevelt: The Making of Modern America* (New York: Rowman and Littlefield, 2022), 158.

Chapter 5: The Opponents

1   Buhite, *FDR's Fireside Chats*, 51, 49.
2   James Patterson, *Congressional Conservatism and the New Deal: The Growth of the Conservative Coalition in Congress, 1933–1939* (Lexington: University of Kentucky Press, 1967).
3   Rita James Simon, ed., *As We Saw the Thirties: Essays on Political and Social Movements of the Decade* (Urbana: University of Illinois Press, 1967).
4   James McGovern, *And a Time for Hope: Americans in the Great Depression* (Westport, Conn.: Praeger, 2000),44–45.
5   Robert Dallek, *Franklin D. Roosevelt and American Foreign Policy, 1932–1945* (New York: Oxford University Press, 1979), 36.
6   Betty Houchin Winfield, *FDR and the Mass Media* (Urbana: University of Illinois Press, 1990), 128.
7   Alan Brinkley, *Voices of Protest: Huey Long, Father Coughlin, and the Great Depression* (New York: Vintage, 1983).
8   Donald Warren, *Radio Priest: Charles Coughlin, the Father of Hate Radio* (New York: Free Press, 1996).
9   Harry Williams, *Huey Long* (New York: Vintage, 1981); Richard White, *Kingfish: The Reign of Huey P. Long* (New York: Random House, 2009).
10   Michael Hiltzik, *The New Deal: A Modern History* (New York: Free Press, 2011), 225.
11   Kennedy, *Freedom from Fear*, 242, 244.
12   Brinkley, *Voices of Protest*, 6.
13   Buhite, *FDR's Fireside Chats*, 48.
14   Si Sheppard, *The Buying of the Presidency?: Franklin D. Roosevelt, the New Deal, and the Election of 1936* (New York: Praeger, 2014); David Pietrusza, *Roosevelt Sweeps Nation: FDR's 1936 Landslide and the Triumph of the Liberal Ideal* (New York: Diversion Books, 2022).
15   William Pederson, *The FDR Years* (New York: Facts on File, 2006), 356.
16   Robert Sherwood, *Roosevelt and Hopkins: An Intimate History* (New York: Harper Brothers, 1948); George McJimsey, *Harry Hopkins: Ally of the Poor and Defender of Democracy* (Cambridge, Mass.: Harvard University Press, 1987); David Roll, *The Hopkins Touch: Harry Hopkins and the Forging of the Alliance to Defeat Hitler* (New York: Oxford University Press, 2013).
17   Gregg Mitchell, *The Campaign of the Century: Upton Sinclair's Race for Governor of California and the Birth of Modern Politics* (New York: Random House, 1992).
18   Kennedy, *Freedom from Fear*, 287.
19   William Leuchtenberg, *The Supreme Court Reborn: The Constitutional Revolution in the Age of Roosevelt* (New York: Oxford University Press, 1995); Marian McKenna, *Franklin Roosevelt and the Great Constitutional War: The Court Packing Crisis of 1937* (New York: Fordham University Press, 2002).
20   Buhite, *FDR's Fireside Chats*, 90.
21   Irving Bernstein, *The Turbulent Years: A History of the American Worker, 1933–1941* (Boston: Houghton Mifflin, 1970); Melvyn Dubofsky and Warren Van Tine, *John L. Lewis: A Biography* (New York: Quadrangle Books, 1977).
22   Ira Katznelson, *From Fear Itself: The New Deal and the Origins of Our Time* (New York: Liveright Publishing, 2003), 173.
23   Kevin McMahon, *Reconsidering Roosevelt on Race: How the President Paved the Way to Brown* (Chicago: University of Chicago Press, 2002).
24   Nancy Weiss, *Farewell to the Party of Lincoln: Black Voters in the Age of FDR* (Princeton, N.J.: Princeton University Press, 1983), 21.

25 Rupert Vance, *The Human Geography of the South: A Study in Regional Resources and Human Adequacy* (Chapel Hill: University of North Carolina Press, 1932); Watkins, *Hungry Years*, 373–74, 380.

26 Arthur Raper, *The Tragedy of Lynching* (Chapel Hill: University of North Carolina Press, 1933), v, 2, 468–84; Harvard Sitkoff, *The Black Struggle for Equality* (New York: Hill and Wang, 2008), 269.

27 *Gallup Poll*, 1:48.

28 Daniel Kato, *Liberalizing Lynching: Building a New Racialized State* (New York: Oxford University Press, 2016), 50.

29 Smith, *FDR*, 402.

30 Goodwin, *No Ordinary Time*, 164.

31 Harvey Klehr, *The Heyday of American Communism: The Depression Decade* (New York: Basic Books, 1984); Frazer Otttanelli, *The Communist Party of the United States: From the Depression to World War II* (New Brunswick, N.J.: Rutgers University Press, 1991); Harvey Klehr and John Haynes, *The American Communist Movement: Storming Heaven Itself* (New York: Twayne, 1992).

32 Klehr and Haynes, *American Communist Movement*, 67.

33 Watkins, *Hungry Years*, 365.

34 Wayne Cole, *Roosevelt and the Isolationists, 1932–1945* (Lincoln: University of Nebraska Press, 1983).

35 Marks, *Wind over Sand*, 18.

36 Steven Casey, *Cautious Crusade: Franklin D. Roosevelt, American Public Opinion, and the War against Nazi Germany* (New York: Oxford University, 2001).

37 Wayne Cole, Charles A. Lindbergh and the Battle against American Intervention in World War II (New York: Harcourt Brace, Jovanovich, 1974).

38 Cole, *Roosevelt and the Internationalists*, 464.

39 Richard Hofstadter, *The American Political Tradition and the Men Who Made It* (New York: Alfred Knopf, 1948), 311.

Chapter 6: The Creators

1 Jerre Mangione, *The Dream and the Deal: The Federal Writers Project, 1935–1943* (Syracuse, N.Y.: Syracuse University Press, 1996); Sharon Ann Musher, *Democratic Art: The New Deal's Influence on American Culture* (Chicago: University of Chicago Press, 2015).

2 Jerre Mangione, *The Dream and the Deal: The Federal Writers Project, 1935–1943* (Syracuse, N.Y.: Syracuse University Press, 1996), 4.

3 Anthony Badger, *The New Deal: The Depression Years, 1933–1940* (Chicago: Ivan Dee, 1989), 218.

4 Mangione, *Dream and the Deal*, 365.

5 Ira Berlin et al., eds., *Remembering Slavery: African Americans Talk About Their Personal Experiences of Slavery and Freedom* (New York: New Press, 1998).

6 Robert Hughes, *American Visions: The Epic History of Art in America* (New York: Alfred Knopf, 1997), 452.

7 Warren French, ed., *The Forties: Fiction, Poetry, Drama* (Deland, Fla.: Everett/Edwards Company, 1969); Peter Conn, *The American 1930s: A Literary History* (New York: Cambridge University Press, 2009); William Solomon, *The Cambridge Companion to American Literature of the 1930s* (New York: Cambridge University Press, 2018).

8 John Steinbeck, *The Grapes of Wrath* (New York: Viking, 1989),

9 Steinbeck, *Grapes of Wrath*, 42, 45.

10 Steinbeck, *Grapes of Wrath*, 50.

11   James McGovern, *And a Time for Hope: Americans in the Great Depression* (Westport, Conn.: Praeger, 2000), 13.

12   Richard Wright, "Blueprint for Negro Writing," in Ellen Wright and Michael Fabre, eds., *The Richard Wright Reader* (New York: Harper and Row, 1978), 37.

13   Conn, *American 1930s,* 4.

14   Richard Lowitt and Maurine Beasley, eds., *One Third of a Nation: Lorena Hickok Reports on the Great Depression* (Urbana: University of Illinois Press, 1981).

15   Michael Golay, *America 1933: The Great Depression, Lorena Hickok, Eleanor Roosevelt, and the Shaping of the New Deal* (New York: Simon and Schuster, 2016).

16   Frank Lloyd Wright, *An Autobiography* (New York: Longman Greens and Company, 1936), 260.

17   David Stowe, *Swing Changes: Big Band Jazz in New Deal America* (Cambridge, Mass.: Harvard University Press, 1996).

18   Thomas Scharz, *The Genius of the System: Hollywood Filmmaking in the Studio Era* (New York: Pantheon, 1989), 159.

19   Andrew Bergman, *We're in the Money: Depression America and Its Films* (Chicago: Ivan R. Dee, 1992); Thomas Scharz, *The Genius of the System: Hollywood Filmmaking in the Studio Era* (New York: Pantheon, 1989); Ina Rae Hark, *American Cinema of the 1930s: Themes and Variations* (New Brunswick, N.J.: Rutgers University Press, 2007); Iwan Morgan and Philip Davies, *Hollywood and the Great Depression: Film, Politics, and Society in the 1930s* (Edinburgh: Edinburgh University Press, 2018).

20   Harlan Lebo, *Citizen Kane: A Film-maker's Journey* (Los Angeles: Angel City Press, 2022).

21   Wheeler Dixon, *American Cinema of the 1940s: Themes and Variations* (New Brunswick, N.J.: Rutgers University Press, 2005).

Chapter 7: The Strides to World War

1   Edgar Nixon and Donald Schewe, eds., *Franklin D. Roosevelt and Foreign Affairs,* 13 vols. (Cambridge, Mass.: Harvard University Press, 1969); Robert Dallek, *Franklin D. Roosevelt and American Foreign Policy, 1932–1945* (New York: Oxford University Press, 1979); Frederick Marks, *Wind Over Sand: The Diplomacy of Franklin Roosevelt* (Athens: University of Georgia Press, 1990); Wayne Cole, *Determinism and American Foreign Relations during Franklin D. Roosevelt Era* (Lanham, Maryland: University Press of America, 1994); Justus Doenecke and Mark Stoler, *Debating Franklin D. Roosevelt's Foreign Policies* (New York: Rowman and Littlefield, 2005).

2   Samuel Rosenman, Working with Roosevelt (New York: Harper Brothers, 1952), 152.

3   Cole, *Roosevelt and the Isolationists,* 114.

4   Cole, *Roosevelt and the Isolationists,* 116.

5   Cole, *Roosevelt and the Isolationists,* 61.

6   Bryce Wood, *The Making of the Good Neighbor Policy* (New York: W.W. Norton, 1967); Frederick Pike, *FDR's Good Neighbor Policy: Sixty Years of Generally Gentle Chaos* (Austin: University of Texas Press, 1995).

7   Dallek, *Roosevelt and American Foreign Policy,* 64.

8   Edgar Nixon, ed., *Franklin D. Roosevelt and Foreign Affairs,* 2 vols. (Cambridge, Mass.: Harvard University Press, 1969), 2:381.

9   Martin Blinkhorn, *Fascism and the Right in Europe, 1919–1945* (New York: Routledge, 2000); Benjamin Hett, *The Death of Democracy: Hitler's Rise to Power and the Downfall of the Weimar Republic* (New York: St. Martin's Griffith, 2020);

Shinichi Kitaoka, *From Party Politics to Militarism in Japan, 1923 to 1941* (New York: Lynne Rienner, 2020); John Foot, *Blood and Power: The Rise and Fall of Italian Fascism* (New York: Bloomsbury, 2022).

10   The best history remains William Shirer, *The Rise and Fall of the Third Reich: A History of Nazi Germany* (New York: Simon and Schuster, 2011), first published in 1959. See also: Benjamin Hett, *The Death of Democracy: Hitler's Rise to Power and the Downfall of the Weimar Republic* (New York: St. Martin's Griffin, 2020); Benjamin Hett, *The Nazi Menace: Hitler, Churchill, Roosevelt, Stalin, and the Road to War* (New York: Griffin, 2021).

11   For overviews of the history leading to Pearl Harbor, see: Herbert Feis, *The Road to Pearl Harbor* (New York: Atheneum, 1963); Dorothy Borg and Shumpei Okamoto, eds., *Pearl Harbor as History: Japanese-American Relations, 1931–1941* (New York: Columbia University Press, 1973); Jonathan Utley, *Going to War against Japan, 1937–1941* (Knoxville: University of Tennessee Press, 1984); Robert, Thompson, *A Time for War: Franklin Delano Roosevelt and the Path to Pearl Harbor* (New York: Prentice-Hall, 1991); Justus Doenecke and John Wilz, *From Isolation to War, 1931–41* (Arlington Heights, Ill.: Harlan Davidson, 1991); Craig Nelson, *Pearl Harbor: From Infamy to Greatness* (New York: Scribners, 2016).

12   Dallek, *Roosevelt and American Foreign Policy*, 117.

13   Alvin Cox and Hilary Conroy, eds., *China and Japan: The Search for Balance since World War I* (Santa Barbara, Calif.: ABC-CLIO, 1978); Iris Chang, *The Rape of Nanjing: The Forgotten Holocaust of World War II* (New York: Basic Books, 1997); Rana Mitter, *China's War with Japan, 1937–1945: The Struggle for Survival* (New York: Penguin, 2014); Richard Frank, *Tower of Skulls: A History of the Asia-Pacific War, July 1937-May 1942* (New York: W.W. Norton, 2020).

14   Manny Goginos, *The Panay Incident: Prelude to War* (Lafayette, Ind.: Purdue University Press, 1967).

15   *Gallup Poll*, 1:71.

16   Smith, *FDR*, 424. William Rock, *Chamberlain and Roosevelt: British Foreign Policy and the United States, 1937–1940* (Columbus: Ohio State University Press, 1988).

17   Owen Booth and John Walton, *World War II: Primary Sources in World Warfare* (New York: Amber Books, 2017), 11.

18   Joseph Persico, *Roosevelt's Centurions: FDR and the Commanders He Led to Victory in World War II* (New York: Random House, 2013), 29.

19   Kennedy, *Freedom from Fear*, 416.

20   Arthur Morse, *While Six Million Died: A Chronicle of American Apathy* (New York: Random House, 1968), 288.

21   Ira Katznelson, *Fear Itself: The New Deal and the Origins of Our Time* (New York: Liveright Publishing, 2003), 44.

22   Steven Casey, *Cautious Crusaders: Franklin D. Roosevelt, American Public Opinion, and the War against Nazi Germany* (New York: Oxford University Press, 2001), 38.

23   Meacham, *Franklin and Winston*, 45.

24   Both quotes from Shirer, *Rise and Fall of the Third Reich*, 470, 474–75.

25   Shirer, *Rise and Fall of the Third Reich*, 634–35.

26   For good overviews of World War II, see: Liddell Hart, *History of the Second World War* (Old Saybrook, Conn.: Konecky and Konecky, 1970); Owen Booth and John Walton, *World War II: Primary Sources in World Warfare* (New York: Amber Books, 2017); Victor Hanson, *The Second World Wars: How the First Global Conflict Was Fought and Won* (New York: Basic Books, 2020).

27   Buhite, *FDR's Fireside Chats*, 149–51.

28   Cole, *Roosevelt and the Isolationists*, 322.

29   Casey, *Cautious Crusade*, 23.

30   Winston Churchill, *Memoirs of the Second World War* (Boston: Houghton Mifflin, 1987), 227.
31   Joseph Lash, *Roosevelt and Churchill, 1939–1945: The Relations that Saved the West* (New York: W.W. Norton, 1976); Warren Kimball, *Churchill, Roosevelt, and the Second World War* (New York: Harper Collins, 1997); Jon Meacham, *Franklin and Winston: An Intimate Portrait of an Epic Friendship* (New York: Random House, 2003); Martin Gilbert, *Churchill and America* (New York: Free Press, 2005); David Stafford, *Roosevelt and Churchill: Men of Secrets* (New York: Overlook Press, 2011).
32   Meacham, *Franklin and Winston*, 38.
33   Smith, *FDR*, 446.
34   Roger Daniels, *Franklin Delano Roosevelt: The War Years, 1939–1945* (Urbana: University of Illinois Press, 2016), 68.
35   Winston Churchill, *Great War Speeches* (New York: Corgi Books, 1957), 25.
36   Goodwin, *No Ordinary Time*, 66.
37   Hart, *Second World War*, 108.
38   Richard Snow, *A Measureless Peril: America in the Fight for the Atlantic, the Largest Land Battle of World War II* (New York: Scribner, 2011); Jonathan Dimbleby, *The Battle of the Atlantic: How the Allies Won the War* (New York: Oxford University Press, 2016).
39   Hansen, *Second World War*, 160.
40   Craig Nelson, *Pearl Harbor: From Infamy to Greatness* (New York: Scribners, 2016), 63.
41   Roger Daniels, *Franklin Delano Roosevelt: The War Years, 1939–1945* (Urbana: University of Illinois Press, 2016).
42   Godfrey Hodgson, *The Colonel: The Life and Wars of Henry L. Stimson, 1867–1950* (New York: Knopf, 1990).
43   Ed Cray, *General of the Army: George C. Marshall, Soldier and Statesman,* (New York: W.W. Norton, 1990); Debi Unger and Irwin Unger, *George Marshall: A Biography* (New York: Harper Brothers, 2014); David Roll, *George Marshall: Defender of the Republic* (New York: Dutton Caliber, 2019).
44   Cole, *Roosevelt and the Isolationists*, 460.
45   Goodwin, *No Ordinary Time*, 187.
46   Richard Moe, *Roosevelt's Second Act: The Election of 1940 and the Politics of War* (New York: Oxford University Press, 2013); Susan Dunn, *1940: FDR, Willkie, Lindberg, Hitler – the Election amid the Storm* (New Haven, Conn.: Yale University Press, 2014); John Jeffries, *A Third Term for FDR: The Election of 1940* (Lawrence: University Press of Kansas, 2017).
47   Goodwin, *No Ordinary Time*, 108.
48   Meacham, *Franklin and Winston*, 69.
49   Charles Peters, *Five Days in Philadelphia: The Amazing "We Want Willkie!" Convention of 1940 and How It Freed FDR to Save the Western World* (New York: Public Affairs, 2005),175.
50   Frank Freidel, *Franklin D. Roosevelt: A Rendezvous with Destiny* (Boston: Little, Brown, 1990), 354.
51   Warren Kimball, *The Most Unsordid Act: Lend Lease, 1938–1941* (Baltimore: Johns Hopkins, 1969).
52   William Pederson, *The FDR Years* (New York: Facts on File, 2006), 395.
53   Buhite, *FDR's Fireside Chats*, 168, 170, 173.
54   Sherwood, *Roosevelt and Hopkins*, 243–46.
55   David Burg, ed., *The Great Depression* (New York: Facts on file, 2005), 343.
56   Moe, *Roosevelt's Second Act*, 327.
57   George Herring, *Aid to Russia, 1941–1946: Strategy, Diplomacy, and the Origins of the Cold War* (New York: Columbia University Press, 1973).

58   Michael Kluger and Richard Evans, *Roosevelt and Churchill: The Atlantic Charter, A Risky Meeting at Sea that Saved Democracy* (London: Frontline, 2022).
59   Keith Sainsbury, *Churchill and Roosevelt at War: The War They Fought and the Peace They Hoped to Make* (New York: New York University Press, 1994).
60   William Nester, *Winston Churchill and the Art of Leadership* (London: Frontline Books, 2020).
61   Winston Churchill, *The Grand Alliance* (Boston: Houghton Mifflin, 1950), 663.
62   Nigel Hamilton, *The Mantle of Command: FDR at War, 1941–1942* (New York: Houghton Mifflin, 2014), 36–39.
63   *Gallup Poll,* 1:244–45.
64   Marks, *Wind over Sand,* 165.
65   Both quotes from Ted Morgan, *FDR: A Biography* (New York: Simon and Schuster, 1985), 540.
66   Roger Daniels, *Franklin D. Roosevelt: The War Years, 1939–1945* (Urbana: University of Illinois Press, 2016), 200.
67   Ronald Lewin, *The American Magic: Codes, Ciphers, and the Defeat of Japan* (New York: Farrar, Straus, and Giroux, 1982); David Alvarez, *Secret Messages: Codebreaking and American Diplomacy, 1930–1945* (Lawrence: University Press of Kansas, 2000).
68   Spector, *Eagle against the Sun,* 446.
69   Alonzo Hamby, *Man of Destiny: FDR and the Making of the American Century* (New York: Basic Books, 2015), 337.
70   Costello, *Days of Infamy,* 152.
71   Alan Schom, *The Eagle and the Rising Sun: The Japanese-American War, 1941–1942: Pearl Harbor through Guadalcanal* (New York: W.W. Norton, 2004), 126.
72   Costello, *Days of Infamy,* 81.
73   Costello, *Day of Infamy,* 259–61.
74   Jeanette Rankin of Montana was the sole nay; she had also voted against Wilson's declaration for World War I.
75   Buhite, *FDR's Fireside Chats,* 199, 205.

Chapter 8: The Opening Campaigns

1   William Johnsen, *The Origins of the Grand Alliance: Anglo-American Military Collaboration from the Panay to Pearl Harbor* (Lexington: University Press of Kentucky, 2016), 243.
2   Martin Gilbert, *Churchill and America* (New York: Free Press, 2005), 252.
3   Meacham, *Franklin and Meacham,* XIX.
4   David Roll, *The Hopkins Touch: Harry Hopkins and the Forging of the Alliance to Defeat Hitler* (New York: Oxford University Press, 2013), 174.
5   Goodwin, *No Ordinary Time,* 311.
6   Robin Edmonds, *The Big Three: Churchill, Roosevelt, and Stalin in Peace and War* (New York: W.W. Norton, 1991); Amos Pearlmutter, *FDR & Stalin: A Not So Grand Alliance, 1943–1945* (Columbia: University of Missouri Press, 1993); Ann Lane and Howard Temperley, eds., *The Rise and Fall of the Grand Alliance, 1941–1945* (New York: St. Martin's Press, 1995); Simon Bethon, *Allies at War: The Bitter Rivalry among Churchill, Roosevelt, and de Gaulle* (London: HarperCollins, 2002); William Johnsen, *The Origins of the Grand Alliance: Anglo-American Military Collaboration from the Panay to Pearl Harbor* (Lexington: University Press of Kentucky, 2016).
7   Mark Stoler, *The Politics of the Second Front: American Military Planning and Diplomacy in Coalition Warfare, 1941–1943* (Westport, Conn.: Greenwood, 1977);

Philip Padgett, *Advocating Overlord: The D-Day Strategy and Atomic Bomb* (Lincoln: University of Nebraska Press, 2018).

8   Kent Greenfield, *American Strategy in World War II: A Reconsideration* (Baltimore: Johns Hopkins University Press, 1963); Eric Larrabee, *Commander in Chief: Franklin Delano Roosevelt, His Lieutenants, and Their War* (New York: Harper and Row, 1987); David Fromkin, *In the Time of the Americans: FDR, Truman, Eisenhower, Marshall, MacArthur – The Generation that Changed America's Role in the World* (New York: Alfred Knopf, 1995); Kenneth Davis, *F.D.R.: The War President, 1940–1943* (New York: Random House, 2000); Joseph Persico, *Roosevelt's Centurions: FDR and the Commanders He Led to Victory in World War II* (New York: Random House, 2013); Nigel Hamilton, *The Mantle of Command: FDR at War, 1941–1942* (New York: Houghton Mifflin, 2014).

9   Mark Stoler, *Allies and Adversaries: The Joint Chiefs of Staff, the Grand Alliance, and United States Strategy in World War II* (Chapel Hill: University of North Carolina Press, 2000); Mark Stoler, *Allies at War: Britain and America against the Axis Powers, 1940–1945* (New York: Bloomsbury, 2007).

10 Kimball, *Juggler*, 67.

11 Larrabee, *Commander in Chief*, 11.

12 Joseph Persico, *Roosevelt's Secret War: FDR and World War II Espionage* (New York: Random House, 2001).

13 Patrick O'Donnell, *Operatives, Spies, and Saboteurs: The Unknown Story of the Men and Women of World War II's OSS* (New York: New Press, 2014).

14 Douglas Waller, *Wild Bill Donovan* (New York: Free Press, 2011).

15 Pascal Zachary, *Endless Frontiers: Vannevar Bush, Engineer of the American Century* (New York: Free Press, 1997).

16 David Hart, *Forged Consensus: Science, Technology, and Economic Policy in the United States, 1921–1953* (Princeton, N.J.: Princeton University Press, 1998).

17 For overviews, see: Richard Rhodes, *The Making of the Atomic Bomb* (New York: Simon and Schuster, 1986); Malcom McPherson, *Time Bomb: Fermi, Heisenberg, and the Race for the Atomic Bomb* (New York: E.P. Dutton, 1986); Cynthia Kelly, *The Manhattan Project: The Birth of the Atomic Bomb in the Words of Its Creators, Eyewitnesses, and Historians* (New York: Black Dog and Leventhal Publishers, 2020).

    For Oppenheimer, see: Kai Bird and Martin Sherwin, *American Prometheus: The Triumph and Tragedy of Robert Oppenheimer* (New York: Alfred Knopf, 2005); Charles Thorpe, *Oppenheimer: The Tragic Intellect* (Chicago: University of Chicago Press, 2008).

18 Rhodes, *Making of the Atomic Bomb*, 520.

19 Hansen, *Second World War*, 231.

20 For the Pacific War, see: Ronald Spector, *Eagle against the Sun: The American War with Japan* (New York: Vintage, 1985); John Dower, *War without Mercy: Race and Power in the Pacific War* (New York: Random House, 1986); Alan Schom, *The Eagle and the Rising Sun: The Japanese-American War, 1941–1942: Pearl Harbor through Guadalcanal* (New York: W.W. Norton, 2004); Ian Toll, *Pacific Crucible: The War at Sea I the Pacific, 1941–1942* (New York: W.W. Norton, 2012); Ian Toll, *The Conquering Tide: The War in the Pacific, 1942–1944* (New York: W.W. Norton, 2016); Ian Toll, *Twilight of the Gods: War in the Western Pacific, 1944–1945* (New York: W.W. Norton, 2021).

21 William Manchester, *American Caesar: Douglas MacArthur, 1880–1964* (Boston: Little, Brown, 1978); Michael Schaller, *Douglas MacArthur* (New York: Oxford University Press, 1989); Arthur Herman, *Douglas MacArthur: American Warrior* (New York: Random House, 2017).

22   Hamilton, *Mantle of Command*, 165.

23   Richard Connaughton, *MacArthur's Defeat in the Philippines* (New York: Abrams, 2003).

24   Manchester, *American Caesar*, 215.

25   Costello, *Day of Infamy*, 269.

26   Michael Norman and Elizabeth Norman, *Tears in the Darkness: The Story of the Bataan Death March and Its Aftermath* (New York: Farrar, Straus, and Giroux, 2009).

27   Spector, *Eagle against the Sun*, 327.

28   Sam Kleiner, *The Flying Tigers: The Untold Story of the American Pilots Who Waged a Secret War against Japan* (New York: Viking, 2018).

29   Charles Romanus and Riley Sunderland, *Stilwell's Mission to China* (Washington D.C.: Military History Department of the Army, 1953); Charles Romanus, and Riley Sunderland, *Stilwell's Command Problems* (Washington D.C.: Army Military History Department, 1956); Charles Romanus and Riley Sunderland, *Time Runs Out in the CBI* (Washington D.C.: Army Military History Department, 1959); David Rooney, *Stillwell the Patriot: Vinegar Joe, the Brits, and Chiang Kai-shek* (London: Greenhill, 2005).

30   Craig Symonds, *The Battle of Midway* (New York: Oxford University Press, 2013).

31   William Manchester, *American Caesar: Douglas MacArthur, 1880–1964* (New York: Little, Brown, 1978), 364.

32   Joseph Wheelan, *Midnight in the Pacific: Guadalcanal – the World War II Battle that Turned the Tide of War* (New York: Da Capo Press, 2017).

33   James Duffy, *War at the End of the World: Douglas MacArthur and the Forgotten Fight for New Guinea, 1942–1945* (New York: Dutton Caliber, 2017).

34   Ralph Levering, *American Opinion and the Russian Alliance, 1939–1945* (Chapel Hill: University of North Carolina Press, 1976); William Taubman, *Stalin's American Policy: From Entente to Détente to Cold War* (New York: W.W. Norton, 1982); Edward Bennett, *Franklin D. Roosevelt and the Search for Victory: American-Soviet Relations, 1939–1945* (Wilmington, Del.: Scholarly Resources, 1990); R.C. Raack, *Stalin's Drive to the West, 1938–1945: The Origins of the Cold War* (Palo Alto, Calif.: Stanford University Press, 1995); Edward Bennett, *Franklin D. Roosevelt and the Search for Security: American-Soviet Relations, 1933–1939* (Wilmington, Del.: Scholarly Resources, 1997).

35   Kimball, *Juggler*, 25.

36   Kimball, *Juggler*, 88.

37   Robert Sherwood, *Roosevelt and Hopkins: An Intimate History* (New York: Harper and Brothers, 1948), 561–63.

38   William Leahy, *I Was There* (New York: McGraw-Hill, 1950), 116.

39   Arthur Funk, *The Politics of Torch: The Allied Landings and the Putsch at Algiers* (Lawrence: University Press of Kansas, 1974); William Brewer, *Operation Torch: The Allied Gamble to Invade North Africa* (New York: St. Martin's, 1988); Norman Gelb, *Desperate Venture: The Story of Operation Torch, the Allied Invasion of North Africa* (London: Hoddert and Stoughton, 1992); Rick Atkinson, *An Army at Dawn: The War in North Africa, 1942–1943* (New York: Henry Holt, 2002); Orr Kelly, *Meeting the Fox: The Allied Invasion of Africa from Operation Torch to Kasserine Pass to Victory in Tunisia* (New York: Wiley, 2002).

40   Hamilton, *Mantle of Command*, 356.

41   Bryn Hammond, *El Alamein: The Battle that Turned the Tide in the Second World War* (London: Osprey, 2012).

42   James Roosevelt, *My Parents: A Differing View* (Chicago: Playboy Press, 1976), 176.

43   E.K.G. Sixsmith, Eisenhower as Military Commander (New York: Da Capo, 1972); Carlo D'Este, Eisenhower: A Soldier's Life (New York: Henry Holt, 2002);

Stephen Ambrose, The Supreme Commander: The War Years of Dwight D. Eisenhower (New York: Anchor, 2012); Jean Smith, Eisenhower in War and Peace (New York: Random House, 2013); Dwight Eisenhower, Crusade in Europe: A Personal Account of World War II (New York: Vintage, 2021).

44 Martin Blumenson, *Kasserine Pass: Rommel's Bloody, Climatic Battle for Tunisia* (New York: Cooper Square, 2000).

45 Both quotes from Atkinson, *Army at Dawn*, 373, 282.

46 Leo Barron, *Patton's First Victory: How General George Patton Turned the Tide in North Africa and Defeated the Africa Korps at El Guettar* (Mechanicsville, Penn.: Stackpole Books, 2017).

47 David Rolf, *The Bloody Road to Tunis: Destruction of the Axis Forces in North Africa, November 1942-May 1943* (London: Frontline, 2015).

48 Michael Howard, *The Mediterranean Strategy in World War II* (London: Greenhill Books, 1993).

49 Charles de Gaulle, *The Complete War Memoirs* (New York: Simon and Schuster, 1964), 399.

50 Smith, *FDR*, 567.

51 Atkinson, *Army at Dawn*, 3.

Chapter 9: The Home Front

1 For overviews, see: Richard Polenberg, ed., *America at War: Homefront, 1915–1945* (Englewood Cliffs, N.J.: Prentice Hall, 1968); Richard Lingeman, *Don't You Know There's a War On?: The American Home Front, 1941–1945* (New York: G.P. Putnam's Sons, 1971); Richard Polenberg, *War and Society: The United States, 1941–1945* (New York: J.B. Lippincott Company, 1972); John Blum, *V Was for Victory: Politics and American Culture during World War II* (New York: Harcourt, Brace, and Company, 1976); Robert Divine, *The Reluctant Belligerent: American Entry into World War II* (New York: Wiley, 1979); David Brinkley, *America Goes to War: The Extraordinary Story of the Transformation of a City and a Nation* (New York: Knopf, 1988); Ronald Takaki, *Double Victory: A Multicultural History of America in World War II* (Boston: Little, Brown, 2000); Allan Winkler, *Home Front U.S.A.: America during World War II* (New York: Wiley Blackwell, 2012).

For economic mobilization and military logistics, see: Elberton Smith, *The Army and Economic Mobilization* (Washington D.C.: Department of the Army, 1949); Alan Gropman, ed., *The Big L: American Logistics in World War II* (Washington D.C.: National Defense University Press, 1997); Robert Coakley and Richard Leighton, *Global Logistics and Strategy, 1943–1945, The United States Army in World War II* (Washington D.C.: U.S. Army, 1989).

2 Lerner, Historical Statistics, 2:1,105.

3 Lerner, *Historical Statistics*, 1:8–9.

4 Katznelson, *Fear Itself*, 338.

5 John Blum, *V Was for Victory: Politics and American Culture during World War II* (New York: Harcourt, Brace, and Company, 1976), 22.

6 Anthony Badger, *The New Deal: The Depression Years, 1933–1940* (Chicago: Ivan Dee, 1989), 107.

7 Polenberg, *War and Society*, 16–18.

8 Polenberg, *War and Society*, 18–19.

9 Polenberg, *War and Society*, 95.

10 Alan Brinkley, *The End of Reform: New Deal Liberalism in Recession and War* (New York: Alfred Knopf, 1995), 211.

11   John Blum, *V Was or Victory: Politics and American Culture during World War II* (New York: Harcourt, Brace, and Company, 1976), 123, 126.

12   Blum, *V Was for Victory*, 135.

13   Brinkley, *End of Reform*, 241.

14   Elberton Smith, The Army and Economic Mobilization (Washington D.C.: Center for Military History, 195), 9–27.

15   Robert Albion and Robert Connery, *Forrestal and the Navy* (New York: Columbia University Press, 1962), 287–88.

16   John Bunker, *Liberty Ships: Ugly Ducklings of World War II* (Annapolis: Naval Institute Press, 1972), 7.

17   John Stover, *The Life and Decline American Railroad* (New York: Oxford University Press, 1970).

18   Hansen, *Second World War*, 109–32.

19   Hansen, *Second World War*, 152.

20   W.J. Holmes, *Undersea Victory: The Influence of Submarine Operations on the War in the Pacific* (Garden City, N.Y.: Doubleday, 1963), 351.

21   Lee Kennett, *G.I.: The American Soldier in World War II* (New York: Scribner's, 1987); Gerald Linderman, *The World within War: America's Combat Experience in World War II* (New York: Free Press, 1997); Gerald Astor, *The Greatest War: Americans in Combat, 1941–1945* (Novato, Calif.: Presidio, 1999).

22   Hansen, *Second World War*, 214–25.

23   Hansen, *Second World War*, 222, 217.

24   Buhite, *FDR's Fireside Chats*, 251.

25   Goodwin, *No Ordinary Time*, 442.

26   For conspiracy theories, see: George Morgenstern, *Pearl Harbor: The Story of the Secret War* (New York: Devin-Adair Company, 1947); Charles Beard, *President Roosevelt and the Coming of the War, 1941* (New York: Transaction Publishers, 1948); Charles Tansill, *Back Door to War: The Roosevelt Foreign Policy, 1933–1941* (Chicago: Regnery, 1952); Robert Theobald, *The Final Secret of Pearl Harbor* (New York: Devin-Adair Company, 1954); Harry Barnes, *Pearl Harbor After a Quarter of a Century* (New York: Arno Press, 1972); John Toland, *Infamy: Pearl Harbor and Its Aftermath* (Garden City, N.J.: Doubleday, 1982); Gordon Prange, *At Dawn We Slept: The Untold Story of Pearl Harbor* (New York: Penguin, 1982); Henry Clausen and Bruce Lee, *Pearl Harbor: Final Judgment* (New York: Crown Publishers, 1992).

27   Roberta Wohlstetter, *Pearl Harbor: Warning and Decision* (Palo Alto, Calif.: Stanford University Press, 1962); John Costello, *Days of Infamy: MacArthur, Roosevelt, Churchill – the Shocking Truth Revealed* (New York: Pocket Books, 1994).

28   Costello, *Day of Infamy*, 241.

29   Robert Dallek, *Franklin D. Roosevelt and American Foreign Policy, 1932–1945* (New York: Oxford University Press, 1979), 225–26.

30   Stephen Fox, *Uncivil Liberties: Italian Americans under Siege during World War II* (Parkland, Fla.: Universal Publishers, 2000); Stephen Fox, *America's Invisible Gulag: A Biography of German American Internment and Exclusion in World War II* (New York: Peter Lang, 2000); John Armor and Peter Wright, *Manzanar* (New York: Times Books, 1988); Greg Robinson, *By Order of the President: FDR and the Internment of Japanese Americans* (Cambridge, Mass.: Harvard University Press, 2001); Richard Reeves, *Infamy: The Shocking Story of the Japanese American Internment in World War II* (New York: Picador, 2016).

31   Eric Yamamoto, Lorraine Bannai, and Margaret Chon, *Race, Rights, and Reparations: Law and the Japanese American Incarceration* (Frederick, Maryland: Aspen Publishing, 2021), 152.

32 Richard Lingeman, *Don't You Know There's a War On?: The American Home Front, 1941–1945* (New York: G.P. Putnam's Sons, 1971), 337.
33 James McCaffrey, *Going for Broke: Japanese Americans Soldiers in the War against Nazi Germany* (Norman: University of Oklahoma Press, 2017); John Armor and Peter Wright, *Manzanar* (New York: Times Book, 1988), 148–49.
34 William Preston, *Aliens and Dissenters: Federal Suppression of Radicals, 1903–1933* (Cambridge, Mass.: Harvard University Press, 1963); Christopher Capozzolla, *Uncle Sam Wants You: World War I and the Making of the Modern American Citizen* (New York: Oxford University Press, 2008).
35 Polenberg, *War and Society*, 49–50.
36 Allen Weinstein and Alexander Vassiliev, *The Haunted Wood: Soviet Espionage in America – the Stalin Era* (New York: Random House, 1999).
37 Beschloss, *Conquerors*, 149–57.
38 Andrew and Gordievsky, *KGB*, 287, 349; Eduard Mark, "Venona's Source 19 and the Trident Conference of 1943: Diplomacy or Espionage," *Intelligence and National Security*, vol. 13, no. 2 (Summer 1998), 1–31.
39 Goodwin, *No Ordinary Time*, 169–70.
40 Joseph Carver, Jerome Ennels, and Daniel Haulman, *The Tuskegee Airmen: An Illustrated History, 1939–1949* (Athens, Georgia: New South Press, 2011).
41 Robert Hill, ed., *The FBI's RACON: Racial Conditions in the United States during World War II* (Boston: Northeastern University Press, 1995).
42 Paul Boyer et al., *The Enduring Vision: A History of the American People* (Lexington, Mass.: D.C. Heath and Company, 1993), 913; Richard Polenberg, ed., *America at War: Homefront, 1915–1945* (Englewood Cliffs, N.J.: Prentice Hall, 1968), 131.
43 Goodwin, *No Ordinary Time*, 41.
44 Margaret O'Brien Steinfels, *Who's Minding the Children: The History and Politics of Day Care in America* (New York: Simon and Schuster, 1973), 67.
45 Goodwin, *No Ordinary Time*, 485.
46 Smith, *FDR*, 584.
47 Hugh Evans, *The Hidden Campaign: FDR's Health and the 1944 Election* (New York: Routledge, 2002); David Jordan, *FDR, Dewey, and the Election of 1944* (Bloomington: University of Illinois Press, 2012); Michael Davis, *Politics as Usual: Thomas Dewey, Franklin Roosevelt, and the Wartime Presidential Election of 1944* (Chicago: Northwestern University Press, 2014).
48 Goodwin, *No Ordinary Time*, 524.
49 Robert Ferrell, *Choosing Truman: The Democratic Convention of 1944* (Columbia: University of Missouri Press, 2000).

Chapter 10: The Conquests

1 Philip Padgett, *Advocating Overlord: The D-Day Strategy and Atomic Bomb* (Lincoln: University of Nebraska Press, 2018), 88.
2 Hamilton, *Mantle of Command*, 202.
3 Michael Howard, *The Mediterranean Strategy in World War II* (London: Greenhill Books, 1993).
4 Martin Blumenson, *Patton: The Man behind the Legend, 1885–1945* (New York: William Morrow, 1985); Carlo D'Este, *Patton: A Genius for War* (New York: Perennial Harper, 1996); Stanley Hirshson, *General Patton: A Soldiers' Life* (New York: Harper Collins, 2002); Gary Bloomfield, *George S. Patton: On Guts, Glory, and Winning* (New York: Globe Pequot, 2017); Nigel Hamilton, *Monty: The Battles of Field Marshal Bernard Montgomery* (New York: Random House, 1994).

5   Rick Atkinson, *The Day of Battle: The War in Sicily and Italy, 1943–1944* (New York: Henry Holt, 2007); Carlo D'Este, *Bitter War: The Battle for Sicily, July-August 1943* (New York: Perennial, 2008).
6   Elena Agarossi, *A Nation Collapses: The Italian Surrender of 1943* (New York: Cambridge University Press, 2000).
7   Jonathan Daniels, ed., *The Complete Presidential Press Conferences of Franklin D. Roosevelt* (New York: Da Capo, 1972), 22.
8   George Botjer, *Sideshow War: The Italian Campaign, 1943–45* (College Station: Texas A and M University Press, 1996); Rick Atkinson, *The Day of Battle: The War in Sicily and Italy, 1943–1945* (New York: Henry Holt, 2007).
9   Angus Konstam, *Salerno 1943: The Allied Invasion of Italy* (London: Pen and Sword, 2007).
10 Jon Mikolashek, *General Mark Clark: Commander of America's Fifth Army in World War II and Liberator of Rome* (New York: Casemate, 2020).
11 Atkinson, *Day of Battle*, 507.
12 Carlo D'Este, *The Fatal Decision: Anzio and the Battle for Rome* (New York: Harper Collins, 1991); John Ellis, *Cassino, the Hollow Victory: The Battle for Rome, January-June 1944* (New York: Arum, 2003); Lloyd Clark, *Anzio: The Friction of War, Italy and the Battle for Rome, 1944* (New York: Headline Publisher, 2007).
13 Atkinson, *Day of Battle*, 431.
14 For an overview of Roosevelt's evolving vision for winning the peace, see: Gabriel Kolko, *The Politics of War: The World and United States Foreign Policy, 1943–1945* (New York: Harper and Row, 1969); John Wheeler-Bennet and Anthony Nicolls, *The Semblance of Peace: The Political Settlement after the Second World War* (London: Palgrave Macmillan, 1974); Gaddis Smith, *American Diplomacy during the Second World War* (New York: Knopf, 1985); John Harper, *American Visions of Europe: Franklin D. Roosevelt, George F. Kennan, and Dean G. Acheson* (Cambridge: Cambridge University Press, 1994); Patrick Heardon, *The Architects of Globalism: Building a New World Order during World War II* (Fayetteville: University of Arkansas Press, 2002).
       For the Cairo and Tehran summits, see: Keith Eubank, *Summit at Teheran: The Untold Story* (New York: Morrow, 1985); Keith Sainsbury, *The Turning Point: Roosevelt, Stalin, Churchill, and Chiang Kai-shek, 1943: the Moscow, Cairo, and Teheran Conferences* (New York: Oxford University Press, 1985).
15 Maurice Matloff, *Strategic Planning for Coalition Warfare, 1943–1944* (Washington D.C.: Government Printing Office, 1959), 341–42.
16 Smith, *FDR*, 587.
17 Marks, *Wind over Sand*, 172.
18 Robert Sherwood, *Roosevelt and Hopkins: An Intimate History* (New York: Harper Brothers, 1948), 344.
19 Bennett Kourig, *The Myth of Liberation: East-Central Europe in U.S. Diplomacy and Politics since 1941* (Baltimore: Johns Hopkins University Press, 1973); Remi Nadeau, *Stalin, Churchill, and Roosevelt Divide Europe* (New York: Praeger, 1990); Lloyd Gardner, *Spheres of Influence: The Great Powers Partition Europe, from Munich to Yalta* (Chicago: Ivan R. Dee, 1993); Elena Aga Rossi, *The Origins of the Bipolar World: Roosevelt's Policy toward Europe and the Soviet Union: A Reevaluation* (Berkeley: University of California Press, 1993).
20 Arthur Morse, *While Six Million Died: A Chronicle of American Apathy* (New York: Random House, 1968); Henry Feingold, *The Politics of Rescue: The Roosevelt Administration and the Holocaust, 1938–1945* (New York: Holocaust Library, 1970); David Wyman, *The Abandonment of the Jews: America and the Holocaust, 1941*

to 1945 (New York: Pantheon, 1984); Robert Rosen, *Saving the Jews: Franklin D. Roosevelt and the Holocaust* (New York: Thunder Mouth's Press, 2008).

21   Wyman, *Abandonment of the Jews*, 72, 73.

22   Smith, *FDR*, 610.

23   Smith, *FDR*, 611.

24   Buhite, *FDR's Fireside Chats*, 241–42.

25   E.B. Potter, *Nimitz* (Annapolis, Maryland: Naval Institute Press, 2013); Trent Hone, *Mastering the Art of Command: Admiral Chester Nimitz and Victory in the Pacific* (Annapolis: Naval Institute Press, 2022).

26   James Hallas, *Saipan: The Battle that Doomed Japan in World War II* (Mechanicsville, Pa.: Stackpole Books, 2019).

27   William Manchester, *American Caesar: Douglas MacArthur* (Boston: Little, Brown, 1978), 369.

28   Samuel Roseman, *Working with Roosevelt* (New York: Harper Brothers, 1952), 456–57.

29   Robert Smith, *Triumph in the Philippines: The War in the Pacific* (Honolulu: University Press of the Pacific, 2005).

30   Thomas Cutler, *The Battle of Leyte Gulf, 23–26 October 1944* (New York: HarperCollins, 1994).

31   Adrian Stewart, *Kamikaze: Japan's Last Bid for Victory* (London: Pen and Sword, 2022).

32   Richard Hallion, "Precision Weapons, Power Projection, and the Revolution in Military Affairs," *Air Force Historical Studies Office*, website, May 29, 1999.

33   Spector, *Eagle against the Sun*, 453, 486–87.

34   Spector, *Eagle against the Sun*, 370.

35   Charles Romanus and Riley Sunderland, *Stilwell's Mission to China* (Washington D.C.: Amry Department of Military History, 1953), 452.

36   Romanus and Sunderland, Time Runs Out in the CBI (Washington D.C.: Amry Department of Military History, 1959), 165–66.

37   Spector, *Eagle against the Sun*, 464.

38   Cornelius Ryan, *The Longest Day: June 6, 1944* (New York: Simon and Schuster, 1994); Max Hastings, *Overlord: D-Day and the Battle for Normandy, 1944* (New York: Pan Books, 2005); Stephen Ambrose, *D-Day, June 6, 1944: The Climatic Battle of World War II* (New York: Simon and Schuster, 2013). For the campaign from Normandy to Germany's defeat, see: Rick Atkinson, *The Guns at Last Light: The War in Western Europe, 1944–1945* (New York: Henry Holt, 2013).

39   Atkinson, *Guns at Last Light*, 23.

40   Richard Davis, *Bombing the European Axis Powers* (Maxwell Air Force Base, Al: Air University Press, 2006); Juan Vasquez Garcia, *Storm over Europe: Allied Bombing Missions in the Second World War* (London: Pen and Sword, 2020).

41   Victor Hansen, *The Second World War: How the First Global Conflict Was Fought and Won* (New York: Basic Books, 2020), 75.

42   Dieter Holsker, *V-Missiles of the Third Reich, the V-1 and V-2* (New York: Monogram Aviation Publishers, 1994); Michael Petersen, *Missiles for the Fatherland: Peenemunde, National Socialism, and the V-2 Missile* (New York: Cambridge University Press, 2011).

43   Atkinson, *Guns at Last Light*, 182.

44   Robin Cross, *Operation Dragoon: The Allied Liberation of the South of France, 1944* (New York: Pegasus, 2019); Antony Tucker-Jones, *Operation Dragoon: The Invasion of Southern France, 1944* (London: Pen and Sword, 2020).

45   Atkinson, *Guns at Last Light*, 221.

46   Cornelius Ryan, *A Bridge Too Far* (New York: Simon and Schuster, 1974); Simon Forty and Leo Marriott, *Operation Market Garden, September 1944* (New York: Casemate, 2018).

47   Simon Berthon and Joanna Potts, *Warlords: An Extraordinary Recreation of World War II through the Eyes and Minds of Hitler, Roosevelt, Churchill, and Stalin* (New York: Da Capo, 2006), 268.

48   Smith, *FDR*, 624.

49   Michael Beschloss, The Conquerors: Roosevelt, Truman, and the Destruction of Hitler's Germany, 1941–1945 (New York: Simon and Schuster, 2002), 60–62, 64.

50   Beschloss, *Conquerors*, 59.

51   Justus Doenecke and Mark Stoler, *Debating Franklin D. Roosevelt's Foreign Policies* (New York: Rowman and Littlefield, 2005), 77.

52   Beschloss, *Conquerors*, 163–64.

53   Kimball, *Juggler*, 45.

54   Richard Gardner, *Sterling-Dollar Diplomacy: The Origins and Prospects of Our international Economic Order* (New York: McGraw, 1969); Alfred Eckes, *A Search for Solvency: Bretton Woods and the International Monetary System, 1941–1971* (Austin: University of Texas Press, 1975); Benn Steil, *The Battle for Bretton Woods: John Maynard Keynes, Harry Dexter White, and the Making of a New World Order* (Princeton, N.J.: Princeton University Press, 2014).

55   Georg Schild, *Bretton Woods and Dumbarton Oaks: American Economic and Political Postwar Planning in the Summer of 1944* (New York: St. Martin's, 1995); Townsend Hoopes and Douglas Brinkley, *FDR and the Creation of the U.N.* (New Haven, Conn.: Yale University Press, 1997); Stephen Schlesinger, *Act of Creation: The Founding of the United Nations, A Story of Superpowers, Secret Agents, Wartime Allies and Enemies, and Their Quest for a Peacefull World* (Boulder, Colo.: Westview Press, 2003).

Chapter 11: The Denouement

1   John Toland, *The Story of the Bulge* (New York: Meridian, 1985); Charles MacDonald, *A Time for Trumpets: The Untold Story of the Battle of the Bulge* (New York: William Morrow, 1997); Peter Caddick-Adams, *Snow and Steel: The Battle of the Bulge, 1944–45* (New York: Oxford University Press, 2014); Christer Bergstrom, *The Ardennes: Hitler's Winter Offensive, 1944–45* (New York: Casemate, 2014).

2   John Rickard, *Advance and Destroy: Patton as Commander in the Bulge* (Lexington: University Press of Kentucky, 2011).

3   Atkinson, *Guns at Last Light*, 488–89; Caddick-Adams, *Snow and Steel*, 649.

4   For overviews, see: Diane Shaver Clemons, *Yalta* (New York: Oxford University Press, 1970); Russell Buhite, *Decisions at Yalta: An Appraisal of Summit Diplomacy* (Wilmington, Del.: SR Books, 1986); S.M. Plokhy, *Yalta: The Price of Peace* (New York: Viking, 2010); Diana Preston, *Eight Days at Yalta: How Churchill, Roosevelt, and Stalin Shaped the Postwar World* (New York: Atlantic Monthly Press, 2022). For the political legacy for America, see: Anthan Theoharis, *The Yalta Myths: An Issue in U.S. Politics, 1945–1955* (Columbia: University of Missouri Press, 1970).

5   Robert Grogin, *Natural Enemies: The United States and Soviet Union in the Cold War, 1917–1991* (New York: Rowman and Littlefield, 2001), 66.

6   Goodwin, *No Ordinary Time*, 585.

7   Smith, *FDR*, 632.

8   H.W. Brands, *Traitor to His Class: The Privileged Life and Radical Presidency of Franklin Delano Roosevelt* (New York: Doubleday, 2008), 808.

9 Samuel Rosenman, *Working with Roosevelt* (New York: Harper and Brothers, 1952), 527.
10 Beschloss, *Conquerors*, 206.
11 David McCullough, *Truman* (New York: Simon and Schuster, 1992), 342.
12 For the best biographies, see: Alonzo Hamby, Alonzo, *Man of the People: A Life of Harry S. Truman* (New York: Oxford University Press, 1995); David McCullough, *Truman* (New York: Simon and Schuster, 1992); Robert Ferrell, *Harry S. Truman: A Life* (Columbia: University of Missouri Press, 1994).

   For his initial year in the White House, see: Robert Maddox, *From War to Cold War: The Education of Harry S. Truman* (Boulder, Colo.: Westview Press, 1988); Robert Moskin, *Truman's War: The Final Victories of World War II and the Birth of the Postwar World* (New York: Random House, 1996).

   For his presidency, see: Alonzo Hamby, *Beyond the New Deal: Harry S. Truman and American Liberalism* (New York: Columbia University Press, 1971); Richard Haynes, *The Awesome Power: Harry Truman as Commander in Chief* (Baton Rouge: Louisiana State University Press, 1973); Robert Donovan, *Conflict and Crisis: The Presidency of Harry S. Truman, 1945–1948* (New York: W.W. Norton, 1977); Robert Donovan, *Tumultuous Years: The Presidency of Harry S. Truman,1949–1953* (New York: W.W. Norton, 1982); Robert Ferrell, *Harry S. Truman and the Modern Presidency* (Boston: Little, Brown, 1983); Michael Lacy, *The Truman Presidency* (New York: Cambridge University Press, 1989).

   For the national security state he forged to fight the Cold War, see: Melvyn Leffler, *A Preponderance of Power: National Security, the Truman Administration, and the Cold War* (Palo Alto, Calif.: Stanford University Press, 1992); Michael Hogan, *A Cross of Iron: Harry S. Truman and the Origins of the National Security State, 1945–1954* (New York: Cambridge University Press, 1998).
13 Lawrence Larson, *Pendergast!* (Columbia: University of Missouri Press, 1997); Robert Ferrell, *Truman and Pendergast* (Columbia: University of Missouri Press, 1999).
14 Edward Judge and John Langdon, *A Hard and Bitter Peace: A Global History of the Cold War* (New York: Rowman and Littlefield, 2018), 21.
15 Alonzo Hamby, "An American Democrat: A Reevaluation of the Personality of Harry S. Truman," *Political Science Quarterly*, vol. 106, no. 1 (Spring 1991), 52.
16 David Robertson, *Sly and Able: A Political Biography of James F. Brynes* (New York: W.W. Norton, 1994).
17 For the two best respective overviews, see: John Toland, *The Last 100 Days: The Tumultuous and Controversial Story of the Final Days of World War II in Europe* (New York: Modern Library, 1994); Richard Frank, *Downfall: The End of the Imperial Japanese Empire* (New York: Random House, 1999).
18 Robert Edsel, *The Monuments Men* (New York: Center Street, 2009).
19 Atkinson, *Guns at Last Light*, 512.
20 Stephen Ambrose, *Eisenhower and Berlin, 1945: The Decision to Halt at the Elbe* (New York: W.W. Norton, 1967).
21 Charles Bohlen, *Witness to History, 1929–1969* (New York: W.W. Norton, 1969), 222–23.
22 Edwin Hoyt, *Inferno: The Fire Bombing of Japan, March 9-August 15, 1945* (New York: Madison Books, 2000); Daniel Schwabe, *Burning Japan: Air Force Bombing Strategic Change in the Pacific* (Lincoln, Ne.: Potomac Books, 2015).
23 Richard Newcomb, *Iwo Jima: The Dramatic Account of the Epic Battle that Turned the Tide of World War II* (New York: Henry Holt, 2002).
24 Spector, *Eagle against the Sun*, 502.
25 Eric Larabee, *Commander in Chief: Franklin Delano Roosevelt, his Lieutenants, and Their War* (New York: Harper and Row, 1987), 619.

26   Robert Smith, *Triumph in the Philippines: The War in the Pacific* (Honolulu: University Press of the Pacific, 2005), 140, 651, 652.

27   Stanley Weintraub, *The Last Great Victory: The End of World War II, July–August 1945* (New York: Dutton, 1995); Douglas MacEachin, *The Final Months of the War with Japan: Signals Intelligence, U.S. Invasion Planning, and the A-Bomb Decision* (Langley, Vir.: Center for the Study of Intelligence, 1998).

28   Charles Mee, *The Meeting at Potsdam* (New York: M. Evans and Company, 1975); Tsuyoshi Hasegawa, *Racing the Enemy: Stalin, Truman, and the Surrender of Japan* (Cambridge, Mass.: Harvard University Press, 2005); Michael Neiberg, *Potsdam: The End of World War II and the Remaking of Europe* (New York: Basic Books, 2015).

29   Harry Truman, *Memoirs: Year of Decisions* (New York: Doubleday, 1955), 458.

30   For the range of scholarly views on the decision to drop the bombs, see: Samuel Walker, "The Decision to Use the Atomic Bomb: A Historiographical Update," Michael Hogan, ed., *America in the World: The Historiography of American Foreign Relations since 1941* (New York: Cambridge University Press, 1995), 83–104.

     Mainstream historians agree that only the atomic bombings forced Japan's fanatical government to surrender when it did, thus preventing all the death and destruction of conquering Japan. Among the best books are: Robert Maddox, *Weapons for Victory: The Hiroshima Decision Fifty Years Later* (Columbia: University of Missouri Press, 1995); Samuel Walker, *Prompt and Utter Destruction: Truman and the Use of Atomic Bombs against Japan* (Chapel Hill: University of North Carolina Press, 1997); Richard Frank, *Downfall: The End of the Imperial Japanese Empire* (New York: Random House, 1999). For succinct articles, see: Henry Stimson, "The Decision to Use the Atomic Bomb," *Harper's Magazine*, vol. 194 (February 1947), 97–107; Herbert Bix, "Japan's Delayed Surrender: A Reinterpretation," Diplomatic History, vol. 19, no. 2 (Spring 1995), 197–225; Brian Vila and John Bonnett, "Understanding Indignation: Gar Alperovitz, Robert Maddox, and the Decision to Drop the Atomic Bomb," Reviews in American History, vol. 24, no. 3 (September 1996), 529–36; Richard Frank, "Why Truman Dropped the Bomb," Weekly Standard (August 9, 2005), 20–25.

     For revisionist views that cherry-pick facts to argue the atomic bombings were unnecessary, see: Gar Alperovitz, *Atomic Diplomacy: Hiroshima and Potsdam – the Use of the Atomic Bomb and the American Confrontation with the Soviet Union* (New York: Penguin, 1985); Gar Alperovitz, *The Decision to Use the Atomic Bomb and the Architecture of an American Myth* (New York: Knopf, 1995); Robert Lifton, and Greg Mitchell, *Hiroshima in America: Fifty Years of Denial* (New York: Putnam's Sons, 1995).

31   John Ellis, *World War II: A Statistical Survey for All the Combatants* (New York: Facts On File, 1993), 253–54.

32   Lerner, *Historical Statistics*, 2:1140.

Chapter 12: The Legacy

 1   Stephen Roskill, *The Art of Leadership* (Hamden, Conn.: Archon Books, 1965); Ann Ruth Willner, *The Spellbinder: Charismatic Political Leadership* (New Haven, Conn.: Yale University Press, 1984); Arthur Schweitzer, *The Age of Charisma* (Chicago: Nelson-Hall, 1984); Jay Conger, *The Charismatic Leader: Behind the Mystique of Exceptional Leadership* (San Francisco: Jossey-Bass, 1989); Keith Grint, *Leadership: Limits and Possibilities* (New York: Palgrave, 2005); Simon Western, *Leadership: A Critical Text* (New York: Sage, 2019); Peter Northouse, *Leadership: Theory and Practice* (New York: Sage, 2021).

 2   Eleanor Roosevelt, *This I Remember* (New York: Harper, 1949), 68.

3   Robert Dallek, *Franklin D. Roosevelt and American Foreign Policy, 1932–1945*
    (New York: Oxford University Press, 1979), 317.
4   Hugh Gallagher, *FDR's Splendid Deception: The Moving Story of Roosevelt's Massive
    Disability and the Intense Efforts to Conceal It from the Public* (New York: Dodd,
    Mead, 1985).
5   Michael Riccards and Cheryl Flagg, *Party Politics in the Age of Roosevelt:
    The Making of Modern America* (New York: Rowman and Littlefield, 2022).
6   William Leuchtenburg, *Franklin D. Roosevelt and the New Deal, 1932–1940*
    (New York: Harper Perennial, 2009), 327.
7   Robert Eden, ed., *The New Deal and Its Legacy: Critique and Reappraisal* (New
    York: Greenwood, 1989); Robert Leighninger, *Long-range Public Investment: The
    Forgotten Legacy of the New Deal* (Columbia: University of South Carolina Press,
    2007).
8   Anthony Badger, *The New Deal: The Depression Years, 1933–1940* (New York:
    Chicago: Ivan Dee, 1989), 73.
9   James McGovern, *A Time for Hope: Americans in the Great Depression* (Westport,
    Conn.: Praeger, 2000), 49.
10 Lerner, *Historical Statistics*, 1:232, 458–63, 468–69; Badger, *New Deal*, 168.
11 Dan Paarlberg, "Tarnished Gold: Fifty Years in New Deal Farm Programs, in
    Eden, *New Deal and Its Legacy*, 42.
12 Buhite, *FDR's Fireside Chats*, 72.
13 Lerner, Historical Statistics, 1:224,135.
14 Lerner, *Historical Statistics*, 1:226–27.
15 Lerner, *Historical Statistics*, 2:1104, 1114, 1102,1117.
16 Lerner, Historical Statistics, 1:457.
17 Lerner, *Historical Statistics*, 1:302; 1:55.
18 Lerner, *Historical Statistics*, 2:1116, 1120,1141.
19 Joseph Persico, *Roosevelt's Secret War: FDR and World War II Espionage* (New
    York: Random House, 2001), 217.
20 Lerner, Historical Statistics, 1:55, 52.
21 Lerner, *Historical Statistics*, 1:55.
22 Allan Winkler, *Home Front U.S.A.: America During World War II* (New York:
    Wiley Blackwell, 2012), 115; Ronald Takaki, *Double Victory: A Multicultural
    History of America in World War II* (New York: Little, Brown, 2000), 41–44.
23 Melvin Dubovsky, Athan Theoharis, and Daniel Smith, *The United States in
    the Twentieth Century* (Englewood Cliffs, N.J.: Prentice Hall, 1978), 323; Lerner,
    Historical Statistics, 1:129, 132.
24 Goodwin, *No Ordinary Time*, 629.
25 Goodwin, *No Ordinary Time*, 163.
26 Eleanor Roosevelt, *Autobiography* (New York: Harper and Brothers, 1961), 214.
27 Dallek, *Roosevelt and American Foreign Policy*, 373.
28 David Kennedy, *Freedom from Fear: The American People in Depression and War,
    1929–1945* (New York: Oxford University Press, 1999), 116.
29 Dallek, *Roosevelt and American Foreign Policy*, 365.
30 Bryce Wood, *The Making of the Good Neighbor Policy* (New York: W.W. Norton,
    1967), 131.
31 Robert Sherwood, *Roosevelt and Hopkins: An Intimate History* (New York: Harper
    and Brothers, 1948), 656.
32 Persico, *Roosevelt's Secret War*, 379–81.
33 Roosevelt to Churchill, March 18, 1942, Warren Kimball, ed., *Churchill and
    Roosevelt: The Complete Correspondence*, 3 vols. (Princeton, N.J.: Princeton
    University Press, 1984), 1:421.

34   Charles Bohlen, *Witness to History, 1929–1969* (New York: W.W. Norton, 1973), 211.

35   Kent Greenfield, *American Strategy in World War II: A Reconsideration* (Baltimore: Johns Hopkins University Press, 1963).

36   David MacIssac, *Strategic Bombing in World War Two: The Story of the United States Strategic Bombing Survey* (New York: Garland, 1976); Michael Sherry, *The Rise of American Air Power: The Creation of Armageddon* (New Haven, Conn.: Yale University Press, 1987); Ronald Schaffer, *Wings of Judgment: American Bombing in World War II* (New York: Oxford University Press, 1995); Philip O'Brien, *How the War Was Won: Air-Sea Power and Allied Victory in World War II* (New York: Cambridge University Press, 2019).

37   Martin Blumenson, ed., *The Patton Papers: 1940–1945* (Boston: Houghton Mifflin, 1974), 681.

38   Victor Hansen, *The Second World War: How the First Global Conflict Was Fought and Won* (New York: Basic Books, 2020), 101.

39   Robert Newman, "Ending the War with Japan: Paul Nitze's 'Early Surrender' Counterfactual," *Pacific Historical Review*, vol. 64, no. 2 (May 1995), 167–94; Barton Berstein, "Compelling Japan's Surrender without the A-Bomb, Soviet Entry, or Invasion: Reconsidering the US Bombing Survey's Early Surrender Conclusions," *Journal of Strategic Studies*, vol. 18, no. 3 (June 1995), 101–48.

40   Charles Romanus and Riley Sunderland, *Stilwell's Mission to China: Stilwell's Command Problems* (Washington D.C.: Military History Department of the Army, 1959), 72.

41   Kimball, *Juggler*, 18.

42   Frank Costigliola, *Roosevelt's Lost Alliances: How Personal Politics Helped Start the Cold War* (Princeton, N.J.: Princeton University Press, 2013), 62; Beschloss, *Conquerors*, 220.

43   Jon Meacham, *Franklin and Winston: An Intimate Portrait of an Epic Friendship* (New York: Random House, 2003), xiv.

44   Averill Harriman and Elie Abel, *Special Envoy to Churchill and Stalin, 1941–1946* (New York: Random House, 1975), 191.

45   Robert Sherwood, *Roosevelt and Hopkins: An Intimate History* (New York: Harper and Brothers, 1948), 363.

46   Jon Meacham, *Franklin and Winston: An Intimate Portrait of an Epic Friendship* (New York: Random House, 2003), xiv.

47   William Nester, *Winston Churchill and the Art of Leadership: How Winston Changed the World* (London: Frontline Books, 2020).

48   Meacham, *Franklin and Winston*, 11.

49   Robert Sherwood, *Roosevelt and Churchill: An Intimate History, 1939–1945* (New York: Harper and Brothers, 1948), 364.

50   Perkins, *The Roosevelt I Knew*, 383.

51   Justus Doenecke and Mark Stoler, eds., *Debating Franklin D. Roosevelt's Foreign Policies, 1933–1945* (New York: Rowman and Littlefield, 2005), 55, 54.

52   Patrick Heardon, *The Architects of Globalism: Building a New World Order during World War II* (Fayetteville: University of Arkansas Press, 2002), 96.

53   Winston Churchill, *World War II: The Grand Alliance* (Boston: Houghton Mifflin, 1950), 663.

54   Kenneth Pendar, *Adventures in Diplomacy: Our French Dilemma* (New York: Dodd, Mead, 1945), 154.

INDEX